THE
IRAQ
WAR

THE IRAQ WAR

ORIGINS AND CONSEQUENCES

JAMES DEFRONZO

University of Connecticut

Westview
PRESS

A Member of the Perseus Books Group

Find us on the World Wide Web at www.westviewpress.com.

Westview Press books are available at special discounts for bulk purchases in the
United States by corporations, institutions, and other organizations. For more information, please contact the Special Markets Department at the Perseus Books
Group, 2300 Chestnut Street, Suite 200, Philadelphia, PA 19103, or call (800)
810-4145, ext. 5000, or e-mail special.markets@perseusbooks.com.

Designed by Pauline Brown

Library of Congress Cataloging-in-Publication Data

DeFronzo, James.
    The Iraq war : origins and consequences / James DeFronzo.
      p.   cm.
    Includes bibliographical references and index.
    ISBN 978-0-8133-4391-4 (pbk. : alk. paper) 1. Iraq War, 2003—Causes.
  2. Iraq War, 2003—Influence. 3. Iraq—History—20th century. 4. United
  States—Foreign relations—Iraq. 5. Iraq—Foreign relations—United States.
  I. Title.
DS79.76D443   2010
956.7044'3—dc22

                                                                2009010797

                         10 9 8 7 6 5 4 3 2 1

Contents

Preface

The invasion of Iraq was in great part the result of a shocking day of violence, the September 11, 2001, terrorist attacks. In turn, the Iraq War led to many stunning developments, including the election of a young opponent of the war, Illinois Senator Barack Obama, as president of the United States. This book attempts to explain why the war took place, central aspects of the conflict, and the war's impacts on Iraq, the United States, the Middle East, and other nations around the world. It also explores the conflict's potential consequences for future rationales for war, foreign policy, the United Nations, and international law and justice.

The book, guided by the principle that awareness of past events is essential to contemporary and future understanding, begins with the early history of Iraq as a new nation formed by Britain from parts of the former Ottoman Empire at the end of World War I. It notes that the belief that "Mesopotamia" contained enormous amounts of oil appeared to play the dominant role in shaping British policies regarding Iraq. America's involvement soon followed Britain's.

The first central theme of this book is that the Iraq War, the justifications for launching it, the lengthy occupation, and the limitations on Iraq's democracy and sovereignty are all best understood in terms of the importance of the country's energy resources. The second theme is the sociological and historical interrelatedness of important sociopolitical developments and the necessity of understanding causal links among them. The book, for example, describes the US and British involvement in oil-rich Iran in 1953 and how this intervention provoked a series of responses and movements that led to the Iran–Iraq War, the Iraqi invasion of Kuwait, the 1991 Persian Gulf War, and ultimately to the invasion and occupation of Iraq.

This book is structured to provide a clear and relatively concise means to significantly expand knowledge of Iraq, the factors and processes that led to the US decision to go to war, the nature of the conflict, the changes that took place in Iraq, and the war's local and international consequences. It is intended to be a central resource for faculty members and students in political science, history, or sociology courses not only dealing specifically with the Iraq War or the Middle East, but also more generally with social conflict, social movements and change, foreign policy, international relations, and the advancement of democracy around the world.

Political scientists may note that the book describes Iraqi politics and political systems since the country's inception, the forces promoting or constraining democracy and sovereignty, and the effects of foreign interventions on later political events.

Historians can find value in the book's providing a basic history of Iraq and US foreign policy important for establishing the context for more fully understanding the Iraq War, the events that followed, and the forces and personalities that would play major roles after the fall of the Baathist regime.

In addition, sociologists may note the effects of Iraq's traditional forms of social organization, its ethnic and religious divides, the nature of contending social movements and the factors that strengthened or weakened them, and the social, political, and economic consequences of the war.

The initial task of the book, toward which the first three chapters are directed, is to introduce the reader to important aspects of Iraq's culture, early sociological characteristics, and political history up to the reign of Saddam Hussein. This includes descriptions of the peoples, cultures, and lands that provided the foundation for the nation of Iraq and how Britain's denial of genuine democracy to the Iraqi people had dire consequences for Iraq's future. The progressive undermining of the British-installed Iraqi royal family by events such as the 1948 Arab–Israeli War, the 1955 Baghdad Pact, and the 1956 Suez crisis is described, as well as the 1958 violent overthrow of the pro-British regime and the profound division between leftist and Arab nationalist revolutionaries that led to the Baathist takeover.

The next section of the book, the fourth and fifth chapters, is oriented toward describing crucial interconnected events, the knowledge of which is essential for understanding the Iraq War and the political actors and organizations that assumed major roles in occupied Iraq. These include Saddam's ascendancy to power, the effects of the Iranian Revolution on Iraq, the Iraqi Shia political-religious movement, the outbreak of the Iran–Iraq War as well as its impacts, Iraq's decision to invade Kuwait, the 1991 Gulf War, how aspects of this conflict motivated Al Qaeda to attack the United States, and the effects of Iraq's defeat.

A central component of the book is the sixth chapter, which describes the impacts of the Bush administration and the 9/11 attacks on America's orientation toward Iraq, the Bush Doctrine of preventive war, the roles of eleven major factors that affected the decision to invade, the war plan, the invasion, and crucial early aspects of the occupation.

The importance of analyzing the American role in Iraq in the context of previous US foreign interventions including Vietnam in terms of factors such as justification for war, the nature of the resistance, military strategy and tactics, and US public opinion is emphasized in the seventh chapter.

The book in the eighth and ninth chapters describes events and developments in Iraq after the US-led invasion, including how different Iraqi social groups responded to the occupation, and the new constitution and political system. It also explains the rise of antioccupation resistance groups and their characteristics. This section of the book further describes US counterinsurgency methods, their application in Iraq, and the role of the 2007 surge in US troop strength and other factors, such as private military firms, in the war. Aspects of US corporate presence and activities are also analyzed along with the 2008 Iraq–US Status of Forces Agreement.

The final chapter describes impacts of the Iraq War on Iraq's people, women's and children's welfare, terrorism, the war in Afghanistan, control of oil, US politics, the news media, the US military, America's international moral standing, the UN, and political developments in other countries. The chapter further considers potential alternate futures for the country and whether and under what conditions the Iraq War can result in a genuinely democratic and sovereign Iraq.

The list of those who played a significant role in the origin of this book includes my own instructors, fellow faculty members, and thousands of students at the University of Connecticut and Indiana University. The reviews and advice of experts in political science, sociology, and history, such as Professor Eliot Dickinson of the Political Science Department of Western Oregon University, who read the manuscript, have been of immense value. I would like to express my thanks to the staff of Westview Press, in particular to Steve Catalano, Karl Yambert, Brooke Kush, Erica Lawrence, Annie Lenth, and Daniel Nasset, and our copyeditor, Antoinette Smith, for all their help and hard work.

Finally, I am deeply indebted to the members of my family and friends, in particular my mother, Mary Pavano DeFronzo, and father, Armand DeFronzo, my aunt Doris Pavano Pitts, aunt Angie Pavano DiFronzo, uncle Francis and aunt Lenneye DiFronzo, my wonderful wife, Jungyun, and her sister Jungha Gil and brother-in-law Namho Kang, Jungyun's nephews Jimin, Jihyun, and Doeun, her parents, Sang-Deuk Gil and Bok-Dan Kim, Jungyun's brothers Chunghoon and Woongchan, and her sister-in-laws, Bo-na Gong and Kyungim Choi, my brother Senator Donald DeFronzo and sister-in-law Diane Bracha DeFronzo, Mr. Anthony Bracha of the United Auto Workers, my sister Margaret Pastore and her friend David Timm, David DeFronzo and Monica Hermanowski DeFronzo, Larry and Teresa Hermanowski, Ralph Maliszewski and Karen DeFronzo Maliszewski, Victoria Maliszewski, Michael Pastore, Miguel Suarez, my cousins Connie Manafort, Carl Tata, Sal and Lynne Romano, Bob and my goddaughter Joy Anello, David and Randi Manafort, Michael and Ginny O'Connor, Jimmy and Jolyn Manafort, Tom and Lil Pitts, Vinnie and Jeanette Pitts, Nancy DiCaprio, Raffaele and Lucy Gironda, Javier and Dori Rathbun, Krista and Mike Hodges, Paul and Elaine Puzzo, Diane DiFronzo Hughes, and my friends Deanna Levanti, who developed the list of documentaries in this book, Al Cohen, Jane Prochnow, Bill Tunmer, Lance Hannon and Monica Cuddy, John and Heather McVarish, Walter and Becky Ellis, Roger Gocking, Thomas and Sue Ryan, Walter and Elizabeth Clebowicz, Dave Fowler and Wendy Kimsey, Ted Rhodes and Joni Pascal, Sue Cook and Ken Ringle, Steve Merlino and Kathy Mangiafico, Stephen Potocny, Jeff Bieber and Deborah Hill, and other good friends for their inspiration and encouragement in fulfilling this project.

— *Jim DeFronzo*

Abbreviations

AQM   Al Qaeda in Mesopotamia (also called Al Qaeda in Iraq)
BBC   British Broadcasting Company
CENTCOM   US Central Command
CPA   Coalition Provisional Authority
DIA   US Defense Intelligence Agency
GAO   US Government Accounting Office
HTS   Human Terrain System
HTT   Human Terrain Team
IAEA   International Atomic Energy Agency
ICP   Iraqi Communist Party
ID   Iraqi dinar
IED   improvised explosive device
IGC   Iraq Governing Council
IIG   Interim Iraqi Government
IMIK   Islamic Movement of Iraqi Kurdistan
INA   Iraqi National Accord
INC   Iraqi National Congress
INOC   Iraq National Oil Company
IOC   international oil company
IPC   Iraq Petroleum Company
ISCI   Islamic Supreme Council of Iraq (new name for SCIRI after May 2007, also known as SIIC, Supreme Iraqi Islamic Council)
ISGR   *Iraq Study Group Report*
IVAW   Iraq Veterans Against the War
JINSA   Jewish Institute for National Security Affairs
KBR   Kellogg, Brown and Root
KDP   Kurdish Democratic Party
KRG   Kurdish Regional Government
METO   Middle East Treaty Organization (the 1955 Baghdad Pact)

NATO   North Atlantic Treaty Organization
NCRC   National Council of Revolutionary Command
NDP   National Democratic Party
OPC   Operation Provide Comfort
OPEC   Organization of Petroleum Exporting Countries
ORHA   Office for Reconstruction and Humanitarian Affairs
PCEG   Policy Counterterrorism Evaluation Group
PKK   Kurdistan Workers Party
PMF   privatized military firms
PSYOPS   US Psychological Operations
PUK   Patriotic Union of Kurdistan
RCC   Revolutionary Command Council
ROTC   Reserve Officers' Training Corps
RPG   rocket-propelled grenade
SCIRI   Supreme Council for the Islamic Revolution in Iraq
SIIC   Supreme Iraqi Islamic Council (new name for SCIRI after May 2007, also known as ISCI, Islamic Supreme Council of Iraq)
SOF   Special Operations Forces
SOFA   Status of Forces Agreement
SWAT   special weapons and tactics
TAL   Transitional Administrative Law
TNA   Transitional National Assembly
UAE   United Arab Emirates
UAR   United Arab Republic
UN   United Nations
UNICEF   United Nations Children's Fund
UNMOVIC   UN Monitoring, Verification and Inspection Commission
UNSCOM   UN Special Commission on Disarmament
VAIW   Veterans Against the Iraq War
WMD   weapons of mass destruction

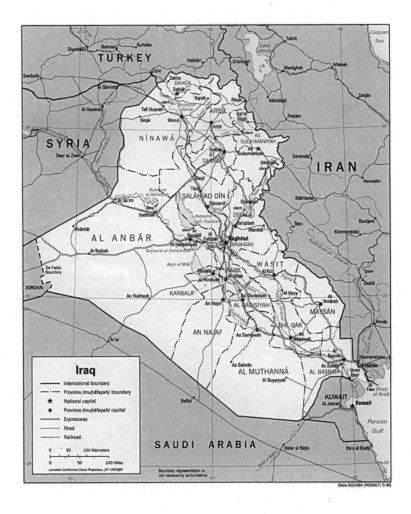

Iraq

- International boundary
- Province *(muḥāfaẓah)* boundary
- ★ National capital
- ◉ Province *(muḥāfaẓah)* capital
- Expressway
- Road
- Railroad

0   50   100 Kilometers

0   50   100 Miles

Lambert Conformal Conic Projection, SP 13N/36N

Boundary representation is
not necessarily authoritative.

Base 802484 (R00667) 5-96

TURKEY

SYRIA

IRAN

JORDAN

SAUDI ARABIA

KUWAIT

Diyarbakır Batman Kurtalan

Şanlıurfa

Al Qāmishlī

Al Hasakah

Dayr az Zawr

Hakkâri Ürümiyeh

Zakho DAHÛK Dahūk
'Aqrah Rāyāt
Tall Huqnah ARBÎL Qal'at Dizah
Sinjār Mosul Arbil
NÎNAWÁ

Tabriz

Lake
Urmia

Marāgheh Mīāneh

Mahābād

Zanjān

Saqqez

Sanandaj

Hamadān

AS
SULAYMÂNÎYAH
As
Sulaymānîyah
Halabjah
Kirkûk AT
TA'MÎM

Bākhtarān

Borūjerd

Khorramābād

Bayjī Tikrīt
SALÂH AD DÎN
Buḥayrat Sāmarrā'
al Qādisīyah Khānaqīn
Al Qā'im DIYÂLÁ
Hadīthah Buḥayrat
ath Tharthār Ba'qūbah Mandalī

Īlām

Akāshāt

AL ANBÂR
Ar Rutbah Ar
Ramādī Fallūjah
Al Habbānīyah Baghdad
Buḥayrat al Habbānīyah BAGHDÂD
Baḥr al Milḥ

De Facto
Boundary

WÂSIT
BÂBIL
Karbalā' Al Kūt
Al Hillah
Al Hindīyah KARBALÂ'
An Nukhayb Ad Dīwānīyah Al Hayy
An Najaf
AL QÂDISÎYAH 'Amārah
MAYSÂN

Dezfūl

Ahvāz

'Ar'ar

AN NAJAF As Samāwah
DHÎ QÂR Nasṣīyah

Rafḥā'

As Salmān
AL MUTHANNÁ Az Zubayr
Al Buṣayyah AL BASRAH
Al
Baṣrah Khorramshahr
Âbādān
Umm
Qaṣr
Al
Fāw Shaṭṭ
al 'Arab

Persian
Gulf

KUWAIT
Al Jahrah Kuwait

Hafar al Bāṭin Ra's al Khafjī

Wādī al Bāṭin

Introduction

On March 20, 2003, the United States, Britain, and an assortment of allies invaded Iraq ostensibly to destroy weapons of mass destruction and Saddam Hussein's regime, which many Americans believed played a role in the 9/11 terrorist attacks, and to establish a democratic political system. However, the support of the American people for the invasion was based largely on false justifications. Saddam's regime was removed, but no WMD and no link between Iraq and 9/11 were found. Furthermore, instead of leaving the Iraqis free to determine their own future without outside interference, the US-led coalition settled in for a lengthy occupation in the face of armed resistance by anti-occupation forces, consisting of Iraqi insurgents as well as an influx of foreign militants.

Apart from the thousands who perished in the initial coalition assault and then during years of insurgent and counterinsurgent attacks, sectarian violence between Sunni and Shia Arabs following the invasion reached a level far worse than at any time in Iraq's history as a nation. While revealing that the main arguments for launching it were false, the invasion in fact created new circumstances used by war advocates as reasons to continue the occupation. Though the levels of insurgent, terrorist, and sectarian violence fell significantly in the second half of 2007 and during 2008, it was not clear what would happen if and when occupation forces were substantially reduced or withdrawn.

Central Themes

The chapters embody two central themes. The first is that the Iraq War, the false premises for its inception, the prolonged occupation, and the limitations on Iraq's democracy and sovereignty are all best understood within the context of the importance of Iraq's energy resources. Removing a regime that could use them to threaten the interests or policies of the United States or its allies and instead establishing conditions of direct or indirect US control was potentially a significant enhancement of American security and international economic and political power. Control of Iraq's resources and long-term US military occupation facilitated American domination of all oil-rich Middle Eastern nations. This had the potential of compensating for Russia's energy surplus in oil and

1

natural gas and also provided a significant advantage over rival economic powers that relied on Middle East oil. US priority for this strategic goal appeared to interfere with postinvasion Iraq's achievement of true democracy and sovereignty.

The second theme, one particularly emphasized in sociological and historical perspectives, is the interrelatedness of crucial sociopolitical developments and the importance of recognizing causal links among major events. In particular, the book explains how US and British intervention in Iran in 1953 set in motion a series of momentous processes, movements, conflicts, and decisions that led to the Iran–Iraq War, the later Iraqi invasion of Kuwait, and eventually to the 2003 US-led invasion of Iraq.

While most American troops occupying Iraq probably believed they were using violence as a necessary measure to liberate the Iraqi people from an oppressive dictatorship and build a democratic society, many Iraqis with a deeper knowledge of their country's history perceived strong similarities between the British colonial and neocolonial roles in Iraq during the 1920s and 1930s and that of the Americans after the 2003 invasion. For them the more significant accomplishment of the occupation was the imposition of American control and the belief that Iraq's internal political changes came at the expense of subjugation to foreign powers.

Chapter Structure and Content

The first chapter begins by describing the area that became Iraq from ancient times through the Ottoman Empire. It briefly explains traditional forms of social organization, the differences and similarities between Iraq's Sunni and Shia Arabs, and the distinctive history and characteristics of the large ethnic minority, the Kurds. The chapter also describes the British-assisted Arab revolt against the Ottoman Empire during World War I and frustrated Arab expectations of self-determination and independence following the war. The apparent reasons for and significance of the British decisions to include the Kurds but exclude Kuwait from the new Iraqi state as well as to continue the Ottoman practice of relying on the Sunnis to administer the country are discussed. The chapter also describes how the 1920 Iraqi rebellion prompted the British to shift from direct colonial rule to indirect rule through importing and establishing a ruling dynasty with a constitution giving the new monarch the capability of dismissing or overruling the Iraqi parliament to ensure that Iraq's obligations to Britain were carried out. Finally, the chapter describes the lasting historical significance of Britain's denial of genuine democracy to the Iraqi people for the sake of its own interests. Many Iraqis viewed the corrupted and hollow political forms the British allowed as a mechanism of imperialism. This had dire consequences for Iraq's future, in inhibiting the development of a democratic political system. It also constituted a historical experience of imperialist machinations with which many Iraqis would equate the political system established under US supervision following the 2003 invasion.

Chapter 2 describes Iraq during the 1920–1932 British Mandate and the period of formal independence under the British-installed monarchy from 1932 to the 1958 revolution, depicting the constrained nature of political conflict and the contending political groups. Essentially, no serious challenge to British interests or the monarchy and no real democracy were tolerated. The chapter describes how the defeat of Iraq and other Arab forces by Israel in the 1948 war in Palestine, the 1955 Baghdad Pact, and the 1956 Suez crisis steadily increased outrage against the monarchy among the Iraqi people and many officers in the Iraqi armed forces, setting the stage for the antimonarchy revolution, which eliminated the royal family.

The third chapter begins by describing the 1958 overthrow of the monarchy by the military, which many Iraqis credited with liberating Iraq from imperialism. But the revolutionaries were split between leftist officers led by General Abd al-Karim Qasim and an opposing group of Arab nationalist officers. At repeated points during the period of General Qasim's leadership, 1958 to 1963, Iraq experienced violent conflict between the Iraqi Communist Party, which supported him, and Arab nationalists including the Baath Party, one of whose young members, Saddam Hussein, participated in a failed attempt to assassinate Qasim. This chapter also describes how the fear of communist influence and the belief that Qasim had betrayed Arab nationalism led to the violent military revolt in 1963 in which Qasim and his top aides were executed and the Iraqi Communist Party was brutally suppressed. A succession of Arab nationalist regimes followed, culminating in the comprehensive coup by Baath Party supporters in July 1968.

The next two chapters describe a series of momentous interconnected developments, the understanding of which is essential for comprehending the Iraq War and the political forces, organizations, and personalities that emerged to play important roles in postinvasion Iraq. Chapter 4 deals with the consolidation of the Baathist regime, the emergence of Saddam as its leader, the regime's nationalization of the oil industry, and economic and social reforms. The chapter also explains the impact of the Iranian Revolution on Iraq, including Iraqi Shia political religious organizations and the outbreak of the Iran–Iraq War. The chapter tracks the course of the war, the involvement of other nations including the United States, how the war ended, and the effects of the war on Iraq.

The fifth chapter describes how the Iran–Iraq War, along with other factors, led to Iraq's decision to invade Kuwait and the 1991 Gulf War, and the consequences of Iraq's defeat. This chapter also explains how the invasion of Kuwait led to events that provoked Al Qaeda to repeatedly attack the United States, including the sensational 9/11 attacks, which provided the opportunity for the George W. Bush administration to invade and occupy Iraq.

Drawing on chapters 4 and 5, chapter 6 begins by describing the impact of the Bush administration and the 9/11 attacks in shifting the United States away from the policy of containing Iraq toward regime change and the so-called Bush Doctrine of preemptive or, more correctly, preventive war. The roles of eleven major actors in the decision for war are analyzed, including the president, Congress, Iraqi exiles, neoconservative officials, US intelligence agencies, the US news media, public opinion, and the UN. The plan for the war and significant aspects of the invasion are described. The chapter concludes with an analysis of the early stages of the occupation and fateful decisions by the occupying authorities.

Chapter 7 examines the American role in Iraq in regard to previous foreign interventions and how these influenced US policies. The major analysis in this chapter compares the Iraq War to the Vietnam War in terms of factors such as justification for war, nature of the resistance, roles of other nations, military strategy and tactics, policy goals, US public opinion, and arguments to continue the wars.

The eighth chapter describes how different social groups in Iraq reacted to the invasion and overthrow of the Baathist regime. It also describes the political arrangements that replaced the old government, the process of developing a new constitution, the first nationwide election under the new system, and key political and social issues. Differences and similarities in the attitudes of Shia and Sunni Arabs toward postinvasion conditions, the occupation, and the occupying forces revealed in social surveys are analyzed. The chapter continues with a description of the rise of antioccupation resistance groups and divisions among them with regard to ideology, goals, and tactics. Counterinsurgency sociological and anthropological methods are presented and compared with those used by American forces in the Vietnam conflict.

Chapter 9 explains the shift in US military strategy from conventional to counterinsurgency warfare and provides a comprehensive analysis of the range of modern counterinsurgency methods, their application in Iraq, and the role of the 2007 surge in US troop strength. The effects of other measures, such as the hiring of tens of thousands of Sunni Arab tribesmen to fight Al Qaeda in Mesopotamia, the truce by antioccupation Shia militiamen, and advanced counterinsurgency technology are also covered. Moving beyond the military dimension, this chapter also explores the activities of US corporations in Iraq and issues of waste, fraud, and corruption. The role of private military firms is described along with their rapid growth in the context of the war on terror and the US occupations of Iraq and Afghanistan. The potential future role of these organizations in US interventions abroad is also considered. The last sections of this chapter deal with issues regarding the US volunteer military, charges of human rights abuse, and the 2008 Iraq–US Status of Forces Agreement, in which Iraq's government consented to extending the US-led military occupation until December 31, 2011.

The final chapter describes major impacts of the Iraq War, including effects on Iraq in terms of loss of life, sectarian violence, women's and children's welfare, and the status of Iraqi Kurdistan. Impacts on the war on terrorism and the war in Afghanistan are also analyzed. The chapter further describes the war's effects on the United States, including the issue of control of oil, economic costs, domestic politics, the news media, the military, and America's international moral standing. Other international consequences covered include the Iraq War's effect on the UN and political developments and policies in other countries. The chapter also considers whether and under what conditions the Iraq War can result in a genuinely democratic and sovereign Iraq and a US government committed to avoiding similar tragic mistakes in the future.

The costs of the Iraq War, a conflict launched through deception of the American people, intentional or not, against a nation that had not attacked the United States and lacked the means to do so have been vast for both Iraq and the United States. The hatred and desire for revenge of many Iraqis and their sympathizers in other countries may result in as yet unanticipated consequences. Coping with the war's effects will undoubtedly continue to be a source of concern and controversy.

I

||||||||||||||||||||||||||||||||||||||||||||||||||||||||||||||||||||||||||||||||||||||||||||||||||||||||||||||||||||||||||||

Culture and
History of Iraq

Ancient Mesopotamia
to the British Mandate

Iraq within its current borders was created shortly after the end of World War I. Which peoples and territories to include or exclude from the new state were in great part decided with the interests of other countries in mind, especially Great Britain. Besides large oil and natural gas reserves, Iraq has rich agricultural lands, but internal and international conflict has often deprived the Iraqi people of fully and securely realizing and enjoying their country's energy and agricultural potential.

The People and Land of Iraq

Great Britain, which occupied much of the former Ottoman Empire at the conclusion of World War I, combined three former Ottoman provinces—Mosul province in the north, Baghdad province in the center, and Basra province in the south—to constitute the new state of Iraq. Britain had earlier detached Kuwait from Basra province and later helped establish it as an independent state.

Approximately 168,754 square miles (437,072 square kilometers), Iraq is bounded by Kuwait and Saudi Arabia in the south, Jordan in the west, Syria in the northwest, Turkey in the north, and Iran in the east. It has access to the Persian Gulf through only two ports, Basra on the Shatt al-Arab (the Arab River), formed by the confluence of the Tigris and Euphrates rivers, and Umm Qasr, which is located on the Persian Gulf where Iraq controls only about 36 miles (58 kilometers) of the coastline. Rain, except in the north of Iraq, falls almost exclusively during winter. Summers tend to be hot and dry with many cloudless days. The US CIA World Fact Book (2008a, 4) indicates that in 2008 Iraq's population exceeded 28 million people. But as many as 2 million people may have fled Iraq in the aftermath of the US-led 2003 invasion.

The origin of the name "Iraq" is unclear. It may have been derived from the ancient Sumerian city of Uruk, once located in what is now southern Iraq.

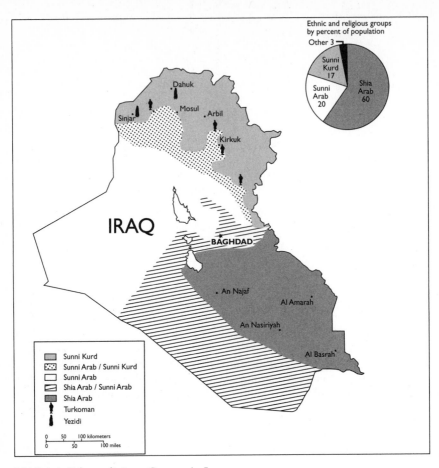

MAP 1.1 Ethnoreligious Groups in Iraq

However, William Polk (2005: 32) suggests that it comes from the Persian expression *erăgh*, meaning "the lowlands."

The population is estimated to be about 75 percent to 80 percent Arab, 15 percent to 20 percent Kurdish (residing mainly in the northeast in areas bordering Turkey and Iran), and about 5 percent other ethnic groups, such as Turkoman, Assyrian, Armenian, or Persian. About 97 percent of Iraq's people are Muslim. An estimated 60 percent to 65 percent are Shia (predominantly in the south, but also the majority in the capital city, Baghdad), 32 percent to 37 percent are Sunni (mainly in central and northern Iraq), and 3 percent Christian or members of other faiths. Most Iraqi Arabs are Shia, but about 75 percent of Kurds are Sunni and 15 percent are Shia (Anderson and Stansfield 2004: 159). Baghdad has a population of over 5 million, the southeastern city of Basra more than 1.5 million, and in the north Mosul has more than 1 million and Kirkuk more than half a million.

The country's diverse terrain and peoples are linked by the Tigris and Euphrates rivers. In the south near the confluence of the twin rivers are considerable wetland and marsh areas. Between the wetlands and Baghdad is the delta territory, home of the Sumerian and Babylonian civilizations of ancient Mesopotamia, a flat area where rain is scarce and farmlands are irrigated by river water. In the northeast the rugged mountains are inhabited almost exclusively by Kurds.

Ancient Civilizations

Mesopotamia is a Greek term meaning "the land between the two rivers." But more generally Mesopotamia included virtually all the land bounded by the Persian Gulf on the south, the Zargos and Anti-Taurus mountains on the west and north, respectively, and the Arabian plateau on the southwest. This encompassed most of modern Iraq and parts of Syria and Turkey. Here the ancient Ubaidians, Sumerians, Akkadians, Babylonians, and Assyrians created revolutionary innovations that greatly influenced the history of humankind, including farming, leading to the development of cities. The Babylonian king Hammurabi (1792–1750 BCE) created one of the first and most historically influential codifications of laws. By setting forth laws in writing, Hammurabi's Code advanced civilization through state-enforced norms that provided uniformity and stability, and reflected a level of common interest that rulers could not arbitrarily ignore. Major contributions of Mesopotamian civilizations to the development of world society, including metalworking, the wheel, writing, and precise calendars, led some modern Iraqi leaders to foster pride in this heritage among the country's diverse ethnic and religious groups in attempts to create a strong national identity.

Persian (Iranian) and Greek (Macedonian) Conquests

In 539 BCE, Cyrus of Persia conquered Babylonia. He was so enamored of the city of Babylon and its achievements that he decided to make it the capital of the Persian Empire and attempted to blend Babylonian and Persian cultures. When Alexander the Great defeated the Persian army and in 330 BCE entered Babylon, he, like Cyrus before him, conceived the idea of uniting cultures, but this time he attempted to unify the culture of the West, Greece, with the cultures of the East, Babylon and Persia. He apparently intended to make Babylon the capital of the world but died there in 323 BCE, after which his empire was subdivided among his top commanders. A new Persian force, the Parthians, captured Babylon in 144 BCE.

Traditional Forms of Social Organization and Authority

From Mesopotamian civilizations to modern Iraq, traditional forms of social organization have played significant roles in economics and politics: the family, the clan, and the tribe. Theoretically, blood relationships are the basis for all three. Family units encompass grandparents, aunts and uncles, and their children (first cousins). The clan (or subtribe) extends beyond the immediate family to include more distant relatives, such as second, third, and fourth cousins, whose existence and relationship to each person may be known to each member of the clan. But unlike the family, face-to-face interaction between clan members is generally more limited. In Iraqi Arab society, a clan often includes several extended family networks that trace their origin to a common father.

The concept of tribe generally refers to a set of clans (often four to six) that are united by a sense of blood kinship and the notion that all of the clans are descended from a common ancestor. In all forms of kinship-based organization, certain members of the kin network are recognized as leaders who have the right to exercise authority over other members. The leader of an Arab tribe is called a sheik, an Arabic word meaning "a man of old age." Among the Shia, a tribal sheik often shares power with a religious leader. The tribal subculture typically emphasizes hospitality and courage. For many, tribal membership provides a sense of identity and a feeling of security, and tribal leaders are often called upon to mediate disputes. Tribalism among Iraq's Kurdish population is similar, with tribal leaders referred to as *aghas*.

As strong central governments emerged in Iraq, providing police, legal frameworks, courts, and various forms of social assistance, the importance and influence of tribes and clans subsided. However, at times when the state lost legitimacy or its ability to provide essential services and security to its citizens, reliance on tribal networks tended to increase. Tribalism, along with ethnicity and religion, has been one of the three major dimensions of group identity in Iraq.

Islamic Iraq and the Shia-Sunni Split

The Prophet Muhammad, born in 571 in Mecca, described experiencing a vision of the angel Gabriel, through whom he received a series of messages to convey to humanity from the one true God. Muhammad's associates assembled those messages into the holy book of Islam, the Quran (Koran). Islam spread rapidly in part because of its principle of social organization, superior to that of tribal society. By proclaiming that only one God existed and that all men who embraced Islam (the state of submission to God) became brothers, Muhammad laid the foundation for a form of social organization based on religious rather than blood kinship (Polk 2005: 38–39). As the "tribe" of Islam grew to include many thousands, it began to overwhelm resistance from traditional tribes. Thus it was not only Islam's message but also the structure and character of the Islamic community that won adherents for the new faith.

The unexpected death of Muhammad in 632 created a leadership dilemma. Prominent Islamic figures elected Abu Bakr, the imam (Arabic for "stood in front") who had led the daily prayers when Muhammad was unavailable, as the first caliph, or successor. In 656 Ali, the Prophet's cousin and the husband of Fatima, the Prophet's daughter, was elected the fourth caliph. Ali, whom many viewed as genuinely concerned about improving the lives of the poor, was faced with an increasingly fractured and internally conflicted Islamic community. In 661 he was assassinated.

Some Muslims proclaimed that Muhammad had actually chosen Ali to be his rightful successor. Furthermore, they believed that only the descendants of Ali and Fatima were to govern the Islamic community. Those who embraced this concept came to be known as the supporters or partisans of Ali, the Shiat Ali or, more simply, Shia. Shia Muslims referred to Ali and certain male descendants of Ali and Fatima, who they believed had the right to rule Islam, as imams (assigning this new meaning to the term other Muslims continued to use for the person who read the daily prayers). The imams were thought by the Shia to be infallible (incapable of religious error). Other Muslims rejected these ideas and believed instead that only the Quran, the most central element of the tradition, or Sunna, of Islam, was infallible. According to the Sunnis, religious leaders could only attempt to interpret the Quran to the faithful in the context of each historical era.

The martyrdom of Imam Hussein in 680 was of great significance for the Shia. Hussein was the grandson of the Prophet and was the third Shia imam after his father, Ali, and his older brother, Hassan. Following Ali's death, the caliphate was assumed by Muawiya Abi Sufian, governor of Syria, who had opposed Ali. When Hussein refused to accept Yazid, Muawiya's son, as the leader of Islam, Yazid's army surrounded and killed Hussein and many of his companions in the Karbala desert of Iraq. Hussein's death symbolized jihad (a struggle carried out for the sake of the Islamic community) and martyrdom (DeFronzo 2007: 277; Hussain 1985: 23–24) for Shia. The date of Imam Hussein's death, Ashura, the tenth day of Muharram (the first month of the year of the Islamic calendar), is commemorated each year as a day of mourning when many Shia make a pilgrimage to the Imam Hussein shrine in Karbala. During the Saddam Hussein era, this event sometimes became an occasion for political protest.

Despite disagreement over succession to Muhammad, the Sunni and the Shia have similar sets of core beliefs. One significant disagreement, though, is that Shia believe the Quran supports the Nikah Mut'ah, or fixed-time marriages that people can enter into with the mutual understanding that the marriage will end on a predetermined date without the need for a divorce. Sunnis reject temporary marriage. Worldwide, the large majority of Muslims are Sunni, while about one-sixth are Shia.

Divisions developed among the Shia concerning how many infallible imams followed Muhammad. The large majority, dominant in Iraq and Iran, are Twelver Shias, who believe the twelfth and last imam vanished in 873, after which there was no longer an infallible leader of Islam. This situation will change, according to Twelver Shia, only when the "hidden imam," or Mahdi, returns to the faithful. Until then Islamic scholars (*mujtahid*) are allowed to issue authoritative opinions. Since Karbala is located in southern Iraq, many people there embraced Shia Islam, and Karbala and Najaf became Shia holy cities. Iraqi political leaders often feared that in times of conflict with Iran, some among Iraq's majority Shia population might side with their Iranian coreligionists.

Mongol Devastation and Ottoman Conquest

With a population of perhaps 1 million by the tenth century (Marr 2004: 5), Baghdad developed into the greatest center of Islamic civilization. But in 1258

Mongol armies captured the city, killing Caliph Mustasim and as many as 800,000 people (Polk 2005: 57). Baghdad was again devastated by the Mongols under Tamerlane in 1401 when tens of thousands more were killed (Al-Qazzaz 2006: 439). The Mongol invasions destroyed major Iraqi achievements in science and technology, and many of the country's most brilliant residents.

Following the Mongol invasions, an Ottoman caliphate was eventually established in Istanbul. After the Persians occupied Baghdad in 1509, the Sunni Ottoman Empire responded in 1534 by seizing the city and later the rest of Mesopotamia. The Ottomans remained in control, except for a brief period of Persian occupation in the seventeenth century, until the British invasion during World War I. What later would be established as Iraq after the end of World War I existed within the Ottoman Empire as three provinces (*vilayats*): Mosul (where many Kurds lived), Baghdad (which included much of what today is central and western Iraq), and Basra (southern Iraq and territory that became the separate country of Kuwait). The Sunni Ottomans preferred fellow Sunnis as administrators and military officers within Mesopotamia. Thus some four centuries of Ottoman rule firmly established Sunni Iraqis in leadership roles rather than the more numerous Shia.

World War I and the Arab Nationalist Revolt

A nationalist movement developed in the early twentieth century to free Arabs from Ottoman rule. When the Ottoman Empire entered World War I on the side of Germany against czarist Russia, Britain, and France, Ottoman conscription of Arabs (people who spoke the Arab language and identified with Arab culture) caused a surge in Arab nationalism.

Desperate for assistance in its war against Germany, Great Britain secretly entered into separate negotiations with several nations and groups over the future of the Ottoman Empire's Arab territories. The British would later be accused of making conflicting but self-serving promises to several of their negotiation partners. Among the most important negotiations regarding Arab territories were the Hussein-McMahon Correspondence, the agreement with Abd al-Aziz abd al-Rahman al-Saud of the Najd region in Arabia, the British-French Sykes-Picot Agreement, and the Balfour Declaration, the British pledge to the Zionist movement to support a Jewish homeland.

The motive behind the Sykes-Picot Agreement of May 1916 seems obvious. Britain, desiring not to offend its ally, France, in the war with Germany and to avoid French interference with British postwar activities in the Middle East, developed a plan for Arab lands that would involve sharing them with the French. The Sykes-Picot Agreement divided the Ottoman Arab provinces between Britain and France, with the French getting Syria and Lebanon and the British getting Palestine and territories that would later become Jordan and Iraq.

The Balfour Declaration of November 2, 1917, committed Britain to creating a homeland for the Jews in largely Arab-populated Palestine. The British, in promising to gratify the aspirations of the international Zionist movement, were apparently hoping to win the support of the world Jewish community in Britain's conflict with Germany. The British might have also hoped that the Balfour Declaration would appeal to Jewish leaders within Russia's 1917 revolutionary government and influence them to keep Russia in the war, forcing Germany to continue to fight a two-front war (Ibrahim 2006: 75).

The agreement with Abd al-Aziz abd al-Rahman al-Saud stated that Britain would recognize al-Saud (future founder of the nation of Saudi Arabia) as the legitimate ruler of the huge Najd section of Arabia in return for al-Saud's assistance against the Ottomans (Ibrahim 2006, 74). The role of al-Saud was significant in that his forces prevented the Ottoman army from receiving supplies through the Persian Gulf.

The British aimed to transform the Arab nationalist movement into a massive revolt against the Ottomans, preventing them from threatening such important British interests as the Suez Canal in Egypt. Arab nationalist groups had been established in Damascus, Syria, and Beirut, Lebanon. One of the most important was al-Ahd (the Covenant), a Damascus-based secret organization that included Syrian and Mesopotamian Arab nationalist officers within the Ottoman army. Since Ottoman forces firmly controlled Damascus and Beirut, the British were unable to negotiate directly with the Arab nationalists there.

The only prominent Arab nationalist leaders the British could effectively communicate with were in the Arabian peninsula, al-Saud in Najd and the Sharif Hussein ibn Ali (sharif means "noble," in the sense of being a descendant of the Prophet) of the Sunni Muslim Hashemite family in Mecca. Sharif Hussein sent one of his sons, Faisal, to Damascus in the spring of 1915. Faisal met with Arab nationalists there and brought back to his father their plan, the Damascus Protocol, for a future independent unified Arab nation that would comprise virtually all of the then Ottoman-dominated Arab territories, including the present-day countries of Iraq, Jordan, Lebanon, Saudi Arabia, Syria, and Palestine (where today Israel is located).

In November 1914, Sharif Hussein began a correspondence with Sir Henry McMahon, British high commissioner in Egypt, regarding the future status of the Arab territories in the Middle East under Ottoman control. According to Ibrahim (2006: 71–73, 76), the basis for Sharif Hussein's demands from the British during these negotiations was the Damascus Protocol.

Through the 1915–1916 Hussein-McMahon Correspondence, the sharif agreed to organize an Arab revolt against Ottoman forces, as well as give the British preference in postwar economic projects in Arab lands, in return for what he apparently thought was a British guarantee that after the war the former Arab territories of the Ottoman Empire, including Syria, Palestine, and Iraq, would be granted immediate independence.

On June 5, 1916, Sharif Hussein launched the Arab Revolt. His army was composed of bedouin from western Arabia, deserters from the Ottoman armies, and Arab nationalist officers who defected from the Ottomans to fight for the promised Arab state. These sharifian officers included Arabs from Mesopotamia (future Iraq), such as Nuri al-Said, who became a major link with the British. The Arab forces were paid and armed by the British and advised by T. E. Lawrence ("Lawrence of Arabia"), who had helped organize the revolt and then joined the Arab forces under the command of Sharif Hussein's son, Faisal. The Arabs did not know that the goal they were fighting for, the establishment of a unified and independent Arab state, was inconsistent with the Sykes-Picot Agreement, the Balfour Declaration, and the British agreement with al-Saud, which helped him move toward creating a separate state of Saudi Arabia rather than joining with a single unified Arab nation. McMahon later claimed that Palestine was excluded from his negotiations with Sharif Hussein, while the sharif indicated that he believed it was included. Ottoman forces surrendered in Jerusalem on December 9, 1917. In October 1918, accompanied by British adviser Lawrence, Faisal and his associates entered Damascus to organize the new Arab nationalist government. But in March 1920, French forces in Syria abolished Faisal's government and he left the country.

Before and during World War I, the British took important actions regarding Iraq. One was the decision to recognize Kuwait as an independent state, even though it was a part of the Ottomans' Basra province, and to declare that it was under British protection. This was in part to provide Britain with enhanced capability to protect its oil interests in Iran (Polk 2005: 67). By the outbreak of World War I, Britain's concern for access to oil intensified because the British navy's ships were converting from coal to oil fuel, much of it coming from the Anglo-Persian Company's Iranian wells (DeFronzo 2007: 278; Hussain 1985: 14). Petroleum-based fuels were also needed for military vehicles and airplanes (Paul 2002: 1).

Access to Kuwait gave Britain increased capability to control the Persian Gulf. Protecting Iranian oil and British communications also motivated the British to invade Mesopotamia. On November 6, 1914, British-Indian forces landed at the port city of Faw on the Shatt al-Arab. But when they attempted to march north against Baghdad in June 1915, they were defeated by Ottoman forces and forced to surrender at Kut in late April 1916. After large reinforcements arrived, the British succeeded in taking Baghdad in March 1917.

At the end of the war, many Arab nationalists soon perceived they were being betrayed. Although US President Woodrow Wilson's Fourteen Points seemed to call for self-determination by the non-Turkish peoples under Ottoman domination, it appeared that Britain and France were dividing the Arab territories between them and that Arab Palestine was being settled by thousands of European Jews intent on creating a Jewish homeland.

British-Controlled Iraq

Although the British and their Indian colonial troops were in control of Mesopotamia at the conclusion of World War I, they sought international legality for a long-term occupation. This was provided by the new League of Nations, which granted Britain a mandate over Iraq under which the British were to prepare the country for independence.

At first the British administered Iraq directly using British and Indian personnel who had served in India's colonial administration. Some saw great agricultural potential through water control and irrigation projects, and Mesopotamia was thought to have large quantities of oil since much of it was geologically similar to Iran, where oil was already being produced. The British high commissioner for Iraq was Sir Arnold Wilson from the British Indian colonial office. Polk (2005: 73) describes Wilson as an extraordinary person, a brave and highly decorated former soldier of integrity who had become familiar with the languages and cultures of the Mesopotamian people. Very efficient, he was accused of using relatively repressive methods.

One of the major issues was exactly which territories to include within Iraq in addition to the former Ottoman provinces of Baghdad and Basra. Much to the resentment of many Iraqis, the British decided to permanently detach Kuwait from Basra province and establish and protect it as a separate entity ruled by a pro-British monarchy (Hiro 1992: 9–48). Maintaining Kuwait as a British affiliated state potentially gave Britain great leverage against a future independent Iraq since once the territory of Kuwait was removed from Basra, Iraq had extremely limited and precarious access to the Persian Gulf.

It was not initially clear whether the Mosul province would become part of Iraq. The British considered turning it over to France or Turkey or using part of it as a new homeland for the Kurdish people. After World War I, the victorious Allied powers had indicated that they would create an autonomous territory for the stateless Kurds that could possibly later become an independent nation. But once it was suspected that Mosul province contained large amounts of oil, the British decided to incorporate it into British-dominated Iraq. That oil existed in at least part of the territory that might have become an independent Kurdish nation sealed the Kurds' fate, despite the potential for future ethnic conflict caused by incorporating them into a predominantly Arab state.

The Kurds

Integrating Kurds into Iraq would prove difficult. Iraqi governments went through cycles of attempting to assimilate the Kurds, appease them, divide them, and/or crush them when they rose in rebellion. The Kurds, who speak an Indo-European language and are likely the descendants of the ancient Medes, live mainly in the northeast mountain ranges, terrain that has helped them survive many conflicts and spawned the saying "the Kurds have no friends but the mountains." They are the fourth-largest ethnic group in the Middle East after the Arabic-, Turkish-, and Persian-speaking peoples and one of the largest in the world with no independent state of their own, making up about 15 percent to 20 percent of Iraqis, and approximately 20 percent of Turks, 10 percent of Iranians, and 5 percent of Syrians. In Iraq they are about 75 percent Sunni, 15 percent Shia, and the rest members of other faiths.

Over time, tribal traditions conflicted with Kurdish political movements in urban areas such as Sulaimaniyya and Arbil. Leftist concepts, such as socialism, and the nationalist goal of suppressing tribal divisions caused city-dwelling professionals and workers to rebel against tribal authority. This tribal-versus-urban split, paralleled by conservative versus leftist ideological orientations, would characterize Kurdish politics in future years.

At the end of World War I, the victorious allies through the Treaty of Sèvres proposed local autonomy for some Kurdish areas and provided "for future consideration of the creation of an independent Kurdish nation" (Bozarslan 2006: 519). According to Anderson and Stansfield (2004: 162–163), the most significant factor that convinced the British to oppose an independent Kurdistan, as noted earlier, was the belief that the Kurdish region of Mosul province contained oil. But having worked cooperatively with Sunnis during World War I, the British also apparently decided to keep the Kurds within Iraq to give the country a larger proportion of Sunnis. A further consideration was that the mountainous Kurdish territory constituted a more easily defensible border for Iraq.

Iraqi Rebellion of 1920

British policies provoked a widespread, though disorganized, rebellion in 1920 lasting about six months, resulting in the deaths of an estimated 6,000 Iraqis and about 500 British and Indian soldiers (Tripp 2000: 44).

The decision to recognize certain cooperative individuals as tribal leaders and grant them title to large landholdings contributed to the revolt. They received private ownership of land that previously had been considered communal tribal property. Poor peasants felt dispossessed of land that their families had cultivated for generations. This explosive British agricultural policy not only provoked class conflict, it also reaccentuated tribalism and tribal divisions.

But the major factor provoking rebellion in 1920 was the perception that Iraq was not going to become an independent nation, but instead had escaped Ottoman rule to be placed under British domination. The announcement that the League of Nations had granted Britain a mandate over Iraq outraged many Iraqis. Thousands took up arms against some 133,000 British occupation troops. The rebellion, in which Sunni Arabs, Shia Arabs, and Kurds all fought the common British enemy, was suppressed with great difficulty. Partly in response, the British decided to move toward more indirect rule of Iraq using cooperative Arabs and Kurds as often as possible in place of British officials. Since Sir Wilson's direct rule had failed, he was replaced as British high commissioner of Iraq by Sir Percy Cox on October 1, 1920.

Modified British Control of Iraq:
Monarchy, Treaty, and Constitution

The new British policies were formulated at the Cairo Conference of 1921, where Britain decided to impose an imported monarchy on Iraq. The decision of a democracy, Great Britain, to install or support monarchies in Arab societies sowed the seeds of future problems. That the royal family of Iraq would be foreign, rather than Iraqi, forced the ruling dynasty to be even more dependent on and cooperative with the British for survival than it otherwise might have been.

The establishment of a monarchy resulted from several considerations. First, the 1920 revolt discredited Sir Wilson's British India colonial approach. Direct rule and precautionary repression to terrorize Iraqis into submission backfired. The fighting, turmoil, expense, and thousands of deaths and injuries during 1920 were unacceptable. The British government turned to a plan advocated by the British Arab Bureau in Cairo, an approach promoted by T. E.

Lawrence and Sir Wilson's rebellious assistant Gertrude Bell: installing a cooperative Arab administration in Iraq in place of direct rule.

The French ouster of Sharif Hussein's son Faisal from Syria made him available for the creation of a pro-British Hashemite monarchy in Iraq as King Faisal I. The Hashemite family name comes from Hashem, the great-grandfather of the Prophet Muhammad. The Hashemites believe they are descendants of the Prophet through his daughter Fatima and her husband, Ali. Though Faisal felt that Britain had betrayed the Hussein-McMahon Correspondence, he was willing to accept the invitation to become king. The British also installed Faisal's brother, Abdullah, as the emir of Transjordan (later king of Jordan).

A monarchy benefited Britain so long as the king and leading members of his government were pro-British. Faisal's regime included al-Ahd veterans, in particular Nuri al-Said, who often would serve as Iraq's prime minister or foreign minister and cooperate with the British. The installation of Faisal as king was to be approved through a referendum. But this occurred only after Sayyid Talib, who called for Iraqis to select their own leaders, was arrested by the British and expelled from the country, leaving no effective opposition (Polk 2005: 79–80). The referendum, described as "well-managed" by Marr (2004: 25), "bogus" by Tripp (2000: 48), and "something of a farce" by Wright (1926: 747), approved Faisal, who became Iraq's first Hashemite king on August 27, 1921. The British high commissioner, Sir Percy Cox, decided to rely heavily on Iraq's Sunni minority to provide, under British supervision, the administrative staff for the monarchy.

The 1922 British-Iraq Treaty

The 1922 British-Iraq Treaty was intended to create the impression that the relationship between Britain and Iraq was based on mutual agreement. The treaty, accepted by the British-approved Iraqi Council of Ministers and signed on October 10, 1922, was described as "the backbone of Britain's indirect rule" (Marr 2004: 26) of Iraq. It stated that the king would support British interests, while Britain controlled Iraq's financial affairs, foreign relations, and army. According to treaty Article IV, "His Majesty the King of Iraq agrees to be guided by the advice of His Britannic Majesty tendered through the (British) High Commissioner on all matters affecting the international and financial obligations and interests of His Britannic Majesty for the whole period of this treaty" (Bourdillon 1924: 281). In the early 1920s, the king relied on British forces, and if he engaged in "unsound administrative policies" the British could refuse to enforce them.

The treaty required that British officials oversee administration of all Iraq's provinces. British "advisers" not only indirectly controlled provincial administrations but also gathered local information. Under British pressure, on the night of June 10, 1924, Iraq's Constituent Assembly formally accepted the treaty by a vote of thirty-seven to twenty-four, with eight abstaining and thirty-one members absent (Bourdillon 1924: 283).

The Iraqi Constitution of 1924

The League of Nations mandate over Iraq called for Britain to develop an "organic law," a constitution, for Mesopotamia: "The Mandatory will frame within the shortest time, not exceeding three years from the date of the coming into force of the Mandate, an Organic Law for Mesopotamia, which shall be submitted to the Council of the League of Nations for approval. . . . This Organic Law shall be framed in consultation with the native authorities, and shall take account of the rights, interests and wishes of all the populations inhabiting the mandated territory. It shall contain provisions designed to facilitate the progressive development of Mesopotamia as an independent state" (Davidson 1925: 42). But while banning discrimination on the basis of race, religion, or language, the constitution enabled Britain to use the monarchy to ensure that obligations of Iraq to Britain specified in the Anglo-Iraqi Treaty of 1922 would be fulfilled regardless of the will of the Iraqi people. Part I, "Rights of the People," Article 18, of the constitution provided for the employment of "foreigners" (British citizens) in Iraqi government positions in accord with the requirements of "Treaties or Agreements."

In Part II, "The Crown," the king is proclaimed the commander in chief of the armed forces and given the right to appoint members of the upper house of the Iraqi parliament, the Senate. Article 26 (c) of Part II gave the Iraqi king the right to make "ordinances which have the force of law," with the consent of the cabinet of ministers, when the Iraqi parliament was not sitting and to disband the parliament. Davidson (1925: 46–47) states, "The King and his Ministers could, in the teeth of an unmanageable Chamber, provide for necessary supplies or decree the legislation necessary to implement . . . treaty obligations on which the very existence of the State depends."

The lower house of parliament, the Chamber of Deputies, was to be elected indirectly by all male voters. Iraqi men could vote through secret ballots in a primary election for electors who would later vote in a secondary election to select the parliamentary deputies. This system allowed the king's administration ample opportunity to influence electors in the secondary election if the primary election had produced results that the monarchy or the British opposed.

Finally, the constitution permitted the king during times of martial law "to entrust" the administration of certain districts to "the Air Officer Commanding British forces in Iraq" (Davidson 1925: 52), in effect, permitting the British military to suppress rebellious Iraqis. The constitution was approved by the Constituent Assembly in 1924. With "a few modifications it provided the country's political and legal structure under the monarchy until the revolution of 1958" (Marr 2004: 28). Many viewed the 1924 constitution as a sham to mask British control that sabotaged any chance to establish real democracy in Iraq for decades.

Economic Change

British policies helped shift the Iraqi economy to produce goods for the world market: First were agricultural products like cotton, but soon oil became the

major export. Previously communally owned or publicly used land was transferred to private ownership. The new owners often occupied central positions
in extended kinship networks. Whether Sunni Arab, Shia Arab, or Kurd, they
could use their economic power and kinship ties to support the monarchy and
British interests. Many peasants were transformed into impoverished rent-pay-
ing tenant farmers. The new landowners were among those most likely to find
their way into the Iraqi parliament.

Irrigated land increased "from about 72 to 4,000 square miles" (Polk
2005: 87), but the lives of many peasants deteriorated significantly. In 1933 an
Iraqi parliament dominated by "urban investors and tribal leaders" passed the
Law Governing the Rights and Duties of the Cultivators (Polk 2005: 87), concerning the legal obligations of peasants. Polk claims that this law effectively
transformed many Iraqi agricultural laborers into serfs. The law expanded the
concept of debt to include a wide range of circumstances, including paying for
any tasks required of the laborer by the landowner that, in the view of the
owner, the laborer did not perform to his satisfaction. Many peasants were consequently continuously in debt to the landowners and, like serfs, had no legal
right to leave the land on which they worked until debts were paid.

British Military Policies

At the 1921 Cairo Conference, the British decided to organize an Iraqi army.
The lower ranks were mostly either Sunni or Shia, but the officers were overwhelmingly Sunni, often veterans of the Ottoman army. The cost of controlling
Iraq was lessened by British airpower, especially effective in an environment
with little natural cover for rebels. The British also created a "Christian" military force from Iraq's tiny Assyrian minority called the Levies. Amazingly, during the mandate period the Iraqi army, whose men were almost entirely Islamic,
as were about 97 percent of Iraq's people, was allowed to be no larger than the
Christian Levies drawn from the less than 1 percent of the population who
were Assyrian. Many Iraqis developed great animosity for the Levies, whom
they viewed as mercenaries for the British. Over time, much of the Iraqi military evolved into an extremely anti-British force because of British failure to
grant genuine independence and the belief that the pro-British monarchy had
betrayed the sacrifice and honor of the armed forces.

Key Factors That Shaped Iraqi Society and History

Social complexity, involving multiple forms of social organization, identification,
and solidarity, has been an important characteristic of Iraq. State-alternative
kinship relationships, ethnic and religious differences, and adherence to varying
political ideologies have led to recurring social conflict. A second significant
aspect of the country's history is that since Shia Islam is the religion of Iraq's giant neighbor, Sunni-dominated Iraqi regimes periodically questioned the loyalty
of many of Iraq's Shia citizens when faced with threats emanating from Iran.

Britain's inclusion of the Kurds and detachment of Kuwait were crucial decisions beneficial to British interests with enormous impacts on Iraq. Conflict

between Kurdish nationalists and the Iraqi central government was a recurrent and destabilizing feature of the country. The separation of Kuwait contributed to frustrating the goal of a united Arab state in the Middle East in which geographically localized resources, in particular oil, could benefit all the Arab people. Kuwait, with about 10 percent of the world's known oil reserves, an indigenous population of about 1,305,000, and an 80 percent foreign workforce (CIA 2008b: 3, 7), is not unlike several other oil-rich ministates in which pro-British monarchies controlled vast energy resources in a cooperative relationship with Britain and its allies. Many Iraqis rejected Kuwait's separate status, and the seizure of Kuwait in 1990 led to Iraq's defeat by a US alliance in 1991 and contributed to the circumstances leading to the 2003 US-led invasion.

Another important factor was the establishment of a monarchy with an imported royal dynasty virtually powerless to take any action opposed by the British. The monarchy became widely despised as an instrument of foreign imperialism. Because the form of government forced on the Iraqis was not a genuine democracy, they could not sufficiently express their aspirations through it or use it as their means of liberation from foreign control. Therefore, the vehicle to achieve true independence for Iraq in the late 1950s was its military, which not only elevated the prestige of the armed forces, but also contributed to a pattern of authoritarian rule in the name of anti-imperialism that ultimately led to the dictatorship of Saddam Hussein.

British reliance on Sunnis to staff top governmental and military posts perpetuated Sunni domination. Many of the most prominent Iraqi Sunni Arabs supported pan-Arabism, the movement for the political unification of Arab peoples and countries. This orientation in government and school textbooks interfered with constructing Iraqi national unity and patriotism. The Kurds were offended by a central government that exalted Arab culture and history. Many Iraqi Shia Arabs were critical of pan-Arabism because, though they were relatively excluded from political power, their population majority status gave them significant economic and religious influence that could be lost in a future unified and overwhelmingly Sunni Arab state. The more Sunni Iraqi leaders pursued pan-Arabism, the more likely they were to provoke ethnic and sectarian conflict.

Summary and Analysis

Iraqis are the descendants of some of the most ancient and creative civilizations in world history, believed responsible for such major contributions to human development as farming, writing, use of the wheel, and written laws. For centuries the Ottomans, who were Sunni Muslims, relied on local Sunnis to administer much of the territory that would become Iraq. During World War I, with major assistance from the British, Arab nationalists launched the Arab Revolt against the Ottoman Empire with the goals of winning independence for the Arab people and establishing a great unified Arab state in the Middle East.

The British, granted a mandate over Mesopotamia by the League of Nations, combined most of three former Ottoman provinces, Baghdad, Basra, and Mosul, into what became Iraq, established a pro-British Iraqi monarchy,

and played a major role in constructing a constitution for the country that required Iraq to satisfy British interests. The form of government the British permitted for the Iraqis, the territories and peoples they did or did not choose to
include in the new state, and their decision to rely mainly on Sunnis to staff administrative and military leadership posts were among the most important factors in the history of Iraq. Though the United States relied more on Shia in
implementing its postinvasion plans, some American policies had striking similarities to those of the British during the mandate period.

References and Further Readings

Abdul-Jabar, Faleh, and Hosham Dawod, eds. 2003. *Tribes and Power: National-
ism and Ethnicity in the Middle East.* London: Saqi.
Anderson, Liam, and Gareth Stansfield. 2004. *The Future of Iraq.* New York: Pal-
grave Macmillan.
Antonius, George. 1938. *The Arab Awakening: The Story of the Arab National
Movement.* London: H. Hamilton.
Atiyyah, Ghassan. 1973. *Iraq, 1908–1921: A Political Study.* Beirut: Arab Institute
for Research and Publishing.
Bourdillon, B. H. 1924. "The Political Situation in Iraq." *Journal of the British In-
stitute of International Affairs* 3, 6: 273–287.
Bozarslan, Hamit. 2006. *"Kurdish Movements."* In James DeFronzo, ed., *Revolutionary Movements in World History: From 1750 to the Present,* vol. 2,
519–528. Santa Barbara, CA: ABC-CLIO.
Bruinessen, Martin van. 2003. "Kurds, States and Tribes." In Faleh A. Jabar and
Hosham Dawod, eds., *Tribes and Power,* 165–183.
Central Intelligence Agency. 2008a. *CIA—The World Fact Book, Iraq.* www.cia.gov/
library/publications/the-world-factbook/geos/iz.html, accessed July 3, 2008.
———. 2008b. *CIA—The World Fact Book, Kuwait.* www.cia.gov/cia/publications/
factbook/print/iz.html, accessed July 3, 2008.
Davidson, Nigel G. 1925. "The Constitution of Iraq." *Journal of Comparative Leg-
islation and International Law* 3rd Ser., 7, 1: 41–52.
DeFronzo, James. 2007. *Revolutions and Revolutionary Movements.* Boulder, CO:
Westview Press.
Dodge, Toby. 2003. "The Social Ontology of Late Colonialism: Tribes and the
Mandated State in Iraq." In Faleh A. Jabar and Hosham Dawod, eds., *Tribes
and Power,* 257–282.
Fromkin, David. 1989. *A Peace to End All Peace: The Fall of the Ottoman Empire
and the Creation of the Modern Middle East.* New York: Avon Books.
Hiro, Dilip. 1992. *Desert Shield to Desert Storm.* New York: Routledge.
Hussain, Asaf. 1985. *Islamic Iran.* New York: St. Martin's Press.
Ibrahim, Ahmed. 2006. "Arab Revolt." In James DeFronzo, ed., *Revolutionary
Movements in World History,* vol. 1, 70–77.
Karim, Thair. 2003. "Tribes and Nationalism: Tribal Political Culture and Behavior
in Iraq, 1914–1920." In Faleh A. Jabar and Hosham Dawod, eds., *Tribes
and Power,* 283–310.

Kedourie, Elie. 1987. *England and the Middle East: The Destruction of the Ottoman Empire, 1914–1921*. Boulder, CO: Westview Press.

———. *The Anglo-Arab Labyrinth: The McMahon-Hussein Correspondence and Its Interpretations, 1914–1939*. London: Frank Cass.

Khalidi, Rashid, Lisa Anderson, Muhammad Muslih, and Reeva S. Simon, eds. 1991. *The Origins of Arab Nationalism*. New York: Columbia University Press.

Kreyenbrock, Philip, and Christine Allison, eds. 1996. *Kurdish Culture and Identity*. London: Zed Books.

Lawrence, T. E. 1935. *Seven Pillars of Wisdom*. Mattituck, NY: Amereon Limited.

Longrigg, Stephen. 1953. *Iraq, 1900 to 1950*. London: Oxford University Press.

Lukitz, Liora. 2006. *A Quest in the Middle East: Gertrude Bell and the Making of the Modern Iraq*. London: I. B. Tauris.

Marr, Phebe. 2004. *The Modern History of Iraq*, 2nd ed. Boulder, CO: Westview Press.

Nakash, Yitzhak. 1994. *The Shi'is of Iraq*. Princeton, NJ: Princeton University Press.

Paul, James A. 2002. "Great Power Conflict Over Iraqi Oil: the World War I Era." *Global Policy Forum*, October 1–3. www.globalpolicy.org/security/oil/2002/1000history.htm.

Pillai, R.V., and Mahendra Kumar. 1962. "The Political and Legal Status of Kuwait." *International and Comparative Law Quarterly* 11, 1: 108–130.

Polk, William R. 2005. *Understanding Iraq*. New York: Harper Perennial.

Roux, George. 1964. *Ancient Iraq*. London: Allen and Unwin.

Sluglett, Peter. 1976. *Britain in Iraq, 1914–1932*. London: Ithaca Press.

Stewart, Desmond. 1977. *T. E. Lawrence*. New York: Harper & Row.

Sykes, Sir Percy. 1951. *A History of Persia*, vols. 1 and 2. London: MacMillan and Company.

Tripp, Charles. 2000. *A History of Iraq*. Cambridge, UK: Cambridge University Press.

Al-Qazzaz, Ayad. 2006. "Iraq Revolution." In James DeFronzo, ed., *Revolutionary Movements in World History*, vol. 2, 427–440.

Wallach, Janet. 1999. *Desert Queen: The Extraordinary Life of Gertrude Bell: Adventurer, Advisor to Kings, Ally of Lawrence of Arabia*. Wilmington, NC: Anchor.

Wilson, Jeremy. 1989. *Lawrence of Arabia: The Authorized Biography*. London: William Heinemann.

Winstone, H. V. F. 2004. *Gertrude Bell*. Manchester, UK: Barzan Publishing.

Wright, Quincy. 1926. "The Government of Iraq." *American Political Science Review* 20, 4 (November): 743–769.

2

||||||||||||||||||||||||||||||||||||||||||||||||||||||||||||||||||||||||||||||||||||||||||||||||||||

From the
British Mandate
to the
1958 Revolution

Following World War I, the League of Nations assigned Britain the task of preparing the new nation of Iraq for independence. A small Iraqi army was organized, led mainly by Sunnis with British advisers. Britain also created the Iraqi Levies, a military force similar in size to the Iraqi army composed of Christian Assyrians, a tiny minority of Iraq's population. Faisal I, a leader of the Arab Revolt against the Ottoman Empire, was installed as Iraq's king.

Since most Iraqis opposed foreign domination, the British promoted the concept that their relationship with Iraq was based on a mutual agreement, the 1922 Anglo-Iraqi Treaty. This was followed by a constitution for Iraq, adopted in 1924, guaranteeing that Iraq would honor the provisions of the treaty and fulfill all of its treaty obligations to Britain. The constitution gave the king control of the Iraqi army and the power to disband parliament and effectively rule by decree. The monarchy and the constitution, with minor modifications, were key elements of the Iraqi regime until the revolution of 1958, when both were abolished as instruments of British imperialism.

Iraq Under the British Mandate

Political and Social Characteristics

The Iraqi political system involved an interdependent relationship between two greatly unequal centers of power: Britain, which militarily controlled Iraq and its increasingly important oil resources, and the Iraqi monarchy, under great pressure to accommodate British interests. Various Iraqi groups groped for the means to influence the nation's destiny within the limits allowed, including political parties organized around specific ideological tendencies, economic interest groups such as urban investors and landowning tribal chieftains, and the

21

armed forces. The number of people allowed to participate in politics was minimized by the poverty and illiteracy of the vast majority of Iraqis.

Wealthy families tended to send their children to more developed countries for education. According to Polk (2005: 92), the preference was not for the occupying power, Britain, but for the United States. Iraqis educated abroad were exposed to political systems and ideologies that contrasted starkly with their homeland. Some Iraqis received training in modern technologies through working for the British, particularly in the developing oil industry.

Many from Iraq's middle and lower middle classes achieved a measure of education and eventually political power through joining the country's armed forces. Since the wealthy dominated the political system, the role the military played in government during specific periods represented a significant form of middle-class participation in national politics. Throughout the era of the monarchy, the royal administration tried to counter urban-based opposition by relying on tribal chiefs to control the largely illiterate rural mass of Iraq's population.

Treaty of 1930

The 1929 election of a Labour Party government in England led to a new treaty with Iraq based on Iraqi independence. The treaty allowed Britain to hold on to its military bases in Iraq and use Iraqi government property until 1957, when the treaty would expire. British technical experts and advisers in the Iraqi government retained their positions, and Britain and its allies continued to develop and control Iraq's oil resources.

Iraqi nationalists opposed the treaty on the grounds that Britain would in reality maintain control. But the monarchy's prime minister, Nuri al-Said, suppressed antitreaty protests, limited press criticism, and had the king dismiss parliament to forestall any effective opposition. Iraq's acceptance of the treaty in November 1930 established Nuri al-Said as Britain's most valued Iraqi political leader (Marr 2003: 34).

Independence

Iraq entered the League of Nations as an independent nation in October 1932, with King Faisal and pro-British Iraqi officials in the royal cabinet of ministers firmly in control. The widespread belief that the country was not genuinely independent, the domination of the political system by the wealthy, and growing economic inequality motivated discontent within sectors of the armed forces and the development of ideologically diverse civilian opposition movements. These movements were mostly in urban areas and generally lacked a mass population base. Political struggles were self-limiting in that most opposition groups did not directly challenge the monarchy. Rather, until 1941, opposition movements mainly sought to reduce British influence, increase political freedom, accomplish economic reforms, and achieve greater national control over Iraq's resources.

Independent Iraq: 1932–1941

The Death of Faisal I

On September 7, 1933, King Faisal I died of natural causes. Although Faisal generally cooperated with the British, he had enjoyed some support because of his leading role in the Arab Revolt against the Ottomans and because he was believed to occasionally resist certain British demands. His son Ghazi became the new king at the age of twenty-one. Ghazi had been educated both in England and at the Iraqi Military College, where he was exposed to the growing Iraqi nationalist, anti-British outlook of many younger Iraqi officers. He was politically inexperienced and lacked the loyalty his father enjoyed among government officials and the pro-British economic elite. During Ghazi's reign, the monarchy's power relative to that of the major British-supported political actors and the Iraqi army declined. However, Ghazi's nationalism and public criticism of British policies in Iraq and the Middle East eventually made him much more popular among ordinary Iraqis than his father had been (Polk 2005: 94).

To reach the Iraqi people, who were mostly illiterate, Ghazi had a radio station constructed in the palace in 1937 and used it to criticize British policies, including Britain's support for a Jewish state in Arab Palestine (Marr 2003: 51). He also broadcast that Kuwait was a part of Iraq split off by British imperialism, and he called upon the Kuwaiti people to oust the ruling sheik and reunite with Iraq (Batatu 1978: 343). To overcome pro-British elements within the Iraqi political and economic establishment, Ghazi began to favor anti-British elements within Iraq's armed forces.

Ascendancy of the Armed Forces

Some nationalists, viewing the political system as a mechanism imposed under threat of British violence through which Britain was able to maintain control, hoped the Iraqi military would be able to end British domination through its own use or threat of force. A key event that enormously increased the military's popularity was its suppression of the 1933 revolt of the Assyrian Levies. Thousands of Assyrian Christians had fled Anatolia (comprising most of modern-day Turkey) during the First World War and had sought refuge in neighboring Iraq. In 1922 the British recruited many into a new force called the Levies. According to Husry (1974a: 164–165), "These were an Imperial force, British-paid and British officered, distinct from the Iraqi army. The martial qualities of the Assyrians made them excellent soldiers; they helped in subduing the Kurdish tribes of the north and in checking the Turks and recovering Rawanduz from them in 1923." According to Polk (2005: 93), many Iraqi Arabs and Kurds developed a deep resentment of the Levies, not because they were Christians, but because of their service to the British.

When the British Mandate came to an end, many Assyrians feared they would be attacked by Iraqi Arabs and Kurds and wanted to leave Iraq for French-controlled Syria or Europe. The Assyrian religious leader, patriarch Mar

Sham'un, entered into negotiations with King Faisal's government. But according to Husry (1974a: 169), Baghdad refused to accept the Assyrian demands for "local autonomy of a special zone, recognition of Mar Sham'un as temporal as well as spiritual head of the Assyrians, and the establishment of a separate Assyrian regiment in the Iraqi army." Iraqis feared that Assyrians would organize their own armed militia for a self-proclaimed independent state on Iraqi territory. When negotiations failed, Iraqi troops attempted to disarm Assyrians and fighting broke out on August 4, 1933. Because the Iraqi military reported that it had been attacked, most Iraqis were outraged and called for the army to strike back at the Assyrians, who they believed still followed British orders. Within a few days, armed Kurds killed "about a hundred Assyrian villagers at Dahuk and Zakhu" (Marr 2003: 39). The worst violence took place on August 11 when a unit of the Iraqi army killed over three hundred unarmed Assyrians at the village of Sumayyil. Husry (1974b: 347) feels the evidence indicates that the massacre at Sumayyil was not ordered by the top Iraqi army officer in the north, the Kurdish Iraqi general Bakir Sidqi, but occurred under the command of a junior officer. Estimates put the number of Assyrians killed in the August fighting and massacres at about 600, but some Assyrians claimed 3,000 perished (Husry 1974b: 353–354).

Many Iraqis believed the army had destroyed a major tool of British imperialism. "On August 26th practically the entire city (of Baghdad) turned out to welcome the army units after completion of their operations against the Assyrians. Thousands upon thousands of men, women, and children filled the streets, squares, and rooftops of the city, bringing everything to a standstill for hours. Immense crowds cheered with delirium as the troops marched through the capital. Men, women, and children showered flowers and rose water on them from the rooftops" (Husry 1974b: 352). Airplanes of the Iraqi air force dropped leaflets reading "Welcome, Protectors of the Fatherland! . . . Stand up to Your Enemies the Tools and Creatures of Imperialism" (Husry 1974b: 352). Crown Prince Ghazi, who had approved the army's campaign against the Assyrians, was "cheered to the heavens" and had become the "darling of the masses."

The army's influence increased further during 1935–1936 after its suppression of Shia tribal rebellions south of Baghdad against policies such as drafting Shia men into the armed forces. The air force bombed rebellious regions and executions were carried out under a state of martial law (Marr 2003: 43). Military power also grew because the armed forces rose from about 13,000 in 1933 to 23,000 in 1936 (Marr 2003: 43).

The 1936 Bakr Sidqi Coup

In 1936 the Iraqi prime minister, Yasin al-Hashimi, an Arab nationalist, provoked opposition by announcing his intention to stay in power for another ten years. In addition, King Ghazi became upset with Hashimi's attempts to restrict his personal life after Ghazi's sister eloped with a hotel servant and renounced Islam (Batatu 1978: 204). Left-leaning political activists, intellectuals, and professionals, generally holding democratic socialist ideas and associated with the liberal newspaper *Al-Ahali* (the Ahali group), accused Hashimi's government of neglecting the poor. Others opposed Hashimi because of his pan-Arabism. Instead they favored the development of a genuine Iraqi sense of patriotism, which Batatu (1978: 203) called "particularist" Iraqi nationalism, designed to appeal to all Iraqis whether they were Sunni Arab, Shia Arab, Kurdish, Christian, or any other minority. General Bakr Sidqi, commander of the First Division, and other Kurdish officers strongly supported the particularist form of Iraqi nationalism and decided to stage a military coup in 1936 against the Hashimi government. (The British described Sidqi as one of the best military commanders in the Iraqi army.) By 1936 Sidqi had become extremely popular among Sunni Arabs and Sunni Kurds for his successes against Assyrians in the north and the tribes south of the capital. On October 29, while airplanes dropped leaflets demanding Hashimi's resignation, General Sidqi's troops marched on Baghdad with, he claimed, the approval of King Ghazi, forcing Hashimi to leave office. Hikmat Sulaiman, linked to the Ahali group, became the new prime minister on October 30.

According to Marr (2003: 44–46), the military coup, the first of several in Iraq's history, reflected two general underlying schools of thought influencing Iraq's educated minority during the 1930s. One was "paternalistic authoritarianism" inspired by Mustafa Kemal of Turkey. Unlike European fascist dictatorships, Kemal's Turkey, where the state promoted education and industry and limited the ability of traditional religious authorities to impede modernization, seemed to provide an appealing Islamic model of a milder, more integrative form of authoritarian rule.

The second perspective, "democratic socialism," the general orientation of the Ahali group, was primarily inspired by the British labor movement. Democratic socialists advocated increased economic and educational opportunities for the mass of Iraq's population and wanted government to become more democratic and overcome the power of the wealthy. Iraqis from these two groups united to overthrow the Hashimi regime. But once they succeeded, their ideological differences brought them into conflict.

Following the coup, General Sidqi became chief of the armed forces. Members or associates of the Ahali group became the heads of most government ministries. Leftist reformers, in power for the first time in Iraq's history, hoped to wrench the country from the control of rural and urban economic elites and revise Iraq's constitution to create a more democratic political system, and also to carry out reforms to benefit the country's underprivileged majority. But the army, having risen up to overthrow civilian leaders, had the potential to do the same to any future government with whose policies it disagreed. The new democracy-oriented, left-leaning government was doomed because of its dependence on the support of military leaders who favored paternalistic authoritarianism.

Prime Minister Sulaiman's government "contained few Arab *sunnis* and not a single advocate of the pan-Arab cause" (Marr 2003: 47). Sulaiman's regime placed improving the welfare of Iraqis above the goal of working for Arab unity. This was called the "Iraq First" policy (Marr 2003: 47; Tripp 2000: 91). The new government also attempted to establish better relations with Iraq's non-Arab neighbors. One of the most pressing problems was the dispute between Iraq and Iran over the Shatt al-Arab (the Arab River), which flowed into the Persian Gulf. The Ottoman Empire had maintained control up to the bank of the river on Iran's side, but in 1932 Iran began to demand that the border be moved from Iran's shore to the "Thalweg" (the center line of the deepest channel in the river), allowing Iran freer access. Arab nationalists were opposed, but the Sulaiman government agreed to a compromise in the Iran-Iraq Frontier Treaty of July 1937. The agreement stated that the border would be the "Thalweg for four miles in the vicinity of the Iranian port of Abadan," but elsewhere the border would remain at the riverbank on the Iranian side (Tripp 2000: 90).

The resolution of the Shatt al-Arab problem permitted the negotiation of a more comprehensive treaty with Iran, Turkey, and Afghanistan, the 1937 Sa'd-abad Pact. This agreement with non-Arab countries further offended Iraqi Arab nationalists but would have potential advantages if it was successful. Good relations with Iran and Turkey, both of which had large Kurdish populations, would decrease the likelihood that either country would assist an Iraqi Kurdish rebellion. Furthermore, improved relations with Shia Iran could eliminate Iraqi Sunnis' fear that members of Iraq's Shia majority might side with Iran over Iraq. The government, however, would fall victim first to its internal ideological division and then to Arab nationalists.

Reformers in Sulaiman's government advocated more democracy, a favorable policy toward trade unions, a minimum wage law, creation of a progressive income tax, land redistribution to the rural poor, and repeal of the repressive Law Governing the Rights and Duties of Cultivators (which had virtually enslaved indebted rural laborers to large landowners). These reforms, however, were opposed by economic elites and top military officers who feared that government encouragement of urban and rural workers to organize unions and demand economic change would disrupt society. In March 1937 General Sidqi "publicly attacked the reformists for being secret communists" (Tripp 2000: 92). Prime Minister Sulaiman attempted to preserve his government by replacing reformers with more conservative cabinet ministers and suppressing workers' strikes. Thus the opportunity to move toward democracy and substantial economic and social reforms was lost.

The Assassination of Sidqi and Overthrow of Sulaiman

General Sidqi did not have long to enjoy his victory over the reformers. A conspiracy among pan-Arab nationalist officers in the Iraqi army developed against the Sulaiman–Sidqi "Iraq First" policy and the particularistic Iraqi nationalism Sidqi supported. These officers felt that Iraq was turning its back on other Arab nations and neglecting international pan-Arab causes, in particular support for the Palestinians, whose land was being used to establish a Jewish homeland. While stopping over at the Mosul airport on August 11, 1937, on his way to visit Turkey, Sidqi was shot and killed. When Sulaiman attempted to punish the assassins, many military commanders refused to cooperate and the government fell. From 1937 to 1941, Arab nationalist military officers dominated Iraqi politics to make sure civilian politicians carried out their policies and to protect their own power.

The Death of King Ghazi

The next major political event was the sudden and mysterious death of King Ghazi. He attempted to arouse Iraq's people by assailing British imperialism and speaking against the creation of a Jewish homeland in Palestine through his broadcasts beginning in 1937 from a palace radio station. His denunciations of Britain's policies became particularly significant as war loomed between the United Kingdom and Nazi Germany. Britain feared that Iraq might stay neutral or even provide Germany with oil for its war effort. Britain's problem with the king ended when he was allegedly killed in a car crash on April 3, 1939. Batatu (1978: 342–343) states that available evidence does not permit a clear determination regarding whether the king's death was an accident or a politically motivated murder and describes some mysterious circumstances suggesting that Nuri al-Said, the British, or both, as many Iraqis believed, had a hand in Ghazi's passing. First, about nine months before the crash, one of Ghazi's close friends was found shot dead within the palace, causing Ghazi to become alarmed that he was the target of an assassination plot. Second, although the king was supposed to have died from a skull fracture while driving his car into an electric light pole, the car and pole seemed to have suffered little damage. Furthermore, Batatu (1978: 343) notes that the disappearance of a servant and the supervisor of the king's radio station, who were "said to have been sitting in the car's back seat," suggested to many Iraqis that the king was murdered.

A regent was selected to fulfill the king's functions until Ghazi's son, Faisal II, reached age eighteen and could assume the crown. Ghazi's estranged wife, Queen Aliyah, claimed that in the event of his death, Ghazi favored her brother, the pro-British Prince Abd al-Ilah, to become regent. Yet it was "widely known in Baghdad that Ghazi hated Abd al-Ilah" (Batatu 1978: 344). When Abd al-Ilah became regent, many Iraqis were further convinced that King Ghazi had been assassinated. In the years leading up to the 1958 antimonarchy revolution, Abd al-Ilah and Nuri al-Said became possibly the most hated figures in Iraq's history.

Impact of World War II

The regent, Prince Abd al-Ilah, "was in some respects positively enthusiastic" about maintaining Iraq's relationship with Great Britain (Tripp 2000: 99), which he viewed as a crucial protector of the monarchy and the Hashemite dynasty. But he distrusted the armed forces, and the idea of military officers of middle- or lower middle–class background participating in national politics, normally dominated by the royal family and wealthy elites, was repugnant to him.

However, serious divisions existed within the military shortly before the outbreak of WWII. Arab nationalist officers had maintained their dominance since Sidqi's assassination. But the level and forms of Arab nationalism varied significantly. Nuri al-Said (repeatedly serving either as Iraq's prime minister or foreign minister) and many of his supporters in the armed forces advocated a relatively mild form of Arab nationalism that could accommodate British interests and, if necessary, even the British-supported establishment of a Jewish homeland in Palestine. But other Arab nationalist officers were far more hostile toward Britain.

Once WWII was under way, following the German invasion of Poland on September 1, 1939, Britain requested that Iraq provide assistance under the terms of the 1930 treaty (Tripp 2000: 99–101), and Prime Minister Nuri al-Said agreed. But Arab nationalist officers, while not openly objecting, invited the leader of the defeated three-year Palestinian revolt against the British, Hajj Amin al-Husani, the mufti (interpreter of Islamic law to the people) of Jerusalem, to come to Baghdad in October. The mufti rejected al-Said's cooperation with Britain and his compromising attitude regarding Palestine. Anti-British feelings intensified, forcing al-Said to resign in March 1940. The new prime minister, Rashid 'Ali al-Kalani, was supported by a group of four Arab nationalist colonels: Salah al-Din Sabbagh, Muhammad Fahmi Sa'id, Mahmud Salman, and Kamil Shabib ("the Golden Square" or "the Four Colonels").

As the Axis powers scored a rapid succession of impressive victories, including the defeat of France in the summer of 1940, disagreement developed among Iraqi political and military leaders regarding whether the British could win (at this point neither the Soviet Union nor the United States had entered the war on Britain's side). Al-Said and his associates felt that Britain, with the resources of its enormous empire and commonwealth, including India, Australia, and Canada, might ultimately triumph. But 'Ali al-Kalani and the Golden Square officers expected the Axis powers to win, in which case providing help to Britain could have negative consequences for Iraq after the war. Given the pro-Axis sympathy in much of the army and government, 'Ali al-Kalani had difficulty fulfilling British requests for assistance. When Iraq delayed permission for British troop movements through Iraq and then refused to go along with Britain's request that Iraq cut diplomatic relations with Fascist Italy, the British feared that Iraq was aligning itself with the Axis powers and demanded that 'Ali al-Kalani be replaced. When he refused to step down, the pro-British regent Abd al-Ilah called for the government's resignation. To avoid a possible civil war, the prime minister resigned on January 31, 1941 (Tripp 2000: 102).

The 1941 Military Coup and War with Britain

The Golden Square officers initially agreed to accept the new prime minister, Taha al-Hashimi, a former army officer with a reputation as an Arab nationalist. But when he moved to disrupt the Golden Square alliance, they, with the support of 'Ali al-Kalani and General Amin Zaki (acting head of the general staff), forced al-Hashimi to resign on April 1, 1941. As military units moved to take control of Baghdad in early April, the regent, with the aid of a US diplomat, escaped capture and reached British-controlled Transjordan. Nuri al-Said also left the country. A "Government of National Defense" led by 'Ali al-Kalani was proposed, and the Iraqi parliament passed a motion to make another member of the royal family, Sharif Sharaf (Tripp 2000: 103), the new regent, hoping to reassure Britain that the monarchy was being preserved and that the government would return to acting within the framework of Iraq's constitution, which required royal conformation of laws approved by parliament.

Doubting Iraq would fulfill its treaty obligations, the British requested consent to land troops. Although 'Ali al-Kalani agreed, the Golden Square officers and cabinet ministers decided to restrict the number of British troops allowed to enter Iraq. Rejecting this limitation, the British entered Basra. In response, Iraqi armed forces moved to the vicinity of the British air base at Habbaniyya, threatening to fire upon any plane attempting to take off. The British commander interpreted their presence as an act of war (Tripp 2000: 105) and attacked Iraqi forces on May 2. After several days of fighting, the Iraqis withdrew to the city of Fallujah. Britain brought in reinforcements from India and Transjordan, and some Shia Arabs, Kurds, and Christian Assyrians aided the British. The Germans and Italians sent only some small arms and about thirty planes to assist Iraqi forces. By the end of May, in the face of the unchecked British offensive, 'Ali al-Kalani and his main military supporters fled Baghdad.

The British Occupation, 1941–1945

In June 1941 British forces entered Baghdad and commenced wartime occupation. Under British protection, Nuri al-Said and Abd al-Ilah, resuming the role of regent, returned. The political system abruptly shifted back to the flawed constitutionalist system that protected British interests. As Marr (2003: 56–57) puts it, "The real significance of the British occupation lay in its reinstatement of the pro-British ruling group. The second occupation indissolubly linked the ruling circles of Iraq, especially the regent and Nuri, to the British." Abd al-Ilah and Nuri al-Said acted to exterminate those who had forced them to flee the country and deter future rebellions.

On January 6, 1942, leaders of the 1941 anti-British Iraqi government and military units were sentenced in absentia to death. While 'Ali al-Kalani and the mufti escaped to Saudi Arabia and Egypt, respectively, the Golden Square officers were captured and killed. The execution of Iraqis who had resisted the British and the persecution of others enraged many Iraqis, particularly Sunni Arabs.

Nuri al-Said, prime minister under British occupation, moved against two institutions that had bred and spread anti-British Iraqi nationalism: the armed forces and the educational system. In addition to the imprisonment or forced retirement of hundreds of Iraqi military men and their replacement by British trained personnel, al-Said slashed the size of the army, which in 1944 was reorganized by a British general to make sure the Iraqi military could never again threaten either the ruling elite or British interests. Strongly nationalistic teachers and textbooks were removed from the educational system. The 1924 constitution was modified to clearly provide the king or regent the authority to oust the prime minister and the cabinet of ministers, giving the monarchy the power of a virtually total dictatorship.

The British alliance with the USSR after the German invasion of the Soviet Union on June 22, 1941, provided an opportunity for the growth of liberal and leftist movements, including the rapid rise in membership and influence of the Iraqi Communist Party (ICP). According to Marr (2004: 58), during WWII, after the defeat of the 'Ali al-Kalani government, the police did not interfere with the distribution of underground communist newspapers, and some leftists achieved important positions in the educational system. Many educated Iraqis became attracted to the ICP or other leftist movements. Unlike other political parties, which organized mainly among educated Iraqis, the communists developed major support among urban workers and oil industry workers. The ICP would, in fact, become Iraq's first significant multi-class, multi-ethnic, cross-sectarian party and eventually wage a war to the death with resurgent Arab nationalists organized in the party of Saddam Hussein, the Baath Party.

The Rise of the ICP

Batatu (1978: 367–386) notes that several people, movements, and organizations contributed to introducing Marxist ideas to the Middle East. These included the leftist members of the Armenian Hentchak (a socialist party active in the Ottoman Empire), Jewish communists in Egypt and Lebanon, individuals linked to the Communist International, and even one activist, Jamil Tuma, associated with the Marxist-oriented Workers' School of Boston, who became active in Baghdad. The ICP was organized nationally through the union of three communist groups in Baghdad with the Basra Communist Circle and the Nasiriyah Communist Circle in the Association Against Imperialism, established in 1935 (Batatu 1978: 415).

The primary organizers of the ICP, who were all male and mostly college educated, included seven Sunnis, four Shia, and five Christians. According to Batatu (1978: 432–433), the "Manifesto of the Association Against Imperialism" included the statements: "Today, the English and the ruling class are partners in . . . perpetuating the oppression and exploitation from which we all suffer. . . . The oil and other raw materials of the country have become a preserve for the English. . . . The ruling class, for its part, plunders the proceeds of taxes, misappropriates lands, and builds palaces on the shores of the Tigris and Euphrates."

In addition to demanding the expulsion of the imperialists and the confiscation of the foreign-owned oil fields, financial banks, and the railroad system, the party called for reducing taxes on the rural poor and eliminating peasant debt, distributing state-owned land to the disadvantaged, and guaranteeing workers freedom of speech, assembly, and trade union activity, and protection against arbitrary dismissal from employment. The ICP also demanded recognition of the eight-hour workday by all domestic and foreign-owned enterprises and the creation of a system to protect workers from poverty and starvation in old age. The ICP central committee decided that the party should basically ignore the issue of religion (Batatu 1978: 409–410).

The ICP opposed terrorism, arguing that assassinations would do nothing to change the system since those killed would be quickly replaced and since violence might alienate the public. Rather, national liberation could be achieved only by organizing the Iraqi people into a mass revolutionary movement that would have the power through numbers to bring about both true independence and a social revolution to benefit the urban workers and rural peasants. The ICP's nationalism was particularist rather than pan-Arab. The party favored developing a sense of Iraqi identity and patriotism inclusive of all of Iraq's ethnic and religious groups.

The party attracted many Shia as well as Sunnis. Batatu (1978: 436–715) describes twelve ICP central committees between 1935 and 1958, with a total of eighty-four members. Their ethnic composition was about 60 percent Arab, 15 percent Kurd, 10 percent Arabized Chaldean, 6 percent Jewish, 2 percent Armenian, and 5 percent mixed ethnic background. One was a woman. Central committee members were overwhelmingly lower middle class (68 percent). Nineteen percent were industrial or transportation workers and about 13 percent were in middle-class occupations. None were peasants. Like other Iraqi political parties during this period, the ICP was almost totally urban based. Batatu (1978: 642) cites sources that indicate fluctuating sizes of ICP membership from 1935 to 1948, possibly in response to levels of repression: a few hundred in 1935; 400 or more in November 1937; 1942, 1,000 or more; January 1948, 3,000 to 4,000; and at the end of 1948, a few hundred. In terms of Iraq's urban population, Shia and Kurds were somewhat underrepresented in the years before 1949.

Iraqi communists initially supported the Sulaiman–Sidqi coup of October 29, 1936, but soon became dismayed by the government's turn against reformers. The party became even more disillusioned when on March 17, 1937, General Sidqi "suddenly and unexpectedly opened an attack on the Communists" (Batatu 1978: 442). At this stage the ICP was a small organization of little political consequence. Sidqi's attack on communists was, rather, a broad warning to all leftists and reformers that they might be dealt with by the armed forces as if they were communists. Repression kept the communist presence in the military relatively limited.

When 'ali al-Kalani and the Golden Square seized power in April 1941, the ICP decided to cautiously offer its support and appealed for the new government to release imprisoned communist military men, which it did. But following the British defeat of the regime, and revenge Arab nationalist attacks on Baghdad Jews, which resulted in about two hundred deaths (Tripp 2000: 105–106), the party announced that its backing for that government had been a mistake (Batatu 1978: 461). But the nationalist sympathies of most Iraqi communists, like many other Iraqis, were grossly offended by the British invasion and takeover in May and June 1941.

Post–World War II Iraq to the 1948 War in Palestine

During the war, economic conditions deteriorated badly. Some were able to make use of their economic resources and political power to earn enormous sums from activities such as selling grain to the British. For most Iraqis, however, the war was economically devastating. The worst problem was inflation.

By war's end, the general inflation index had climbed by over 400 percent (Bantatu 1978: 470–471). For most people, wage increases were far below increases in the cost of living.

Economic hardship combined with heightened anger toward the monarchy, swelling urban populations, and a surge in jobless men as the British shut down military support operations that had employed many Iraqis to set the stage for explosive political protests and the surge of membership in opposition parties. An increase in the student population also fueled growth in opposition political activity. The number of college students climbed from 77 in 1927 to 4,212 in 1948, and high school students went from 1,086 to 23,047 (Batatu 1978: 477). The ICP gained support among students, urban workers, professionals, intellectuals, and discontented civil servants and in the late 1940s began to emerge as a significant political force.

Temporary Liberalization and the New Parties

As the British military presence in Iraq declined after the end of WWII, the regent, Abd al-Ilah, tried to increase support for the regime by promising more political freedom and to replace the 1930 treaty with one more acceptable to the people. He promised to allow the creation of some political parties.

Of the new legal parties (the ICP remained illegal), the National Democratic Party (NDP), established in 1946, was center-left, descended from the Ahali organization (Marr 2004: 63). The NDP advocated policies to benefit the disadvantaged, including new tax laws to achieve a redistribution of wealth, the dismantling of business monopolies, and a more democratic political system. This moderate socialist party opposed foreign domination of Iraq and rejected pan-Arabism in favor of developing a uniquely Iraqi identity, making the party attractive to the Shia and minorities. The NDP, whose influence was limited mostly to urban people with some level of education, took part in uprisings against the regime in 1948, 1952, and 1956 and played a significant role in the Revolution of 1958.

While the NDP sprang from a wider movement, which included the ICP, to bring about significant socioeconomic reform, the Istiqlal (Independence) Party, also created in 1946, was a manifestation of the other major ideological tendency in Iraq, Arab nationalism. It also operated mainly among educated urban Iraqis, and some of its members had fought against the British in 1941. The party was led by a Shia, Muhammad Mahdi Kubba, but most of its members were Sunnis who favored a pan-Arab orientation rather than a purely Iraqi nationalism.

Despite being illegal, the ICP in 1946 was the country's "best organized" party (Marr 2004: 63) and played a major role in mass protests that summer. On June 28 two communist-influenced groups, the League Against Zionism and the National Liberation Party, staged a demonstration in Baghdad in which some 3,000, mainly workers and students, protested injustices against the Arab Palestinians and called for expelling the British from Iraq. Then in Kirkuk on July 3, where oil workers were infuriated by low wages and inflation, the ICP supported a strike of approximately 5,000 employees of the Iraqi Petroleum

Company. A police attempt to disrupt workers' meetings on July 12 resulted in shootings "killing at least ten, and wounding twenty-seven" (Batatu 1978: 533), the Kirkuk Massacre of 1946. The British and the monarchy were shocked at the Kirkuk strike and the power of organized and defiant workers, so the regime increased efforts to crush the ICP.

On January 18, 1947, the charismatic ICP leader, Yusuf Salman Yusuf, "Comrade Fahd," was arrested. According to Batatu (1978: 485), "Fahd succeeded where many had failed. From the founding of the party in 1935 to the year 1941, the efforts of the communists recurrently lapsed into individualism, discord, and spinelessness. Between 1941 (when Fahd became party leader) and 1947, however, Fahd turned the party into a compact and effective political force and built a mass base of support and belief." The Iraqi political police feared Fahd because he had "strong powers of persuasion and the gift of explaining things in a clear and simple manner" (from a statement by the head of the monarchy's political police, Bahjat 'Atiyyah, to Hanna Batatu in June 1958, Batatu 1978: 486).

Fahd was born in 1901 in Baghdad into a lower middle–class Chaldean Christian family (Batatu 1978: 416–417). He attended the Syrian Church School in Basra and then the American Mission School (1914–1916), and later KUTV, the Communist University for the Toilers of the East (1935–1937) in Moscow. Working as a clerk, a mechanic, and an ice seller, he was profoundly affected by the 1920 rebellion against the British. He joined the communist movement in 1927, eight years before the ICP was founded. Working effectively to spread the movement to workers and others in various parts of Iraq, Fahd was elected ICP general secretary in 1941. The success of his efforts contributed to the July 1946 Kirkuk oil workers' strike and, consequently, to his arrest. Coincidentally, the head of Iraq's political police was a former classmate at the American Mission School, Bahjat 'Atiyyah, from a well-to-do landowning family. ('Atiyyah was later executed by the 1958 revolutionary government.)

Fahd was charged with subversion (communicating communist concepts), armed insurrection (although Fahd claimed that the ICP did not provide weapons to members), and spreading communist ideas to Iraqi military personnel (an offense for which the penalty was death and for which Batatu [1978: 540] states the evidence "was conclusive"). On June 23, 1947, Fahd received a death sentence, commuted to life imprisonment in July. However, Fahd and other jailed communists turned their prison at Kut into a school for revolutionaries and established communication with party members on the outside.

The 1948 Wathbah

When the regent attempted to increase popular support for the regime by negotiating a new treaty with Britain, he discovered that many Iraqis simply wanted no treaty at all. But he and the British hoped that by stating in the new agreement that British troops would leave and that Britain's Iraqi air bases would come under Iraqi control, most people would eventually accept it. Representatives of the regime and the British government signed the new treaty at Britain's Portsmouth naval base on January 15, 1948.

The Portsmouth Treaty, however, ignited an explosion of outrage. It stated that if Britain went to war, Iraq would return the air bases, thus involving Iraq in a war on Britain's side whether the Iraqi people approved or not. The treaty also stipulated that Iraq's military would receive its training and supplies from Britain. And whereas the 1930 treaty would have expired in nine years, the Portsmouth Treaty was to stay in effect for another twenty-five, until 1973.

Students in Baghdad began protesting in early January. After the treaty was signed, a new demonstration took place on January 16. Police fired on demonstrators, killing four, wounding others, and outraging many. Further protests resulted in more deaths and injuries. This series of demonstrations by students and workers became known as the *wathbah* ("leap," here referring to a mass insurrection), the most widespread protests against the regime in the monarchy's history. Police violence on January 27 may have resulted in as many as three hundred or four hundred deaths (Batatu 1978: 557). Police claimed communist activists played leading roles in the demonstrations, but the regent was forced to cancel the Portsmouth Treaty. Batatu (1978: 557–566) states that the popularity of the wathbah and its success in getting the Portsmouth Treaty canceled and the pro-treaty prime minister ousted increased support, at least temporarily, for the ICP until the party's spectacular blunder later in 1948 regarding the issue of Palestine.

British interests and military presence in Iraq, however, were still guaranteed by the 1930 treaty, which remained in effect. Marr (2004: 66) observes that following the wathbah, a "new cycle of politics ensued." The regent would react to opposition demands by allowing political moderates to form a cabinet, but then when the government seemed to be moving against the monarchy's interests, Nuri al-Said would be brought back as prime minister to reverse unacceptable developments and control the situation to the regent's satisfaction. More Iraqis came to believe that the political system was so corrupt that the only options available to the regime's opponents were street protests and nonconstitutional actions, including promoting rebellion within the military.

The regime was so frightened by the level of participation and emotion of the wathbah and by the ICP's prominent role that Fahd and two other party members, Zaki Basim and Hussain Muhammad ash-Shabibi, were tried on the new charges of leading the ICP from prison and attempting to bring about a revolution. All three were hanged in February 1949 with the bodies displayed publicly at government buildings for about two days to discourage other regime opponents.

Impact of the War in Palestine

After the Nazi Holocaust against Europe's Jews, governments around the world agreed that the Jewish people required their own nation. But instead of taking land to create a Jewish homeland from Germany or other European nations that had played roles in persecuting and destroying Jews, in 1947 the United Nations voted to partition Palestine and, as long advocated by the Zionist movement, establish a Jewish state, Israel. The new state would be where ancient Israel once had existed, and would be alongside a separate state for Arab

Palestinians. Most Arabs opposed this plan on the grounds that Palestinians were being deprived of much of their territory because of Europe's inhumanity to its Jews, and that the Jews in Palestine, 80 percent of whom were relatively recent immigrants from Europe and who made up about one-third of Palestine's population and occupied approximately 5.7 percent of the land, were receiving about 56.5 percent (including the "more fertile" land) of Palestine (Batatu 1978: 597). As noted by Marr (2004: 66–67), opposition to Zionism (the movement to establish a homeland for the Jews in Palestine) and the partition of Palestine had the potential to unite much of Iraq's diverse population. When the first Arab–Israeli War broke out in May 1948, the Iraqi regime, responding to popular demand, sent troops. The Israelis, however, won the war and preserved their new state.

These events had major impacts. Many Iraqis felt humiliated by the Arab defeat and the inability to help the Palestinians. They also felt betrayed by the United Nations. Even the Soviet Union had supported the establishment of Israel, reversing its long opposition to the Zionist movement and offering the fanciful explanation that in an independent state, Jewish communists would someday overcome Israeli capitalists and bring about a communist government there. Within a few years the Soviet Union returned to its previous policy, but by then Israel was firmly established.

The Soviet Union's UN vote in favor of creating Israel shocked most ICP members. For a time the party rejected the USSR's new position and clung to its arguments that creating Israel was part of Western imperialist strategy, that Zionism was racist and reactionary, that Jews and Arabs should live together in the same state, and that an Israeli state would increase religious and racial animosities and reduce the possibility for peace in the Middle East.

But on July 6, 1948, the majority of the ICP leadership who were not in prison decided to go along with the Soviet Union and support the partition. This move divided the party, caused many members to leave, lost the huge boost in popular support the communists had gained during the wathbah, and played into the hands of their enemies, the Arab nationalists who sought to portray the communists as traitors to the Arab cause and to Islam and as tools of a foreign power, the Soviet Union, which they claimed wanted to take over Iraq. Coupled with the execution of Comrade Fahd and increased regime repression, the ICP's temporary support for the partition of Palestine seriously, though only briefly, diminished its size and influence.

One of the major impacts of the defeat in Palestine was the belief among many Iraqi officers and soldiers that they had lost the war because they had been betrayed by their own government. According to Polk (2005: 98), Iraq's "soldiers had been marched off to fight in that war with little training; many did not even have guns and ammunition; some did not even have shoes or jackets." According to Al-Qazzaz (2006: 432), "Many Iraqis accused the government of scheming with Britain and other Western powers to establish the state of Israel." The Iraqi army's experience in Palestine, along with the pro-Western Baghdad Pact in 1955 and the Suez crisis and war of 1956, eventually combined to provoke the armed forces to do what the opposition political parties could not: destroy the monarchy and free Iraq from British domination.

Iraq: 1948–1958

Oil and Economic Development

The Iraqi monarchy's regime responded to the growing internal threat with multiple strategies, including rewarding business and landowning elites for continued support, and repressing opponents. To prevent a coup, military units were often ordered not to carry ammunition and were kept away from major political centers. A key approach to holding on to power was to calm the population by using Iraq's oil wealth to accelerate economic development.

When the British-controlled Iraq Petroleum Company began significant commercial production of oil at Kirkuk in 1927, the Iraqi government received only a small fraction of the earnings. As the amount of oil the British company extracted increased dramatically and educated Iraqis realized the value of their country's resources, they began to criticize the government for not demanding a bigger portion of the profits. In response to criticism and in order to launch major economic development projects, Nuri al-Said convinced the British to significantly increase Iraq's profit share, to 50 percent, in 1952 (Tripp 2000: 128).

By approving the new arrangement, the British hoped to protect the regime. Furthermore, providing Iraq with half the profit of the increasingly valuable oil, the production of which was continuously expanding, was far preferable to what had happened in 1951 in neighboring Iran, where a nationalist-dominated parliament had simply nationalized the Anglo-Iranian Oil Company. But some Iraqis demanded the total expropriation of the oil industry. Others objected to the inclusion of British and US members on the board that was to assign development funds and oversee infrastructure projects, such as communication and transportation facilities, dams, and irrigation systems.

However, wealth, resources, and economic opportunities remained highly concentrated in a small minority of the population. According to Marr (2004: 69), "In 1958 some 3 percent of large and very large landholders controlled almost 70 percent of the land." Most cities and towns lacked safe drinking water, electricity, or sewage treatment. By 1958 higher educational institutions in Iraq were graduating only a little more than one thousand students per year (Marr 2004: 70).

Regrowth of the ICP

Batatu (1978: 465–482, 659) notes that the conditions that originally drew Iraqis to Marxist-Leninist ideas continued to persist, including tremendous inequality, social injustice, and the perception that Iraq's ruling class served foreign imperialists. Despite severe repression, the ICP continued to attract new members among both workers and intellectuals. After the summer of 1949, the ICP began to rebound, this time establishing a major presence in Kurdistan and recruiting more heavily among urban lower-income groups, including Shia Arabs and Kurds (Batatu 1978: 700). By the early 1950s, the ICP had revived to again become a significant opposition force.

The 1952 Intifada (Uprising)

In 1952, Iraq experienced its worst violence since the 1948 wathbah. The conditions underlying the intifada, or uprising, included continuing inflation and the failure of improvements to keep pace with people's expectations, which had risen after it was announced that Iraq would get a bigger share of oil revenues. Many were inspired by neighboring Iran, where the parliament had seized British oil facilities and had reduced the power of the British-supported Iranian shah (king).

In addition, the 1952 Egyptian Revolution, in which a group of young officers overthrew the British-supported Egyptian monarchy, encouraged opponents of the Iraqi regime. Similar to younger officers in the Iraqi military, Egyptian officers whose army had also been defeated in the 1948 war with Israel believed that the Egyptian government had betrayed its fighting forces by "providing Egyptian soldiers with defective weapons" leading to the shame of defeat (Gorman 2006: 249). By the end of 1949, a group led by a young army officer, Gamal Abdel Nasser, began creating a revolutionary leadership organization within the military called the Free Officers, aimed at liberating Egypt from British control. On July 23, 1952, the Egyptian Free Officers took control without bloodshed. They quickly established a ruling military council and forced the Egyptian king, Faruq, to abdicate on July 26. Egypt was officially declared a republic on June 18, 1953, and Nasser became the country's second president in March 1954 following the 1953–1954 presidency of General Muhammad Nagib.

The Egyptian Revolution, economic distress, and a lack of democratic reform played major roles in sparking the 1952 Iraqi intifada. The first action was an August 23 strike by Basra port workers, followed by a new wave of protests that commenced with a student strike at the College of Pharmacy on October 26 (Marr 2004: 71–72). The general atmosphere of rebellion expanded the scope of demonstrations, and antiregime riots spread to other cities. The American Information Office was attacked, revealing that in the minds of many, the United States, five of whose oil companies owned 23.7 percent of the stock in the Iraq Petroleum Company (Al-Qazzaz 2006: 439), was collaborating with the British in dominating Iraq.

To restore order, the regent appointed the head of the Iraqi armed forces, General Nur al-Din Mahmud, as prime minister on November 23. The new military government declared martial law in Baghdad province, "banned all political parties, imposed a curfew, suspended seventeen newspapers, and arrested more than 300 leaders of the opposition parties" (Al-Qazzaz 2006: 432). These actions further demonstrated the undemocratic nature of the regime and convinced Iraqis opposed to the regime that only violent methods could free the country from foreign control, but also demonstrated to disaffected officers that the military could run the country.

Faisal II Becomes King

Although when he turned eighteen on May 24, 1953, Faisal II became king, the power of the monarchy continued to be exercised by Abd al-Ilah. The regent had created a patronage network that looked to him, now titled crown prince, as the true power behind the throne. The young king, educated primarily by British tutors, was not attractive to the large sector of Iraq's population yearning to be free of British control. Young, inexperienced, and used to relying on the regent, he posed no real threat to al-Ilah.

Repressing the Opposition—The 1954 Elections

After a little over two months of military rule, the monarchy appointed a civilian government on January 29, 1953, that allowed political parties to become openly active again in September. Apparently believing the opposition had been disrupted and intimidated, Abd al-Ilah called for a new parliamentary election to take place in June 1954. The relegalized (licensed) leftist National Democratic Party and the Arab nationalist Istiqlal Party decided to form a united opposition National Front with the illegal Iraqi Communist Party. The ICP was represented in the Front by its associated licensed party, the Peace Partisans. Despite significant disadvantage in rural areas, where much of the population was illiterate and under the influence of conservative tribal leaders, the National Front was able to win fourteen seats in the 135-member parliament (Tripp 2000: 136), provoking concern from the regent and the establishment. Militant opposition representation in parliament appeared to signify new anti-monarchy and anti-British momentum just as the 1930 treaty between Britain and Iraq was approaching its 1957 expiration. A new treaty had to be negotiated quickly to safeguard Britain's interests and protect the monarchy. However, the government feared a repetition of the 1948 wathbah, which had doomed the Portsmouth Treaty, if the new treaty was put forward while the National Front had a forum in parliament to oppose it.

To avoid another explosion of street protests, Nuri al-Said was once again installed as prime minister. The new parliament was dismissed, and in early August the government began another systematic repression under the guise of fighting communism, banning all political parties in the process. Nuri al-Said became a virtual dictator and was able to play a major role in creating the Baghdad Pact (the Middle East Treaty Organization, METO), a British-sponsored and US-supported anti-communist Cold War alliance of Turkey, Iran, Pakistan, Britain, and Iraq. Most Iraqis strongly opposed this alliance, and this animosity contributed significantly to bringing about the 1958 anti-monarchy Iraq Revolution.

The Baghdad Pact

Prime Minister Nuri al-Said sought agreements with Iraq's non-Arab neighbors to secure Iraq's borders and deny support from either Iran or Turkey to any Kurdish groups contemplating rebellion. He also anticipated that negotiating an alliance with Shia Iran would reduce the possibility of discontent from segments of Iraq's majority Shia population. His solution to constructing a pro-Western alliance with Britain and Iraq's neighbors, Turkey and Iran, and replacing the 1930 Anglo-Iraq Treaty, was the Baghdad Pact.

The Baghdad Pact allowed Iraq to run the British air bases at Habbaniyya and Shu'aiba while Britain retained the right to fly through Iraqi air space and use the air bases for refueling. Britain continued to provide weapons and train Iraq's armed forces, preserving British leverage over the military and oversight of Iraqi officers. The pact maintained the aspects of the 1930 treaty Britain most valued, while allowing al-Said to portray British rights as features of a regional alliance among equal partners, rather than as an instrument of continued British domination.

Reaction from several Arab countries and most Iraqis, however, was hostile. Egyptian President Nasser immediately condemned the pact as a betrayal of Arab unity and neutrality in the Cold War. Egypt became committed to overthrowing the al-Said government, and the Cairo-based radio station the Voice of the Arabs launched an attack against the Iraqi regime that was almost impossible to silence. Any Iraqi with a radio could pick up the broadcasts and hear how negatively other Arab governments viewed the Iraqi government and its new alliance with Britain and non-Arab states, spreading discontent through the countryside and much of the military.

The Suez Crisis

As tensions grew in Iraq over the Baghdad Pact and pressing social issues, President Nasser nationalized the largely British- and French-owned Suez Canal Company on July 26, 1956, leading Britain, France, and Israel to attack Egypt in October. Many nations were appalled at this action, including the United States, which pressured invading forces to withdraw. Egypt accommodated several concerns of the attacking nations but retained control of the canal. As a result Nasser emerged as an even greater hero of the Arab world. According to Al-Qazzaz (2006: 432), "Nasser's success had momentous effects among the Arab masses, including the Iraqis."

The attack against Egypt precipitated major demonstrations in many Iraqi cities, including Baghdad, Mosul, and Najaf. Although the Iraqi government had no choice but to publicly criticize the invasion, it increased repression and declared martial law. Since the Baghdad Pact had reconfirmed Iraq's bond with Britain, the regime was further undermined domestically and vilified by other Arab governments. The Suez crisis "hastened the government's downfall" (Al-Qazzaz 2006: 432).

The Baath Party

Another political party emerged in Iraq to oppose the regime. The Baath Party, an Arab nationalist organization, was created primarily by two Syrians, Michel Aflaq, an Orthodox Christian Arab, and Salah al-Bitar, a Sunni Muslim, both sons of merchants who first met in 1929 while attending the Sorbonne in Paris. According to Devlin (1991: 1397), both enthusiastically embraced the pan-Arab ideology to which they had been previously introduced while in Syrian schools. As students in France "they shared the same experiences, read the same authors—Nietzsche, Mazzini, André Gide, Romain Roland, Marx, and

Lenin, among others—and were caught up in the same Marxist wave that swept over the European campuses during the world-wide slump and financial crisis of 1929–1932" (Batatu 1978: 725). They came to believe that socialist concepts explained major social and political problems afflicting the people of the world, including Arabs, and they were attracted to France's leftist political parties, the Communists and the Socialists, because they seemed sympathetic to the welfare of Arabs in French-controlled Syria.

Aflaq went home to Damascus in 1933 and became a history teacher, while al-Bitar returned in 1934 as a physics instructor. But their attraction to the communists ended after the French Communist and Socialist parties became members of France's governing coalition in 1936 and France failed to increase political freedom in Syria or establish Syria as an independent country. They accused the Syrian Communist Party of acting like a puppet of the French communists and became further alienated from the communist movement by the Soviet Union's pursuit of self-serving policies rather than helping to liberate the peoples oppressed by European nations. The view that communists were agents of the USSR attempting to impose a new form of imperialism on Arabs would partially account for the ferocious hostility of Iraqi Baathists toward the ICP in the 1960s.

Aflaq and al-Bitar proposed a new ideology, movement, and organization to liberate the Arab peoples. They began to attract students to their secret political activities, and the core of what would later become the Baath Party was formed around September 1940. In 1941 the group adopted the title Arab Baath (Arab Renaissance) but as late as 1943 may have had fewer than ten members (Batatu 1978: 727). However, after the French shelled and bombed Damascus in May 1945, party membership grew rapidly. In April 1947, when the first Baath Party congress was held, official membership was in the hundreds, mostly students, teachers, lawyers, medical doctors, and other intellectuals. At the 1947 party congress, members of the Syrian Alawis, a Muslim sect related to Shiism, also joined the movement.

Following Israel's 1948 victory, many more joined the Baath Party. The party's central goals included Arab nationalism (*freedom, hurriyah*, of Arab peoples from foreign domination), *unity* (*wihdah*, the goal of uniting the Arab peoples despite local cultural and social differences, in a single Arab state), and *socialism* (*ishtirakiyah*, "which they interpreted as social justice for the poor and underprivileged") (Devlin 1991: 1397). Farouk-Sluglett and Sluglett (2003: 89) state that Baathism, like Nasser's form of Arab nationalism, "is essentially non-Marxist, and in fact anti-Marxist, in the sense that it stresses the primacy of the national-ethnic identity and rejects the notion of antagonistic social classes." Liberation of Arabs from imperialism and their unification were expected to result in reduced class conflict and restored Arab greatness. Another contrast between Baathist and communist ideologies was with regard to private property. While the communists called for abolition of much private property, the Baath Party constitution described private ownership and inheritance of property as natural rights that should be respected except in cases that conflicted with the interests of nationalism.

Syrian teachers brought Baath concepts to Iraq in 1949. By 1951 the Baath movement in Iraq had grown to about fifty members led by Fu'ad al-Rikabi, a Shia engineer from Nasiriyah. Since al-Rikabi recruited a number of his friends and family members to the movement, many of the original members of the Iraqi Baath Party were Shia. The Baath membership list seized by Iraqi police on June 25, 1955, indicated that the party at that point had 289 members, 102 of whom were students.

The United National Front

Despite their differences, the Baath Party and the ICP decided to cooperate against the common enemy, the Iraqi monarchy. In February 1957 a new opposition alliance, the United National Front, was created to coordinate the efforts of four parties—Iraqi Communist, National Democratic, Istiqlal, and Baath—against the regime. The Front called for abolishing martial law, establishing a democratic political system, withdrawing Iraq from the Baghdad Pact, and creating a neutral foreign policy (Al-Qazzaz 2006: 432; Tripp 2000: 143). In addition, some members of the Front parties developed relationships with discontented military officers who would play decisive roles in the July 1958 revolution.

The United Arab Republic

In pursuit of Arab unity, Egypt and Syria merged in what was called the United Arab Republic. Although it lasted only from February 1958 to September 1961, the republic was viewed as a threat by the monarchies of Iraq and Jordan, which feared that their subjects would demand to join the republic and eliminate their regimes in the process. In response, the Jordanian and Iraqi rulers created their own version of Arab nationalism, a federation of the two monarchies. But rather than protect the Iraqi regime, this provided an opportunity for its overthrow.

Summary and Analysis

From 1920 to 1932, Britain controlled Iraq under the authority of the League of Nations. In 1932 Iraq was declared an independent nation, but many Iraqis believed they were still dominated by Britain, which maintained military bases there and controlled the Iraq Petroleum Company. Following the death of King Faisal I in 1933, the influence of the Iraqi military grew.

Opposition to the British was manifested through two types of nationalism. One was particularistic, in that it aimed to develop a distinctive sense of patriotism that included all of Iraq's religious and ethnic groups. The other was pan-Arab nationalism, which had the goal of creating a united Arab state.

In 1936 Iraqi army General Bakr Sidqi, of Kurdish ancestry, successfully led the first military coup in Iraq's history, supported by liberal reformers. The new government pursued the particularistic form of Iraqi nationalism. When

established economic interest groups resisted proposed liberal reforms to benefit workers and peasants and the threat of political instability grew, Sidqi turned
against the economic reformers in the government in part to appease upper-class
interests. But in August 1937 he was assassinated by Arab nationalist officers.

The outbreak of World War II in Europe precipitated an overt rupture between the militant Arab nationalist sector of the military and the pro-British
regent. In April 1941, Arab nationalist officers staged a coup and refused to accommodate British demands, resulting in a brief war and Britain's reoccupation
of Iraq. The British reinstalled the pro-British regent, Abd al-Ilah, and their
most valued Iraqi politician, Nuri al-Said, who proceeded to brutally repress
opponents. During WWII, when Britain was allied with the Soviet Union, the
Iraqi Communist Party, while not permitted legal status, experienced a level of
tolerance and grew significantly. The war and its aftermath brought economic
hardship to wide sectors of the population.

The attempt to replace the 1930 Anglo-Iraq Treaty with a new treaty negotiated at Portsmouth, England, in January 1948, which would have extended
British prerogatives in Iraq long after the earlier treaty was set to expire, coupled with difficult economic conditions, led to the outbreak of the antiregime
wathbah mass protests. The government blamed the Communist Party and responded by imprisoning or executing party leaders and smashing much of the
party's organizational network, as well as generally repressing dissent. In May
1948, poorly equipped Iraqi soldiers were sent to join the fight against newly
independent Israel. Along with other Arab forces, they suffered a humiliating
defeat, and many officers believed Iraq's pro-British rulers had betrayed the
armed forces.

In the early 1950s, as exploitation of the country's oil resources expanded
dramatically, Iraq benefited from an increased share of oil profits, much of
which was directed toward infrastructure development. The regime alternated
between promising greater levels of political freedom and repressing dissent
when opposition forces appeared to be gaining too much momentum. The ICP,
though still not permitted legal status, grew once again into a significant political group. Opposition parties with legal status included the Arab nationalist Istiqlal and the leftist National Democratic Party. During the 1950s another Arab
nationalist group began to attract members, the Iraqi Baath Party. Founded in
Syria, the Baath movement spread to Iraq in 1949. Its anti-imperialism stance,
call for unity of Arab peoples, and advocacy of social reform attracted many recruits, who organized into a secretive cellular network similar to the organizational structure of its rival, the ICP.

In 1955, to replace the 1930 Anglo-Iraqi Treaty, which was nearing its
1957 expiration date, pro-British Iraqi officials brought Iraq into a new US-
supported multination alliance, the Baghdad Pact, with Britain and three non-
Arab nations, Turkey, Iran, and Pakistan. This alliance placed Iraq clearly on
Britain's side in the Cold War and was widely opposed within Iraq and throughout much of the Arab world. The joint British, French, and Israeli attack on
Egypt in October 1956 further undermined Iraq's pro-British monarchy.

In February 1957, growing animosity toward the monarchy and its supporters motivated the creation of the antiregime United National Front, which

included the leftist National Democratic and Iraqi Communist parties, along with the Arab nationalist Istiqlal and Baath parties. But the most crucial elements in the developing revolutionary situation were outraged Iraqi military leaders, who would launch a revolution and annihilate the regime in July 1958.

References and Further Readings

Batatu, Hanna. 1978. *The Old Social Classes and the Revolutionary Movements of Iraq*. Princeton, NJ: Princeton University Press.

Davidson, Nigel G. 1925. "The Constitution of Iraq." *Journal of Comparative Legislation and International Law* 3rd Ser., 7, 1: 41–52.

Devlin, John E. 1991. "The Baath Party: Rise and Metamorphosis." *American Historical Review* 96 (December): 1396–1407.

Farouk-Sluglett, Marion, and Peter Sluglett. 1988. "The Iraqi Ba'th Party." In Vicky Randall, ed., *Political Parties in the Third World*, 57–74. London: Sage.

———. 2003. *Iraq Since 1958*. London: I. B. Tauris Publishers.

Gorman, Anthony. 2006. "Egyptian Revolution of 1952." In James DeFronzo, ed., *Revolutionary Movements in World History: From 1750 to the Present*, 246–253. Santa Barbara, CA: ABC-CLIO.

Husry, Khaldun S. 1974a. "The Assyrian Affair of 1933 (I)." *International Journal of Middle East Studies* 5 (2): 161–176.

———. 1974b. "The Assyrian Affair of 1933 (II)." *International Journal of Middle East Studies* 5 (3): 344–360.

Ismael, Tareq. 2007. *The Rise and Fall of the Communist Party of Iraq*. Cambridge, UK: Cambridge University Press.

Khalidi, Rashid, Lisa Anderson, Muhammad Muslih, and Reeva S. Simon, eds. 1991. *The Origins of Arab Nationalism*. New York: Columbia University Press.

Long, David E., and John A. Hearty. 1986. "Republic of Iraq." In David E. Long and Bernard Reich, eds., *The Government and Politics of the Middle East and North Africa*, 93–111. Boulder, CO: Westview Press.

Longrigg, Stephen. 1953. *Iraq, 1900 to 1950*. London: Oxford University Press.

Marr, Phebe. 2004. *The Modern History of Iraq*. Boulder, CO: Westview Press.

Pillai, R. V., and Mahendra Kumar. 1962. "The Political and Legal Status of Kuwait." *International and Comparative Law Quarterly* 11 (1): 108–130.

Polk, William R. 2005. *Understanding Iraq*. New York: Harper Perennial.

Al-Qazzaz, Ayad. 1976. "The Iraqi British War of 1941: A Review Article." *International Journal of Middle East Studies* 7: 591–596.

———. 1996. "The Ahali Group." In Reeva S. Simon, Phillip Mattar, and Richard W. Bulliet, eds., *The Encyclopedia of the Modern Middle East*, vol. 1, 60–61. New York: Macmillan Reference USA.

———. 2006. "Iraq Revolution." In James DeFronzo, ed., *Revolutionary Movements in World History*, 427–440.

Sluglett, Peter. 1976. *Britain in Iraq, 1914–1932*. London: Ithaca Press.

Tripp, Charles. 2000. *A History of Iraq*. Cambridge, UK: Cambridge University Press.

3

The Iraq Revolution
and the Establishment
of the Baathist Regime

The political system many Iraqis viewed as an instrument of foreign imperialism would be swept away in the 1958 revolution. A revolutionary left-leaning government led by General Abd al-Karim Qasim attempted to strengthen Iraqi patriotism and accomplish economic and social reforms. But opposition from Arab nationalists and conservative Islamic clergy led to his overthrow and execution in February 1963. The new government was led by Arab nationalist General Abd al-Salam Arif. After the coup, Baath Party militia killed many ICP members and other leftists. The high level of violence caused months of social turmoil and generated resentment against Baath leaders, leading to the removal of most Baath Party members from government. After Abd al-Salam Arif died in a helicopter crash in 1966, his brother, Abd al-Rahman Arif, became president. The second Arif was ousted on July 17, 1968, and on July 30, the Baath Party staged another coup, removing several non-Baathist officers and taking exclusive control of government. A respected Baathist military officer, Ahmad Hasan al-Bakr, became president. But behind the scenes a younger Baathist leader, Saddam Hussein, controlled the party organization, a role that would lead to his becoming Iraq's supreme leader.

The Revolution of July 14, 1958

Setting for Revolution

Although Iraq's oil revenues had grown, long-standing inequalities remained largely unchanged. The British-supported regime had repressed and killed anti-imperialist Arab nationalists and leftists, including ICP leaders, in the late 1940s. Animosity toward the regime surged in response to the 1955 Baghdad Pact binding Iraq into a new alliance with Britain, and then in reaction to the 1956 British, French, and Israeli attack on Egypt. The monarchy's domestic support narrowed to only some businessmen and conservative tribal chieftains.

Egyptian and Syrian antimonarchy radio broadcasts reached illiterate Iraqis, further weakening the regime.

The Revolutionary Process

Four opposition political parties—the NDP, the ICP, Istiqlal, and Baath—formed the United National Front (UNF) alliance in February 1957, with the support of many professionals and students, as well as oil and transportation workers. A number of military officers wanted revenge for the executions of those who had resisted the British in 1941 and/or for the perceived betrayal of the armed forces in the 1948 war in Palestine, so they formed secret revolutionary committees of Free Officers. These included three future leaders of Iraq: General Qasim and the Arif brothers, Abd al-Salam and Abd al-Rahman. By 1957, the Free Officers groups had unified under the leadership of the highest ranking member, General Qasim. The fourteen-member Free Officer central committee consisted of largely Sunni Arabs (only two Shia Arabs and no Kurds). Most were from middle-class families, but Qasim came from the lower class. Although the two hundred Free Officers represented less than 5 percent of all officers (Farouk-Sluglett and Sluglett 2003: 48), lack of opposition to the 1958 revolution indicated that support for the movement in the armed forces was widespread. The Free Officers' eclectic ideology included, according to one member, combating imperialism, removing foreign bases, freeing peasants from exploitation and feudal conditions, creating a republic, drafting a democratic constitution, supporting Kurdish and other minority rights, cooperating with and achieving unity with Arab nations, and returning Palestine to its people (Marr 2004: 83–84).

However, security agents became aware of secretive groups within the armed forces. Fearing a military revolt, the regime refused to allow most units to carry ammunition. The Free Officers overcame this by having Naji Talib, director of military training, redirect training ammunition to the units that would carry out the revolt, whose timing was determined by an uprising in Lebanon.

The rebellion's key leaders were General Qasim, commander of the Nineteenth Brigade of the Iraqi army, and Colonel Abd al-Salam Arif, commander of one of the battalions of the Twentieth Brigade. The Iraqi regime, fearing fighting could spread from Lebanon and threaten the Jordanian monarchy, which was federated with Iraq, ordered Iraqi forces to Jordan. Qasim and Arif used this opportunity to move troops to destroy the Iraqi monarchy. On July 13, Arif took command of the entire Twentieth Brigade and marched toward Baghdad. Early on July 14, he seized a radio station in Baghdad and broadcast that the revolution was under way and that Iraq would be free from "the corrupt crew that imperialism installed" (Farouk-Sluglett and Sluglett 2003: 49). Units from his battalion were sent to the royal palace and to the residence of Nuri al-Said, and around 8 A.M. soldiers killed King Faisal II, former regent Abd al-Ilah, and other members of the royal family, effectively annihilating the Iraqi Hashemite dynasty. Qasim's forces arrived in the city by early afternoon. Nuri al-Said was spotted on July 15 and immediately shot and killed.

The Revolutionary Government

Although Qasim and Arif were the most powerful figures in the revolution, the official leadership was the three-person Sovereignty Council, composed of a Shia Arab of the Istiqlal Party, Muhammad Mahdi; a Kurdish former military officer, Khalid al-Naqshabandi; and a Sunni Arab military officer, Najib al-Rubai'i.

The revolutionary government abolished the monarchy and the constitution that supported its existence. Persons considered hostile to the revolution were removed from high positions in the armed forces, police, and government bureaucracies. However, most in the middle and lower levels of the military and police, many of whom were very conservative, stayed.

Foreign policy abruptly changed. Federation with Jordan ended, and Iraq withdrew from the Baghdad Pact and established relations with the USSR and the People's Republic of China. Fearful of provoking Britain, which had organized an international boycott of Iranian oil after that country's parliament nationalized the Anglo-Iranian Oil Company in 1951 and two years later, with US assistance, helped to overthrow Iran's nationalist government to reinstall the Iranian shah as a virtual absolute monarch, the new government took no immediate action regarding the British-controlled Iraq Petroleum Company. The British–United States intervention in Iran is widely thought to have given birth to modern political Islamic fundamentalism (DeFronzo 2007: 275–324, 325–342; Sariolghalam 2008: 430) that played the leading role in Iran's 1979 revolution, which in turn had enormous consequences for Iraq (see chapters 4 and 7).

In postmonarchy Iraq, Qasim became commander of the armed forces, prime minister, and minister of defense. Arif became deputy commander, deputy prime minister, and minister of the interior. The cabinet had two NDP members, one each from the Baath and Istiqlal parties, a Kurd, and a person described as a Marxist, but none from the ICP.

A temporary constitution stated that Iraq was a republic in which the Sovereignty Council exercised presidential powers and the Council of Ministers acted as a legislature. Many Free Officers, however, did not receive posts in the new government, and soon a power struggle developed between Qasim and Arif.

General Qasim's background appeared to make him the ideal leader for building a unified Iraq and accomplishing social reforms. He was born in Baghdad in 1914 into a lower-class family. His father was a Sunni Arab who worked as a carpenter, and his mother was a Shia Kurd (known as a Faili) (Al-Qazzaz 2006: 439). Although Qasim identified himself as Sunni, his birth family represented a blending of Iraq's two major religious orientations and ethnic groups, and he seemed motivated to improve the welfare of Iraq's urban and rural poor. His approach, however, was to attempt to lift up the disadvantaged without drastically dispossessing the upper classes. After high school Qasim taught briefly at a primary school and then enrolled in the military college. He became an officer in 1938 and served in the 1948 Arab–Israeli War, blaming defeat in Palestine on corrupt Arab governments that in reality served British interests.

Abd al-Salam Arif, who spearheaded the revolution and later claimed primary responsibility for it, was born into a lower middle–class Sunni Arab family in Baghdad in 1921 (Batatu 1978: 779). He attended the military college and in 1941 became an officer. Like Qasim, he served in the 1948 war in Palestine and similarly blamed the Iraqi and other Arab governments for the defeat. His Sunni family background may have contributed to his Arab nationalism, compared with Qasim's Iraqi nationalist outlook.

Conflict Between Qasim and Arif

Qasim and Arif disagreed over whether Iraq should join the United Arab Republic (UAR). Colonel Arif, the Baath and Istiqlal parties, and many in the Free Officers' movement favored joining the UAR, which would continue to be led by Egypt's President Gamal Abdel Nasser. Qasim and the National Democratic and Communist parties supported cooperating with Egypt and Syria, but not unification. They favored building a strong sense of national identity among Iraq's different religious and ethnic groups, economic development, and social reforms. In addition, while Arif was willing to accept Nasser as leader, Qasim was not. The communists also feared that Nasser would repress the ICP.

Qasim gained the upper hand partly because the communists supported him and organized mass demonstrations against joining the UAR. When Arif continued to call for rapid unification with Egypt and Syria, Qasim dismissed him from his positions on September 30 and sent him to West Germany as Iraq's ambassador. But Arif returned to Iraq on November 4, allegedly to participate in a plot to assassinate Qasim. Arif was arrested on November 5, tried, and given a death sentence, later commuted to a prison term.

General Qasim's Regime: 1958–1963

Qasim and the Communists

Although Qasim was supported by many of Iraq's people because of his role in the revolution, his commitment to social reform, his humble origins, and his mixed ethnic ancestry, he had several crucial weaknesses. Unlike Arif and later Saddam Hussein, Qasim lacked the assistance of a large extended family network. He also did not have a mass political party whose views he could accept. In some respects, his outlook was similar to the social democratic NDP. But the NDP, having only a few hundred members, was not a mass political movement like the ICP. Furthermore, many NDP members became disappointed that Qasim did not rapidly implement a democratic political system, and the party soon split between those favoring and those opposing him. Though the ICP backed his government, Qasim did not agree with aspects of its ideology and often viewed this crucial component of his support as a potential threat to political stability. He appeared to fear that the perception of too much ICP influence in his government could provoke intense domestic opposition from Arab nationalists and religious leaders, and might also bring about foreign intervention from Western capitalist nations. As noted earlier, Qasim and his associates were well aware that in 1953 in neighboring Iran a nationalist alliance of parties led by Mohammad Mossadeq had been overthrown in a military coup assisted by British agents and the US CIA. Mossadeq's government had nationalized the Anglo-Iranian Oil Company, enraging the British, who persuaded US leaders that Mossadeq was a threat to US security interests. In an attempt to reduce the likelihood of a US–British intervention against his government, Qasim did not nationalize foreign-owned oil companies and repeatedly refused to legalize the Iraqi Communist Party.

The ICP, however, continued to enthusiastically support Qasim. While the party advocated a future socialist economy, its immediate focus was to work for reforms, such as improved health care, expanded educational opportunities, and reduced inequality within Iraq's capitalist system. The communists widely used the title "Sole Leader" for Qasim not only to rally their supporters but also to recruit more people to their party by capitalizing on Qasim's popularity. Over the course of his regime, Qasim was forced to rely organizationally on the ICP while often trying to publicly distance himself from it.

Qasim's Oil Policy

After failing to convince the Iraq Petroleum Company to either grant Iraq 20 percent ownership or give up 90 percent of the territory in the company's concession, increase Iraq's share of the profits, and partner with Iraq in exploiting the other 10 percent of the concession, Qasim proclaimed Public Law 80 on December 11, 1961, which simply removed 99.5 percent of the concession area from the company's control (Marr 2004: 102). The government created the Iraq National Oil Company to develop the former concession territory. The Iraq Petroleum Company was allowed to continue pumping and selling oil, from which Iraq received a share of the profits, from the 0.5 percent of the original concession area the Iraq Petroleum Company had already developed. Though this ensured that Iraq would continue to receive oil revenue, the Iraq Petroleum Company responded to Public Law 80 "by slowing down the rate of production," causing Iraq's revenues to grow at a slower pace than they would have (Farouk-Sluglett and Sluglett 2003: 78). But Public Law 80 was extremely popular among the Iraqi people.

Development and Reforms

The Qasim government was committed to accelerating economic and social development through central planning and investment in industrialization and related projects. State-directed economic development was endorsed by the NDP, the ICP, and the Baath Party. Education funding was nearly doubled, and the percentage of young people in school increased significantly from primary level through college. The state also provided funds for improvements in health care and workplace conditions. A land reform program greatly weakened the political power of large landowners in the countryside, limiting their holdings to a maximum of 1,236 rain-fed acres or 618 irrigated acres (Farouk-Sluglett and Sluglett 2003: 76). Appropriated land was to be given to landless peasants in amounts of twenty to forty acres. The notorious Law of the Rights and Duties of Cultivators, which had in effect enslaved many rural laborers to landlords, was abolished, as was the Tribal Disputes Code, which had permitted tribal leaders to oversee their own system of law separate from that of the state. Much low-cost housing for the urban poor was constructed, and middle-class and lower middle–class workers were given access to relatively low-interest home loans.

Qasim's reforms ensured that he remained popular with a wide sector of the population, particularly the poor. Qasim also moved to bring about greater gender equality. In December 1959, the Personal Status Law was revised to eliminate child marriage, protect women against arbitrary divorce by husbands, and give women an improved right of inheritance. The new law, however, provoked opposition from conservative religious leaders.

Regime Instability

Arab Nationalists

Qasim alienated Arab nationalists first by appointing only a few Free Officers to government positions; second by refusing to join the UAR and instead focusing on developing a strong sense of Iraqi patriotism; and third by arresting and imprisoning Abd al-Salam Arif, whom many regarded as the real hero of the July 1958 revolution. (Qasim, believing that others had misled Arif into a coup plot, lifted the death sentence.) These events increased polarization between the pro-Qasim "left" and the Arab nationalist "right," with whom anti-communists among the economic establishment, military, and police began to ally. Many Shia clergy, alarmed that Shia youth were joining the communist movement, also sided with Arab nationalists against Qasim.

The Mosul Coup Attempt

Mosul, with the exception of its Christian and Kurdish residents, was a relatively conservative Arab nationalist–oriented city. After Arif was sentenced to death in February 1959, Arab nationalists and antileftist groups, such as the Sunni Muslim Brotherhood, formed an anti-Qasim alliance. Large landowners, threatened by the left-leaning government, also lined up against Qasim.

A number of officers, including Rif'at al-Haij Sirri, Baghdad military intelligence chief; Nazim al-Tabaqchali, commander of the Kirkuk garrison; and Abd al-Wahhab Shawwaf, commander of the Mosul garrison, organized a coup attempt. According to Batatu (1978: 871–872), Colonel Shawwaf, son of a wealthy landowning family, was to launch the coup. Then Tabaqchali at Kirkuk and Sirri at Baghdad would declare their support for the coup. Sirri was supposed to arrest Qasim and either exile or eliminate him.

Batatu (1978: 871–879) suggests that the coup planners chose Mosul as the site to begin the coup because of its conservative and Arab nationalist orientations and because many disenchanted Free Officers were stationed there or close by. He claims that the communists had become aware of the coup plot, warned Qasim about it, and in fact chose Mosul for the site of the communist-affiliated Peace Partisans' nationwide rally to foil the coup. On February 23, 1959, the communist newspaper *Ittihad al-Shaab* (People's Unity) announced the march would be held in Mosul on March 6. The plotters, however, waited to launch the coup until the march was over and many out-of-town leftists had departed the city.

At the time, Mosul was a city of some 180,000. ICP membership there was estimated as being from below 400 to as many as 2,000 (Batatu 1978: 874). On March 5 thousands of participants arrived at Mosul, many on specially scheduled trains. On the 6th, the march took place relatively smoothly with an official estimate of 250,000 taking part, chanting slogans such as "Our Sole Leader is Abd al-Karim Qasim!" (Batatu 1978: 880). By noon of the 7th, most Peace Partisans had left Mosul, but many out-of-town communists remained, staging demonstrations, while Baathists and other anti-communists staged counter-demonstrations and burned leftist bookstores and a coffeehouse known as a favorite meeting place for local communists.

At 7 A.M. on March 8, an announcement over Radio Mosul declared that General Qasim had betrayed the July Revolution and the Free Officers' movement, created chaos, and sided with people (the communists) whose political ideology had "no appeal for Iraqis" (Batatu 1978: 881). The pro-coup broadcast also stated that Qasim had attacked Arab nationalism and allowed newspapers and radio stations to criticize the UAR.

But the coup quickly began to fail. Neither General Tabaqchali in Kirkuk nor Colonel Sirri in Baghdad was able to help Colonel Shawwaf because they were kept under close surveillance by Qasim supporters. In Mosul, Shawwaf faced opposition from many enlisted soldiers within his own Fifth Brigade who were from poor families, identified with Qasim, and had benefited from Qasim's pay raise for enlisted soldiers. In addition, some of them were Kurds and had leftist rather than Arab nationalist sympathies. The army engineering regiment in Mosul attempted to resist the coup, but its pro-Qasim commander was killed and Shawwaf's forces temporarily gained control of the city.

At 8 A.M. the next day, planes of the Iraqi air force, commanded by Communist Colonel Jalal al-Awqati since the July Revolution, bombed the Fifth Army Brigade headquarters in Mosul, wounding Shawwaf. Later he was killed, apparently by a soldier or soldiers opposed to the coup (Batatu 1978: 883). At times the fighting took on the characteristics of an all-out civil war but with interclass, interethnic, and intertribal dimensions. A turning point in the violence occurred when news spread that Arab nationalists had murdered in prison "the much-loved Peace Partisan leader," Kamil Qazanchi (Farouk-Sluglett and Sluglett 2003: 68). Qazanchi, who was both a poet and a lawyer, "had spectacularly defended Comrade Fahd at his trial in 1947" and had led the successful massive demonstrations against the proposed Portsmouth Treaty in 1948. In retaliation, "the Communists and their supporters began to wage a campaign of indiscriminate revenge against suspected 'nationalists'" (Farouk-Sluglett and Sluglett 2003: 68). Two hundred or more people were killed in several days of violence.

Trial of the Mosul Coup Plotters

Qasim's government had established a People's Court to try members of the prerevolutionary regime accused of serious crimes. Four of them were executed, including the notorious Bahjat 'Atiyya, former head of the monarchy's Criminal Investigation Department who had persecuted communist leaders, including Comrade Fahd. After the Mosul coup, the court tried the surviving leaders, and televised the proceedings, including statements of the accused. General Tabaqchali made an impressive speech on the reasons he and his associates had staged the coup attempt. But he, Colonel Sirri, and eleven others were sentenced to death and executed on September 20, increasing Arab nationalist animosity and thirst for revenge toward Qasim and the communists.

Communists' Surge and Qasim's Response

The events in Mosul in March 1959 had a number of consequences beyond increasing hostility between Qasim's supporters and Arab nationalists. First, Qasim's regime removed a number of Arab nationalists from the military and government ministries. Second, the popular appeal of the Communist Party increased significantly. ICP membership, which had been about 500 nationally in the mid-1950s, increased to between 20,000 and 25,000 (Marr 2004: 95). Communist leaders demanded that the People's Resistance militia, which had been established to protect the revolution after the overthrow of the monarchy and had come under communist control, be fully armed. The People's Resistance grew from about 11,000 in August 1958 to approximately 25,000 in May 1959.

On May 1, 1959, the May Day workers' holiday, hundreds of thousands marched through Baghdad's streets, many of them calling for the ICP to be officially represented in Qasim's government. But Qasim perceived the growing communist movement as a threat to stability, potentially setting the stage for a civil war or even foreign military intervention if the British felt that their oil interests in Iraq were about to fall under the control of a communist government. Qasim hoped to calm conservatives by proving that the communists were not going to take power or be allowed the means to do so. He refused to arm the communists or the People's Resistance militia they dominated. Qasim's fear of the political repercussions of the communists' capturing a large share of the vote probably played a role in his decision not to permit a democratically elected parliament. A communist-dominated parliament might have provoked a new Arab nationalist rebellion or some type of intervention from Britain and the United States.

After realizing that Qasim would not give them a significant role or create a democratic political system that might allow them to be elected to power, some communist leaders considered whether to take advantage of their strength after the Mosul conflict to seize the government (Farouk-Sluglett and Sluglett 2003: 69). However, most ICP leaders believed that such a step would result in a civil war they would lose because other political groups and religious conservatives would unite against them, very likely with foreign military assistance.

The only realistic, though frustrating, choice for the communists was to go on building the party and its affiliated organizations, support Qasim's regime against the possibility of a far worse government, and attempt to win Qasim over to their point of view.

Despite Qasim's refusal to give in to ICP demands, many Arab nationalists and religious conservatives simply lumped Qasim and the ICP together as different manifestations of the same communist enemy that had to be destroyed.

Kirkuk Violence

While Qasim moved to limit the ICP's military potential by retiring some prominent communist officers, he decided to allow the party to have some minor representation in his government by appointing an ICP member as minister of municipalities and two pro-ICP people to other ministries.

But the ICP's influence would diminish significantly after July violence in Kirkuk. The communists decided to follow the big demonstration in Mosul with another massive ICP display of strength in Kirkuk on the first anniversary of the July 14 revolution. Kirkuk had an economically prominent Turkoman population, but Kurds, drawn to Kirkuk's growing oil economy, began to challenge Turkoman domination. Ethnic identities tended to correspond to class divisions, with employers typically Turkomans and employees more often Kurds. And while Turkomans tended to be politically conservative, many Kurds were Communist Party members or supporters of the Kurdish Democratic Party, then allied with the ICP.

Violence broke out along the march route, often deadly and even savage. According to Batatu (1978: 912), 31 people were killed, of whom 28 were Turkomans, and 130 injured, of whom 124 were Turkoman. The perpetrators were thought to be overwhelmingly Kurds. Although the tragic events in Kirkuk in 1959 seem dwarfed by the levels of interethnic and sectarian killings in later years, at the time accounts of the violence had a devastating impact on the ICP. Opponents of the party used radio broadcasts to claim that the killings showed the barbaric nature of the communists. Qasim seized on the "Kirkuk Massacre" to harshly criticize the communists and justify his restrictions on the party. ICP leaders themselves issued a statement highly critical of problems within the party, including the questionable character of many who had joined during the huge surge in membership. Though remarkably honest, the public admissions probably damaged the party's popularity.

The Baath Assassination Attempt

Enraged by Qasim's perceived betrayal of the Arab nationalist cause and his alliance with the communists, the Baath Party planned to assassinate him. The problem they faced after the Mosul coup attempt was that the growth in ICP strength had been so great that they feared that assassinating Qasim in the spring or summer of 1959 would most likely have resulted in a communist takeover of the government, so they waited for political conditions to change. The diminished appeal of the communists after the July Kirkuk events significantly reduced the probability of a communist takeover if Qasim were killed. In addition, the televised speeches at the People's Court of the soon-to-be-executed Arab nationalist officers involved in the Mosul rebellion won the sympathy of a large sector of the public. Qasim's own actions seemed to further increase his vulnerability. As he turned away from his key supporters, the communists, and limited their military capabilities, he attempted to attract political moderates and even allowed more than a dozen Arab nationalist officers who had been purged after the Mosul rebellion to return to the armed forces.

The Baathists concluded that the time was right to eliminate Qasim. On October 7 a group of Baathists, including twenty-two-year-old Saddam Hussein, shot and killed Qasim's driver but only wounded Qasim as they were driving on Rashid Street in Baghdad. The attackers and many involved in planning the assassination attempt escaped, most to Syria. Saddam Hussein was wounded in the event but made his way out of the country. His role in the attack would become a significant asset to his rise within the Baath Party. Seventy people were captured, and some used their trials to effectively express their political views, helping to increase the Baath Party's appeal to other Arab nationalists. Six received death sentences, but, unlike the Mosul defendants, were never executed.

Qasim was gratified when after the assassination attempt huge crowds spontaneously poured into the streets and shouted his name and their thanks that the "son of the people" had been spared. Surviving the attack may have led him to believe that Allah had saved him because he was divinely chosen to build the Iraqi nation. He may also have felt that his popularity would protect him from any future assassination or coup attempt. This may partially explain some of his later seemingly incompetent and even suicidal political decisions, such as continuing to try to make peace with the far-too-alienated Arab nationalists while suppressing the communists. In reality this strategy "merely served to undermine his only secure source of support" (Farouk-Sluglett and Sluglett 2003: 74) while providing his real enemies with new means and opportunities to destroy his regime.

Legalizing Political Parties

In 1960 Qasim allowed the legalization of a number of political parties. But with the exception of the Kurdish Democratic Party, only relatively insignificant groups attained legal status. The ICP remained illegal and had no option but to continue supporting Qasim while his government simultaneously maneuvered to oust ICP members from control of student groups and labor unions and shut down pro-communist newspapers.

Shia Opposition to Qasim

Communist support for Qasim, coupled with the generally secular nature of his regime and the impact of several of his major reforms, provoked opposition from a number of Shia clergy, tribal leaders, and landlords. Some objected to Qasim's Personal Status Law, which provided increased rights to women. Qasim's land reform, while well received among poor Shia peasants, threatened the wealth of the traditional Shia elite and, indirectly, the income of the Shia clergy, to whom the wealthy paid religious taxes. The clergy also feared the appeal to Shia youth of the ICP and the Baath Party, both of which had significant numbers of Shia members.

One important step in awakening Shia political activism was the 1960 fatwa (religious ruling) by the primary *marjah* (religious authority), Grand Ayatollah Muhsin al-Hakim, opposing participation in the ICP. In addition, two important Shia Islamic groups were created, the Society of Ulama (clergy) and the Dawa (Islamic Call) Party. The Society of Ulama, composed of clerics from the theological center of Najaf, was formed in 1960 mainly to counter the communist movement and Qasim's Personal Status Law, and to reemphasize Shia religious doctrine.

The Dawa is thought to have been organized around 1958 by younger Shia clergy and laypeople in part to diminish the appeal of the Communist and Baath parties and to modify Shia Islam to fit the realities of the modern world. A young cleric, Muhammad Baqir al-Sadr, emerged as the Dawa's intellectual leader and published works on Islamic philosophy and economics in 1959 and 1961, respectively, which helped politically mobilize Shia.

The Kurds

During the 1920s the combination of British airpower and the Iraqi army suppressed Kurdish rebellions. The Russian military occupation of Iranian Kurdistan during World War II provided an opportunity for Iranian Kurds and Iraqi Kurdish fighters to establish an autonomous Kurdish republic, the so-called Mahabad Republic in Iranian territory. But the republic depended on the presence of Soviet forces for its existence, and when they were withdrawn, Iranian troops crushed it and executed its leader in 1947 (Bozarslan 2006: 519, 523, 527). However, an Iraqi Kurd involved in forming the republic, Mustafa Barzani, escaped to the Soviet Union.

Most Kurds welcomed the 1958 Iraqi revolution and Qasim's temporary constitution, which stated that Arabs and Kurds were to be "partners in the Iraqi homeland and their national rights are recognized within the Iraqi state" (Farouk-Sluglett and Sluglett 2003: 79). That Qasim's mother and one of the members of the three-man Sovereignty Council were both Kurdish was also encouraging. Qasim allowed Barzani to return to Iraq partly for support against the Arab nationalists. The Kurdistan Democratic Party of Iraq (KDP-Iraq), originally founded in 1946, cooperated with the ICP against Arab nationalists. But Barzani, a conservative tribal leader who had been fighting for Kurdish autonomy since 1931, soon worried Qasim, who feared that autonomy would lead to a push for a fully independent Kurdish state. Barzani could command the loyalty of hundreds of tribal fighters, and his legendary determination and guerrilla fighting skills resulted in his election as leader of the KDP in 1960, the same year Qasim allowed the party to be legalized.

Marr (2004: 105–106) describes deep-seated differences within the KDP: "Barzani represented the landed establishment and the wealth and power of the aghas." The other wing of the party was led by urban intellectuals, mainly the middle-class leftist lawyers Ibrahim Ahmad and his son-in-law Jalal al-Talabani, who were interested in significant economic reforms to help the disadvantaged. Both branches of the party, however, were united behind the goal of winning autonomy for Iraqi Kurdistan.

Discontent among Kurdish tribal leaders and landlords rose in response to Qasim's land reform program, a policy generally supported by the leftists within the KDP. Barzani entered into negotiations with Qasim's government but in January 1961, dissatisfied by the lack of progress, began to prepare for armed conflict. In August Barzani demanded that Qasim establish a democratic political system and agree to Kurdish autonomy.

When Kurdish tribal fighters occupied the city of Zakho in northern Iraq, a full-scale war for Kurdish autonomy commenced with both sections of the KDP participating, although Barzani commanded more fighters (*peshmergas*, those who face death) than the leftist branch of the KDP. The Barzani rebellion continued off and on until 1975, when Iran decided to prevent Iraqi Kurds from using its territory for regrouping or receiving aid.

Once the fighting started, many Kurdish soldiers in the Iraqi army defected to the rebels. Marr (2004: 106–107) estimated that by the end of 1963, "for every three Kurds fighting for the government, there were four fighting for Barzani." Qasim's support was eroded by the revolt and by the inability of the army, although about two-thirds of its troops were deployed to the Kurdish region, to defeat it. The war absorbed valuable resources, slowed development, and diverted attention from other important problems.

The Baathists made an offer to the KDP that if Qasim was overthrown, the Kurds could have autonomy. This appears to have been mainly an attempt to convince the Kurds not to interfere with an Arab nationalist coup against Qasim. Although the Kurdish war was not solely Qasim's fault, his alienation of the Kurds—who, as Farouk-Sluglett and Sluglett (2003: 81) note, logically should have remained among his key allies—resembles Qasim's somewhat self-defeating turn against his main allies, the communists.

Foreign Affairs

The World. The 1958 revolution that destroyed the pro-Western monarchy in oil-rich Iraq shocked the British. According to Marr (2004: 108), both Britain and the United States "considered military action against the regime, urged on by regional allies such as Turkey, Iran, Jordan and Israel." But such intervention was "soon rejected as impractical." The United States remained hostile to Qasim because he was supported by the ICP, which seemed to be growing rapidly.

Qasim had to find a new source for the weapons, machinery, and economic aid that had previously come from Britain and the United States. His government turned to the USSR for arms, technology, and assistance with new development programs. By the end of 1959, Iraq had purchased Soviet MIG fighter planes, helicopters, and transport aircraft, as well as at least one hundred tanks (Marr 2004: 108). In addition, nearly eight hundred young Iraqis were studying in the USSR, many on scholarships provided by the Soviets.

Kuwait. In June 1961 Britain allowed Kuwait to become an independent nation. While some Arab governments recognized its independence, Qasim asserted, as King Ghazi had in the late 1930s, that Kuwait was a part of Iraq's Basra province.

Fearing Iraqi military action, British troops landed in Kuwait, followed by forces from several Arab countries. However, Iraq's capacity to attack Kuwait was almost nonexistent since most of its troops were in the north fighting rebellious Kurds. Qasim's only recourse was to try convincing other countries not to recognize Kuwait's independence by using the virtually inconsequential threat that Iraq might break diplomatic relations with them. Predictably, this warning was largely ignored, and Kuwait was admitted to the Arab League on July 20, 1961, and then the UN on May 14, 1963.

Some governments doubted the validity of Iraq's claim to Kuwait, but others believed that Britain's long-term separation of Kuwait from Basra had created a new political reality that was impossible to reverse. Also, several Arab monarchies likely did not want to see a precedent set in which a revolutionary republic destroyed a monarchy and incorporated its territory. The United States and Britain strongly preferred keeping Kuwait's oil under a pro-Western monarchy dependent on them for its continued existence. The way in which Qasim went about pressing Iraq's claim to Kuwait further called into question his political judgment.

Overthrow of Qasim's Regime

Disillusionment with Qasim increased during 1961. The war in Kurdistan continued and most people lost hope that Qasim would establish democracy. The ICP, Qasim's principal source of mass support, was still strong, but party members were bewildered by Qasim's efforts to weaken them.

By February 1963, Baathist and other Arab nationalist officers devised a plan to topple Qasim by taking advantage of the absence of most of the armed forces in the north and the fact that Qasim had not armed the communist-led People's Resistance. Communication facilities and military bases were to be quickly seized and Qasim and several of his military supporters killed. Resistance to the coup, dispirited after Qasim's death, would be crushed and the leadership and organizational structure of the ICP was to be destroyed to ensure political stability of the post-Qasim Arab nationalist regime.

Several days before the coup, communists warned Qasim that a military rebellion was about to take place, but he took only mild precautions. One of the first coup actions occurred at 8:30 on the morning of February 8 when the head of the Iraqi air force, communist General Jalal al-Awqati, was shot and killed as he exited his car at a confectionery shop with his child (Batatu 1978: 974). The conspirators took control of several military bases and began bombing the Ministry of Defense, Qasim's headquarters. At about 9:40 A.M. the plotters announced their coup against Qasim over the radio, referring to him as "the enemy of the people" (Batatu 1978: 975–976). But the television station showed Qasim, who had been visiting his mother's house on Rashid Street, being wildly cheered "by the communists and the humbler classes of Baghdad." At about 10:30 A.M.

Qasim arrived at the Ministry of Defense, where crowds had assembled calling for weapons to fight against the coup, but Qasim declined to provide them with arms. At 3 P.M. the battle for the Defense Ministry began. Intense fighting lasted until noon on February 9. At 12:30 P.M. Qasim was forced to surrender unconditionally and at about 1:30 he and three of his associates were executed by a firing squad. Resistance to the coup, largely from people living in poor neighborhoods, especially the largely Shia al-Thawra area of Baghdad (Makiya 1998: 58–59), and from some communist soldiers and civilians, was suppressed.

Assessment of Qasim's Regime

Quite a few of Qasim's decisions seem hard to explain. Some feel that he was incompetent politically, others that he somehow became mentally unstable, and a number feel that his main purpose was to hold on to power. The question also arises as to whether Qasim sabotaged or at least failed to take advantage of Iraq's last real opportunity to build a democratic state within the borders of post–British Mandate Iraq. There may be some validity to one or more of these arguments. But the totality of the evidence suggests that other factors probably affected his behavior.

Qasim may have tried to serve the Iraqi people to the best of his ability and understanding. The Baathists and other Arab nationalists who overthrew and killed him searched in vain for evidence that Qasim had deposited money in foreign bank accounts or was otherwise corrupt. But instead they found the opposite. According to Batatu (1978: 981), when a lieutenant colonel participating in the coup inspected Qasim's private papers in the Ministry of Defense, he discovered that Qasim's salary "was being regularly dispensed to certain needy families of Baghdad." It is possible that his policies were guided by a set of principles that he clung to despite the fact that other choices might have proved more effective in preserving him in power.

Qasim tried to avoid political actions that would provoke a civil war. This likely explains why he refused to back the communists although they were his main supporters and why he was, with the exception of the Mosul conspirators, exceptionally lenient toward Arab nationalists. He was trying to maintain a political balance rather than allow one faction to gain a dominant position, potentially provoking another faction to violence. Ironically, this might also be why Qasim did not permit the construction of a genuinely democratic political system. He may have feared a rebellion from Sunni Arab nationalists or conservative Shia or foreign intervention if elections brought the communists into a dominant political role, or led to the victory of a pro-independence party in Iraq's Kurdish provinces. Regarding Kuwait, Qasim, like most Iraqis, believed that its detachment from Basra was an act of British imperialism.

Qasim's greatest failure was his unwillingness to take the risk of establishing a genuine democratic political system and institutions. Tripp (2000: 170) notes that Qasim, possibly by virtue of his mixed family background, "was particularly sensitive to the diversity of Iraq's population" and concerned with developing a "sense of national community" among all of the country's people.

But he was not perceptive enough to understand that a strong sense of Iraqi patriotism was unlikely to take root unless all Iraqis felt that their interests were being effectively "represented in institutions which they could trust" (Tripp 2000: 170). The Iraqi people would suffer greatly from the brutality of the authoritarian regimes that followed Qasim.

Arab Nationalist Rule, 1963–1968

The National Guard, an armed Baath-controlled militia under the command of Colonel Mundhir al-Wandawi and estimated at about 5,000 at the time of the coup (Farouk-Sluglett and Sluglett 2003: 85) but which grew to about 34,000 by August, began an intense onslaught against the communists. The repression from February through the summer reflected a high level of coordination, apparently aided by lists identifying communist leaders and where they lived, possibly supplied by the CIA (Arnove 2007: 51). The head of the party and some members of its central committee were executed. According to Farouk-Sluglett and Sluglett (2007: 86), "It is certain that some of the Ba'th leaders were in touch with American intelligence networks" and that a number of groups in the Middle East "had a strong vested interest in breaking what was probably the strongest and most popular communist party in the region." Batatu (1978: 985) observes that communist sources estimated that 5,000 people "were killed in the fighting from 8 to 10 February, and in the relentless house-to-house hunt for communists that immediately followed." An alternate figure was provided by a foreign diplomatic source that estimated that about 1,500 people perished. Arrests and killings went on from February until at least November, when most Baathists were temporarily ousted from the government by other Arab nationalists. Batatu (1978: 988) states that by November 1963, 7,000 communists were in prison.

Baathists had played a major role during and after the coup for several reasons. First, most Arab nationalists were not members of an organized party. But in 1963 the Baath Party included some 850 members and about 15,000 supporters (Farouk-Sluglett and Sluglett 2003: 83). This allowed Baathists to organize military officers who were not Baath Party members and to coordinate the coup. Second, unlike other Arab nationalists, the Baathists had their own party militia, the National Guard, that could arrest and kill people separate from the actions of the armed forces. Third, as an international movement, the Baathists had branches in Syria, Jordan, and Lebanon they could count on for assistance. And as an anti-communist force, it is probable that the Baathists received aid or at least encouragement from US and/or British intelligence services. Finally, of the Arab nationalists the Baathists had a relatively coherent ideology (described in chapter 2) that was not only anti-imperialist, but also explicitly oriented to bring about a more socially just society. Marr (2004: 115) explains that Baath ideology "combined an almost mystic belief in Arab unity with a call for the social and economic transformation of society. Thus the party had succeeded in combining the two strains of thought that had divided the intelligentsia in Iraq since the 1930s."

Baath Domination: February–November 1963

Following the coup, the Baath Party held twelve of the twenty-one cabinet positions, including the most important (Marr 2004: 117). Abd al-Salam Arif, the Arab nationalist hero of the 1958 revolution, became president and was elevated to the rank of field marshal. The Baathist general Ahmad Hasan al-Bakr from Tikrit was selected as prime minister and also served as Arif's vice president, while Baath Party leader Ali Salih al-Sadi became deputy prime minister and minister of the interior. Most power, however, was held by the National Council of Revolutionary Command (NCRC), formed at the start of the 1963 coup. The NCRC had eighteen members, ten military and eight civilian. Abd al-Salam Arif was one of only two who were not Baath Party members. The NCRC acted as the commander in chief of the armed forces and had the authority to select or abolish cabinets.

During much of 1963 the Baathists demonstrated they were adept at capturing, imprisoning, torturing, and killing communists and other Qasim supporters. They were aided by anti-communist personnel in the police who had served the monarchy. The brutality far exceeded the Qasim government's actions.

The Baathists did not immediately enact new economic reforms to avoid offending wealthy interests that had supported the coup. The new regime had better relations with the United States, which had been concerned about communist influence in the Qasim government. Iraqi relations with Nasser's Egypt also improved. The government dropped Qasim's claim to Kuwait and instead signed an agreement in October accepting Kuwaiti independence. In response Kuwait provided an interest-free loan of 30 million Iraqi dinars (Marr 2004: 119).

The Baath Regime and the Kurds

Barzani expected full autonomy from the new regime. And the KDP demanded that Iraqi Kurdistan include the provinces of Arbil, Kirkuk with its major oil fields, and Sulaimaniyya, as well as districts with Kurdish majorities in Diyala and Mosul provinces. All central government officials serving in Iraqi Kurdistan were to be Kurds and the region was to have its own legislature, executive structure, and military, a Kurdish branch of the Iraqi armed forces. The Kurds also demanded financial autonomy through the power to collect taxes in the Kurdish areas and a guaranteed proportion of oil revenues. Further, there was to be a Kurdish vice president for the central government. A major reason the KDP wanted a high level of autonomy was in case the new regime fulfilled its Arab nationalist agenda by unifying with other Arab states.

Baghdad refused the terms and the war resumed in June 1963. The government adopted a more aggressive approach than Qasim had, but Kurdish peshmergas, aided by Iranian Kurds, were able to withstand the onslaught. The failure provoked discontent among Iraqi officers unhappy that the Baath government, like Qasim before, could neither negotiate a peaceful settlement nor defeat the Kurds.

The Baath Regime and Arab Unity

Efforts were soon under way to unify Iraq with other Arab nations, the mission Qasim had been accused of betraying. This temporarily pacified the non-Baathist, pro-Nasser Arab nationalist officers who supported the coup. During the existence of the UAR, Egypt had dominated the union, provoking Syria to secede in September 1961. Shortly after the February 1963 Iraq coup, a military coup occurred in Syria in March (Lawson 1998: 473–475). This raised the possibility that Egypt, Iraq, and Syria could unite into one Arab state. Negotiations soon ran into problems, however, since the Baath parties in Iraq and Syria were unwilling to surrender power to Egypt's Nasser.

Divisions in the Ruling Arab Nationalist Coalition

From the start, the post-Qasim regime was beset with divisions, among the Baathists themselves and between the Baathists and other Arab nationalists. The expressions in the Baathist slogan, "Freedom, Unity and Socialism," could have separate interpretations to different Baathists. Some officers had joined the party to overthrow Qasim and had little interest in economic reform. But Baath party leader al-Sadi publicly identified with the more socialist-oriented branch of the party.

Amazingly, given the vicious suppression of the communists through the spring and summer of 1963, in September al-Sadi suddenly announced that he was a Marxist, perhaps in part to convince the Soviet Union to renew its developmental aid and military assistance, which had been cut off during the ferocious anti-communist rampage.

General Arif's Anti-Baath Coup

Conservative Baath and other Arab nationalist officers ousted al-Sadi on November 11. He and four of his associates were flown out of the country to Madrid (Batatu 1978: 1023). In response, al-Sadi's ally al-Wandawi bombed the Rashid military base and had the Baath National Guard seize Baghdad. But on November 18, General Abd al-Salam Arif ordered the armed forces to attack and disband the National Guard. Within a matter of hours Arif had won (Tripp 2000: 175).

Arif then became chairperson of the NCRC as well as maintaining his positions as president and armed forces commander. He created a well-equipped force, the Republican Guard, primarily to deter or quickly suppress any coup attempts by dissident factions within the armed forces. Later the Republican Guard would be expanded into whole Republican Guard divisions. The initial Republican Guard unit, which was stationed near Baghdad and had its own tank regiment, was commanded by a relative of Arif, Colonel Said Slaibi, who recruited many Guard members from Arif's al-Jumaila clan.

Arif maintained power primarily by developing and strengthening "personal bonds of trust" (Tripp 2000: 177), which he considered more important and dependable than either political ideology or a strong civilian political party. He built a network of relationships within the military, government, and economy through two interrelated strategies. One was appointing family, clan, and tribal members to important positions in all three institutions. The other was through a patronage system in which the positions and benefits one received explicitly depended on loyalty to Arif.

He removed most Baathists from important positions, including the Baath senior military officer, Ahmad Hasan al-Bakr, and relied instead mainly on pro-Nasser officers. Arif seemed to have been preparing Iraq for unification with Egypt by creating a new constitution resembling Egypt's that "provided that Iraq would be democratic, socialist, Arab and Islamic," with "more emphasis to Islam and less to socialism" in the case of Iraq (Marr 2004: 125). To bring Iraq's economic system more in line with Egypt's, in July 1964, Iraq nationalized all insurance companies and banks. A joint military command was also established.

Obstacles to Iraqi-Egyptian Unification

Arif and Nasser, however, both came to realize that unification would be extremely difficult. Iraq differed in major ways from Egypt. First, unlike Egypt, oil production was a significant part of Iraq's economy and the oil sector was privately owned and foreign controlled. Another difference was that Iraq had proved far more politically unstable than Egypt, with repeated military coups and coup attempts and multiple episodes of intense civil violence. In addition, the majority of Iraq's population was Shia, while Egypt was almost totally Sunni. Many Shia religious leaders held that socialization (government nationalization) of businesses violated Islamic protection of private property. The nationalizations abruptly shifted the clergy's perception of Arif, whom they had previously viewed as a good Muslim since he required the population to more strictly observe Islamic law and had agreed to changes in Qasim's Personal Status Law they demanded. Furthermore, Shia religious leaders felt threatened by the consequences of unifying with secular, socialist, Sunni Egypt, where the government had significant control over religious institutions. The possibility of a rebellious Shia population within a unified state was alarming to Sunni leaders in both countries.

Another important impediment to unification was Iraq's large Kurdish population. Arif had worked out a cease-fire with Barzani in February 1964, but the nationalizations and Iraq's apparent interest in unifying with Egypt provoked new concern from Barzani and his tribal allies, who objected to the socialist policies of Arif's government, as they had to land reform under Qasim. Furthermore, the Kurds feared that unity with Egypt would threaten Kurdish aspirations for cultural and political autonomy. The war in Iraqi Kurdistan resumed in March 1965, and again the Iraqi army had only limited success.

Prime Minister al-Bazzaz

On September 21, 1965, Arif appointed Abd al-Rahman al-Bazzaz as the first nonmilitary prime minister since July 1958. Al-Bazzaz was a lawyer and a professor with a reputation as a moderate Arab nationalist. The NCRC was replaced by the military National Defense Council, which oversaw the cabinet of ministers who were allowed to carry out legislative-like functions previously confined to the NCRC. Following the 1963 coup, and later coups and attempts, the armed forces had been purged of most of its ideologically oriented or party-affiliated officers. Many remaining officers were tied to Arif's patronage network, and the Republican Guard served as a powerful deterrent to further coups.

Within the context of enhanced stability, the new prime minister moved toward liberalizing the political system, including permitting elections for a parliament, and improving conditions for private enterprise. Al-Bazzaz increased compensation for socialized property and proposed maintaining a mixed economy in Iraq under the slogan of "prudent socialism" (Tripp 2000: 184).

Abd Al-Rahman Arif's Regime

The death of President Arif in an April 1966 helicopter crash undermined al-Bazzaz's administration. Arif's supporters selected the deceased president's brother, General Abd al-Rahman Arif, as the new president on April 17. Abd al-Rahman Arif tried to copy his brother's method of governing but lacked a personal relationship to many key figures and did not have as much skill maintaining the patronage networks.

Following several Kurdish victories over Iraqi army units, Prime Minister al-Bazzaz made a new attempt to stop the fighting. A cease-fire was declared in May 1966, and negotiations led to an agreement in June 1966 in which the prime minister announced that Iraq was a binational state and "promised full representation and self government to the Kurds within the framework of a parliamentary democracy in Iraq" (Tripp 2000: 187). The terms constituted the best offer yet the Kurds had received from any Iraqi government, and they accepted it as the basis for ending the conflict.

Some military leaders were concerned, however, that such a strong recognition of Kurdish national rights would lead to full independence. Others believed the prestige of the armed forces would suffer if so much was conceded to the Kurds following Iraqi defeats. Also, a number of officers feared for their careers and the future of Iraq and its armed forces if al-Bazzaz succeeded in ending the war, reducing military spending, and instituting a parliamentary form of government. Faced with intense pressure from military officers, al-Bazzaz resigned and Abd al-Rahman Arif decided to replace him with a new prime minister with a military background, former Free Officer Naji Talib. Negotiations with Barzani ended.

Talib proved ineffective, leading Arif himself to become prime minister in May 1967. But within weeks Iraq was shocked by Israel's rapid victory in the six-day Arab–Israeli War (the Third Arab–Israeli War) in June. The Iraqi regime, like other Arab governments, was humiliated by the huge Israeli victory. Iraq's inability to provide significant assistance to Arab forces in the war cast doubt on the competency of its succession of military-run governments. Yet Arif appointed another officer, Tahir Yahya, prime minister in July. US and British support for Israel led Iraq to turn further toward the USSR and to

France for assistance, including helping the Iraq National Oil Company develop its resources.

Doubt about the effectiveness of Iraq's military leadership was compounded by the army's inability to defeat the Kurds and by the emergence of an armed guerrilla movement organized by an ICP splinter group, Aziz al Hajj's Communist Party Central Command, in the southern marshes and the south mid-Euphrates area.

Hajj's rebels provoked a new fear of communism among both Shia and Sunni religious leaders. Baath Party members took advantage of the situation to reestablish the party's appeal by participating in anti-communist demonstrations in Baghdad and elsewhere. Since being removed from government in November 1963, the party had changed significantly. In 1964 al-Sadi and a number of his associates who had led the Baathists during their brutal repressive actions in 1963 were expelled from the party. Ahmad Hasan al-Bakr and other members of the Baath Military Bureau took over party leadership. Al-Bakr put his younger cousin Saddam Hussein in charge of reorganizing the party in the summer of 1964.

After a Baath coup attempt against Abd al-Salam Arif in the fall of 1964, both al-Bakr and other Baathists were arrested. Saddam Hussein was held in prison until 1966. But the party was able to recruit many new members, including within the military. In the fall of 1966 al-Bakr named Saddam deputy secretary-general of the Regional Command of the Baath Party in Iraq, and Saddam played a leading role in creating a new Baath Party militia (Tripp 2000: 190). And he took advantage of the demonstrations at the time of Israel's June 1967 defeat of Arab forces to increase party membership and expand its organizational structure.

The New Regime: al-Bakr and Saddam

The Baath Coups of July 1968

Mounting factionalism in the armed forces and among Iraq's elites created a desire for some type of overarching organizational structure to restore stability and discipline. The Baathists began planning a new coup and formation of a new Baath-led government. Success required that four key military officers either support the plan or at least be effectively neutralized. Three lieutenant colonels, Abd al-Razzaq al-Nayif, chief of military intelligence; Ibrahim Abd al-Rahmann al-Daud, then head of the Republican Guard; and Sadun Ghaidan, commander of the Republican Guard tank regiment, had lost confidence in Arif and agreed to turn against him. They were willing to work with the Baathists because they believed that the party's network inside the military, as well as among civilians, would provide necessary additional support.

July 17, 1968, was chosen as the coup date because the fourth key officer, General Slaibi, who would have opposed the coup, was in London having medical tests. The coup plotters seized the Ministry of Defense, Republican Guard headquarters, and the broadcasting center. Arif was flown out of the country. Al-Bakr became the new president, al-Nayif prime minister, al-Daud minister of defense, and Baathist Salih Mahdi Ammash minister of the interior. Another Baathist, Hardan al-Tikriti, became chief of staff of the armed forces and head of the air force. Ghaidan assumed leadership of the Republican Guard.

As in past government takeovers, however, the coup allies soon turned against one another. According to Tripp (2000: 191), the Baathists realized that unless they acted quickly they would lose power because most officers in the armed forces were not Baathist. Securing Ghaidan's support, as well as that of the commander of the Baghdad garrison, a tribal relative of al-Bakr, the Baathists staged a second successful coup on July 30, while al-Daud was out of Iraq. The Baath Party would control Iraq until the 2003 US-led invasion.

In the absence of elite willingness to construct a democratic system, alternatives for the Iraqi people were limited. They had rejected British occupation and the British-imposed monarchy. Military government was plagued by successive coups. Another option was a political system dominated by a mass political party. The Baath Party, with its Arab nationalist socialist ideology and program, would succeed in providing a level of stability that previous political arrangements had failed to deliver.

Summary and Analysis

In 1958, the military revolutionaries of the Free Officers' movement overthrew the Hashemite monarchy and established a self-described anti-imperialist regime. As in many revolutions, disagreements arose regarding postrevolution policies. The leading figures, Qasim and Arif, represented opposing coalitions. Qasim, whose parents came from Iraq's two main ethnic groups, Arab and Kurd, and religions, Sunni and Shia Islam, was backed by two leftist parties, the social democratic National Democratic Party and the ICP. He prioritized achieving major social reforms and economic growth, and developing a strong sense of Iraqi patriotism among the country's different ethnic and religious groups. In contrast, Arif, backed by many members of the Free Officers' movement, gave priority to Arab nationalism. His view was supported by the other two political parties that had been part of the antimonarchy revolutionary alliance, the Istiqlal and the Baath. The conflict between the "leftists," who championed the "Iraq First" approach, and the "rightists," who pushed for Arab unity, intensified, spurred on by the bloody events in Mosul and Kirkuk in 1959. Religious leaders and former supporters of the overthrown monarchy, fearful of the growing Iraqi communist movement, began to align with the Arab nationalists. Qasim, attempting to appease these groups, turned on his main organizational base of mass support, the ICP. He did not legalize the ICP or allow totally democratic elections, which might have resulted in a communist-dominated parliament, leading to a rebellion by anti-communist Iraqis or British or American intervention. And he unwisely allowed officers who had tried to overthrow him to reenter the armed forces, where they finally succeeded during the violent February 1963 coup, which killed Qasim and many others.

The new Baath-led Arab nationalist regime launched a ferocious assault against the communists and other Qasim supporters. But the social turmoil their tactics caused, coupled with Baathist failures regarding the Iraqi Kurds and Arab unity, prompted Arif and other Arab nationalist officers to oust the Baathists in November 1963.

Arif created a special government protection military unit, the Republican Guard, which would later expand into a central component of the Iraqi armed forces. He also constructed a patronage network to protect his power and had members of his family and clan placed in important positions and in the Republican Guard. Ironically, Arif, who claimed Qasim betrayed Arab nationalism, shifted his point of view toward more of an Iraq First position over time. The patronage- and kinship-supported political system that Arif built proved incapable of surviving his 1966 death. Within about two years, his brother's regime was overthrown in a new Baath-led coup on July 17, 1968. The Baathists staged a second coup on July 30, in which they removed non-Baathist military officers who had helped them take power two weeks earlier.

The new Baath regime was led by a well-respected senior Baathist officer, Ahmad Hasan al-Bakr, and behind the scenes by his younger cousin Saddam Hussein, who was the leading figure in reorganizing and expanding the Baath Party and its militia. In the absence of a democratic political system, or an effective dictatorship, or an occupying power using overwhelming military strength to enforce social order, a fourth option to bring stability and economic progress to Iraq was the installation of a government controlled by a single political party. The Baathists built such a state, which soon fell under the total control of the party leader, Saddam Hussein.

References and Further Readings

Agwani, M. S. 1969. *Communism in the Arab East*. Bombay: Asia Publishing House.

Arnove, Anthony. 2007. *Iraq: The Logic of Withdrawal*. New York: Henry Holt.

Baram, Amazia. 1989. "The Ruling Political Elite in Baathi Iraq, 1968–1986: The Changing Features of a Collective Profile." *International Journal of Middle East Studies* 21 (4): 447–493.

Batatu, Hanna. 1978. *The Old Social Classes and the Revolutionary Movements of Iraq*. Princeton, NJ: Princeton University Press.

Bozarslan, Hamit. 2006. "Kurdish Movements." In James DeFronzo, ed., *Revolutionary Movements in World History: From 1750 to the Present*, vol. 2, 519–528. Santa Barbara, CA: ABC-CLIO.

Dann, Uriel. 1969. *Iraq Under Qassem: A Political History, 1958–1963*. London: Praeger.

DeFronzo, James. 2007. *Revolutions and Revolutionary Movements*. Boulder, CO: Westview Press.

Devlin, John E. 1991. "The Baath Party: Rise and Metamorphosis." *American Historical Review* 96 (December): 1396–1407.

Farouk-Sluglett, Marion, and Peter Sluglett. 1988. "The Iraqi Ba'th Party." In Vicky Randall, ed., *Political Parties in the Third World*, 57–74. London: Sage.

———. 1991. "The Historiography of Modern Iraq." *American Historical Review* 96 (5): 1408–1421.

———. 2003. *Iraq Since 1958*. London: J. B. Tauris Publishers.

Galvani, John. 1972. "The Baathi Revolution in Iraq." *Middle East Report* 12 (September): 3–11, 14–22.

Gorman, Anthony. 2006. "Egyptian Revolution of 1952." In James DeFronzo, ed., *Revolutionary Movements in World History*, 246–253.

Ismael, Tareq. 2007. *The Rise and Fall of the Communist Party of Iraq*. Cambridge, UK: Cambridge University Press.

Khadduri, Majid. 1960. *Independent Iraq 1932–1958: A Study in Iraqi Politics*. Oxford, UK: Oxford University Press.

———. 1969. *Republican Iraq: A Study in Iraqi Politics since the Revolution of 1958*. Oxford, UK: Oxford University Press.

Lawson, Fred H. 1998. "Syrian Revolution (1963)." In Jack A. Goldstone, ed., *The Encyclopedia of Political Revolutions*, 473–475. Washington, DC: Congressional Quarterly Inc.

Long, David E., and John A. Hearty. 1986. "Republic of Iraq." In David E. Long and Bernard Reich, eds., *The Government and Politics of the Middle East and North Africa*, 93–111. Boulder, CO: Westview Press.

Makiya, Kanan (Al-Khalil, Samir). 1998. *Republic of Fear: Saddam's Iraq*. Berkeley: University of California Press.

Mattar, Philip. 2004. *Encyclopedia of the Modern Middle East and North Africa*. New York: Macmillan Library Reference.

McDowell, D. 2004. *A Modern History of the Kurds*. London: I. B. Tauris.

Pillai, R. V., and Mahendra Kumar. 1962. "The Political and Legal Status of Kuwait." *International and Comparative Law Quarterly* 11 (1): 108–130.

Polk, William R. 2005. *Understanding Iraq*. New York: Harper Perennial.

Al-Qazzaz, Ayad. 1967. "Military Regimes and Political Stability in Iraq, Syria and Egypt." *Berkeley Journal of Sociology* 12 (Summer): 44–54.

———.1969. "The Story of the July Fourteen 1958 Revolution." *Middle East Forum* 45 (4): 63–71.

———. 1971. "The Changing Patterns of Politics of the Iraqi Army." In Morris Janowitz and Jacques Van Doorn, eds., *On Military Interventions*, 335–361. Rotterdam, Netherlands: Rotterdam University Press.

———. 2006. "Iraq Revolution." In James DeFronzo, ed., *Revolutionary Movements in World History*, 427–440.

Sariolghalam, Mahmood. 2008. "Iran in Search of Itself." *Current History* 107 (713): 425–431.

Tripp, Charles. 2000. *A History of Iraq*. Cambridge, UK: Cambridge University Press.

4

||||||||||||||||||||||||||||||||||||||||||||||||||||||||||||||||||||||||||||||||||||||||||||||||||||||||||

Saddam Hussein,
the Iranian Revolution,
and the Iran–Iraq War

The Baath coup of July 30, 1968, established a government led by an esteemed senior military officer, Ahmad Hasan al-Bakr, a member of the Free Officers. But while al-Bakr was the public face of the Baathist regime, his much younger cousin, Saddam Hussein, led the party. Saddam shared certain characteristics with the notorious Russian leader Joseph Stalin, whom he reportedly came to admire. Both came from lower-class backgrounds and had difficult, abusive childhoods. Both engaged in violent activities as revolutionaries. Neither had served in their countries' armed forces, which they later came to command. For both the path to power was through playing a central role in organizing and leading their expanding revolutionary parties. And just as Stalin determined the ultimate outcome of the Bolshevik Revolution, Saddam shaped the structure of the institutions that resulted from the Iraqi Revolution.

The 1979 Iranian Revolution shocked Iraq. As the threat increased that Iraq's Shia clergy would follow the example of Iran's fundamentalist leader, Ayatollah Ruhollah Khomeini, and organize a Shia uprising in Iraq, Saddam became Iraq's president. Perceiving that Iran was politically divided and weakened militarily in the wake of its revolution, Saddam and his associates decided to launch what they anticipated would be a short, victorious war against the Iranian Islamic Republic. They expected that Iran would quickly be forced to accept Iraq's conditions for peace and that the transnational advance of Islamic fundamentalism would be halted. Instead the attack resulted in a tragic and enormously destructive eight-year war.

The Baathist Regime, 1968–1979

The New Baath Party

As it took control of Iraq at the end of July 1968, the Baath Party still clung to the goal of uniting all Arabs in a single state. Its leaders continued to believe that their aims in Iraq and for all Arabs would be achieved through the party acting as the vanguard for the Arab masses (Batatu 1978: 1078). But the party had changed in significant ways. One was the shift in the religious background of party leaders. Shia had played the leading role introducing the Baath movement into Iraq. Batatu (1978: 1078) reports that between 1952 and November 1963, the top party leaders were 53.8 percent Shia Arabs, 38.5 percent Sunni Arabs, and 7.7 percent Kurds. Between November 1963 and 1970, however, 84.9 percent of the fifty-three main party leaders were Sunni Arabs, 7.5 percent Kurds, and only 5.7 percent Shia Arabs. So party leadership went from being roughly representative of the country's religious composition in the 1952–1963 period to overwhelmingly Sunni Arab during 1963–1970.

Batatu (1978: 1078–1079) claims that two main factors helped cause the shift in party leadership and membership. First, many Sunni Baathists blamed Shia Baath Party leader Ali Salih al-Sadi's brutal and disruptive policies for provoking the anti-Baathist coup of November 1963. Shia Baathists largely supported al-Sadi in the subsequent internal party struggle. When al-Sadi lost and was expelled from the party, many Shia Baathists left with him.

But probably the more important reason for the decline in Shia membership was the largely Sunni composition of the police forces that repressed the Baath Party during the governments of the two Arif brothers. Batatu claims that the police tended to be far harsher on Shia Baath members than on Sunni Baathists. This was because the police and Sunni Arab members of the Baath Party often came from the same hometowns and tribal groups. Since the police often tended to treat Sunni Arab Baathists with more leniency, they were more likely to stay in the party than the Shia.

Another important trend was the increasingly significant role that Sunni military officers from Tikrit began playing in the Baath Party from 1963 onward. This was primarily due to al-Bakr and Saddam, both from Tikrit, assuming party leadership. According to Batatu (1978: 1084), although al-Bakr was born in 1914 and Saddam in 1937, they were ideologically from "the same mold" although during much of 1964 through the mid-1970s al-Bakr had "the last word." The combination of al-Bakr and Saddam was essential to bringing the Baath Party to power in 1968 and transforming Iraq into a one-party state. Their kinship supplemented their ideological affinity, and their reputations, talents, and personal charisma complemented one another to produce a potent political force. Al-Bakr convinced many military officers to join or support the Baathists and attracted significant popular support for the party. Saddam had shown his dedication, risking his life in the failed assassination attempt against Abd al-Karim Qasim. Respected by many and bolstered by the support of his widely admired cousin al-Bakr, Saddam was able to use his considerable intelligence and political skills to reorganize and expand the party, estimated at only about 5,000 members in 1968 (Marr 2004: 140), so that the civilian branch of the party could eventually assume governmental control from the military.

Following the July Baath takeover, al-Bakr held the positions of chairman of the governing Revolutionary Command Council (RCC), president, prime minister, and secretary-general of the Baath party. The five members of the RCC, which controlled the government, the armed forces, and the party, were all

Sunni military officers. On November 9, 1969, the RCC was expanded to fifteen members and after that varied in size through 1977, but all of its members through these years were Sunni Arabs except one who was an "Arabized" Sunni Kurd (Batatu 1978: 1085–1088). After 1969, civilians outnumbered officers, but according to Batatu (1978), the votes of the military members carried more weight than those of civilians, except for Saddam. When he joined the RCC in November 1969, it was as deputy chairman, officially making him the second most powerful man in Iraq after al-Bakr. He was also assistant secretary-general of the Baath Party.

Military officers from Tikrit held three of the five positions on the RCC from July 30, 1968, to November 9, 1969, and six of the fifteen positions on the next RCC. A major reason for the power of Tikritis in the military was that they were disproportionately represented in the rank and file of the armed forces. Because of limited opportunity in Tikrit, many Tikritis migrated to Baghdad to find employment, and some "were able to gain admission into the cost-free Royal Military Academy" and became army officers (Batatu 1978: 1088). Their rise to high rank was due to repetitive purges of the armed forces in the years after the 1958 antimonarchy revolution.

Al-Bakr's Consolidation of Power

Trials and Executions of Conspirators and Spies

Baath control was strengthened by a series of prosecutions of Iraqis accused of such offenses as conspiring to overthrow the government or spying for foreign enemies. The trials removed possible enemies of the regime and deterred many others from opposing al-Bakr's government. In October 1968 the regime announced that a "Zionist spy ring" had been discovered in Basra (Makiya 1998: 49). More than a dozen, including a number of Iraqi Jews, were arrested and charged with spying for Israel, Iran, and the United States. President al-Bakr addressed the nation in a live two-hour television speech, charging that Iraq was threatened by American imperialism, which had recruited disloyal Iraqis to create an internal division and to carry out sabotage and even killings to divert Iraq from "the great battle with the Zionist enemy." Fourteen of those convicted were executed in Baghdad's main square with some 500,000 witnessing the hangings.

Shortly after the spy trials, an antiregime plot was uncovered involving pro-Western Iraqis thought to be sponsored by the US-supported Iranian monarchy. In January, thirty-seven people accused of attempting to overthrow the government were executed. One alleged conspirator was given the death sentence in absentia and later assassinated in London in 1978, according to Makiya (1998: 13) by Istikhbarat (Iraqi Military Intelligence).

The Baathists also moved against the diminished ICP when it decided to criticize the government in the spring of 1970, imprisoning several hundred communists (Marr 2004: 142). Previously, in 1969, the regime had crushed the splinter communist rebellion in the south led by Aziz al-Hajj, who after being captured made a televised statement rejecting violence and accepting the Baath government.

The Military

The Baath regime attempted to ensure that it would not be threatened by the armed forces. As a number of non-Baathist officers were pressured to retire, many Baath Party members received military training and entered the armed forces as officers. By the end of 1970, 3,000 new officer commissions were announced (Farouk-Sluglett and Sluglett 2003: 120). Many acted as political commissars watching over the actions and noting the political sentiments of other officers. The Baath regime enacted a law forbidding any other political party from trying to spread its ideas to members of the military or recruit party members in the armed forces under penalty of death. This law was used to arrest and execute a number of ICP members. Special units, including the Republican Guard, were assigned to protect the regime. In addition, the Baath Party equipped its large militia with new weapons to further deter any coup. Saddam had himself appointed to the rank of army general, and as the armed forces progressively fell under the near total control of the Baath Party and relatives of al-Bakr and Saddam, the number of officers in positions of government leadership gradually declined.

Seducing the ICP

Remarkably, the Baathist regime attempted to establish an alliance with the ICP, many of whose members its fanatical militia had killed in the process and aftermath of overthrowing Qasim in 1963. There appeared to be several reasons for this surprising invitation. The communists were still an influential political force whose members had leadership roles in several mass organizations, such as labor unions and student groups. The ICP also had supporters among intellectuals. According to Farouk-Sluglett and Sluglett (2003: 127), "It was of the utmost importance for the Ba'th to be able either to weaken or in some way to absorb the Kurdish and communist movements, which were still the two most important political forces within the country, without giving them any concessions in terms of actual power sharing, in order to expand its own power base." An alliance between the Arab Socialist Baath Party and the ICP would unify the reformist sector of Iraqi politics against conservative internal and foreign opponents. It would also provide crucial additional popular support for the regime and remove a threat to political stability. Furthermore, Baathists could learn from the communists how to assemble and lead mass organizations. In addition, by gaining public communist acceptance of the regime, the Baathists could broaden their appeal to the traditional constituencies of the ICP, such as urban and oil field workers and students, and certain groups of civil servants, and perhaps gradually win them over from the internationalist socialist ideology of the communists to the Arab socialism of the Baathists. Finally, Iraq wanted to purchase large quantities of weapons from the USSR, and the Soviets would be more likely to cooperate if the ICP announced its support for the Baathist regime.

Al-Bakr and Saddam attempted to convince the communists to join a Baath-dominated coalition on several grounds. First, they argued that with communist support the government was more likely to succeed in carrying out the sweeping social and economic reforms that the communists advocated to help disadvantaged Iraqis. They also claimed the Baathists were just as anti-imperialist as the communists and that by supporting the Baath government the ICP could better protect Iraq from foreign exploitation and aggression. The regime further attempted to convince the communists that the Baath leadership now supported the Iraq First approach that the ICP had long favored and a milder form of Arab nationalism that in the foreseeable future involved cooperating with and helping other Arabs, such as the Arab Palestinians, rather than trying to pursue the impractical goal of immediately unifying all Arabs in one state.

Al-Bakr offered the communists two cabinet ministries as part of the alliance. But most ICP leaders, suspicious of promises and still outraged at Baath atrocities, initially rejected the offer. They demanded that the ICP be legalized and that the government guarantee "freedom of speech, freedom to organise, and the release of all political prisoners" (Farouk-Sluglett and Sluglett 2003: 127). The regime responded with more repression.

Ultimately, however, the ICP decided to take part in the government and in May 1972, two communist ministers entered the cabinet. In July 1973 the ICP leadership consented to joining the Baathist-led political coalition, the National Patriotic Front. Although distrustful of the Baathists, the ICP leadership felt compelled to join the alliance because Baathist efforts to help the poor, nationalize the oil industry, and establish weapons and oil agreements with the USSR were all policies the ICP supported. The communists were given some freedom to recruit new members and circulate their publications. But since the Baathists dominated the government, military, and police, the ICP could do little more than try to influence government policies through persuasion of Baath leaders.

Some communists thought the alliance would give the ICP the opportunity to significantly increase its membership and allow members who had fled Iraq to return. Others, however, feared that allying with the Baath Party would prevent the ICP from voicing criticism of Baath policies and that the ICP's reputation would suffer since Baathists had brutalized and killed so many of its members. They also argued the ICP would be blamed for government actions over which, in reality, the communists had no control. Communists also opposed aspects of Baathist ideology that implied Arab cultural, if not racial, superiority to other peoples. And many communists worried that the Baath Party was simply using the ICP to increase its mass base and would eventually turn against the communists when their support was no longer needed. Although after the alliance was formed, communists were released from prison or allowed to regain their civil service jobs, the ICP was still barred from engaging in any sort of political activity among members of the armed forces.

Defeat of a Deadly Coup Attempt

While al-Bakr and Saddam pushed for reconciliation with the ICP, the regime almost fell victim to a lethal plot to wipe out the government's top leadership in a mass assassination. The June 1973 conspiracy was organized by Nazim Kazzar, the Shia Baathist head of Iraq's security police, who had a reputation "as a sadistic torturer and murderer" (Farouk-Sluglett and Sluglett 2003: 160). Kazzar may have resented Sunni domination of the party, but probably more important, he was intensely hostile toward both the ICP and Kurdish militants. He opposed the alliance with the communists and their participation in the government, and efforts to negotiate a settlement with Kurdish rebels by granting some of their major demands. Farouk-Sluglett and Sluglett (2003: 161) note that Kazzar probably also feared that al-Bakr and Saddam were going to remove him as head of security operations and decided to eliminate them first.

Kazzar's plan was to assassinate President al-Bakr, Saddam, and others at Baghdad Airport on June 30, 1973, as al-Bakr and his associates returned from Eastern Europe. Additional top government officials would also arrive at the airport to greet al-Bakr, providing a rare opportunity to eliminate almost all the top leadership of the Baath regime simultaneously. As head of security, Kazzar would then seize power during the ensuing turmoil and get rid of any remaining rivals. Kazzar's men went to the airport to carry out the political massacre. The plane, however, was late, causing Kazzar's men to mistakenly conclude that President al-Bakr had somehow been informed about the plot. Witnessing on television the safe arrival of the plane and its passengers, Kazzar tried to escape to Iran using two captured RCC members, Lieutenant General Hammad Shihab, minister of defense, and Lieutenant General Sadun Ghaidan, minister of the interior, as hostages. Near the Iranian border, however, Kazzar and his associates were intercepted by Iraqi soldiers. One of the hostages, Shihab, was killed and the other badly wounded. But Kazzar and many of his fellow conspirators were caught. By July 9, Kazzar and thirty-five others had been tried, found guilty by a specially appointed court, and executed.

The elimination of Kazzar allowed al-Bakr and Saddam to accuse him and his agents of much of the brutality blamed on the Baathists, including atrocities against the communists. ICP leaders believed the failure of Kazzar's plot probably prevented a new wave of anti-communist repression. Soon after the conspiracy was defeated, the alliance between the Baathists and the communists was finalized. The attempted assassinations provided an excuse for Saddam to have Sadun al-Tikriti and Saddam's younger half brother, Barzan Ibrahim al-Tikriti, reorganize the Iraqi intelligence services. With the Left largely united with the Baathists in the National Patriotic Front, the next major goal for the regime was to successfully resolve the Kurdish situation.

Baathists and Kurds

President al-Bakr appointed two members of Mustafa Barzani's faction of the KDP and one from Jalal al-Talabani's leftist section of the KDP as cabinet ministers. Barzani, however, objected to what he viewed as the Baathists playing the two factions off against each other (Tripp 2000: 199). His forces resumed fighting and in March 1969 used long-range artillery, apparently supplied by Iran, to launch a devastating attack on the Kirkuk oil facilities (Farouk-Sluglett and Sluglett 2003: 129).

The government sent Saddam to negotiate with Barzani's representatives. The result was the Manifesto of March 1970, in which the government offered to grant Kurdish militants more of their demands than ever before, including recognizing "the distinct national identity of the Kurds." The Baathist regime also promised that the Kurds would play the central role in the administration of their region (Tripp 2000: 200), which was to include all districts with a Kurdish majority as determined by a population census. The manifesto, which was to be implemented by 1974, temporarily ended the conflict and allowed the Baath government to claim that it had solved the Kurdish problem, permitting it to gain time to deal with other important issues and further secure its power.

But the government refused to allow the Kurds to have their own military force. Furthermore, the regime encouraged Arabs to move into the Kirkuk oil-producing area so that when the census took place it would show an Arab majority there and result in Baghdad's maintaining direct control of Kirkuk's oil. The regime also deported about 45,000 Shia Kurds (Faili) to Iran (Marr 2004: 155). Barzani, the target of assassination attempts in 1971 and 1972, for which he suspected the regime was responsible, once again prepared to fight.

While in the early 1970s Iraq was an anti-imperialist republic governed by the Baath Party allied with the Communist Party, Iran was a monarchy supported by Western capitalist powers. Iraq's republican revolution had annihilated a monarchy accused of being a tool of imperialism. The shah's security forces were attempting to suppress revolutionaries who wanted to similarly destroy his regime and had no desire to see them encouraged by a successful leftist regime in neighboring Iraq. One option for the shah was to attempt to destabilize the Iraqi regime by assisting rebellious Iraqi Kurds. According to Marr (2004: 155), Barzani's Kurdish forces also received help from the US CIA and Israel.

While the manifesto census was delayed, possibly because it would have indicated a Kurdish majority in the Kirkuk oil-producing area, Barzani and the KDP pushed for the inclusion of Kirkuk in the autonomous region. The Baath government refused and offered a more limited autonomy plan, which the KDP rejected. On March 11, 1974, the Baath regime declared that its autonomy plan would go into effect, and the Kurdish nationalists resumed the war in April. After the Iraqi army achieved several victories, Iran provided antitank missiles and artillery to the KDP. By the spring of 1975, the war was stalemated. Iraq, realizing it could not defeat KDP forces as long as they were aided by the shah's government, entered into negotiations with Iran.

Iran had no desire to see the war actually result in an independent Iraqi Kurdistan, which might then encourage and aid Iranian Kurds to rebel. On March 6, 1975, Saddam, representing Iraq, and the shah reached an agreement in Algiers (Hiro 1991: 16–18). The Iranians agreed to stop aiding Barzani's forces in return for concessions from the Iraqis. First, Iraq would agree that the boundary at the Shatt al-Arab was the midline of the deepest channel in the river. Second, Iraq would renounce any claim to the Arab-speaking province of Iran, Khuzistan, as well as to Iranian-occupied islands in the Persian Gulf. Immediately after the Algiers Agreement, Iran began removing artillery from the war zone. Deprived of assistance from Iran, Barzani decided to give up the fight, and he died in the United States in 1979. Iraq granted amnesty to Barzani's peshmergas, and most accepted the offer.

The failure of Barzani's rebellion "was a major trauma for the Kurds" having significant consequences (Bozarslan 2006: 523). First, the defeat led to the creation of more leftist revolutionary Kurdish movements, in particular the Patriotic Union of Kurdistan (PUK), formed under the leadership of Jalal al-Talabani and other urban intellectuals. The PUK initially had a Maoist rather than pro-Soviet orientation because the USSR aided the Baathist regime (although the PUK "adopted a social-democratic and more and more Kurdish nationalist program later on" [Bozarslan 2006: 527]). The PUK organized its own guerrilla army, which from 1975 to 1991 fought Iraqi forces and, in 1994 to 1996, the KDP in the Kurdish civil war. A second result was increased anti-Americanism among the Kurds internationally because they viewed the withdrawal of aid to Barzani's peshmergas by the United States and the US-supported Iranian monarchy as an American betrayal.

The Baath plan for autonomous Kurdistan excluded Kirkuk. In the early 1980s, the Kurds were allowed to elect a fifty-member assembly. The Iraqi president appointed a president of Kurdistan from among assembly members and had the power to dismiss him as well as the entire Kurdish assembly. The government built new factories, hospitals, schools, roads, and communications facilities in the Kurdish region. The student population rose from about 112,000 in 1975 to 332,000 in 1979 (Marr 2004: 158). Land reform redistributed approximately 670,000 acres from landlords to Kurdish peasants, economically weakening tribal leaders who had supported Barzani. Baghdad funded other tribal leaders to revitalize a proregime force called Fursan, which included Kurdish veterans of the Iraqi army. Antiregime Kurds derisively referred to Fursan soldiers as *jash*, meaning "young donkeys." All Kurdish villages for a depth of five to fifteen miles along the eight hundred–mile border with Turkey and Iran were destroyed, and hundreds of thousands moved to settlements close to Kurdish cities.

Nationalization of Oil

The Baath regime began to develop southern oil-rich areas expropriated from the Iraq Petroleum Company by Qasim. Soviet, US, and West German companies were recruited to drill oil wells or build pipelines and new port facilities. Iraqis believed the Iraq Petroleum Company was slowing oil production to punish Iraq for taking most of its concession territory. Iraq's share of oil produced in the Gulf area had fallen since 1960, while those of the monarchies cooperating with the Western-owned oil companies, Saudi Arabia, and Iran, had risen (Marr 2004: 159). In response to the Iraq Petroleum Company's failure to restore oil production levels, the Baath government proclaimed Public Law 69 on June 1, 1972, nationalizing the Iraq Petroleum Company. Following the 1973 Arab–Israeli War, the regime seized all remaining foreign oil concessions, and the temporary Arab oil embargo in response to Western aid to Israel during the war caused oil prices to rise dramatically (Hiro 2007: 111).

Iraq doubled its oil production by the end of the decade, causing oil revenue to rise from $575 million in 1972 to $26 billion in 1980 (Marr 2004: 161). The regime's popularity increased since it had freed Iraq's oil from foreign control and used much of the vast increase in revenue to improve the material well-being of the people.

Social and Economic Reforms

Baath Party "socialism" envisioned mainly state ownership of large industrial and financial enterprises, with private ownership of smaller businesses. The government was to oversee the economy and society as a whole, intervening when necessary to bring about social justice. In May 1969, President al-Bakr modified land reform by declaring that peasants who had or would in the future receive land would no longer pay compensation to former landowners, removing a major burden from the lives of many poor farmers. Then in 1970 a new reform distributed land to more than 200,000 peasants for cooperative farming (Marr 2004: 163).

The ratio of doctors improved from 1 for every 4,200 citizens in 1968 to 1 for every 1,790 citizens in 1980, and life expectancy increased from forty-six to fifty-seven years (Marr 2004: 164). Medical care was free, as was education through the university level. In 1980 there were about 100,000 Iraqis in colleges and universities after total educational enrollment doubled from 1968.

Economic Development

The government built new industries to diversify the economy, including petrochemical, steel, aluminum, and plastics facilities. Iraq's defense budget climbed from $500 million in 1970 to $4.5 billion in 1975 (Marr 2004: 165–166). The regime acquired antiaircraft missiles, fighter planes, tanks, and artillery, and built underground shelters to shield military equipment. In 1974 a three-person Strategic Development Committee, led by Saddam, was created to manufacture weapons of mass destruction, including chemical and nuclear weapons. France agreed to sell Iraq two nuclear reactors, ostensibly for research purposes, and Italy sold equipment "capable of separating plutonium" (Marr 2004: 165). Iraq recruited hundreds of engineers and scientists from various Arab countries and sent Iraqis to other nations to be trained in science and technology. Israel impeded Iraq's nuclear program when in 1979 its agents "destroyed reactor cores being shipped to Iraq from France" (Marr 2004: 166). Then in 1981, Israeli planes attacked and demolished Iraq's large Osiraq reactor.

Per capita income rose from about 120 Iraqi dinars in 1970 to approximately 1,181 in 1980 (Marr 2004: 164), and an estimated "one-fifth to one-fourth of the population eventually worked directly or indirectly for the government" (Marr 2004: 166). Income levels were higher in urban areas, where by 1977 64 percent of the population resided. The country's middle class greatly expanded as more Iraqis became highly educated and entered modern occupations such as medicine, engineering, and teaching. One estimate put Iraq's middle class at approximately 50 percent of the urban population in 1977 (Marr 2004: 167).

Shia Political Religious Movements

There were significant political and religious differences among Iraqi Shia. Many impoverished Shia had joined the Communist Party or had been enthusiastic supporters of economic and social reforms, and some died resisting the coup against Qasim. Highly educated Shia tended to have a secular outlook. Further, Shiism was decentralized, and individual Shia were relatively free to follow the religious interpretations and rulings of particular ayatollahs. Differences among ayatollahs included whether and to what degree clergy should be involved in politics, and level of affinity toward Persian coreligionists in Iran versus Iraqis who were fellow Arabs but Sunni.

Shia clergy were concerned that many government officials came from the relatively secular oriented, leftist branch of the Baath Party. Many objected to land reform and the end of compensation payments from land recipients to the former landowners who provided financial support to the clergy.

In reaction to suspected Iranian involvement in the 1968 antiregime plot described earlier in this chapter, approximately 20,000 Iraqis, allegedly of Iranian descent, were expelled. In response, Ayatollah Muhsin al-Hakim, the leading Iraqi Shia cleric, led thousands in a protest march from Najaf to Baghdad. After the ayatollah's son was arrested on a charge of spying for Israel, Shia protests increased.

President al-Bakr requested in April 1969 that Ayatollah al-Hakim openly side with Iraq in its dispute with Iran over the Shatt al-Arab. When he refused, al-Bakr ordered all Iranian religious students in Iraq deported from the country, thus depriving clerical teachers of many students.

The regime, fearing the development of an anti-Baathist Shia-Sunni religious front, arrested a number of Shia and Sunni clerics, seized the endowments of religious institutions in Najaf, closed Islamic schools in some mainly Shia-populated towns, and banned religious processions (Tripp 2000: 203). The reading of the Quran on government radio stations was prohibited, as was Islamic instruction in state-run educational institutions. These actions provoked more antigovernment protests, especially in Najaf, Karbala, and Basra. Ayatollah al-Hakim proclaimed a fatwa banning membership in the Baath Party.

Security forces disclosed early in 1970 that they had uncovered and crushed a plot connected to Iran to overthrow the Baath government. A number of military officers, government officials, and members of both Sunni and Shia religious organizations were arrested and executed. When Ayatollah al-Hakim died in the summer of 1970, he was replaced as the top Iraqi Shia leader by Ayatollah Abu al-Qasim al-Khoei, who tended to be a more traditional cleric and typically avoided political involvement and confrontation with the government.

Many of al-Hakim's followers then turned to Muhammad Baqir al-Sadr, a founder of the Dawa Party. Shia began to discuss al-Sadr's ideas and the possible ways and degree to which religion should be involved in politics and the economy. Around the same time, exiled Iranian Shia fundamentalist leader Ayatollah Khomeini, who had been expelled from Iran by the shah for criticizing the regime, was giving a series of lectures in Najaf on his concept of an Islamic government. According to Khomeini, separation of church and state was fundamentally un-Islamic (Hiro 1991: 31) and removing Islam from government morally weakened the people and made them easier for non-Islamic imperialist nations to control and exploit.

In contrast, in an Islamic republic the leading role would be played by clergy representing Allah's sovereignty over the political system. The Iraqi government initially tolerated Khomeini because he attacked the Iranian regime and its supporters, Britain and the United States. However, it was soon obvious that some of the criticisms Khomeini directed against the Iranian shah could also apply to the Iraqi regime and incite Iraq's own fundamentalists.

In 1974 more than two dozen Shia were tried for plots against the government, and five Dawa Party members were executed (Marr 2004: 173). Then in February 1977, the regime attempted to prevent a Shia religious procession from Najaf to Karbala, leading to a protest by some 30,000 people and a confrontation with security forces in which sixteen were killed. Two thousand were arrested, and eight people were sentenced to death for their actions during the protest.

In addition to trying to discredit, exile, or eliminate defiant religious leaders, the government used oil revenue to bring new benefits to the Shia population and recruit allies against the Shia clerical leadership. And more Shia Baathists were appointed to prominent party and government positions and to the RCC. According to Marr (2004: 173), by 1977 about 24 percent of those in the party's "higher leadership levels" were Shia. The regime also extended aspects of its patronage network into the Shia south. But despite these efforts, the challenge of the Shia political-religious movement intensified with the success in early 1979 of the Islamic Revolution in Iran. The ability of a movement led by a Shia religious scholar, Ayatollah Khomeini, to defeat a US-backed monarchy whose military was armed with billions of dollars' worth of advanced weaponry provided enormous encouragement to Iraq's Shia militants. By the end of the 1970s, the regime viewed politically oriented Shia organizations, rather than Kurdish militants, as the most serious internal threat.

Impact of the Iranian Revolution

While Ayatollah Khomeini resided in Iraq, pilgrims to Shia holy places there often returned to Iran with audiotaped copies of Khomeini's sermons attacking the shah. But because it became apparent that Khomeini's ideas also threatened the Baathist regime, when the shah requested that Iraq expel Khomeini in 1978, it complied. Khomeini ended up in France, where he had access to world media that reported his messages almost instantly to his millions of followers in Iran and his admirers in Iraq.

After the triumph of Iran's revolution in February 1979, the new constitution gave ultimate power to the religious leadership. Iraqi Ayatollah Muhammad Baqir al-Sadr supported Khomeini's revolution, looked ahead to new Islamic triumphs, and even made suggestions to Khomeini on the content of Iran's Islamic constitution. Khomeini viewed al-Sadr as the potential leader of an Islamic revolution in Iraq. Like Ayatollah al-Hakim before him, al-Sadr issued a fatwa against joining the Baath Party. During late May and early June 1979, the Dawa Party organized demonstrations in Najaf calling for people all over Iraq to take an oath of allegiance to Ayatollah al-Sadr. In response, the Baath regime arrested al-Sadr and hundreds of Dawa members on June 12. Al-Sadr's sister, Bint al-Huda, then called for the people to rescue her brother. The resulting mass protests gained al-Sadr's release, but the Dawa organization was severely repressed.

The Baath leadership became divided on how to deal with the protests. President al-Bakr favored leniency, while Saddam preferred harsher treatment (Hiro 1991: 25). But after a bomb assassination attempt against a major Baath leader and RCC member, Tariq Aziz, on April 1, 1980, in which he was wounded and several people died, al-Sadr, his followers, and the Iranian Islamic government were blamed, and the regime launched a major crackdown (Hiro 1991: 35).

The Baathists had learned a lesson from the Iranian Revolution. The shah had arrested Khomeini but deported instead of executed him, leaving him alive to lead the Iranian Revolution. Ayatollah al-Sadr and his sister were executed on April 8, leaving his movement virtually leaderless and in disarray. But their executions provided martyrs for their movement, and their reputations contributed to the rise decades later of their cousin Ayatollah Muhammad Sadiq al-Sadr's son, Moqtada al-Sadr, as a major Shia political religious leader and opponent of the occupation following the 2003 invasion.

The failure of Islamic revolution in Iraq after the successful Iranian Revolution was due to additional factors as well. One was that Iran's revolution was not only a religious movement, but also a nationalist revolution against perceived foreign control. Therefore, it involved a strong anti-imperialist revolutionary alliance among secular leftists, Islamic leftists, and Islamic fundamentalists. In contrast, the Iraqi movement was more narrowly based on a fundamentalist interpretation of Islam against a government that could in no way be viewed as a tool of imperialism. In fact, the Baath regime used nationalism against Shia fundamentalism by portraying it as a form of Persian (Iranian) aggression, or at least subversion. The Iraqi Shia revolution eventually succeeded, in a limited way, only because the 2003 invasion destroyed the Baath-dominated state.

The substantial impact of the Iranian Revolution on Iraq set the stage for the Baath regime's enormous miscalculations leading to the eight-year Iran–Iraq War, the consequences of which motivated Iraq's disastrous invasion of Kuwait in 1990.

Onset of Saddam's Reign

Saddam–Stalin Parallels

The lives of Saddam Hussein and Iosif Vissarionovich Dzhugashvilli, better known as Joseph Stalin, a man Saddam apparently came to admire, have striking similarities. Both were born into poverty and had difficult childhoods characterized by abusive father figures, which likely affected their outlooks on the world and their inclination toward violence. Both Saddam and Stalin had to leave their immediate-family households to receive an education, Saddam to live with relatives and Stalin to enroll in a seminary to train for the priesthood. As opponents of existing regimes, both engaged in violence in pursuit of revolutionary goals, Saddam as a would-be assassin and Stalin as a bank robber to get funds for the Bolsheviks. The route to power for both was through taking the leading role in administering and structuring their revolutionary parties during periods of rapid growth in party membership. Control of the revolutionary party was crucial to each man's attainment of complete power. Saddam and Stalin also both benefited from having important sponsors, President al-Bakr and Vladimir Lenin, respectively, who recognized their talents and provided them with unique opportunities but apparently came to realize too late that their protégés were leading their revolutions in directions of which they did not approve.

Saddam: Impoverished Child to Revolutionary

Saddam Hussein was born in 1937 into deep poverty near the town of Tikrit, north of Baghdad. His mother was seven months pregnant with him when her husband died, and she had also lost a son to illness. The name she gave him, Saddam, means in Arabic "he who confronts." With no means of support, his mother sent Saddam to live with her brother, Khairallah Talfah, a military officer. Saddam stayed with his uncle for four years in Tikrit, a city on the banks of the Tigris River. In 1941 Saddam's uncle participated in the unsuccessful war against the British, and when Iraqi forces were defeated, he was dismissed from the military and imprisoned. Saddam was returned to his mother, who by that time had married her deceased husband's brother. But her new husband was reportedly both physically and psychologically abusive toward Saddam and would not let him go to school. Instead he demanded that Saddam, though still a child, work to make money for the family. At age ten, Saddam ran away to rejoin his uncle, who had been released from prison. In explaining his reasons for fighting against the British and opposing the pro-British monarchy, his uncle was instrumental in inspiring Saddam to become an anti-imperialist revolutionary. Living in his uncle's household, he was finally able to go to school.

Saddam's uncle took him to Baghdad in 1956, when the city was stirred by Egyptian President Gamal Abdel Nasser's defiance of the British in the Suez crisis. Nasser's actions inspired many young Arabs to enter the world of politics. In Saddam's case, this meant joining the Baath Party.

Bitterly disappointed when, after the 1958 antimonarchy revolution General Qasim failed to immediately fulfill the Arab nationalist dream of unifying Iraq with other Arab countries, Baath Party leaders decided to assassinate him, choosing twenty-two-year-old Saddam to participate in the ambush. Saddam was wounded in the October 7, 1959, attempt. Sought by the police, he was able to escape to Cairo. He enrolled in Cairo University law school, while in Iraq he was sentenced to death in absentia. In Egypt, Saddam married his first cousin, Sajida Talfah, the daughter of his uncle Khairallah. Saddam and Sajida eventually had five children: two sons, Uday and Qusay, and three daughters, Rana, Raghad, and Hala. The 1963 coup overthrowing Qasim permitted Saddam to return to Iraq. After the Baathists were forced out of the government in November 1963, Saddam was recruited for a new coup, this time to overthrow

Abd al-Salam Arif. When the coup failed, Saddam was put in prison from 1964 to 1966, where he formed strong relationships with other imprisoned Baathists and helped plan the party's future seizure of power.

Once out of prison, he went back to work as a party organizer. Israel's devastating 1967 defeat of Arab forces shocked millions of Arabs, many of whom concluded their leaders were incompetent. Existing governments, including that of Abd al-Rahman Arif in Iraq, lost support. Saddam and the Baath Party took advantage of the situation to seize control of Iraq in July 1968.

Saddam's Rise to Power

When Saddam reentered Iraq in 1963 he had two major assets: his reputation as a committed Baathist and the support of his cousin, General al-Bakr. He used these resources, combined with his intelligence, charm, and capacity for violence, not only to build the Baath Party and regime, but also to prepare his way to power. Steps in achieving his goals included helping to convince the communists to support the Baath government, temporarily ending the Kurdish rebellion through the 1975 Algiers Agreement with Iran, and repressing the Iraqi Shia political-religious movement.

The Iranian Revolution and the apparent intention of Ayatollah Muhammad Baqir al-Sadr to create a second Islamic republic in Iraq prompted Iraqi security agents to place al-Sadr under house arrest in June 1979, provoking huge protest demonstrations. In the midst of heightened fear of a greater Shia anti-regime mobilization, al-Bakr announced on July 16, 1979, that he was immediately resigning as president in favor of Saddam, whom he described as the best person for the job. Although the transition of the presidency to Saddam had been in process for some time, the timing of the announcement might have been influenced by the discovery of an alleged Syrian-backed plot. When a Shia member of the RCC, Muhyi al-Din Abd al-Hussein, was arrested on July 12, he provided the names of many other conspirators. The coup plot was revealed to Baath Party members and the country at the July 22 televised meeting of the Iraqi Baath Party leadership. The names of conspirators were announced to the assembled party leaders, including four additional members of the RCC (Hiro 1991: 30), and a number of the accused were present and immediately taken into custody. A special court of loyal RCC members sentenced twenty-two people, including Muhyi al-Din Abd al-Hussein and the other four accused members of the RCC, to death. Thirty-three were sentenced to prison terms and thirteen were acquitted (Marr 2003: 179).

Opposition to Saddam's becoming president apparently was motivated by a number of factors, including concern that he was developing "a dynastic power base" (Farouk-Sluglett and Sluglett 2003: 209). Some objected to his opposition to unifying with Syria. If the two states merged before he assumed the presidency, al-Bakr would have been president of the new federation and Syria's leader, Hafix al-Asad, second in command, with Saddam third in rank, making al-Asad, rather than Saddam, next in line to replace al-Bakr in the presidency. But by preventing unification, the way was open for Saddam to succeed al-Bakr. Still another reason for some to have plotted against Saddam was the difference between his and al-Bakr's orientation toward Shia militancy in the south and toward the new Islamic Republic in Iran. Al-Bakr seemed to favor flexibility toward Iraq's Shia activists and Iran. In contrast, Saddam advocated decisive repression of the Iraqi Shia political-religious movement and a more hostile approach toward Iran, whose religious leadership he believed was promoting a fundamentalist revolution in Iraq.

Among those executed were several people who previously had been among Saddam's closest associates. This suggested that some of the people who knew Saddam best feared what would happen if he became president. Their execution showed that having been close to him was no guarantee of safety.

According to Marr (2004: 180), Saddam's assumption of the presidency in July 1979, coupled with the removal of government and Baath Party officials who opposed him, meant that the Iraqi regime "became a more personal autocracy." Al-Bakr's retirement "eliminated a check and a balance on the actions of Saddam, one that was never restored" (Marr 2004: 180). The Baath Party virtually ceased to exercise an independent role and served in part to thinly veil the family and tribal networks that increasingly characterized his government. Saddam appointed himself field marshal of the armed forces, his cousin Adnan Khair Allah Talfah became deputy commander in chief, and his half brother, Barzan Ibrahim al-Tikriti, was made head of the Mukhabarat (the Security Directorate of the Baath Party).

Ironically, as Iraq moved steadily from one-party rule toward a one-man dictatorship, the regime proclaimed a law establishing a 250-member national assembly in March 1980 that would be elected every four years. In reality it would have little power independent of Saddam. The first assembly election, held on June 20, 1980, resulted in a large majority for the Baath Party. A Shia Baathist, Na'im Haddad, who was also an RCC member, was elected assembly speaker.

The Iran–Iraq War

There were several major reasons for Iraq's decision to launch what was intended to be a short, limited war with Iran on September 22, 1980. Probably most important was the fear of a dangerous upsurge of fundamentalist revolutionary activity in Iraq, inspired by the Iranian Revolution and Ayatollah Khomeini's call to establish an Iraqi Islamic republic (Wright 1989: 110). Saddam was also concerned that widespread Shia protests or rebellion could encourage Kurdish separatists to take up arms again and "plunge Iraq into a debilitating civil war" (Hiro 1991: 37–38). Farouk-Sluglett and Sluglett (2003: 257) believe that Baath leaders overestimated the extent to which the Iraqi Shia "population as a whole was in sympathy with, or prepared to support, the establishment of a theocratic regime in Iraq." They suggest that Saddam overreacted in part because of his inability to tolerate any significant increase in resistance to his regime.

A second factor was perception of Iranian weakness. The revolution had disrupted Iran's armed forces. Some officers had been executed by religious courts, and many fled the country. The Iranian military shrank from around 400,000 to about 200,000, and both the United States and Great Britain, from whom the overthrown monarchy had purchased aircraft, tanks, missile systems, and other weapons, cut off sale of military equipment, preventing Iran from buying new missiles or replacement parts, such as aircraft or tank engines. The Iraqi leadership believed that Iran would have no choice but to agree to Iraq's demands almost immediately.

But Iran partially compensated for deficiencies in its professional armed forces by rapidly expanding its Islamic Revolutionary Guard (IRG). This volunteer force, filled with religiously fervent young men, was initially intended to protect fundamentalist leaders of the Iranian Revolution from attack by other factions in the anti-shah alliance or from a military coup.

Hundreds of thousands in the IRG proved determined fighters. Iran was able to obtain some spare parts for its American-made weapons from Vietnam, which had large amounts of equipment that the United States had left behind after the Vietnam conflict (Hiro 1991: 71–72). In addition, Hiro (1991: 83) claims that Israel provided weapons aid to Iran. Iraq also did not anticipate that the United States would violate its own embargo and secretly sell weapons to Iran during the war.

The Iraqi leadership expected the defeat of Iran's Islamic revolutionary regime to be well received by the United States, which feared the spread of fundamentalist revolution to its Arab allies. But the Iraqis may have underestimated the extent to which Israeli interests influenced US policy. It is hard to conceive that Israel would have been content with a quick, decisive Iraqi victory over Iran, given Baathist hostility toward Israel and commitment to supporting the Palestinians. A relatively unscathed and triumphant Iraq, supported by the Arab masses, would have represented a significant threat to Israel.

Another motive for war was the disagreement concerning the boundary between Iraq and Iran along the Shatt al-Arab. In the 1975 Algiers Agreement, desperate to get Iranian cooperation in ending the war in Iraqi Kurdistan and faced with Iranian military superiority, Saddam had consented to drawing the border at the midline of the deepest channel. But he now asserted that the boundary should return to Iran's shoreline.

Lead-Up to War

Soon after the revolution, Iran stopped effectively patrolling its border with Iraqi Kurdistan, permitting KDP forces to reorganize. In response, Iraq began supporting rebellion by Arab groups in the largely Arab-speaking and oil-rich Iranian province of Khuzistan.

More threatening to the Iraqi regime were calls from Iranian Islamic leaders for Iraqi Shia to overthrow the Baathist government. Faced with a surge in Shia activism, in March 1980 the Iraqi government made membership in the Dawa Party punishable by death. Frightened by the April attempt to kill Tariq Aziz, a Christian (Chaldean Catholic) RCC member, the regime, as noted earlier, quickly executed Ayatollah Baqir al-Sadr and his sister, Bint al-Huda, an Islamic scholar.

Iraq's leaders depicted themselves as the defenders of the Arab world, Arab socialism, and modernity against the threat of Persian imperialism and a medieval religious movement.

Ayatollah Khomeini claimed his movement had nothing to do with Persian imperialism and that it was not restricted to Shiism, but rather was intended to reinvigorate all of Islam in part by removing un-Islamic governments—whether secular republics, as in Iraq, or monarchies, such as Saudi Arabia—and replacing them with Islamic republics (Hiro 1992: 32). Some of Iraq's Baathist leaders believed that if they did not act to remove the fundamentalist government from much larger Iran while it was still weakened by the disruption of revolution, they would be faced with a far more serious threat once Iran's government was consolidated and its armed forces revitalized.

The Iraqis had provided funds to opponents of Khomeini's fundamentalists to overthrow the Islamic government and replace it with a moderate regime friendly to Iraq. The failure of these efforts limited Iraq's options. The belief that the United States would not assist Iran in the event of war was reinforced when young Iranian militants, believing that the shah's admission into the United States on October 22, 1979, for cancer treatment was in reality part of a plot to reestablish his dictatorship, stormed the US embassy in Tehran on November 4, and took about fifty US citizens hostage. The hostage crisis, which would last 444 days, appeared to make it extremely unlikely that the United States would help Iran.

The Iraqi plan was for an overpowering attack that would crush Iranian forces near the common border, leaving Iran no choice but to make peace on Iraq's terms, perhaps delegitimizing Iran's fundamentalist government and resulting in its downfall.

When the attack took place, the US government, in contrast to its extreme condemnation of the Soviet intervention in Afghanistan, "neither condemned the Iraqi aggression of Iran nor identified Iraq as the instigator" (Milani 1994: 208). "The logic of the U.S. strategy was to permit him [Saddam] to become just strong enough to contain the Islamic Revolution" (Milani 1994: 208–209) so the two potentially dangerous nations could become entangled in a hugely destructive, exhausting war, with neither being allowed to decisively defeat the other. Instead the aim was "to assure that there would be two losers in one war" (Milani 1994: 209).

Iranian provocations apparently contributed to the Iraqi decision to go ahead with a major invasion. Iranian artillery attacked the Iraqi cities of Khanaqin and Mandali on September 4, 1980, causing many civilian casualties (Marr 2004: 184). On September 17, Saddam "officially abrogated" the 1975 Algiers Agreement and stated that Iraq would enforce control over the entire Shatt al-Arab. Then on September 19, Iranian artillery and airplanes attacked Iraqi facilities on the Iraqi side of the river as well as merchant ships. According to Marr (2003: 184), "This was the trigger Saddam had been waiting for." On September 22, the date widely viewed as the start of the war, Iraq launched air raids on ten Iranian airfields (Hiro 1991: 40). But many Iranian planes were located at airfields beyond the range of Iraqi aircraft or were protected in hardened shelters (Bergquist 2002: 57). The next day Iraqi ground forces crossed into Iranian territory.

The War: 1980–1982

Having captured a mostly narrow band of Iranian territory extending south from near the southern part of Iraqi Kurdistan to the besieged Iranian city of

Abadan, with significant Iraqi penetration into the oil-rich Iranian province of Khuzistan, the Iraqi leadership ceased the offensive, apparently expecting Iran to concede control of the Shatt al-Arab and promise to end Iranian interference in Iraqi internal affairs, in exchange for return of captured Iranian territory.

Iran's response, however, was defiant. Tens of thousands of Iranians volunteered to fight the Iraqi invasion. Instead of weakening the Iranian government, the attack strengthened it by motivating most Iranians to temporarily forget their differences and unite to face an external threat. Even most Arab-speaking and Sunni Iranians seemed to remain loyal to Iran. A similar phenomenon occurred in Iraq, with the large majority of Shia Iraqis staying loyal to Iraq and their Arab heritage rather than siding with their Persian coreligionists. Only some members of the "traditional religious families" (Farouk-Sluglett and Sluglett 2003: 258) of the Iraqi holy cities of Najaf and Karbala and some captured Iraqi Shia soldiers chose to support Iran. Throughout the war, the Iranians sustained two to three times the casualties of the Iraqis, yet continued to fight. Iran was able to push the Iraqis back in Khuzistan and then advance toward the captured city of Khorramshahr.

Saddam and his associates soon realized they had made major miscalculations regarding Iranian military resources, the impact of the war on Iran's government, and their own military capabilities. While Jordan, Saudi Arabia, Kuwait, and the United Arab Emirates supported Iraq (Hiro 1991: 76), eventually helping Iraq with huge loans, Syria and Libya sided with Iran. Since Basra was within the war zone, much of Iraq's international commerce was conducted by way of Kuwait during the war (Farouk-Sluglett and Sluglett 2003: 259).

In May 1982 Iran recaptured Khorramshahr (Hiro 1991: 59–60). This Iranian victory prompted Saddam to propose a settlement of the war in June. He stated that Iraq and Iran should stop fighting so they could help Lebanon, which Israel had invaded on June 6, 1982. Iraq was prepared to withdraw its forces to internationally recognized boundaries. However, Ayatollah Khomeini demanded that any peace agreement include not only many billions of dollars in reparations to Iran, but also the removal from power of the man he blamed for starting the war: Saddam Hussein. Khomeini also wanted an end to the Baath Party government (Hiro 1991: 64). Iraq refused.

Rejecting alternate proposals for peace, including the Arab League Peace Plan, which "called for an immediate cease-fire, complete withdrawal of Iraqi troops from Iran, and compensation of some $70 billion to Iran through the Islamic Reconstruction Bank" (Milani 1994: 209), the Iranians now repeated "the mistake that Saddam Hussein had made earlier" (Marr 2004: 186). They decided to invade Iraq to overthrow Saddam and install an Iraqi Islamic republic. In July 1982 Iranian forces pushed into Iraqi territory to the outskirts of Basra. There the advance was halted with both sides sustaining great loss of life. The war entered a new phase in which ground combat would be fought largely in Iraq.

The War: 1982–1985

The Iraqis, fighting from strong defensive positions, repeatedly repelled Iranian assaults, inflicting many casualties. Iraq was initially able to shield most of the country's population from the war's effects, relying on about $30 billion in its foreign currency reserves (Tripp 2000: 235). But by 1983 Iraqi reserves had fallen to about $3 billion. The country's oil revenues declined from $26 billion in 1980 to approximately $9 billion in 1982 after the pro-Iranian Syrians closed Iraq's oil pipeline through Syria in April 1982 and the Iranians destroyed Iraq's Faw oil terminal (Tripp 2000: 235). Iraq's foreign debt grew to about $25 billion in 1983.

Beginning that year, major construction projects were slowed down or halted, the cost of living started to rise rapidly, and citizens were called upon to donate to the war effort. With finances devastated by the war, the government moved away from socialism and encouraged an expansion of the private sector. Due in part to an agricultural labor shortage caused by the large number of men serving in the armed forces, the government had to increase food imports. Despite a new oil pipeline through Turkey, Iraq's economy was also damaged by a decline in international oil prices during the 1980s.

The Iraqis turned to other oil-rich Arab states for tens of billions of dollars in assistance. European countries rescheduled debt payments and issued Iraq new credit, while the United States provided agricultural credits. By 1983 the United States began to fear an Iranian victory, which might put Iraq's oil in the hands of a new anti-American Iraqi Islamic Republic and threaten the pro–United States monarchies of Saudi Arabia, Kuwait, and other Persian Gulf states. In November 1983 the United States removed Iraq from its list of terrorist nations and in January 1984 replaced it with Iran (Hiro 1991: 120).

The conflict became further internationalized when in 1984 Iraqi planes targeted tankers heading for Iranian ports. The Iranians then launched attacks against tankers heading for Iraq's financial allies, Saudi Arabia and Kuwait (Karsh 1989: 37–39; Rubin 1989: 124, 127), causing tanker insurance rates to skyrocket (Hiro 1991: 129–132). By 1986 Iran held about three hundred square miles of Iraqi territory, including an artificial Iraqi island, Majnun, the site of newly discovered oil. In the 1984 battle for Majnun, the Iraqis were accused of using chemical weapons, such as mustard gas. Despite these repeated accusations, few Western nations issued any significant protests (Marr 2004: 187).

The Iraqi regime apparently was not seriously threatened during the war. The officer corps was committed to preventing an Iranian victory, and the three possible significant opposition groups—the Shia religious leadership, the KDP, and the ICP—were internally divided and could not work together because of differing ideologies and goals.

The War: 1986–1988

After years of stalemate and mutual devastation, a series of dramatic events began to move the war toward a climax. The first occurred in February 1986 when Iran captured the Faw Peninsula (Hiro 1991: 167). From Faw, Iran could launch Chinese-made Silkworm missiles against ships or into Kuwait. This again raised the possibility of an Iranian victory, establishment of a fundamentalist republic in Iraq, and perhaps in Kuwait and Saudi Arabia, and the loss of billions loaned to Iraq by other nations including France and the Soviet Union.

Iraq responded to the Faw defeat by giving its military command more freedom of action, preparing to go on the offensive, and expanding the Republican Guard from three brigades to twenty-eight (Marr 2004: 188).

Iran, encouraged by taking Faw, decided to launch a new effort to capture Basra. During January and February 1987, in a ferocious battle, Iranians advanced to within about ten miles of the city when the Iraqis stopped them. The defeat of the Basra offensive was devastating for Iran because it lost so many experienced officers and large quantities of military equipment it was unable to replace. The Iranians were also discouraged by the support major powers provided Iraq. The United States reportedly began supplying satellite photographs of Iranian forces to the Iraqis to help them plan their military operations more effectively (Marr 2004: 195).

There were indications that the United States was at times aiding both sides, which may have convinced both countries to keep on fighting in the hope of victory. Many observers reached such a conclusion after a Lebanese publication in 1986 disclosed that the United States had been violating its own arms embargo by selling missiles to Iran (Hiro 1991: 215–221). This became known as the Iran-Contra scandal because much of the profits from the weapons sales were used to help support counterrevolutionary forces, or contras, attempting to overthrow the Sandinista government in Nicaragua after the US Congress had cut off funds for this Reagan-administration project. According to Milani (1994: 209), Washington's objective seemed to be the "mutual destruction of belligerents," similar to Great Britain's apparent orientation during World War II while Germany and the Soviet Union waged massive land warfare against each other between 1941 and 1944.

A turning point in the war occurred on May 17, 1987, when an Iraqi plane hit the US frigate *Stark* with two French-made Exocet missiles, killing thirty-seven members of its crew. Although the Iraqi government declared the incident an accident and paid compensation, it is possible that the attack on the *Stark* was deliberate, either an Iraqi retaliation for what was viewed as US treachery in providing arms to Iran while also aiding Iraq, or a tactic for provoking US intervention to protect Saudi and Kuwaiti tankers earning oil revenues to support the Iraqi war effort. In response to the *Stark* attack, the United States speeded up its plan to reflag the Kuwaiti tankers as US ships and put them under US naval protection (Hiro 1991: 186).

The United Nations had been attempting since at least March 1985 to end the war. Finally in July 1987 the UN Security Council adopted Resolution 598, calling for a cease-fire and withdrawal to internationally recognized borders, exchange of prisoners of war, and a commission to determine who was responsible for starting the conflict (Marr 2004: 190). Failure to accept the resolution would result in UN action to end the war. Though the Iraqis consented, it would take a year for Iran to fully accept the resolution.

US military actions contributed to convincing Iranians they could not win. After Iran attacked a US reflagged vessel with a Silkworm missile on October 16, 1987, the United States struck an Iranian Revolutionary Guard communications facility. Then after a US warship hit a mine laid by Iranian boats in

April 1988, the United States attacked two offshore Iranian oil platforms. Iran responded by having its high-speed boats attack United Arab Emirates oil platforms. In retaliation, the United States sank two of Iran's frigates, which constituted half of Iran's major naval vessels (Marr 2004: 190).

Benefiting from loans and credits, and increased oil revenue from expanded pipelines, Iraq was able to purchase new military equipment giving it as much as a four to one advantage over Iran in tanks and artillery. In 1987 Iraq was estimated to have approximately five hundred combat aircraft to Iran's approximately sixty-five (*The Economist* 1987: 49). Iraq's armed forces in 1988 included about 130 divisions with 1.3 million military personnel (Marr 2004: 190).

In early 1988, the Iraqis attempted to demoralize their adversary by launching missile attacks on Iranian cities. Between February 22 and April 20, approximately 150 modified Scud B Hussein missiles hit Tehran while about 50 hit other Iranian cities. Iran retaliated in Iraqi Kurdistan by taking the town of Halabja. The Iraqis attacked Halabja on March 16 using both mustard gas and nerve gas, killing between 3,500 and 5,000 people. Fearing a similar chemical attack by rocket-borne warheads, which never actually occurred, an estimated 1.5 million fled Tehran, a city of about 8 million, creating a difficult internal refugee problem for the Iranian regime.

The Iraqis launched a surprise attack to retake the Faw Peninsula on April 16, the beginning of Ramadan, catching the Iranians off guard. After four days, Iraqi Republican Guard forces and the regular army's Seventh Corps succeeded in retaking Faw. In June, Iraq recaptured Majnun, then Iraqi forces again advanced into Iranian territory.

The next devastating blow to Iran was almost certainly an accident, although many Iranians believed it was intentional. On July 3, 1988, the USS *Vincennes*, a Ticonderoga-class AEGIS guided-missile cruiser, mistakenly identified an Iranian airliner with 290 people on board as a hostile warplane and destroyed it with ship-to-air missiles, killing everyone on board (Hiro 1991: 211).

Faced with these reverses, the Iranian leadership concluded that the only option was to end the war. On July 17, Iran informed the UN that it would accept Security Council Resolution 598. Though the fighting ended, negotiations to formally conclude the war continued for some time.

Consequences of the Iran–Iraq War

The Iraqi Shia

Most Iraqi Shia did not support the *vilayat-e faqih*, the central governing principle of the Iranian Islamic Republic, that gave ultimate political authority to the selected representative of the Shia clergy in Iran. This apparently was one reason why Shia desertion rates during the war were similar to those of Sunnis. In fact, many Shia "officers were promoted to positions of prestige and responsibility in which they demonstrated their competence and loyalty to the regime in the war against Iran" (Tripp 2000: 247).

To reinforce the allegiance of the country's Shia, Iraq declared as a national holiday the birthday of Imam Ali, who the Shia believed was Muhammad's rightful successor. Saddam even claimed he was a descendant of Ali's. At the end of the war, many Shia Arabs shared with Sunni Arabs a heightened sense of pride and patriotism and a feeling that they had been able to withstand and to some extent defeat much more populous Iran.

But some Iraqi Shia did side with Iran. Shia groups that opposed the Iraqi government during the war included the Dawa Party, many of whose members fled to Iran, and the Supreme Council for the Islamic Revolution in Iraq (SCIRI), led by Muhammad Baqir al-Hakim. SCIRI, formed on November 17, 1982, as an umbrella confederation of Shia groups opposing the Baath regime, was supported by Iran and initially included the Dawa Party. (After the US-led invasion in 2003, SCIRI and Dawa emerged as separate Shia political parties.) SCIRI favored adopting the vilayat-e faqih principle of the Iranian Islamic Republic, which put supreme political power in the hands of Shia religious leaders, while other Shia opposition groups, such as Dawa, did not. With Iranian help, al-Hakim was able to create an armed force, the SCIRI militia called the Badr Brigade, some of whose members were recruited from Iraqi prisoners of war held by Iran, which played a limited role in military operations against the Iraqi army, mainly in Kurdistan (Tripp 2000: 247). In 1983, after al-Hakim and associates set up a so-called Iraqi government in exile in Tehran, the Iraqi regime arrested dozens of his family members remaining in Iraq, executing six who were Shia religious leaders, including three of his brothers (Marr 2004: 197). But SCIRI's collaboration with Iran alienated it from much of the Iraqi Shia population who "had no desire to be liberated by Tehran or incorporated in a new Islamic empire" (Marr 2004: 199).

The Iraqi Kurds

There were four main military organizations of Kurds during the war. Kurds served as soldiers and officers in the Iraqi armed forces. They also participated in the Fursan, the proregime Kurdish militia that by the summer of 1986 had an estimated 150,000 members. And they fought in the two Kurdish armies opposing Baghdad: the PUK and the KDP.

The KDP, led by members of the Barzani family, allied with Iran. Many KDP fighters had stayed in Iran following the defeat of the Barzani rebellion in 1975 and "forged close ties with the new Iranian regime" (Marr 2004: 199). In October 1983, the KDP joined in an Iranian attack that succeeded in occupying territory in Iraqi Kurdistan, in effect opening a northern front in the war. In response, according to Marr (2004: 199), the Baath regime "rounded up some 8,000 male members of the Barzani clan and sent them to an unknown destination; they were never heard from again." The Fursan helped the Iraqi army secure urban areas and communication routes in the Kurdish region.

Masud Barzani of the KDP, son of Mustafa Barzani, and Jalal al-Talabani of the PUK organized an opposition coalition including the KDP, the PUK, the Kurdish Socialist Party (KSP), the Communist Party, and the Assyrian Democratic Movement, which came into existence in May 1987. By that time, the KDP controlled almost all of the Iraqi border with Turkey and the PUK controlled much of the border with Iran. The Iraqi government responded by carrying out the brutal repression during 1987 and especially 1988 that came to be known as Anfal ("spoils"). While temporarily suppressing the rebellion and killing thousands of Kurds, the Anfal alienated many more and intensified the drive for either extensive Kurdish autonomy or outright independence.

The person thought to be primarily responsible for the Anfal was Ali Hasan al-Majid, Saddam's cousin, who was appointed governor of the Kurdish provinces on February 28, 1987. The goals of the repression were to destroy the Kurdish insurgents and any villages providing them support or recruits. During April through June 1987, more than five hundred villages were demolished in the lowlands and along highways (Marr 2000: 201), and people refusing to leave were sometimes killed. The harsh policy resulted in many Fursan soldiers defecting to the KDP or PUK.

In January 1988, the Iranians attempted a breakthrough in the north, seizing more of Iraqi Kurdistan with the aid of peshmergas. Iraq retaliated with coordinated attacks between February and September involving conventional high-explosive bombs and chemical weapons. Once enemy forces had been killed or forced to flee, Iraqi soldiers were sent in. Children, women, and the elderly from nearby villages were sent to detention camps. It's suspected that many captured men were executed.

At least 50,000 to 100,000 Kurds were killed during the Anfal, although some estimates are as high as 200,000 (Farouk-Sluglett and Sluglett 2003: 270). Although at war's end Baghdad militarily controlled Iraqi Kurdistan, the costs to the regime would prove extremely damaging. Many Kurds who had supported the government in the Iran–Iraq War turned against it. And as reports of the Anfal, and especially the use of lethal chemical weapons, spread around the world, Iraq lost much of the international support it had enjoyed during its struggle with Iran.

Political Effects

The war appeared to increase the concentration of power in Saddam's hands. The government promoted a Saddam personality cult so that, despite his mistakes, veneration of the president would put him beyond the reach of rational criticism. By the end of the war, the Baath Party had become a mass organization oriented toward mobilizing support for government policies. Membership was viewed as a significant asset for admission to top schools and advancement in government employment or professional careers. The party's share of the vote, however, declined from the first national assembly elections in 1980, when it won about 75 percent of the seats, to the 1989 election, when it barely kept a majority. The strident Arab nationalism of the original Baath Party was further eroded as during the war the regime stressed Iraqi patriotism in an attempt to bind together Iraqi Shia Arabs, Sunni Arabs, and Kurds.

Wartime support from the United States and other Western countries appeared to moderate Iraq's orientation toward the Israeli–Palestinian conflict. As early as 1981, Iraqi officials, including Saddam, indicated that Iraq would support a settlement of the conflict acceptable to Palestinians.

Iraq's Armed Forces and Security

By 1988 the total Iraqi armed forces had grown from a few hundred thousand to approximately 1.3 million personnel organized in 130 divisions (Marr 2004: 190). Between 1979–1980 and 1987–1988, Iraq went from about 1,900 to 6,310 tanks; from 339 to more than 500 combat aircraft; and from 231 to 422 helicopters (Farouk-Sluglett and Sluglett 2003: 271–272). The battle-tested, well-equipped, and, in the sense of protecting the country, victorious Iraqi armed forces concluded the war with a relatively high level of morale and confidence, probably the most effective Arab military at that time.

The war made the entire country dependent on the skills and leadership of its military officers, potentially threatening Saddam, who had no formal military experience. In an apparent attempt to prevent the emergence of popular military heroes, "the generals commanding the various fronts were rotated regularly, and rarely mentioned by name in the official press" (Farouk-Sluglett and Sluglett 2003: 264). Danger to the regime was limited by the wartime increase in the size and heterogeneity of the officer corps, which made it more difficult for a small group of officers to carry out a coup (Tripp 2000: 249).

Iraqi security agencies protecting the regime—including General Security (Amn al-Amm) of the Interior Ministry, Military Intelligence (Istikhbarat) of the Ministry of Defense, the Security Directorate (Mukhabarat) under the Baath Party, and the Special Security Organization (SSO or Amn al-Khass) under the president of the republic—may have had between 60,000 and 200,000 members (Marr 2004: 211).

Economic, Demographic, and Sociological Effects

The war claimed the lives of about 125,000 Iraqis and left 255,000 wounded (Marr 2003: 207). Iran's war dead may have been about three times Iraq's (Farouk-Sluglett and Sluglett 2003: 271). These figures do not include Iraqi Kurds killed in the Anfal campaign.

Much of Iraq's oil production infrastructure was destroyed by the Iranian air force, especially in Basra province. The Shatt al-Arab became unusable for several years because it was blocked by sunken ships and other wreckage. In the year before the war started, Iraq earned $26 billion for its oil, and in the month the war began, September 1980, the country was producing about 3.5 million barrels a day (Marr 2004: 203). But oil production fell to fewer than 1 million barrels a day in 1982, and in 1983 oil revenue was only about $10 billion. After two years of war, Iraq cut back construction projects and imports by about 50 percent (Farouk-Sluglett and Sluglett 2003: 264).

Wartime assistance from Arab nations probably totaled between $40 billion and $50 billion. Iraq also owed tens of billions more to non-Arab countries. Oil prices had fallen considerably, so Iraq earned only about $13.16 billion for its oil in 1988 (Farouk-Sluglett and Sluglett 2003: 275), half its 1980 oil revenue.

The government allowed many men to postpone military service while they completed their educations, to protect the country's most talented and skilled youth, but the length of the war meant that many of them eventually perished in the conflict.

Since the war created a labor shortage, the regime invited about 2 million Indians, Filipinos, Koreans, and Egyptians to fill jobs. The percentage of Iraqi women in the nonagricultural workforce rose from about 17 percent in the 1970s to about 25 percent in the 1980s (Marr 2004: 207).

The war economically devastated middle-class Iraqis employed by the government, since salaries could not keep pace with wartime inflation. Desperate for money and increased productivity, the government, departing from Baath socialist ideology, began selling off state-owned industries and land, and, through Law 113 of 1982, facilitated privatization by offering tax concessions and low-interest loans as investment incentives to private industrial companies (Farouk-Sluglett and Sluglett 2003: 265). As a result, individual businessmen and landlords, Sunni Arabs, Shia Arabs, and Kurds, became wealthy through owning newly privatized properties. Economic inequality increased. Dependent on ties to the Baath government for their continued prosperity, the self-interested allegiance to Saddam of flourishing capitalists helped bond segments of their religious and ethnic communities to the regime.

The overall financial costs of the war were estimated to be as much as $453 billion for Iraq and $644 billion for Iran, including infrastructure damage, lost oil revenue, and reduced gross national product (Farouk-Sluglett and Sluglett 2003: 271).

Final Peace Agreement

When Iran's July 17, 1988, acceptance of UN cease-fire Resolution 598 was announced, "Iraqis came out on the streets to celebrate with a sense not only of relief but also of victory" (Marr 2004: 212). Many Iraqis believed they had defeated the threat of fundamentalist extremism on behalf not only of Arabs, but of all humanity as well. According to Hiro (1991: 257), the war increased the sense of "national unity" among many Iraqis. The government immediately began a reconstruction program for Basra, Faw, and other locations in the south. The level of financial damage the war caused was not yet understood by most Iraqis and perhaps by the country's leadership, which believed that Arab states should treat the billions they gave Iraq as nonrepayable grants, rather than loans, since Iraqis had fought and died to stop a common enemy.

The final peace agreement stalled over issues such as creating a commission to establish responsibility for the war. Final settlement came on August 15, 1990, two weeks following Iraq's invasion of Kuwait. Then, apparently to secure Iranian neutrality in the conflict over Kuwait, Saddam consented to both the complete implementation of UN Resolution 598 and to designating the border where Iran wanted it, at the midline of the deepest channel of the Shaat al-Arab.

Summary and Analysis

Rather than establish an Iraqi state with full sovereignty and a truly democratic political system, the British installed a monarchy with a pliant, elite-dominated parliament constrained by a treaty and constitution that served British interests. When secular nationalists in Iraq's huge neighbor Iran tried to free their nation from its pro-British monarchy and take control of their nation's oil resources and armed forces, British and American agents, whose governments publicly claimed to promote democracy, helped overthrow the nationalists in 1953 and reinstall the Iranian shah as a virtually absolute monarch protected by a new, brutal secret police force. Some Iraqis, once they ousted their own monarchy in 1958, feared foreign intervention and were concerned that a totally democratic political system was too vulnerable to subversion or overthrow by Britain, the United States, or other nations. They concluded that only a disciplined one-party-dominated state could prevent reimposition of foreign control. Baathists created such a system in Iraq. The Baath Party defeated the first Iraqi anti-imperialist mass movement, the ICP, through repression and by portraying it as a tool of another foreign power, the USSR. The Baath Party offered the Iraqi people the benefits of socialism promised by the ICP coupled with a genuinely anti-imperialist pan-Arab-oriented government.

After the Baath Party seized control in 1968, the two major figures in power were Ahmad Hasan al-Bakr and his young cousin Saddam Hussein. Al-Bakr, a respected Baathist military officer, was crucial in convincing other important officers to support the Baath regime. Saddam took the leading role in reorganizing and expanding the party. The regime removed potential opponents from the military and made it a capital crime for any other party to recruit from the armed forces. A key mechanism for regime consolidation was placing extended-family members of al-Bakr and Saddam in key party, government, and military positions.

The Baath government nationalized oil resources, contributing to a rapid increase in the country's revenue. Health care, housing, educational opportunities, and the social welfare system were greatly improved and Iraq's economic base was diversified through new industries. The regime succeeded in convincing the main party to its left, the ICP, to support its reforms, removing a significant political threat and allowing the Baathists to assume a major role in labor and student organizations, where the communists once dominated.

The Baathist regime also tried to accommodate Kurdish militants seeking autonomy. When negotiations broke down, Saddam worked out an agreement with Iran that cut off aid and closed the border to the Kurds in return for Iraq's accepting Iran's preferred boundary on the Shatt al-Arab and other Iraqi concessions. The KDP had no choice but to temporarily give up the fight.

The regime also faced a threat from Shia clerical leaders who objected to the Baathists' secular orientation and certain reforms. The Shia population, however, was diverse, with internal theological, class, and tribal divisions. Many Shia were Baathists, and the government rewarded Shia willing to cooperate, incorporating them into its patronage network.

Many Iraqis experienced dramatic improvements in their income levels and living conditions during the 1970s. But the government felt threatened by the 1979 Iranian Revolution, whose leaders were intent on spreading Islamic revolution to other countries (Hiro 1991: 27–28). Several Iraqi Shia leaders who expressed support for establishing an Islamic republic in Iraq were imprisoned, killed, or forced to flee the country. As concern over Iran increased, al-Bakr retired and Saddam became president.

Iraq decided to launch what it anticipated would be a short, successful war against Iran to undermine Iran's Islamic government and halt the advance of fundamentalism. Most Iranians, however, reacted to the Iraqi invasion by rallying to defend their country. The fundamentalist government appeared strengthened, rather than weakened, by the attack.

During September 1980 to mid-1982, Iraq initially scored significant victories, followed by successful Iranian counterattacks, forcing the Iraqis to give up much of the territory they had seized. Then in July 1982 Iran took the war into Iraq. During much of 1982 through 1985, the conflict was a stalemate that included the beginning of the so-called tanker war and some use of chemical weapons. From 1986 to 1988, Iran scored major victories, including the conquest of Iraq's Faw Peninsula and the occupation of territory in Iraqi Kurdistan. But then the Iranians suffered catastrophic personnel and equipment losses in their unsuccessful attempt to take the major Iraqi city of Basra. With greatly superior quantities of aircraft, tanks, and artillery the Iraqis successfully counterattacked. Iran's military reverses on land were accompanied by losses at sea due to US naval and air actions. Iran concluded that with Iraq enjoying a great advantage in military equipment as well as benefiting from US intervention in the Persian Gulf, it had to agree to a cease-fire in July 1988, essentially concluding the eight-year conflict.

Saddam's hold on power at the end of the war seemed as strong as ever. Many Iraqis, Sunni and Shia, felt they had won the war by holding off the much larger Iran and stopping the advance of fundamentalism. But the regime's brutally repressive measures in Iraqi Kurdistan during the war alienated more Kurds than ever before, significantly widening Iraq's major ethnic divide. Of critical importance, Iraq found itself deeply in debt with revenue limited partly because of the fall in oil prices in the late 1980s. Faced with a mounting economic crisis, Iraq turned to its large, battle-tested armed forces. The country would soon launch a new military adventure that would bring more hardship to the Iraqi people and ultimately doom the Baath regime.

References and Further Readings

Algar, Hamid (translator and annotator). 1981. *Islam and Revolution: Writings and Declarations of Imam Khomeini*. Berkeley, CA: Mizan.

Batatu, Hanna. 1978. *The Old Social Classes and the Revolutionary Movements of Iraq*. Princeton, NJ: Princeton University Press.

Bergquist, Ronald E. 2002. *The Role of Airpower in the Iran-Iraq War*. Honolulu, HI: University Press of the Pacific.

Bozarslan, Hamit. 2006. *"Kurdish Movements."* In James DeFronzo, ed., *Revolutionary Movements in World History: From 1750 to the Present*, vol. 2, 519–528. Santa Barbara, CA: ABC-CLIO.

DeFronzo, James. 2007. *Revolutions and Revolutionary Movements.* Boulder, CO: Westview.

Devlin, John E. 1991. "The Baath Party: Rise and Metamorphosis." *American Historical Review* 96 (December): 1396–1407.

The Economist. 1987. "The Arming, and Disarming, of Iran's Revolution." (September): 49 (US edition).

Farouk-Sluglett, Marion, and Peter Sluglett. 1988. "The Iraqi Ba'th Party." In Vicky Randall, ed., *Political Parties in the Third World*, 57–74. London: Sage.

———. 1991. "The Historiography of Modern Iraq." *American Historical Review* 96 (5): 1408–1421.

———. 2003. *Iraq Since 1958.* London: J. B. Tauris Publishers.

Galvani, John. 1972. "The Baathi Revolution in Iraq." *Middle East Report* 12 (September): 3–11, 14–22.

Hiro, Dilip. 1987. *Iran Under the Ayatollahs.* London: Routledge and Kegan Paul.

———. 1991. *The Longest War: The Iran-Iraq Military Conflict.* New York: Routledge.

———. 1992. *Desert Shield to Desert Storm.* New York: Routledge.

———. 2007. *Blood of the Earth: The Battle for the World's Vanishing Oil Resources.* New York: Nation Books.

Hussain, Asaf. 1985. *Islamic Iran.* New York: St. Martin's.

Ismael, Tareq. 2007. *The Rise and Fall of the Communist Party of Iraq.* Cambridge, UK: Cambridge University Press.

Joffé, George. 2006. "Islamic Fundamentalist Revolutionary Movements." In James DeFronzo, ed., *Revolutionary Movements in World History*, 452–464.

Karsh, Efraim. 1989. "From Ideological Zeal to Geopolitical Realism: The Islamic Republic and the Gulf." In Efraim Karsh, ed., *The Iran-Iraq War: Impact and Implications*, 26–41. New York: St. Martin's.

Khadduri, Majid. 1969. *Republican Iraq: A Study in Iraqi Politics since the Revolution of 1958.* Oxford, UK: Oxford University Press.

Makiya, Kanan (Al-Khalil, Samir). 1998. *Republic of Fear: Saddam's Iraq.* Berkeley: University of California Press.

Marr, Phebe. 2004. *The Modern History of Iraq.* Boulder, CO: Westview.

McDowell, D. 2004. *A Modern History of the Kurds.* London: I. B. Tauris.

Milani, Moshen. 1994. *The Making of Iran's Islamic Revolution: From Monarchy to Islamic Republic.* Boulder, CO: Westview Press.

Nakash, Yitzhak. 1994. *The Shi'is of Iraq.* Princeton, NJ: Princeton University Press.

Polk, William R. 2005. *Understanding Iraq.* New York: Harper Perennial.

Al-Qazzaz, Ayad. 1967. "Military Regimes and Political Stability in Iraq, Syria and Egypt." *Berkeley Journal of Sociology* 12 (Summer): 44–54.

———. 1971. "The Changing Patterns of Politics of the Iraqi Army." In Morris Janowitz And Jacques Van Doorn, eds., *On Military Interventions*, 335–361. Rotterdam, Netherlands: Rotterdam University Press.

———. 2006. "Iraq Revolution." In James DeFronzo, ed., *Revolutionary Movements in World History*, 427–440.

Rubin, Barry. 1989. "The Gulf States and the Iran-Iraq War." In Efraim Karsh, ed., *The Iran-Iraq War*, 121–132.

Smith, Craig S. 2004. "Major Creditors in Accord to Waive 80% of Iraq Debt." *New York Times* (November 22). www.nytimes.com.

Tripp, Charles. 2000. *A History of Iraq*. Cambridge, UK: Cambridge University Press.

Weiss, Martin A. 2004. "Iraq: Paris Club Debt Relief." *Congressional Research Service—The Library of Congress*, www.fas.org/sgp/crs/mideast/RS21765.pdf.

Wright, Robin. 1989. "The War and the Spread of Islamic Fundamentalism." In Efraim Karsh, ed., *The Iran-Iraq War*, 110–120.

5

||||||||||||||||||||||||||||||||||||||||||||||||||||||||||||||||||||||||||||||||||||||||||||||||||||||||||

The Invasion of Kuwait and the 1991 Persian Gulf War

The Iranian Revolution led to the Iran–Iraq War. Iraq viewed the billions of dollars provided by Arab nations during the war not as loans but as contributions to the defense of all Arabs against Iranian fundamentalist extremism. When Kuwait demanded repayment and in addition appeared to market oil in excess of an international agreement, thus reducing the price and Iraq's badly needed export income, Iraq accused its monarchy of collaborating with the United States. The crippling of Iraq's economy would, in the view of Iraqi leaders, ultimately degrade the Arab peoples' foremost military power, leaving the Middle East dominated mainly by Israel and pro-Western Arab governments.

The Kuwaiti royal family, which ruled a country of around 1 million people in 1990, was thought by Iraqis to control as much as twenty times the amount demanded as loan repayment from Iraq. This was especially aggravating because most Iraqis viewed Kuwait as a part of their country that Britain had split off as a separate state to serve British interests. Saddam Hussein attempted to resolve the problem by invading and annexing Kuwait as Iraq's nineteenth province. Most nations, however, condemned Iraq's action and demanded immediate withdrawal. The United States, Britain, and other nations assembled an overpowering military force and, with virtually total control of the air, carried out devastating attacks, forcing Iraq to withdraw.

Many Iraqi Shia soldiers, disgusted with what they viewed as the pointless slaughter of their comrades because of Saddam's military folly, rebelled against the regime in the south and were soon joined by Shia religious militants. But loyal troops repressed the southern insurrection, as well as a Kurdish rebellion in the north.

The UN punished Iraq for its seizure of Kuwait by imposing severe economic sanctions, which could be removed only by the supervised destruction or surrender to UN authorities of all weapons of mass destruction and long-range missiles, as well as Iraqi recognition of Kuwaiti sovereignty. Though Iraq was eventually permitted to market some of its oil with the UN controlling use of revenues, the sanctions, which were thought to have contributed to the deaths of several hundred thousand Iraqis due to malnutrition and the degradation of the country's health care system, had not been fully lifted at the time of the 2003 US-led invasion.

Saddam's government survived internal rebellion, assassination plots, and coup attempts, some involving groups aided by the US CIA. The regime also weathered sensational betrayals and scandals within Saddam's own family.

The Invasion of Kuwait

Causes

Economic Difficulties and Debt

The Iran–Iraq War endangered Iraq's health and educational systems, once among the best in the Middle East. During the conflict, much property shifted from state to private ownership, resulting in the growth of a wealthy minority while the lifestyle of the middle and lower classes deteriorated (Farouk-Sluglett and Sluglett 2003: 278). A central postwar problem was that Iraq owed tens of billions of dollars to non-Arab nations and had received approximately $40 billion to $50 billion from Arab countries. The Iraqi government informed Arab nations that had provided assistance that it considered their war funding a non-refundable investment in their own peoples' security. Instead of asking for repayment, Iraqi leaders believed, oil-rich Arab states should contribute to repairing the war damage Iraq suffered (Tripp 2002: 252). Kuwait's continued demand for repayment led Iraqi leaders to accuse its monarchy of betraying the Arab cause by trying to weaken Iraq.

Iraq also asked other oil-producing Arab countries to limit their output in order to drive prices up, allowing Iraq to earn more so that it could pay back loans to those countries on whose technological assistance it depended, and re-build the country. A year after the 1988 Iran–Iraq cease-fire, Iraq's military imports amounted to more than $5 billion, its civilian imports to about $12 billion, and debt repayments to $5 billion. However, its oil income amounted to only about $12 billion, resulting in an approximately $9–$10 billion budget shortfall (Marr 2004: 219).

Kuwait

Saudi Arabia appeared willing to forgive Iraq's debt, but Kuwait refused (Marr 2004: 220). Iraq accused Kuwait and the United Arab Emirates (UAE) of producing oil beyond national quotas set by the Organization of Petroleum Exporting Countries (OPEC) so that Iraq would earn less for its oil (Hiro 1992: 88–90). OPEC nations were supposed to limit production in 1990 to 22 million barrels per day but in fact were marketing 24 million, with Kuwait and the UAE responsible for 75 percent of the excess production (Marr 2004: 221). Oil in January 1990 was about $21 per barrel but by March was under $18, falling in the summer to around $11. According to Hiro (1992: 88), Iraqi foreign minister Tariq Aziz stated that for every dollar less in the price per barrel of oil, Iraq's annual revenue dropped by about $1 billion. Saddam claimed that economic warfare was being waged against his country.

Other disagreements between Iraq and Kuwait concerned the location of their mutual border and the possession of two Kuwaiti-controlled islands, Warba and Bubiyan. Iraq wanted Kuwait to turn over the islands as well as territory near the Iraqi port of Umm Qasr to allow it more land access to the Persian Gulf.

Changes in the International Environment

As Iraq faced enormous economic problems, revolutions in Eastern Europe replaced communist regimes with less friendly governments. And since the Soviet Union was experiencing its own economic crisis, it could not provide much assistance to Iraq.

Further, other countries undermined Iraq's weapons development plans. Shipments of equipment, apparently related to Iraq's nuclear weapons program, were intercepted. And Iraq experienced a blow to its missile program when Dr. Gerald Bull, a famous Canadian ballistics and missile engineer, was shot and killed entering his Brussels hotel room on March 22, 1990. Bull had designed a supergun for Iraq that when completed could have launched explosive shells hundreds of miles, and he was helping the Iraqis improve the range of their surface-to-surface missiles. Many believed that Israeli Mossad intelligence agents were responsible for the killing (Hiro 1992: 71).

Decision to Occupy Kuwait

Iraq's leaders believed that after their country, at enormous cost, had greatly diminished the threat of Iranian-inspired fundamentalism, the United States and Great Britain turned sharply against Iraq, using their most dependent and compliant allies among the Arab states, the oil monarchies, to impair Iraq's reconstruction and economic revival. Kuwait seemed to be playing a key role by demanding repayment of wartime aid and driving down the price of oil. Furthermore, the Iraqis claimed that Kuwait was drilling into the southern end of the Rumaila oil field, which extended into Kuwaiti territory, and extracting Iraqi oil (Hiro 1992: 88–89).

Despite the potential benefits of seizing Kuwait, why did Iraq believe that it could succeed? Saddam expected that his popularity among the people in many Arab countries would prevent their ruling elites from interfering. Furthermore, Iraqi leaders believed most Arabs had negative views of Kuwait as the epitome of a puppet monarchy sitting on enormous oil wealth, as much as 86 percent of the proven oil reserves of Iraq with about one-twentieth of Iraq's population (excluding the approximately one-half of its residents who were foreign workers or family members). Since Kuwait had a small population, the Kuwaiti ruling family could afford relatively low prices for its oil, regardless of the damage to other countries that desperately needed higher revenue because of their much larger populations. Instead of Kuwait's oil wealth being available to the

Arab people as a whole, the ruling family could decide how much to share with the Arab poor in other countries, or spend on Kuwait's citizens, or maintain in foreign investments benefiting oil-consuming nations. Saddam believed that many Arabs preferred Kuwait's oil to be in the hands of the Iraq republic rather than the Kuwaiti ruling family and the foreign interests it was widely perceived to serve.

In regard to the United Nations, Iraqi leaders may have counted on a continuation of its pattern of inaction and feeble measures. From their point of view, Israel had been relatively free to defy the UN and ignore its resolutions regarding territories the Israeli army captured in the 1967 war. Further, the UN was relatively ineffective in dealing with internationally condemned US actions regarding Nicaragua in the 1980s, the US occupation of Grenada on October 25, 1983, or the US invasion of Panama on December 20, 1989 (Blum 2004: 305–314). Although the Panama attack had resulted in hundreds of casualties and was condemned by the Organization of American States and criticized in the UN General Assembly, the United States was successful in removing a government it opposed so that one viewed as more favorable to US interests, in particular the Panama Canal, could take its place. Iraqi leaders apparently thought they were entitled to follow the US example and use military force to deal with what they perceived as the immensely greater threat to Iraq's well-being posed by the actions of the Kuwaiti monarchy.

Preceding the final decision to invade, Iraq appealed to the Kuwaiti regime in July 1990 to respect the OPEC oil production quota and also brought its complaints to the Arab League. Around the same time, battle-hardened units of the Republican Guard moved toward the Kuwait border.

Concerned about a possible US military response, Saddam held a meeting with US Ambassador to Iraq April Glaspie on July 25 (Hiro 1992: 91–94). According to an Iraqi-released transcript of the interview published in the *New York Times* on September 23, 1990, Saddam describes Iraq's complaints about Kuwait's behavior. He states that "when planned and deliberate policy forces the price of oil down without good commercial reasons, then that means another war against Iraq. Because military war kills people by bleeding them, and economic war kills their humanity by depriving them of their chance to have a good standard of living. As you know, we gave rivers of blood in a war that lasted eight years. . . . We do not accept that anyone . . . (should be allowed to) . . . injure Iraqi pride or the Iraqi right to have a high standard of living. Kuwait and the U.A.E. were at the front of this policy aimed at lowering Iraq's position and depriving its people of higher economic standards. . . . The price at one stage had dropped to $12 a barrel and a reduction in the modest Iraqi budget of $6 billion to $7 billion is a disaster." According to the transcript, Glaspie expresses concern about the large number of Iraqi troops near the Kuwait border and indicates that the dispute should be resolved through negotiations. However, the transcript shows that instead of providing firm warnings against Iraqi military action or indicating US use of force in retaliation, Glaspie is reported as making statements such as, "You should have the opportunity to rebuild your country. But we have no opinion on the Arab-Arab conflicts, like your border disagreement with Kuwait." Glaspie then asks about Iraq's intentions regarding Kuwait. Saddam replies that Iraqis want to find a fair solution but that their patience is "running out." He describes the policies of Kuwait and the UAE as "harming even the milk our children drink," the pensions of war widows, "and the pensions of the orphans who lost their parents." Saddam states that Iraq agreed to a meeting arranged by Saudi Arabia at Jidda on July 10 and 11 among the oil ministers of Iraq, Kuwait, and other Arab oil-producing countries. He indicates that although Iraq compromised to reach a settlement, within about two days the Kuwaiti oil minister appeared to contradict the agreement.

Saddam goes on to describe how the "oil people," who were supposed to help other Arabs like the Egyptian people, "were mean beyond belief" and that "some of them are disliked . . . because of their greed." He later specifically refers to "Kuwaiti greed." The transcript concludes with Saddam describing another forthcoming meeting with Kuwaiti officials to be hosted at Jidda on July 30 to try to work out differences. This appears to reassure Glaspie that a peaceful solution could be reached. Saddam states that Iraq would not do anything if the meeting with the Kuwaitis produced hope, but warns that "if we are unable to find a solution, then it will be natural that Iraq will not accept death."

The transcript suggests that Glaspie was diplomatically trying to ignore Saddam's warnings about resorting to force and instead responding mainly to his positive statements. Saddam also seems to respond selectively by focusing on Glaspie's statements about the United States' not having an opinion on inter-Arab conflicts. While the ambassador does stress the desirability of using nonviolent means to resolve the conflict, it is possible that a clear threat of US military retaliation might have prevented the Iraqi attack on Kuwait or at least limited it to occupying only disputed territory.

Marr (2004: 228) states that the Kuwaitis might have been willing to compromise on some issues at the July 30 Jidda meeting, but the Iraqis insisted that Kuwait stop demanding repayment of its wartime assistance, provide Iraq with reconstruction aid, agree to territorial concessions, and pay for the oil Iraq claimed Kuwait stole from the Rumaila field. Failure to resolve the disagreements led to Iraq's decision to attack Kuwait.

At first Iraqi leaders may have planned for a limited attack in which Iraqi forces would seize only a northern thirty- to fifty-kilometer span of Kuwait bordering Iraq and the two disputed offshore islands (Marr 2004: 226). But this would have left the Kuwaiti royal family in control of the rest of Kuwait and would not have resolved the debt issue.

The decision to totally occupy Kuwait was most likely made either by Saddam alone or by him and a few close associates. Iraqi deputy prime minister Tariq Aziz claimed that when he first heard of the full invasion plan, he brought up the possibility of US military intervention by stating that "the Americans may come to Saudi Arabia and counterattack. Why don't we go all the way and take Saudi Arabia too?" (Cockburn and Cockburn 1999: 8). By linking his concern about a US military response with the unrealistic suggestion of conquering Saudi Arabia at the same time as Kuwait, Aziz hoped that Saddam would be warned but not offended. Instead of understanding his intended point, Saddam mildly scolded him for proposing such an extreme course of action. After Saddam was captured by US forces in 2003, he told his Arabic-speaking FBI interrogator that before making the final decision to seize Kuwait he had sent Iraq's foreign minister to Kuwait to try to find solutions to problems between the two countries. But according to Saddam, after Kuwait's ruler told the Iraqi foreign minister "that he would not stop doing what he was doing until he turned every Iraqi woman into a $10 prostitute," he decided to invade (CBS *60 Minutes* 2008; Tyson 2008).

Invasion

The Iraqi invasion commenced on August 2, 1990, and Kuwait was completely occupied within about twenty-four hours (Hiro 1992: 102–103). Most of the ruling family, including Kuwait's leader, Shaik Jabir al-Sabah, fled to Saudi Arabia, along with about 300,000 other Kuwaitis (Tripp 2002: 252). The invasion was estimated to have cost the lives of more than 1,000 Kuwaitis (Marr 2004: 234). While Republican Guard units were involved in the attack, much of the occupation force was made up of conscripted Shia Arab and Kurdish soldiers (Cockburn and Cockburn 1999: 13).

A pro-Iraqi provisional government was established. But within a matter of days, Iraq declared that Kuwait would be annexed as its nineteenth province to reverse one of the great crimes of British imperialism.

The reaction of most governments to Iraq's occupation of Kuwait, including some Arab regimes, was much more hostile than Iraqi leaders anticipated. In many countries both Kuwaiti and Iraqi assets were frozen. The UN Security Council passed Resolution 660 on the same day as the invasion, calling for Iraq to immediately withdraw. Resolution 661, passed on August 6, banned all trade and financial transactions with Iraq except for "food, medicine, and the necessities of life" (Marr 2004: 231). Iraqi oil pipelines through Turkey and Saudi Arabia were shut down.

Saudi Arabia and the other Arab oil monarchies were shocked at the possibility that Iraq would target them next. With the addition of Kuwait's oil reserves and financial assets, Iraq could challenge Saudi Arabia's leading role in OPEC. The Saudis agreed to allow US forces into their territory for protection and for future military operations against Iraq.

The Bush administration began sending US forces to Saudi Arabia within days of the invasion, first ostensibly to protect the kingdom in Operation Desert Shield and then to prepare for an offensive against Iraqi forces in Operation Desert Storm. The number of US military personnel in Saudi Arabia grew to over half a million in about six months (Tripp 2002: 253).

The Arab League convened in Cairo on August 7 to consider the Kuwait situation. The Arab states generally most dependent on the United States for military or other assistance, such as Saudi Arabia, the other Persian Gulf monarchies, and Egypt, along with Syria, which had favored Iran during the Iran–Iraq War, and Morocco, opposed Iraq's action and were inclined to support US-led military intervention. In contrast, Yemen, Sudan, Algeria, the Palestinians, and Jordan tended to oppose US involvement. Twelve out of twenty league governments voted for the Iraqis to withdraw and for the return of the

Kuwaiti ruling family. Some also expressed a willingness to send their own armed forces to defend Saudi Arabia.

Saddam responded that any Iraqi consideration of withdrawal could occur only after Israel withdrew from occupied Palestinian, Syrian, and Lebanese territories and Syria exited the parts of Lebanon it occupied, events that had no chance of occurring in the foreseeable future. Faced with mounting international opposition, Iraq attempted to guarantee that its huge neighbor Iran, hundreds of thousands of whose soldiers it had recently killed in the eight-year war, would remain neutral in any coming military confrontation.

Iranian leaders, who believed that the United States had encouraged Iraq to attack Iran in 1980 and that US aid to Iraq had prevented Iran from winning the war, agreed to stay out of the conflict over Kuwait for a price. In return for Iranian neutrality, Iraq agreed to accept Iran's position regarding sharing the Shatt al-Arab in the August 15, 1990, final settlement of the Iran–Iraq War. The Iranian reconciliation with Iraq had a surprising aspect: Once the war began, Iran allowed many Iraqi aircraft to take refuge in its territory (Gordon 1991; Hiro 1992: 338–339).

On August 28, Iraq designated Kuwait as its nineteenth province. The islands of Warba and Bubiyan, as well as the northern span of Kuwait, however, were detached and joined to Basra province, indicating that if Iraq was forced to give up the rest of Kuwait, it intended to hold on to these territories. Iraq was able to confiscate only about $2 billion from Kuwait's central bank. Iraqi security agents and soldiers also removed industrial, electronic, and communications equipment, and other valuable property for shipment to Iraq. With pipelines closed, Iraq's exports declined by 97 percent (Marr 2004: 234), and imports dropped by 90 percent. Iraq resorted to rationing as prices surged.

The 1991 Persian Gulf War

Decision for War

After Iraq refused to withdraw, the George H. W. Bush administration decided on October 30, 1990, to dramatically increase US forces in Saudi Arabia to shift from simply defending the kingdom (Operation Desert Shield) to attacking Iraq (Operation Desert Storm). At the request of the United States, the UN Security Council voted twelve to two (Cuba and Yemen opposing, and China abstaining) in favor of Resolution 678, which authorized the use of force to end the Iraqi occupation of Kuwait. The deadline was January 15, 1991, giving Iraq about forty-five days to withdraw.

Having granted Iran its territorial demands and thereby securing Iranian noninterference in the conflict over Kuwait, Saddam may have been reluctant to withdraw without some significant gains or a fight. Underestimating coalition airpower and weapons technology, Iraqi leaders hoped their forces could inflict unacceptably high losses on US-led forces. The Iraqi regime positioned Republican Guard divisions to defend central and northern Iraq and impede an attack from the south.

The war began on January 16 (January 17 Iraqi time) with a devastating air attack (Hiro 1992: 320), far beyond anything the Iraqis had experienced in the war with Iran, designed to wreck major components of the country's infrastructure and destroy military equipment so Iraq would lack the capability to effectively resist the coalition ground attack. For six weeks coalition air forces attacked Iraqi air force bases, command centers, military-industrial facilities, power stations, and oil refineries. Iraq's communications systems were disrupted and production of electricity dropped by about 75 percent (Marr 2004: 235). Powerless to counter the aerial assault, Iraq launched mobile ground-to-ground missiles against Israel (not a member of the US coalition, but in whose interest the Iraqis believed the war against them was being waged) and against Saudi Arabia and US military forces there. The Iraqis apparently hoped to provoke Israel into attacking Iraq, making it difficult for Egypt and Syria to remain members of the US-led coalition. Israel, however, did not militarily retaliate.

Another desperate Iraqi plan was an attempt to start the ground war while its units still had significant capability to inflict many casualties on coalition soldiers, forcing a negotiated settlement that would achieve some of Iraq's goals. Thus Iraqi forces went on the offensive, attacking coalition forces in Saudi Arabia's Eastern Province on January 29 and taking and holding the Saudi city of Khafji for about two days. But after heavy losses from air attacks, Iraqi units withdrew. The fighting at Khafji confirmed that control of the air and weapons technology superiority were decisive factors in a largely flat, open environment.

Following the failure of the Iraqi ground offensive, the USSR put forward a proposal on February 21 stating that Iraq would withdraw from Kuwait in return for the UN's lifting the trade restrictions once the withdrawal was two-thirds completed. The United States rejected this and instead gave Iraq one week to withdraw unconditionally from Kuwait without any fixed date for when sanctions might be ended. Iraq's offer to withdraw from Kuwait further demoralized Iraqi soldiers stationed there by raising the question of why they should risk death to defend a territory they were going to abandon anyway.

Beginning on February 22 the Iraqis began setting fire to or blowing up about eight hundred Kuwaiti oil wells, storage tanks, and refineries. This appeared to be mainly an attempt to use smoke from the fires to interfere with coalition air operations and use of precision guided weapons.

The coalition ground offensive, which began on February 24, had several main components. One was a deception that was apparently successful in convincing Iraqi defenders that the main attack on their positions in Kuwait would be an amphibious assault from the sea. But the real attack came by land from Saudi Arabia and with relative ease broke through Iraqi defenses degraded by weeks of aerial bombardment. Thousands surrendered and others attempted to flee to Iraq. Virtually defenseless against air attacks, many were killed on the road leading north, the so-called highway of death from Kuwait City to Basra.

Another coalition assault advanced rapidly into the Iraqi southern desert from the west in an attempt to cut off and destroy or force the surrender of the Republican Guard divisions that had been deployed to defend against a coalition invasion of Iraq from the south. On February 27, as units of three Republican Guard divisions attempted to escape north to avoid encirclement, the Second Brigade of the Iraqi Republican Guard Medina Luminous Division, equipped mainly with Russian-made T-72 and T-55 tanks, was assigned to delay the advance of the US 1st Armored Division and its powerful Abrams M1A1 tanks. The Iraqi commander positioned his tanks on a low ridge so they would be difficult to see or be hit from long distances by the American tank guns, which had a range of about two miles, twice that of the Iraqi tanks. This allowed the Iraqis to briefly slow the US advance in what turned out to be the biggest tank battle of the war, the so-called Battle of Medina Ridge. The attacking US forces included antitank Apache helicopter gunships and air force A-10 tank-killer jets. According to one of the participants in the battle, Sergeant John Saglione of the US First Armored Division, "Every time we shot, you could see a massive explosion. . . . The turrets were flipping forty, fifty feet in the air. Eleven tons of steel just—it was incredible to see a gun tube and the turret just spinning up in the air and landing hundreds of yards away from the vehicles. We took very few prisoners at Medina Ridge, very few. . . . Most of the people I saw were dead. . . . I have never seen such destruction in my life" (PBS 1997). About three hundred Iraqi tanks and other armored vehicles were destroyed at Medina Ridge along with many of their crews, while one American was killed from friendly fire and four tanks were damaged from Iraqi hits.

The Battle of Medina Ridge clearly demonstrated the immense technological superiority of US over Iraqi forces, but also the courage of Republican Guard soldiers. This sacrifice in the face of overwhelming odds might in part explain the insurgency against US forces following the 2003 invasion. At the time, the battle seemed to show that nothing could prevent a total coalition victory.

End of the War

The coalition offensive, however, did not press on to annihilate the Baathist government (Hiro 1992: 392–393). UN Security Council Resolution 686 of March 2 stated that Iraq would have to accept all of the twelve previous UN resolutions concerning Kuwait before a cease-fire would be declared. This included Iraq's agreeing to abolish all laws having to do with the annexation of Kuwait, release all coalition and Kuwaiti prisoners, pay for war damage, and return all Kuwaiti property. On behalf of the Iraqi government, Tariq Aziz immediately agreed. On March 5 Iraq eliminated all laws relating to the annexation of Kuwait and agreed to send back stolen property and pay war reparations. In response, on April 3 the UN approved Resolution 687, which ended the war.

Despite the defeat, Saddam's regime survived for several reasons. First, the UN authorized only the removal of Iraqi forces from Kuwait and restoration of the preinvasion government, not the conquest of Iraq or the elimination of its government. Second, it is doubtful that the coalition would have held together, especially its Arab components, if the United States had proceeded to a full-scale invasion of Iraq. Third, the United States likely intended to preserve a significant Iraqi military as a counterweight to Iran. Finally, there was concern that the destruction of the Baathist regime might result in the disintegration of

Iraq, leading to Iran's seizing the oil-rich Shia southern part of Iraq or the establishment of Iraqi Kurdistan as an independent nation, which might destabilize Turkey and Iran by encouraging their Kurdish populations to rebel.

The Baathist regime attempted to portray the outcome of the war as at least a partial victory for Iraq since it had faced the military forces of thirty-one nations, including those with the most advanced weaponry, and survived.

Impacts of the War

Costs

Estimates of Iraqis killed in the 1991 Persian Gulf War range from under 30,000 (Marr 2004: 239) to 100,000 or more soldiers and civilians and as many as 300,000 wounded (Farouk-Sluglett and Sluglett 2003: 288; Hiro 1992: 396). Iraq lost approximately 2,100 tanks in Kuwait, about 90 percent simply abandoned (Cockburn and Cockburn 1999: 14). Major Republican Guard units, as well as much of the regular army, escaped coalition forces.

Iraq failed to solve its debt problem, was ordered to pay billions of dollars in war damage reparations, and was handicapped by UN-imposed sanctions. Billions of dollars of its industrial, transportation, and communications infrastructure had been destroyed (Farouk-Sluglett and Sluglett 2003: 288).

As conditions deteriorated, thousands of Iraq's best educated left the country, further impairing the economy and government bureaucracies, whose task it was to optimize the delivery of diminished resources to the people. The sanctions, reduced government services, and seemingly irrational international restrictions that, for example, allowed some components of health care equipment to enter the country only to be rendered useless because other essential parts deemed to have a dual-use function (medical or possibly military) were barred, led to the deaths of tens of thousands (Cockburn and Cockburn 1999: 299).

The Kuwait war increased Iraq's international isolation. This became more significant late in 1991 when the Soviet Union, a longtime Iraq supporter, disintegrated. The new Russian state faced its own extreme economic difficulties and its leaders seemed to have less sympathy for Iraq.

Much of the ordnance used by the United States and Britain was made of depleted uranium instead of tungsten (Bertell 1999: 1). Depleted uranium anti-tank shell hits often dispersed a mist of tiny radioactive particles into the air. Those who salvaged metal from armored vehicles destroyed by these weapons were also likely exposed to radiation. The destruction of chemical weapons may further have damaged the environment. Many Iraqis and US Gulf War veterans suffered health problems possibly due to either radiation or toxic chemicals.

Restrictions on Sovereignty

UN constraints on Iraq's sovereignty were set forth in Security Council Resolution 687, adopted on April 3, 1991 (United Nations 1991). This resolution, "the longest and most comprehensive in UN history" (Marr 2004: 240), required Iraq to accept a permanent border with Kuwait, to be determined by a special international committee. It also mandated that a UN peacekeeping force be stationed on the fixed boundary line. Section C, paragraph 8, stated that "Iraq shall unconditionally accept the destruction, removal, or rendering harmless, under international supervision, of: (a) All chemical and biological weapons" and related materials including production equipment, and "(b) All ballistic missiles with a range greater than 150 kilometers" along with parts and manufacturing facilities. Paragraph 9 required that Iraq provide the UN "Secretary-General, within fifteen days of the adoption of the present resolution, a declaration of the locations, amounts and types of all the items specified in paragraph 8 and agree to urgent, on site inspection." Paragraph 12 stipulated that Iraq agree "unconditionally not to acquire or develop nuclear weapons" or material related to the development of such weapons and that Iraq provide the UN secretary-general and the director-general of the International Atomic Energy Agency with the locations, amounts, and types of all nuclear-related items.

Section E stated that Iraq was responsible for all debts existing before August 2, 1990, and for "any direct loss, damage, including environmental damage and depletion of natural resources, or injury to foreign Governments, nationals and corporations, as a result of Iraq's unlawful invasion and occupation of Kuwait." A percentage of Iraq's oil revenues was to pay its debt and war reparations, "taking into account the requirements of the people of Iraq." Section H, paragraph 32, "requires Iraq to inform the Security Council that it will not commit or support any act of international terrorism or allow any organization directed towards the commission of such acts to operate within its territory and to condemn unequivocally and renounce all acts, methods and practices of terrorism." Iraqi compliance with the provisions of the resolution would be reviewed every sixty days to determine whether the sanctions should be lifted. After Iraq accepted Resolution 687, coalition troops were withdrawn from Iraq on May 9.

The sanctions remained in effect to some degree until the end of the Baathist regime. The issue of whether Iraq was satisfactorily fulfilling its Resolution 687 obligations not only affected the continuation of sanctions, but ultimately played a major role in the rationale given by the George W. Bush administration for invading Iraq in 2003.

The 1991 Gulf War and 9/11

One of the major consequences of the Kuwait war was the reorientation against the United States of an organization, Al Qaeda, created in 1988 by Islamic fighters against Soviet forces in Afghanistan. A Saudi volunteer, Osama bin Laden, the son of a billionaire construction company owner, and his associates created a data set and communication network, Al Qaeda, "the base" for the thousands of foreign volunteers who had fought in Afghanistan. Islamists ultimately won and Soviet forces withdrew in 1989.

Bin Laden, who embraced the concept that Muslims lost their former power because they ceased waging jihad against foreign imperialists and the corrupt regimes in Muslim countries that served their interests, returned in 1989 to Saudi Arabia, where he was initially regarded as a hero. But soon Iraq invaded Kuwait and appeared to threaten Saudi Arabia. Bin Laden, hostile to Iraq's Baath Party government and Saddam, offered to recruit as many as 35,000 Al Qaeda members to defend Saudi Arabia. The Saudi royal family declined bin Laden's offer and instead allowed the United States to use Saudi Arabia as a base of operations. Neither the United States nor the monarchy wanted a reconcentrating of tens of thousands of battle-hardened Islamic fundamentalist fighters, self-confident after defeating the Soviets, on Saudi territory.

Having just fought a long war to drive the Soviets from one Islamic nation, bin Laden and other Sunni fundamentalists were outraged by the presence of non-Islamic armed forces in the nation with the holiest sites of Islam. Bin Laden claimed that the United States was establishing a permanent occupation of the Middle East. Because of his criticisms, he was forced to leave the country.

Al Qaeda launched attacks against the United States, including the 1993 truck bombing of New York's World Trade Center. In August 1998, Al Qaeda associates bombed US embassies in Kenya and Tanzania, and in 2000, suicide bombers using a small boat struck the USS *Cole*. Then on September 11, 2001, Al Qaeda carried out what has been described as the most destructive terrorist attack in history by using hijacked passenger airliners to destroy the World Trade Center towers in New York and to attack the Pentagon in Washington, DC.

Anxious to strike back at someone, many Americans would support the Bush administration's decision to attack Iraq in 2003, although evidence would later prove the country had no role in 9/11. But ironically it was a consequence of Iraq's invasion of Kuwait, the huge deployment of US armed forces to Saudi Arabia triggering Al Qaeda's 9/11 terrorism, that provided the impetus and opportunity for the Bush administration's occupation of Iraq.

Rebellions in the South and North

The outcome of the Kuwait invasion undermined regime support, particularly among demoralized Shia soldiers from southern Iraq. Many became enraged at Saddam for provoking a war in which thousands of their comrades died and they suffered a humiliating defeat (Cockburn and Cockburn 1999: 14). Streaming north from Kuwait, they rose against the government in what became known as the intifada, or uprising, beginning on March 1, 1991, and lasting until about April 1, 1991. The southern insurrection was soon accompanied by a Kurdish rising in the north (Allawi 2006: 45–48).

The rebels were encouraged by the perception that Saddam's government was politically weakened and by the expectation that the United States would provide help to the rebellion because President George H. W. Bush had called upon the Iraqi armed forces and people to overthrow Saddam (Marr 2004: 242–243). The failure to provide effective assistance to the rebels led to a deep sense of betrayal against the United States among many who had participated in the intifada.

One report stated that the relatively spontaneous rebellion in Basra on March 1 started when an Iraqi soldier entering the city's central square fired his tank gun on a large Saddam portrait (Marr 2004: 243–244). Rebellions then broke out on or before March 4 in Najaf and Kufa, and on March 7 in Karbala. In about one week, rebels controlled parts or all of a number of cities and towns south of Baghdad province (Hiro 1992: 400). In Basra city mutinous soldiers were the main rebel force. But Shia militants took the lead elsewhere, as in Najaf, where rebels called for an Islamic revolution.

The southern intifada, which was almost exclusively urban, failed in part because most Iraqi soldiers remained loyal to the regime. Since there were apparently no cases in which entire military units, such as whole regiments, joined the intifada (Marr 2004: 246–248), the rebellion lacked the coordination or level of weaponry that such defections might have provided. Popular support for the rebellion waned because of its anarchic destructiveness and revenge killings of regime officials that appalled large numbers of people, Sunnis and Shia alike, and because secularly oriented Shia feared that some rebels sought to impose a fundamentalist Islamic regime. Finally, the uprising was crushed in part because the United States permitted the regime to use helicopter gunships in coordination with loyal ground forces to repress the rebels.

The Kurdish rebellion began on March 5 in Raniyya, a city of about 50,000, spread to Sulaimaniyya on March 7, where four hundred or more Baathists were killed (Marr 2004: 250), and reached its greatest extent with the seizure of Kirkuk on March 20. The northern intifada involved both spontaneous participation and planning and leadership by the KDP and the PUK (Cockburn and Cockburn 1999: 18). Furthermore, much of the proregime Kurdish militia, the Fursan, alienated by the brutality of the Anfal campaign against fellow Kurds, defected to the rebel side (Hiro 1992: 404–409). The goal of northern rebels was to establish self-government for Kurdistan, and only secondarily to change the government in Baghdad.

The Kurdish Front, composed of the KDP, the PUK, and five smaller parties, declared the creation of a legislative council for regional self-government on March 13. Since Kirkuk's mixed Arab, Kurdish, and Turkoman population did not join the intifada, the Front launched an attack on the city, which, after an estimated 3,000 casualties, fell to the rebels.

In contrast to the south and north, the central provinces of Iraq remained relatively quiet. But Iranian support for the southern intifada offended Iraqi nationalists, who, after the killings of hundreds of regime supporters, feared more massacres if the rebels succeeded. The Kurdish seizure of Kirkuk also shocked Sunni Arabs into launching a major effort to repress the northern rebellion. Thus many Iraqis, regardless of feelings about Saddam or the Kuwait disaster, fought the rebellions to protect a flawed regime against the threat of something they perceived as far worse. In some Iraqi military units there was also a desire for revenge against rebels considered traitors who had stabbed the nation in the back after its defeat by the US-led coalition.

By March 29, after three weeks of fighting, the regime crushed the southern intifada. The rebels probably killed thousands of people, but the number who perished in suppressing the rebellion may have exceeded 30,000 (Marr 2004: 251–252). Government forces using helicopter gunships attacked Kurdish rebels in Kirkuk on March 28 and retook the city. The regime also recaptured Arbil and Sulaimaniyya and held all of Iraqi Kurdistan's large urban areas by early April.

Baghdad Loses Control of Iraqi Kurdistan

Baghdad's victory in the north caused as many as 2 million Kurds to flee their homes, most heading for Iran and some to Turkey (Marr 2004: 253). Many refugees were unprepared for the very cold conditions in the mountains and perished. The plight of the refugees provoked concern from around the world. In desperation, Kurdish leaders appealed to both the United States and Baghdad for assistance.

The Iraqi government feared that the size of the humanitarian crisis might result in coalition attacks and was anxious to find a solution. European coalition members wanted to help the refugees without resuming the war. Coalition assistance, Operation Provide Comfort (OPC), began with US planes dropping supplies to refugees on April 7. To protect relief planes, the United States banned Iraqi aircraft from flying north of the thirty-sixth parallel latitude, which covered much Kurdish territory, including Arbil. The air drop had only limited success. On April 16, the United States decided to send ground troops into Iraqi Kurdistan to provide safety for refugees in a security zone near the Turkish border. After Baghdad granted amnesty to Kurdish rebels and agreed to allow the UN to establish humanitarian relief centers in the Kurdish region, most Kurds were able to go home.

The Kurdish leadership decided to negotiate with Baghdad now that refugees were returning home and its cause had earned sustained international attention. But opposing views on the same issues that wrecked many previous negotiations, such as the regime's refusal to allow Kirkuk to become part of the Kurdish autonomous region, led the Kurds to break off talks in January 1992. Fighting resumed and Kurdish forces were able to take several towns. In the fall Baghdad, which could no longer provide its ground troops with air support due to the new northern no-fly zone, agreed to a cease-fire and withdrew its forces from Sulaimaniyya and Arbil but held on to Kirkuk. The Baath regime decided to concentrate its forces on maintaining the most crucial areas of Iraq, the Sunni-dominated central provinces, the oil-rich Shia south, and the Kirkuk area. Baghdad attempted to limit trade with the Kurdish region, mistakenly anticipating that under economic pressure the Kurds would decide to reintegrate with the rest of Iraq and settle for a reduced level of autonomy. But the Kurds held fast and, for the first time since they had been promised self-government by the victorious powers following World War I, finally had a totally autonomous, in reality de facto independent homeland in what had been a large part of northern Iraq. And so another outcome of the regime's failed attempt to annex Kuwait was the loss of most of its Kurdish-speaking areas.

From Defeat to the Eve of Occupation

Political and Social Adaptation

Baghdad pardoned surviving rebels of the southern intifada in April 1991. But the Baath Party in the south had lost many mid- and lower-level party leaders. New party elections in August 1991 replaced some of them.

Around the country people began to rely more heavily on extended kin to adapt to the decline in state resources resulting from the country's debt and UN sanctions. The regime recognized the increased role of tribal networks in people's welfare and in maintaining government control in areas where Baath Party personnel had been decimated during the intifada.

Since most Arab nations turned against Iraq during the Kuwait crisis, the regime moved even farther away from pan-Arabism. Saddam portrayed Iraq's predicament as the result of a coordinated effort by Western imperialist nations and Zionists to besiege Iraq, overthrow its anti-imperialist government, and ultimately gain control of Iraq's oil. The Iraqi people were asked to courageously endure hardships for the sake of humanity with the understanding that Iraq was being targeted because it resisted imperialism. Religious imagery was employed to depict Saddam as divinely selected to lead the anti-imperialist struggle.

Sanctions

Restrictions on oil sales and trade were to remain in effect until Iraq fulfilled Resolution 687 requirements. Although the resolution was approved by a majority of UN Security Council members, pressure from several especially powerful nations could preserve the sanctions long after other governments that originally supported them no longer did. Resolution 688, which required Iraq to end repression of its people, intensified intrusions on Iraq sovereignty. The US coalition used this resolution to justify requiring Iraq to observe the northern no-fly zone. Then in August 1992, to protect southern Shia, it was used to legitimize banning Iraqi aircraft from flying south of the thirty-second parallel.

Despite vigorous objections, the Iraqi National Assembly was forced on November 10, 1994, to accept the UN border commission's decisions favorable to Kuwait on land and sea boundaries, as specified in UN Resolution 833.

The most disputed aspect of the cease-fire agreement was UN inspections for detecting and eliminating Iraq's weapons of mass destruction (WMD), which began in May 1991. According to Marr (2004: 267), "By the end of June [1991] Saddam Hussein had set up a high-level concealment plan to destroy, in secret, much of the forbidden weaponry in order to hide and preserve those elements Iraqis considered essential." This might have prevented inspectors from discovering how far advanced work on WMD had been and how quickly Iraq could reconstruct WMD once circumstances became more favorable. The Iraqis appeared to be engaged in a process of partial compliance and disclosure, mixed with selective deception, frustrating UN inspectors and periodically leading to sensational confrontations and punitive US military strikes.

Iraqi reluctance to fully comply with UN requirements was partly due to the belief that information on Iraq's weapons programs, key scientific personnel, and important military and security installations, whether relevant to WMD or not, was being provided by the UN inspectors to the US CIA and Israel. For example, in an incident on September 24, 1991, UN inspectors showed up at the Iraqi Central Records Office in Baghdad to photograph documents. Iraqi officials soon arrived to demand the return of the copies, stating that they included the identities and personal information on a number of Iraqi scientists who they feared would be targeted by Israeli Mossad intelligence agents for assassination (Cockburn and Cockburn 1999: 105–106). Iraqi concerns achieved some credibility when an inspector was accused of repeatedly sending information on findings to the CIA and Israel (Farouk-Sluglett and Sluglett 2003: 293).

Reports were submitted every six months by the UN Special Commission on Disarmament (UNSCOM) and the International Atomic Energy Agency (IAEA) to the UN on Iraqi compliance with Resolution 687 regarding satisfactory inspections and sufficient proof of the location and destruction of all WMD and related equipment. As long as these agencies refused to certify that Iraqi compliance was satisfactory, sanctions would remain in effect. Between 1991 and 1994 the IAEA documented three Iraqi uranium-enrichment processes being pursued among at least some of the forty identified nuclear research operations (Marr 2004: 267). But after the main nuclear facilities were destroyed in 1992, the IAEA was able to certify that Iraq's nuclear project had been shut down.

UNSCOM disposed of more than 148,000 tons of chemical weapons materials, including sarin, mustard gas, and tabun. In October 1994, however, the former head of Iraqi military intelligence, Wafiq al-Samarrai, defected and claimed that, unknown to UN inspectors, the CIA, or British intelligence, Iraq had produced the extremely deadly nerve poison VX (Cockburn and Cockburn 1999: 111).

Iraq admitted that it had a biological weapons project but claimed that it had destroyed all toxic agents. UNSCOM inspections did not detect any remaining biological warfare materials. However, suspicions that Iraq was concealing some WMD programs or materials, and assertions that it was not providing satisfactory lists or evidence of the weapons it claimed to have destroyed, contributed to the maintenance of UN sanctions.

Sanctions' Effects

Since the sanctions prevented weapons or weapons-related technologies from reaching Iraq, the capabilities of Iraq's armed forces deteriorated. Oil production dropped by about 85 percent between 1990 and 1991 (Marr 2004: 268). Per capita income, which had been about $2,000 in 1989, declined to $609 by 1992. Many highly educated middle-class Iraqis who had skills they could market internationally, especially to other Arab countries, left Iraq. One estimate indicated that 3 million Iraqis were living outside the country by 1996, close to 15 percent of the population (Farouk-Sluglett and Sluglett 2003: 294). Often less competent people were left to run the country's institutions, delivering the meager government resources available and the permitted humanitarian aid. The government provided food rations, which helped many avoid starvation.

Agricultural productivity, important because of Iraq's reduced ability to pay for imported food, was impaired by restrictions on purchasing foreign agricultural machinery, fertilizers, pesticides, and other materials that might also have a military application. Medical supplies declined and infant mortality climbed to rates characteristic of Iraq forty years earlier (Tripp 2002: 261). Child mortality in general was estimated at five times the presanction level by 1995 (Marr 2004: 268). Inflation was devastating. Before the war one Iraqi dinar had been the equivalent of about $3.20, but by 1996 the ratio was approximately 2,600 dinars to $1.

The UN had expected the harsh sanctions to quickly force Iraq to agree to satisfactory inspections. But when UNSCOM repeatedly reported that it could not guarantee that Iraq was in full compliance, the sanctions persisted far longer than expected. The regime survived, but many Iraqis suffered greatly and directed much of their resentment at the foreign powers keeping the sanctions in place. The level of punishment seemed hypocritical and even racist compared to the treatment of other nations accused of violations of international law. As this sentiment spread internationally, Iraq received significant help in smuggling some of its oil out of the country. By 1995 Iraq was able to export as much as 110,000 barrels of petroleum products per day to or through Jordan, Turkey, and other countries in the region, which, at discount prices, probably earned Iraq somewhat less than $1 billion per year (Marr 2004: 269).

The UN passed Resolution 706 in August 1991, allowing Iraq to sell $1.6 billon in oil in six-month renewable periods. The proceeds were to be deposited in an internationally monitored fund from which 30 percent would go to war reparations (Tripp 2002: 261). Iraq rejected this as an unacceptable limitation of its sovereignty. Later in 1995 the UN passed Resolution 986, known as the oil-for-food resolution, which allowed Iraq to market specified quantities of its oil for food purchases. Iraq initially refused to go along with this resolution, expecting, mistakenly, that UNSCOM was about to approve the removal of the entire sanctions program. However, in 1996 the regime agreed, permitting Iraq to market $2 billion worth of oil every six months (Tripp 2002: 262). After increases in the oil limit, Iraq was allowed to sell $8.3 billion during May–November 1999 with the UN controlling the oil revenue. After preset percentages of revenue went to war reparations, UNSCOM expenses, and Iraqi Kurdistan, Iraq received the rest (Farouk-Sluglett and Sluglett 2003: 291; Tripp 2002: 262). The UN was to oversee the distribution of the food and other supplies purchased with oil revenue to ensure that the benefits reached all sectors of Iraq's population.

Many observers blamed Saddam's regime for continued sanctions because it did not totally comply with UN Resolution 687. Some believed too much of Iraq's limited resources were used for the military instead of more effectively helping people cope with the sanctions' effects. Others, such as Pope John Paul II, criticized the sanctions (BBC 2000) because of their harmful effects on the Iraqi people.

Opposition to the Regime

The government was threatened by assassination attempts, rebellions, and coup plots. And members of Saddam's own family also contributed to potentially destabilizing the regime.

The Shia

Despite persistent discontent in the south, the regime was able to contain Shia opposition movements. Most of the top leaders of SCIRI and the Dawa Party were outside the country. Shia clerics advocating fundamentalist concepts, especially those tainted by accepting Iranian assistance, seemed to have dwindling appeal to young Shia who had received relatively secular educations.

Some Shia groups were able to continue attacks, using the southern marshes as a conduit for travel between Iraq and Iran and for concealment. The regime sent troops to cut down vegetation that often towered several feet above the heads of soldiers, and much of the marsh dried up after the government built two large drainage canals. As many as 250,000 people were moved out of the area, many of them resettled in and around Kirkuk, increasing the percentage of Kirkuk's Arab population. SCIRI and the Dawa Party would resume playing important political roles in Iraq only after the US-led invasion destroyed the Baath regime in 2003.

The Kurds

After the imposition of the no-fly zone over most of Iraqi Kurdistan and the establishment of UN humanitarian centers, Kurdish leaders were able to defy the regime when negotiations broke down in February 1992 and simply declare that they would hold elections and create a new government for the Kurdish region. The election for the 105-member Kurdish parliament took place on May 19, 1992. Seats were awarded based on the vote percentage each party received, as long as this was at least 7 percent of the votes cast. But five seats were set aside for minorities. The results indicated that Barzani's KDP won fifty-one of the one hundred contested seats and Jalal al-Talabani's PUK forty-nine. Of the five seats set aside for minorities, the Assyrian Democratic Movement took four. The PUK complained about the accuracy of the results and refused to concede defeat. In an attempt to preserve unity, the KDP gave up one seat to the PUK.

Following the election, the Kurdish Regional Government (KRG) was established on July 4. In an additional attempt to structure a unified government, the Kurdistan Council of Ministers was set up so that when a member of one of the major parties was designated as a government minister, a member of the other major party would be selected as the deputy minister. This arrangement, coupled with the equal number of KDP and PUK seats in the parliament, contributed to government deadlocks. In response to Kurdish defiance of Baghdad, the Baath regime restricted trade with the Kurdish region and reduced its food rations and electricity supply.

International nongovernmental organization (NGO) and UN assistance to the Kurdish region helped delay a collapse of the Kurdish government. The economic difficulties, however, contributed to worsening tensions between the KDP and PUK. The KDP was strongest in the largely rural northern section of Kurdistan where the Kurmanji dialects of the Kurdish language dominated, while PUK support was strongest mainly in the south where the Surani Kurdish dialect was common, especially in the city of Sulaimaniyya. The KDP's control of the north gave it an economic advantage since this area had much fertile farmland and had suffered less from the Anfal, and because the KDP controlled the border with Turkey at Khabur where an estimated 700 to 1,000 trucks crossed each day (Farouk-Sluglett and Sluglett 2003: 298). This yielded significant customs revenue, including from smuggling oil and other goods, that the KDP refused to share with the PUK, whose territory had been more severely damaged by Anfal and had the much less profitable border crossings with Iran (Tripp 2002: 272).

The economic confrontation was a primary reason for outbreak of the Kurdish civil war between the KDP and the PUK in May 1994. An estimated 1,000 Kurds had perished by August (Marr 2004: 280). During the conflict, a third group, the Islamic Movement of Iraqi Kurdistan (IMIK), took control of Halabja, Banjwin, and Khurmal and surrounding territory. When the fighting subsided, Kurdistan no longer had a unified government. The PUK controlled the two major urban centers, Sulaimaniyya and Arbil, and about two-thirds of Kurdistan, while the KDP held the north, including the border with Turkey and part of the border with Iran.

The KDP, disappointed by the lack of effective US intervention to settle the civil war, surprisingly requested military assistance from Saddam's government on the grounds that the PUK was receiving military assistance from Iran. Saddam sent some 30,000 to 40,000 Iraqi troops (Farouk-Sluglett and Sluglett 2003: 299; Tripp 2002: 273), mostly Republican Guard units, to help the KDP seize Arbil on August 31, 1996. A week later the KDP took Sulaimaniyya and then most Iraqi troops withdrew within a few weeks. With Iranian assistance, the PUK was able to launch a counterattack and retake Sulaimaniyya in October, in effect restoring a balance between the KDP and the PUK. Under pressure from the United States, the KDP and the PUK again agreed to cooperate, although in reality they continued to dominate their separate regions. In the Washington Agreement of September 1998, the KDP agreed to share its revenues with the PUK, and the semblance of a unity government was restored through the reconvening of the Kurdish Assembly (Tripp 2002: 274).

External Opposition Groups

The Iraqi exile community provided a fertile environment for the emergence of groups opposed to Saddam's regime. There were an estimated 1.5 million Iraqi exiles before the Kuwait war, growing to as many as 3 million following the war, the suppressed intifada, and the effects of the UN sanctions. The two most important Western-assisted antiregime Iraqi exile groups were the Iraqi National Accord (INA) and the Iraqi National Congress (INC).

The INC, formed in Vienna in June 1992, began as a collection of anti-Saddam groups. Its leader was a Shia from a wealthy banking family, Ahmed Chalabi, who had been educated in the West as a mathematician and had been away from Iraq for many years. Unlike the Iraqi Shia opposition leaders in Iran, Chalabi had a relatively secular outlook. He had organizational ability, was skillful in dealing with Western political leaders and officials, and was an articulate spokesperson for the exile opposition. Western governments tended to overlook his being accused of involvement in major banking fraud in Jordan. They considered him and the INC potentially important assets in their quest to get rid of the Baathist regime. INC leaders moved their operational headquarters into Iraqi Kurdistan to claim greater legitimacy than other opposition groups by being based inside Iraq, and to be better able to infiltrate the rest of Iraq and launch attacks against the regime.

Receiving funds from the CIA, the INC attracted people from inside Iraq who had turned against the regime, including military defectors. Many were organized into the INC militia. On March 3, 1995, the INC force, along with PUK peshmergas, attacked Iraqi army units in the Kirkuk area, forcing the surrender of seven hundred soldiers (Marr 2004: 275). However, without help from the KDP and air support from the United States, the INC could not proceed further. In addition, the INC failed to induce any significant defections from the Iraqi armed forces or provoke uprisings among the people, although its military efforts enhanced its reputation among regime opponents.

During the Kurdish civil war, however, the INC, along with CIA operations in Iraqi Kurdistan, suffered a devastating blow when the Iraqi army, allied with the KDP against the PUK, seized Arbil on August 31, 1996. Iraqi forces arrested as many as seven hundred regime opponents and executed ninety-six (Marr 2004: 286). Some 5,000 to 6,500 Iraqis and Kurds fled as the CIA left, and many later settled in the United States (Farouk-Sluglett and Sluglett 2003: 299; Tripp 2002: 273).

The United States considered the intervention by Iraqi troops in Kurdistan a violation of the Gulf War cease-fire. But on September 2, instead of taking action in the north to aid the INC or the PUK, it launched dozens of cruise missiles at Iraqi military installations in the south of Iraq and extended the southern no-fly zone from the thirty-second to the thirty-third parallel.

The other major CIA-assisted exile opposition group, the INA, also suffered a catastrophic defeat. The INA was mainly composed of former Baath Party members. It was led by Ayad Allawi, a secularly oriented Shia, and was based in London.

In contrast to the INC approach of attacking Iraqi army units, the INA, which included some high-level Baathist military veterans, tried to organize a coup against the regime from inside the armed forces. A retired Iraqi special forces general living in Jordan, Muhammad Abdullah al-Shawani, met INA leader Ayad Allawi and decided to work with the group against the regime. Al-Shawani appeared to be just the person the INA and the CIA were looking for. His three sons, Anmar, Ayead, and Atheer, were officers in the Republican Guard, a major, a captain, and a lieutenant, respectively (Cockburn and Cockburn 1999: 223–224). All three had reputations as committed Baathists and were seemingly beyond suspicion. Al-Shawani explained that he and his sons wanted to organize a coup against Saddam from within the Republican Guard. Soon top British and US officials were encouraged by knowledge of a developing coup within Saddam's most trusted military units.

By the end of 1995, the al-Shawani brothers sent word that they had succeeded in establishing a network of sympathetic officers. CIA operatives in Amman attempted to solve the problem of how to communicate quickly and secretly with the coup organizers. There were only two ways to exchange messages between Amman and Baghdad, and both were subject to Iraqi regime surveillance. International telephone calls went through a facility north of Baghdad where they were taped for Iraqi security agents to review. The other method was to send a message with a professional driver who had to be approved by the Baath security agency Mukhabarat. Thus the conspirators had to recruit an officially approved driver willing to collaborate in the plot to physically deliver their messages to Jordan. The CIA agents assigned to coordinate with the coup organizers decided to provide them with special satellite communication and encryption equipment that would allow a rapid and secure exchange of messages.

Although it is possible that the regime already knew of the plot through infiltration of the INA, the interception of the driver returning to Baghdad with the communications equipment during either January or February 1996 guaranteed disaster. The coup, apparently scheduled for the third week of June, never occurred. Iraqi security agents began arresting about 120 officers beginning around June 20 (Cockburn and Cockburn 1999: 228). The accused were reportedly all Sunni members of the Special Republican Guard, the Republican Guard, the General Security Service, and the army. Later, members of the Mukhabarat were also taken into custody, and after about three months as many as eight hundred had been arrested. Cockburn and Cockburn (1999: 229) report that Iraqi intelligence informed the CIA of the destroyed plot through a message sent on the captured satellite communications equipment.

The US Congress, despite the Iraq exile groups' defeats, provided them with $5 million in May 1998 and $97 million more through the Iraq Liberation Act on October 31 of the same year (Iraq Liberation Act of 1998). Some members of these organizations would play at least temporary political roles after the ouster of the Baath regime in 2003.

Saddam's Family Problems

Saddam's son Uday in 1988 had beaten his father's trusted aide, food taster, and friend, Kamal Hanna Jajjou, to death at a party reportedly because he believed Jajjou had arranged for Saddam to have an extramarital affair, distressing Uday's mother. Saddam was outraged and sent Uday out of the country on a supposed diplomatic assignment. But Saddam's affection for Uday, despite his repeatedly embarrassing, disruptive, and even criminal behavior, eventually led to his being rehabilitated to the regime and given some important responsibilities.

Allowing Uday to regain power apparently contributed to a sensational event, the defection of Saddam's sons-in-law, General Hussein Kamal al-Majid and his younger brother, Lieutenant Colonel Saddam Kamal, to Jordan on August 7, 1995. It is not clear whether Saddam's daughters knew that their husbands were defecting rather than just visiting Jordan, where the older brother had undergone medical treatment in 1994.

Hussein Kamal, who had led some Republican Guard units in the war with Iran and managed several military industries, had multiple reasons for defecting. Uday had publicly criticized him in an apparent effort to undermine his power. However, Hussein Kamal gave other reasons for leaving Iraq, including his concern about Iraq's economic problems. He said Iraq would be much better off cooperating with the United States and not going to war with its neighbors (UNSCOM/IAEA 1995, www.fair.org/press-releases/kamel.pdf).

On August 22 Hussein Kamal was interviewed by UNSCOM and IAEA officials. His statements had an important impact on the UN weapons inspections program, the continuation of sanctions, and, eventually, the 2003 invasion. The interviewers included Rolf Ekeus, executive chairman of UNSCOM; Professor Maurizio Zifferero, director of IAEA; and Nikita Smidovich, a Russian who led UNSCOM's ballistic missile inspection group.

Kamal's assertions led his interviewers to believe that Iraq had been deceiving them. He described unknown aspects of Iraq's nuclear program and indicated that Iraq was concealing and preserving information on its nuclear and other WMD programs as well as blueprints and molds for long-range missiles. He also revealed that toward the end of the Iran–Iraq War, Iraq had developed and weaponized VX nerve gas. But he also stated that Iraq had destroyed all its WMD.

Some governments claimed Kamal's statements proved that Iraq had not complied with UN requirements for lifting sanctions. But they seemed to ignore that he also told his interviewers that all weapons of mass destruction, "biological, chemical, missile, nuclear were destroyed" (UNSCOM/IAEA 1995, www.fair .org/press-releases/kamel.pdf; FAIR 2003, www.fair.org/index.php?page=1845). After Kamal's defection but two days before the interview, Iraq gave UNSCOM records on the nuclear development project, claiming that it was the defector, Hussein Kamal, who had on his own authority hidden these documents.

Hussein Kamal's defection provided an opportunity for Jordan's government to shift farther away from its previous pro-Iraq orientation. Jordan had remained friendly to Iraq during the Gulf War mainly because most Jordanian residents are Palestinians and pro-Iraqi. But when the Kuwaiti ruling family returned to power and expelled hundreds of thousands of Palestinian workers, most ended up in Jordan, placing a huge burden on that small country, which had lost aid from the angry Saudi and Kuwaiti monarchies (Cockburn and Cockburn 1999: 195). By providing a refuge for Hussein Kamal, Jordan assisted UNSCOM and improved relations with the United States and Saudi Arabia.

Saddam worked hard to repair damage to the regime caused by the defection and to get his daughters and their children back to Iraq. He realized that Uday's insults to Hussein Kamal had contributed to the defection and, thereby, the continuation of sanctions. In addition, on the night of Kamal's defection, Uday had shot and wounded his uncle during an argument at another party. Also angered by Uday's acquisition of luxury cars for personal use, Saddam decided to remove him from some of his powerful positions and turn toward his younger son, Qusay, reliable and loyal, as the most suitable person in the family to become Iraq's future leader.

In Jordan, Hussein Kamal became disillusioned with his situation. UNSCOM officials neglected him once they had all the useful information they thought he had, and Iraqi opposition exile groups showed little interest in offering him a leadership role. Kamal missed the power he used to wield in Iraq and was facing a serious legal action after he was accused of threatening to kill a Jordanian journalist who wanted to publish critical remarks Kamal had made about Jordan's king.

To the disbelief of people around the world, Hussein Kamal decided to accept a pardon from Saddam and return to Iraq on February 20, 1996. The Kamal brothers were required to come to the presidential palace, where Saddam demanded that they agree to divorce his daughters. They reportedly refused (Cockburn and Cockburn 1999: 209). But on the 23rd news reports indicated that their wives, Raghad and Rana, had divorced them, saying they had been taken to Jordan against their will.

When the Kamal brothers left Iraq, they had been condemned by members of their own al-Majid clan. Hussein Kamal's uncle, Ali Hassan al-Majid, denounced him for treason, and his extended kin publicly stated that they would not seek revenge on anyone who killed him. After their meeting with Saddam, the Kamal brothers went to their sister's home. About forty armed men showed up and surrounded the house, all members of the al-Majid clan and members of the presidential guard. Claiming to be acting to restore family honor tarnished by the defection, they prepared to attack the house. But according to Cockburn and Cockburn (1999: 209), out of respect for tribal tradition, they first delivered a supply of automatic weapons and ammunition for the Kamals to use to defend themselves. The subsequent battle lasted for about thirteen hours, reportedly resulting in the death of everyone in the house and two of the attackers.

The killing of the Kamal brothers was followed by an assassination attempt against Uday by an internal resistance organization, al-Nahdah, or "the Awakening." This group was created by highly educated young Iraqis, who supported democracy and opposed sectarian or ethnic conflict, in 1991 in the aftermath of the Kuwait war. Believing that because of tight security it was impossible to kill Saddam, the group ambushed Uday on his way to a party on December 12, 1996. Uday was badly wounded but not killed, and all the would-be assassins escaped. Uday's resulting disabilities coupled with his past behavior meant that his more capable younger brother would assume the more prominent leadership roles. By the end of the 1990s Qusay was supervising major security operations including his father's personal guard, the Special Security Organization, and the Special Republican Guard (Marr 2004: 285), helping to stabilize the regime as it entered the twenty-first century.

Iraq from 1996 to 2003

Inspection Disputes and Sanction Modifications

When the UN Security Council passed Resolution 986 in 1995 allowing Iraq to market $2 billion worth of oil every six months under UN restrictions, some Iraqis felt the regime should accept it, believing that gradually this policy would be expanded and the sanctions eliminated. But Saddam believed that UNSCOM was about to certify that Iraq no longer had WMD, which would result in a total lifting of sanctions. Hussein Kamal's defection and statements to UNSCOM about concealed information, however, contributed to the continuation of inspections and sanctions.

Worsening economic conditions finally convinced the regime to accept the oil-for-food plan, and Iraq's economy began to gradually improve. UN Resolution 1153, adopted on February 20, 1998, raised Iraq's permitted oil sales to $5.2 billion every six months and permitted expanded imports, including such civilian infrastructural needs as electric power generation and delivery equipment and water purification systems. In December 1999 UN Resolution 1284 removed all limits on Iraq's oil exports. These changes helped raise GDP per capita for Iraqis from about $725 in 1997 to $1,385 in 2000, although as oil prices temporarily declined it fell to $1,078 in 2002.

In 1997 Ekeus was replaced as UNSCOM director by Richard Butler, an Australian arms control specialist. Inspectors were still concerned about not finding all of the documentation on some WMD programs as well as possibly some VX nerve toxin or materials to make it. Although the Iraqis claimed that these items had been destroyed, UNSCOM decided to conduct more comprehensive searches of government buildings, such as palaces where they thought some WMD records or components might be stored. The Iraqis objected to some of these searches, claiming that certain UNSCOM agents were in fact spies for the United States or Israel, and that the inspections now had little to do with WMD and were mainly a cover for gathering information for future US or Israeli attacks or covert operations, including possibly targeting key personnel for assassination.

Disclosures in the second half of 1998 indicated that UNSCOM "had been cooperating with Israel on intelligence and using U.S. intelligence intercepts" (Marr 2004: 289). At the end of October, Iraq stopped cooperating with UN inspectors and refused to hand over certain documents when UNSCOM attempted to resume inspections in November. UNSCOM personnel were pulled out of Iraq, and the United States and Britain conducted air attacks December 16 through 19, called Operation Desert Fox. However, Saudi Arabia, Russia, France, and other European nations objected to the new military actions. These events effectively ended UNSCOM and the inspections program.

Party and Government

By 1998 the Revolutionary Command Council (RCC) and top Baath Party leaders were about 28 percent Shia Arabs and 61 percent Sunni Arabs. Approximately one out of four came from Tikrit (Marr 2003: 292). The party firmly embraced religion during the Iran–Iraq War. As economic conditions deteriorated due to the effects of sanctions, party and regime identification with Islam increased. Due to inflation and reduced government revenue, the salaries of civil servants had such little purchasing power that many had to hold two or more jobs, impairing delivery of government services. The armed forces' strength declined to about 400,000. The best-trained and best-equipped were the seven Republican Guard divisions, with about 60,000 to 70,000 soldiers.

Kurdish Self-Government

While the KDP and PUK controlled most of Iraqi Kurdistan, the Islamic Movement in Kurdistan-Iraq (IMKI) and other Islamic groups carved out a small fundamentalist enclave in about 5 percent of the region's territory. The return of Kurds affiliated with Al Qaeda from the successful jihad against the Soviets in Afghanistan meant that by 2003 the more radical Ansar al-Islam (Supporters of Islam) had supplanted the IMKI.

After the spring of 1998, cooperation between the KDP and the PUK increased as Kurds benefited from their share of Iraq's oil revenues, customs collections at the Turkish and Iranian borders, and international aid. Self-government took firm root. School lessons were taught in Kurdish, and Arabic and English were offered as second languages. Students were taught that Kirkuk with its oil was rightfully a part of Kurdistan. Many Kurds appeared to favor a totally independent Kurdistan, probably a large majority, according to the results of an unofficial referendum on the issue in February 2005 (Galbraith 2005).

The Regime and Shia Militancy

The government attempted to increase support among Iraqi Shia by allowing pilgrimages to resume to the Shia holy cities after a 1997 agreement with Iran. The influx of pilgrims improved the economy of the south, including the well-being of clergy. Southern Iraq also benefited from increasing oil revenues.

Saddam supported Grand Ayatollah Muhammad Sadiq al-Sadr, the cousin of Ayatollah Muhammad Baqir al-Sadr, whom the regime had executed in 1980, to head Hawza, the main institution for Shia education in Iraq, located in Najaf. Saddam favored him because he was an Arab Shia and Saddam was interested in purging the teaching center of its non-Arab religious authorities (Welsh 2004), and because he displayed great public animosity toward the United States and toward Israel using the slogans "No, no to America," "No, no to Israel," and "No, no to the devil" to begin his Friday sermons (Raphaelli 2004: 1; International Crisis Group 2006: 5).

Sadiq al-Sadr, however, called on the regime to release Shia prisoners and began to advocate that Iraq conform more closely to Islamic teachings. Some believe the regime began to fear that he could become the leader of a new political religious movement. But al-Sadr also had differences with other Shia clerical leaders, who were more closely affiliated with Iran, and with some in the quietist orientation, who shunned the level of involvement in politics inherent in al-Sadr's approach. He launched an antiquietist movement, accusing much of the clerical leadership of not providing all young Shia with a knowledge of basic religious doctrine and of failing to speak out after the execution of his cousin, Muhammad Baqir al-Sadr.

On February 18, 1999, Grand Ayatollah Sadiq al-Sadr and two of his four sons, Mustafa and Muammal, who were his assistants, and their driver were all killed by machine-gun fire as they drove home from Friday prayer services.

Many believed government agents were responsible, although the regime denied this. Thousands of Shia protested the killings, including in the large Shia section of Baghdad that was later renamed Sadr City after the assassinated grand ayatollah. The government tried and executed three alleged killers, blaming the murders on other Shia and foreign agents (Raphaelli 2004: 2). Sadiq al-Sadr's older surviving son immersed himself in religious studies, but his youngest, Moqtada, worked hard to replace his father as a political activist and leader of his own large Shia organization, the Mahdi Army, after the 2003 invasion.

Sliding Toward Invasion and Occupation

The terrorist attacks on September 11, 2001, provided a new international framework, energized by an enraged and apprehensive US public oriented to strike preemptively at potential threats. The Bush administration more decisively moved US policy toward Iraq from containment to regime elimination and a US-orchestrated restructuring of the country, using to justify launching a war what was described as Iraq's failure to comply with UN Resolution 687 regarding WMD.

In 2002, under pressure from the United States, the UN passed Resolution 1441, which stated that Iraq was in violation of the Gulf War cease-fire terms and demanded the return of inspectors and complete Iraqi cooperation. Fearing a US-led invasion, Iraq accepted the new resolution. In November 2002 the UN inspectors returned to Iraq as the United Nations Monitoring, Verification and Inspection Commission (UNMOVIC).

If Iraq could have satisfied UN inspectors regarding WMD, the US and British governments might have found it more difficult to launch the 2003 invasion. But many believe that the invasion was inevitable because the primary motivation was to gain control of Iraq's oil from an unfriendly government. In this regard, eighteen-year US Federal Reserve Chair Alan Greenspan, a Republican, stated in 2007 that "I am saddened that it is politically inconvenient to acknowledge what everyone knows: the Iraq war is largely about oil" (Paterson 2007, www.timesonline.co.uk).

Summary and Analysis

Iraq claimed that it had defended other Arab nations from the threat of Iranian fundamentalist extremism and that the tens of billions of dollars Arab oil monarchies provided to buy weapons should be treated as grants, not loans. Kuwait rejected this concept, which angered many Iraqis who regarded Kuwait as a part of Iraq detached by Britain to serve its interests. Furthermore, Iraq accused Kuwait of producing oil beyond OPEC quotas to lower the price and, therefore, significantly reduce Iraq's oil revenue.

Saddam Hussein decided to solve Iraq's economic problems by using the main asset left over from the Iran–Iraq War, Iraq's heavily armed military, to seize Kuwait in August 1990. The United States, most nations in the UN Security Council, and most Arab states condemned Iraqi occupation of Kuwait and demanded withdrawal. Iraq's failure to do so by the UN deadline resulted in an overwhelming US-led military assault that devastated Iraq's armed forces and badly damaged its infrastructure. To obtain a cease-fire, Iraq agreed to accept Kuwaiti independence, give up all weapons of mass destruction and long-range missiles, and allow UN inspections to guarantee compliance with cease-fire terms. Rebellions broke out in the Shia south and the Kurdish north following Iraq's defeat. Although the uprisings were suppressed, international intervention resulted in the establishment of Kurdish self-government.

The UN imposed sanctions on Iraq until its compliance with cease-fire requirements could be verified. Since inspectors never confirmed that Iraq fully complied, the sanctions lasted for more than a decade, contributing to the deaths from malnutrition and disease of an estimated half-million people. In the latter part of the 1990s, Iraq was allowed to sell increasing amounts of its oil under UN supervision and experienced some limited economic recovery.

The Iranian Revolution had led to the Iran–Iraq War, which in turn created conditions contributing to Iraq's decision to invade Kuwait. That invasion brought a huge American military force to Saudi Arabia, turning the Al Qaeda organization decisively against the United States. As a result of Al Qaeda terrorism, the Baathist regime would be destroyed, not by an internal coup or rebellion, but by US reaction to 9/11.

References and Further Readings

Allawi, Ali A. 2006. *The Occupation of Iraq: Winning the War and Losing the Peace*. New Haven, CT: Yale University Press.

BBC. 2000. "Pope's Prayer for Iraq." March 19. http://news.bbc.co.uk/2/hi/middle_east/682407.stm.

Bertell, Rosalie. 1999. "Gulf War Veterans and Depleted Uranium." *Hague Peace Conference, May*. www.ccnr.org/du_hague.html.

Blum, William. 2004. *Killing Hope: U.S. Military and CIA Interventions Since World War II*. Monroe, ME: Common Courage Press.

CIA World Factbook: Iran. www.cia.gov/library/publications/the-world-factbook/geos/ir.html.

CIA World Factbook: Iraq. www.cia.gov/library/publications/the-world-factbook/geos/iz.html.

CIA World Factbook: Kuwait. www.cia.gov/library/publications/the-world-factbook/geos/ku.html.

CIA World Factbook: Saudi Arabia. www.cia.gov/library/publications/the-world-factbook/geos/sa.html.

Cockburn, Andrew, and Patrick Cockburn. 1999. *Out of the Ashes: The Resurrection of Saddam Hussein*. New York: Harper Perennial.

Congressional Research Service. 2005. "Iraq Oil: Reserves, Production, Potential Revenues." *CRS Report for Congress*, April 13. www.fas.org/sgp/crs/mideast/RS21626.pdf (accessed September 21, 2007).

FAIR (Fairness & Accuracy in Reporting). 2003. "Star Witness on Iraq Said Weapons Were Destroyed." www.fair.org/index.php?page=1845.

Farouk-Sluglett, Marion, and Peter Sluglett. 2003. *Iraq Since 1958*. London: J. B. Tauris Publishers.

Galbraith, Peter W. 2005. "As Iraqis Celebrate, the Kurds Hesitate." www.ny times.com/2005/02/01/opinion/01galbraith.html.

Gordon, Michael. 1991. "War in the Gulf: Iraqi Air Force; Harboring Iraqi Planes by Iran Calls Its Neutrality into Question." *New York Times*, January 29. http://query.nytimes.com.

Hiro, Dilip. 1992. *Desert Shield to Desert Storm: The Second Gulf War*. New York: Routledge.

International Crisis Group. 2006. "Iraq's Muqtada Al-Sadr: Spoiler or Stabiliser?" *Middle East Report 55* (July). www.crisisgroup.org/Library/documents/middle_east_north_africa/Iraq_iran_gulf/55_iraq_s_muqtada_al_sadr_spoiler_or_stabiliser.pdf.

"Interrogator Shares Saddam's Confessions." 2008. CBS *60 Minutes*, January 27. www.cbsnews.com/stories/2008/01/24/60minutes/printable3749494.shtml.

Iraq Liberation Act of 1998. www.iraqwatch.org/government/US/Legislation/ILA.htm.

Katz, Mark N. 2002. "Osama bin Laden as Transnational Revolutionary Leader." *Current History* 101, no. 652: 81–85.

Marr, Phebe. 2004. *The Modern History of Iraq*. Boulder, CO: Westview.

New York Times. "U. S. Ambassador April Glaspie's Interview with President Saddam Hussein, July 25, 1990." 1990. September 23. www.chss.montclair.edu/english/furr/glaspie.html (accessed September 6, 2007).

"Osama bin Laden: In the Name of Allah." 2001. *Biography*. http://store.aetv.com/html/product/index.jhtml?id=70644.

Paterson, Graham. 2007. "Alan Greenspan Claims Iraq War Was for Oil." Times Online. www.timesonline.co.uk.

Polk, William R. 2005. *Understanding Iraq*. New York: Harper Perennial.

Public Broadcasting Service (PBS). 1997. *The Gulf War*, part 2. www.pbs.org/wgbh/pages/frontline/gulf.

Raphaeli, Nimrod. 2004. "Understanding Muqtada al-Sadr." *Middle East Quarterly* (Fall): 1–10. www.meforum.org/pf.php?id=655.

Tripp, Charles. 2002. *A History of Iraq*. Cambridge, UK: Cambridge University Press.

Tyson, Ann Scott. 2008. "FBI Agent: Hussein Didn't Expect Invasion." *Washington Post*, January 26. www.washingtonpost.com.

United Nations. 1991. "Resolution 687 (1991)." www.fas.org/news/un/iraq/sres/sres0687.htm.

UNSCOM/IAEA. 1995. Transcript of UNSCOM and IAEA Interview with Hussein Kamal, August 22, 1995. www.fair.org/press-releases/kamel.pdf.

Welsh, May Ying. 2004. "Al-Sadr City: Support from the Impoverished." *News Arab World*, April 28. www.thewe.cc/contents/more/archive2004/april/al_sadr_city.htm.

6

||||||||||||||||||||||||||||||||||||||||||||||||||||||||||||||||||||||||||||||||||||||||||||||||||||||||||||||||||

The Iraq War

Causes, Invasion, and Postinvasion Policies

From 1993 to 2001 the Clinton administration emphasized containment: limiting Iraq's capabilities and deterring Iraqi aggression. US policy changed dramatically in 2001 due to two events: the beginning of the George W. Bush administration and the September 11 terrorist attacks. The first brought to power people intent on eliminating Saddam Hussein's government. The second provided them with the public support necessary to act. The Bush administration argued that the Iraqi regime should be removed because it possessed WMD, was supporting terrorism, and was brutalizing the Iraqi people.

The large majority of people surveyed in most countries around the world opposed an invasion of Iraq. Russia, China, and France, which had the ability to veto any UN action, refused to support an attack on Iraq. This left the United States and Britain the option of acting without UN authorization. The invasion began on March 20, 2003, and US forces captured Baghdad on April 9, effectively ousting the Baath government. But hundreds of unguarded arsenals were raided by many thousands of Iraqis seeking weapons for self-protection or for use in the coming resistance to occupation forces.

Most Sunni Arabs were hostile to the invasion. Many Iraqi Shia Arabs supported or at least tolerated the attack as necessary to get rid of Saddam but did not favor an indefinite US occupation. Iraq's Kurdish ethnic minority overwhelmingly supported the invasion as a means of helping them secure political autonomy.

A number of factors contributed to the development of organized resistance to the occupation. Among the most important were the occupation authority's decisions to remove tens of thousands of Baath Party members from their government positions and the disbanding of the Iraqi armed forces. These actions impaired reconstruction and left unemployed hundreds of thousands of embittered men with weapons and military training.

When no WMD or connections between Saddam and Al Qaeda and the 9/11 attacks were found, the US public's support for the war declined rapidly.

Containment Policy

The United States did not want Iraq's defeat in the 1991 Gulf War to result in either an independent Iraqi Kurdistan or Iranian domination of Iraq's oil-rich Shia south. Iraq was to be left with sufficient military resources to discourage an attack from Iran. Both the George H. W. Bush and Clinton administrations hoped that the Baath regime would be overthrown by Iraqi officers outraged by Saddam's disastrous miscalculations leading first to war with Iran and then defeat following Iraq's invasion of Kuwait.

US containment policy included continual aerial surveillance as well as enforcement of northern and southern no-fly zones, where Iraqi aircraft were forbidden. Although the Iraqi defector Hussein Kamal claimed that Iraq had destroyed all WMD and long-range missiles, his other statements led the UN to suspect that Iraq was concealing WMD information. When the UN intensified inspections, Iraq objected, claiming some inspectors were spying for the CIA and Israel rather than looking for WMD. The Iraqis ended their cooperation with UNSCOM in 1998, leading to a new US and British military retaliation, the four-day missile and bomb attack called Operation Desert Fox. This was the most powerful enforcement of the containment policy from 1991 to the 2003 invasion (Ricks 2006: 19). Beginning on December 16, 1998, the bombardment included 415 cruise missiles (the United States fired only 317 in the entire 1991 Gulf War) and 600 bombs. The ninety-seven targets included suspected weapons production and storage sites and government command and intelligence headquarters. Some US officials doubted whether Operation Desert Fox was effective and a number of Republican officials thought it might have been a ploy by President Bill Clinton to divert attention from the scandal involving his sexual relationship with a White House intern. But in reality Desert Fox had caused great damage and apparently came close to destabilizing the regime. This reinforced US CENTCOM commander Marine General Anthony Zinni's belief that the containment policy was effective (CENTCOM is the acronym for Central Command, covering the Middle East and parts of central Asia and eastern Africa).

But Iraq's success in halting UN inspections angered US legislators who complained that containment was failing. This led to the passage of the Iraq Liberation Act of 1998, which funded Iraqi exile groups and officially committed the United States to working for regime change and the establishment of a democratic Iraqi government. However, given the regime's strength, the legislation seemed inadequate to bring about Saddam's downfall.

Why, many have asked, didn't Iraq totally cooperate with UN inspectors, since it had apparently destroyed all its WMD more than ten years before the 2003 invasion? One reason was that the regime believed its cooperation was sufficient and anticipated that UN inspectors would rapidly verify that it had no WMD, resulting in an end to sanctions. Saddam repeatedly expected the sanctions to be lifted. Since there were no WMD, the Iraqis came to believe that the inspections had essentially become spy missions for the CIA and Israel so that key personnel and purely defensive infrastructure could be targeted in future covert operations or war. Some observers also believe it's possible that

Iraq wanted to leave some doubt in the minds of Iranian leaders so that they would be intimidated from launching an attack on Iraq for fear of WMD. Saddam apparently expressed such a concern about deterring Iran to the FBI agent who interrogated him regarding WMD after he was captured by US forces (CBS *60 Minutes* 2008).

Impact of the Bush Administration and 9/11

When George W. Bush became president in January 2001, a number of his major foreign policy advisers were convinced that the containment policy was failing. The UN had greatly increased the oil Iraq could market and removed many restrictions on the nonmilitary goods Iraq was allowed to purchase. Russia, France, and China, all in line to be awarded oil development contracts by Iraq, pushed for reduction or elimination of UN sanctions. One of the US officials advocating regime removal was new Deputy Secretary of Defense Paul Wolfowitz. Before 9/11, he had supported providing the Iraqi National Congress (INC) with air support so it could launch a more effective military campaign to overthrow the Baath government. General Zinni considered this proposal unrealistic, even referring to it pejoratively as Wolfowitz's "Bay of Goats," likely to suffer an ignominious defeat similar to the CIA's 1961 Bay of Pigs fiasco against Cuba (Ricks 2006: 22).

The situation changed dramatically following the Al Qaeda attacks against New York and Washington on September 11, 2001, when the American people, outraged at the deaths of almost 3,000 people, clamored to strike back. On September 20 President Bush gave a powerful televised address to a joint session of Congress setting the stage for the invasion of Afghanistan, where Al Qaeda's 9/11 terrorists had trained, and providing a framework for attacking other countries aiding terrorists.

Bush began by praising the passengers of United flight 93 for their bravery in preventing the fourth plane with 9/11 terrorists from reaching Washington and asserted that other Americans would also respond courageously to the attacks. "Al Qaeda," he said, "is to terror what the mafia is to crime. But its goal is not making money; its goal is remaking the world—and imposing its radical beliefs on people everywhere" (Bush 2001). The president asked, "Why do they hate us?" But in his answer he ignored the reasons given by Osama bin Laden: that the United States was occupying Saudi Arabia and would never leave the Middle East willingly; that the United States was favoring Israel over the Arab Palestinians; and that the United States was persecuting Iraqi Arabs. Instead, Bush stated that Al Qaeda hated America's democratic way of life. "They hate our freedoms—our freedom of religion, our freedom of speech, our freedom to vote and assemble and disagree with each other." Thus he depicted the terrorist attacks as motivated not by opposition to US foreign policy, as bin Laden claimed, but to the democratic essence of US society, which, unlike US foreign policy, no American could sacrifice or refuse to defend.

After announcing an unconditional ultimatum to Afghan Taliban leaders to immediately turn over all Al Qaeda members and allow US forces "full access to terrorist training camps," Bush stated, "Our enemy is a radical network of terrorists, and every government that supports them. . . . And we will pursue nations that provide aid or safe haven to terrorism. Every nation, in every region, now has a decision to make. Either you are with us, or you are with the terrorists. From this day forward, any nation that continues to harbor or support terrorism will be regarded by the United States as a hostile regime." He concluded by asserting, "We'll meet violence with patient justice—assured of the rightness of our cause."

Reaction to the 9/11 attacks and the impressive speech boosted the president's approval rating to an astounding 90 percent. Millions put their trust in his administration to identify and punish the terrorists responsible for 9/11. However, many around the world would soon accuse the Bush administration of betraying the concept of justice by taking advantage of a relatively unquestioning public and congressional support to invade a country that had played no role in 9/11 and kill thousands of its soldiers and civilians.

Arguments Justifying War

Bush administration officials cited Iraq's unwillingness to permit unrestricted inspections as an indication that it possessed WMD. The specter of Iraq using WMD against the United States or supplying WMD to terrorists, after witnessing how much damage nineteen men with knives and box cutters using hijacked airliners could cause, convinced many Americans to support an invasion.

Suspicion that Saddam was involved in 9/11 was also used to justify attacking Iraq. Some asserted that the 9/11 operation was too well coordinated to be carried out by Al Qaeda alone, that Iraq's intelligence service must have been involved, and that no one had a stronger motive than the Iraqis to launch such a vicious attack on the United States.

President Bush also cited the desirability of removing Saddam's regime because of its human rights violations. But it was clear that this third argument alone could not convince either the American people or Congress to support war, especially in the face of UN opposition.

Arguments Against War

The Oil Issue

The almost universal response from Bush administration critics was that the real reason for invading Iraq was oil. This was admitted by some war advocates, but mainly in the sense of eliminating a dangerous regime that could again become powerful because of its control of enormous energy resources. War opponents, however, believed the Bush administration intended to seize Iraq's oil and use Iraq as a base to increase influence over neighboring oil-rich countries.

The importance of Iraqi and other Middle East oil is difficult to overstate (Hiro 2007: 137–139). In 2006 the Middle East had about 61.5 percent of the world's known oil reserves (BP Statistical Review of World Energy 2007). This amounted to a 79.5-year supply of oil at the 2006 level of annual production (proven reserves divided by annual production). Middle Eastern oil is also relatively cheap to produce, estimated at between 50 cents and $2.50 per barrel compared to over $13.75 per barrel for oil production in Europe or the United States (Kubursi 2006: 248). While an increase in oil price is typically born by individual consumers in the form of higher costs for gasoline, home heating oil, or jet fuel, governments that have influence over the Middle Eastern regimes can benefit from high oil prices not only through their oil companies but also by selling products, including military equipment and advanced technologies, to the oil-exporting countries.

Control of Iraq and its oil became more important for several reasons. One was that the United States had developed greater dependency on Middle Eastern oil. In 1985 it was less than 8 percent of US oil imports (Kubursi 2006: 255) but in 2003 had risen to about 21 percent and was expected to go significantly higher if US domestic oil production remained unchanged. Another reason was that a continued huge US military presence in Saudi Arabia might prove destabilizing to the regime. This had been one of the major factors Al Qaeda used to recruit Saudi Arabians, including fifteen of the nineteen 9/11 terrorists. By seizing Iraq, the United States could move personnel and equipment there from Saudi Arabia (Cashman and Robinson 2007: 349).

Control of Mesopotamia had been a major concern of the British during World War I even though no oil had yet been found there. But the Anglo-Persian (later Anglo-Iranian) Oil Company was producing oil in Iraq's neighbor Iran and it was clear that much of Iraq was geologically similar to Iran and likely possessed enormous quantities (Paul 2002: 1). Oil was becoming increasingly important militarily for fueling naval ships, army trucks and other vehicles, and airplanes, and was viewed as crucial to the future growth of the civilian economy. Sir Maurice Hankey, secretary of the British War Cabinet, wrote to British Foreign Secretary Arthur James Balfour in 1918 that "the only big potential supply that we can get under British control is the Persian and Mesopotamian supply. . . . The control over these oil supplies becomes a first class British war aim" (Maugeri 2006: 26). After World War I, Britain was pressured to allow US oil companies to participate in Iraq oil operations (Paul 2002: 2–3), and British and US interest in Iraqi oil persisted from World War I forward.

In the period leading up to the Iraq War, a number of issues regarding Iraq's vast energy resources appear to have influenced the decision to invade, remove the Baathist government, and occupy the country. One, as noted above, was the desire to remove a hostile government from control of strategically important energy resources that, after further relaxation of UN sanctions or their total elimination, could be used to increase revenues allowing Iraq to rearm and/or to counter US economic leverage over certain other countries around the world.

A further concern was that an invasion would create circumstances acceptable to the United States and Britain to modernize Iraq's oil industry, open untapped wells, and use technologically advanced techniques to explore for as yet undiscovered oil deposits. This would create the potential for Iraq to quickly increase the world supply if necessary to prevent catastrophic rapid increases in international oil prices.

While giving a speech at the London Institute of Petroleum in 1999, Dick Cheney (2004) stated, "While many regions of the world offer great oil opportunities, the Middle East, with two thirds of the world's oil and the lowest cost, is still where the prize ultimately lies." Ferraro (2003) noted that Judicial Watch (2003) obtained documents indicating that before the war Vice President Cheney's energy task force became concerned that Iraq had signed contracts with a number of oil companies from other countries, including Russia, China, and France, that would have access to enormous reserves of Iraqi oil as UN sanctions continued to erode or were completely removed. This possibility reportedly distressed several major multinational oil corporations that feared that the companies with Iraqi contracts would expand Iraqi oil production, but in an uncontrolled self-serving way, pumping and selling as much oil as fast as possible and, in the process, damaging the profits of American oil companies. If the United States occupied Iraq, it or a new Iraqi government under its influence could regulate both contracts and oil production, increasing or decreasing supply as desired.

One strategy through which US corporations could gain control over much of Iraq's oil would be for a new Iraqi government to permit the privatization of the country's oil facilities and deposits and then allow foreign companies to purchase them. Such a process could restore foreign domination of Iraq's energy resources, similar to the situation that existed before the 1958 Iraqi Revolution. Klare (2005: 3) reports that the US State Department recruited a group of exiled Iraqi oil experts that formulated "plans for the privatization of Iraq's state-owned oil company and its acquisition by foreign firms." He also noted that US military units moved to capture Iraqi oil fields at the beginning of the war and in April 2003 seized the Iraqi Oil Ministry headquarters in Baghdad while appearing to generally ignore the extensive looting that followed the capture of Baghdad.

The invasion also created an opportunity for the United States to establish major long-term military bases in Iraq, which could function not only to control Iraq, but also to influence the internal politics and policies of major neighboring oil-producing nations, including Saudi Arabia and Kuwait. As Zunes (2006) notes, a continuing large-scale US military ground force in the Middle East constitutes a potentially significant advantage for the United States against energy resource–deficient economic competitors, such as the European Union, China, and Japan.

No Iraq Role in 9/11

Despite the knee-jerk reaction among some Americans that Iraq must have been involved in 9/11, experts on Al Qaeda realized that this was extremely unlikely (Risen 2006: 72). The Baath regime had repressed fundamentalist movements and, while adopting a more religious public image to appeal to the faithful, continued to be relatively secular by Al Qaeda standards. Furthermore, bin Laden opposed Saddam Hussein and had offered to assemble Al Qaeda forces from around the Islamic world in Saudi Arabia to defend against a possible Iraqi attack after Iraq seized Kuwait. In interviews in the late 1990s bin Laden referred to Baathists as "communists" because they had seized lands from religious leaders, suppressed fundamentalists, and secularly organized Iraqi society (policies similar to those of the leftist Afghan regime allied to the Soviets he had fought in the 1980s).

Another rather obvious reason for Iraq not to have been involved in 9/11 was that the United States would almost certainly respond by invading Iraq, toppling the Baathist regime, and killing Saddam. In other words, carrying out 9/11 would have been willful suicide for both the Baathist regime and Saddam personally. Only a relatively stateless organization like Al Qaeda could have hoped to survive American retaliation.

Indications Iraq Did Not Possess WMD

In all the many UN inspections carried out since 1991, no WMD had been found in Iraq. As noted earlier, Hussein Kamal, Saddam's son-in-law, apparently considered credible by UN interviewers, clearly stated that all WMD and banned long-range missiles had been destroyed. Tahir Jalil Habbush, a very high-ranking Iraqi intelligence official who was secretly an informant for the British, also claimed well before the invasion that Iraq had no WMD (Suskind 2008: 361–369). Like the idea of Iraq participating in 9/11, continued possession of WMD, much less their use, would have amounted to regime suicide.

Critics of the Bush administration noted the suspicious sources for the supposed evidence of Iraqi WMD, largely Iraqi exiles with strong reasons to fabricate false information. The US Senate Select Committee on Intelligence indicated that data on Iraq WMD were misrepresented or exaggerated and the evidence that WMD did not exist tended to be ignored. These intelligence mistakes appeared to virtually all be in the direction of reinforcing the claim that Iraq posed a serious security threat (Cashman and Robinson 2007: 342).

The Questionable Significance of WMD

Another issue raised by critics of US policy was whether Iraqi WMD would really have constituted a serious threat. Iraq did not use its WMD against the United States during the 1991 Gulf War. It used WMD in the Iran–Iraq War only when it faced an enemy with three times its population but that did not possess nuclear weapons with which to retaliate. Iraqi use of WMD against nuclear-armed nations, such as the United States or Israel, would have constituted an act of intentional self-destruction. Furthermore, there are other reasons why no Islamic nation would find it acceptable to use nuclear weapons offensively against Israel. One is that Jerusalem is a sacred location for Islam. Another is that Arab Palestinians, many of whom reside within Israel or nearby, would die as the result of such an attack and much of the land turned into an uninhabitable nuclear wasteland, leaving surviving Palestinians homeless.

There were only two reasons why Iraq or other Islamic nations in the Middle East could have benefited from possessing nuclear weapons. The first was to deter an attack from the United States or Israel by having the capability to inflict politically unacceptable casualties. This is a lesson that Saddam admitted he learned too late (that Iraq should not have seized Kuwait until after it had a nuclear weapon) and that North Korea acted on after the US-led occupation of Iraq, proving to the world through a nuclear test that it had succeeded in developing nuclear weapons.

Iraq or other Islamic nations might also have perceived a benefit from possessing nuclear weapons to neutralize the intimidation effect of Israel's nuclear weapons. Faced with one or more nuclear-armed adversaries, Israel might have proved more ready to allow the establishment of a viable Arab Palestinian state.

Why Single Out Iraq's Dictatorship?

War opponents could not deny that Saddam's regime was a brutal dictatorship. But if the United States was going to use military force to remove repressive, undemocratic governments, why begin with or limit the effort to Iraq? Why not start with or at least equally pursue regime change in the Gulf monarchies so dependent on US assistance? One answer is that Iraq was targeted because of its oil, geographic position bordering other oil-producing states, military weakness, and defiance (Zunes 2006: 28–30).

From Containment to Preemptive Strike to Preventive Attack

The impact of 9/11 on the US government and public provided an opportunity for those preferring the removal of Saddam's regime over the containment policy. Some advocating invading Iraq embraced the neoconservative (new-conservative or neocon) perspective. Neoconservative ideology called for propagating capitalism, free-market trade policies, and democratic political systems around the world, and tended to justify US military action even without UN permission. In contrast, more traditional US conservatives were often more concerned with threats to traditional social and moral institutions, rather than foreign military interventions. Neoconservatives, such as Deputy Secretary of Defense Paul Wolfowitz, Chairman of the Defense Policy Board Richard Perle, and Under Secretary of Defense for Policy Douglas Feith, were often closely aligned with Israel's foreign policy perspectives. Perle and Feith served on the Jewish Institute for National Security Affairs (JINSA) advisory board (Vest 2002: 2–4). JINSA was established in 1976 by neoconservatives worried that Israel was losing support to the extent that the United States might not assist it in a future Arab–Israeli war. Some critics claimed that JINSA often portrayed US and Israeli interests as essentially identical.

While neoconservatives publicly supported the spread of democracy, they were accused of attempting to use US power to force governments around the world to submit to American and Israeli interests. A more traditional conservative, Patrick Buchanan, referred to neoconservative influence as tending to push the United States into a state of continual war (NBC Nightly News Oct. 25, 2007). Packer (2006: 26) notes that almost all those who planned the Iraq War had managed to avoid military service in Vietnam. Some opponents felt that few politicians deserved the label "chicken-hawks" (people who advocate war while avoiding military service themselves) more than the neoconservatives who advocated invading Iraq.

A number of Iraqi defectors and exiles provided the Bush administration and receptive journalists with stories of having seen Iraqi WMD. Others claimed to have information on ties between the Baath regime and Al Qaeda. These reports served as much of the pre–Iraq War "intelligence" that found its way into presidential speeches or addresses by other government officials. Well-known journalists fell for the fabrications of certain Iraqi exiles, convincing many Americans that the fraudulent concoctions were true.

The Bush administration relied on preemption, the idea that a nation about to be attacked by another country has the right to attack that country first in self-defense. However, when postinvasion investigations indicated that Iraq did not have WMD or connections to 9/11, some invasion supporters shifted to a preventive-attack rationale (Cashman and Robinson 2007: 332, 360). This view, which is referred to as the Bush Doctrine (Kinsley 2003), held that the United States should be allowed to unilaterally attack another country, even one that lacks the capability to attack the United States, as long as that country has a government that is hostile and might one day obtain such a capability.

Major Actors in the Decision for War

The President

President George W. Bush appeared to hold a personal grudge against Saddam for allegedly attempting to assassinate his father during the senior Bush's visit to Kuwait in 1993. According to Isikoff and Corn (2006: 116–117), the president expressed great hostility toward Iraq to members of Congress because of Saddam's contempt for the United States and said, "that's why we're going to get rid of him." Such an attitude likely constituted one of the key reasons for the war and why the Bush administration decided to target Iraq's government, from among the numerous repressive regimes around the world. The president's tendency to alternate among justifications for invading Iraq raised questions concerning his integrity or capacity for personally beneficial self-deception.

Although Risen (2006: 106) indicates that important CIA-acquired information indicating that Iraq did not have WMD apparently never reached the president, he also notes that top CIA officials felt they were under great pressure to support the Bush administration.

Bush's immense popularity following 9/11 gave him enormous leverage in convincing the American people that destroying the Iraqi regime should be an essential component of the war on terrorism. The president accomplished this in part through a series of speeches in which he presented false information that Iraq possessed WMD, and in which he referred to the possibility that the country could provide WMD to terrorists. In his January 29, 2002, State of the Union address, Bush referred to North Korea, Iran, and Iraq, along with what he referred to as "their terrorist allies," as components of an "axis of evil"

(Bush 2002a). He also claimed that "Iraq continues to flaunt its hostility toward America and to support terror. The Iraqi regime has plotted to develop anthrax, and nerve gas, and nuclear weapons for over a decade." As the administration became more committed to invading Iraq, the president's speeches contained more explicit claims regarding what in reality were nonexistent WMD.

In his October 7, 2002, speech at the Cincinnati Museum Center, the president claimed Iraq was defying the UN by continuing to possess WMD. He stated that Iraq "possesses and produces chemical and biological weapons" and "it is seeking nuclear weapons" (Bush 2002b). He added that "Iraq's weapons of mass destruction are controlled by a murderous tyrant" and "Saddam Hussein is harboring terrorists and the instruments of terror, the instruments of mass death and destruction." He also claimed that "the world has tried limited military strikes to destroy Iraq's weapons of mass destruction capabilities— only to see them openly rebuilt, while the regime again denies they even exist." As the president continued, he demanded that "the Iraqi regime must reveal and destroy, under UN supervision, all existing weapons of mass destruction." Finally, Bush's January 28, 2003, State of the Union address set the stage for the rapidly approaching invasion with further false assertions about Iraqi WMD. "Today, the gravest danger in the war on terror, the gravest danger facing America and the world, is outlaw regimes that seek and possess nuclear, chemical, and biological weapons. These regimes could use such weapons for blackmail, terror, and mass murder. They could also give or sell those weapons to terrorist allies, who would use them without the least hesitation" (Bush 2003a).

Later in the speech the president began to focus on the coming military target, Iraq. "Twelve years ago, Saddam Hussein faced the prospect of being the last casualty in a war he had started and lost. To spare himself, he agreed to disarm of all weapons of mass destruction. For the next 12 years, he systematically violated that agreement. He pursued chemical, biological, and nuclear weapons, even while inspectors were in his country. Nothing to date has restrained him from his pursuit of these weapons—not economic sanctions, not isolation from the outside world, not even cruise missile strikes on his military facilities." As the speech continued, the president described uranium from Africa and aluminum tubes, about which some US and foreign intelligence agents had great doubts. "The British government has learned that Saddam Hussein recently sought significant quantities of uranium from Africa. Our intelligence sources tell us that he has attempted to purchase high-strength aluminum tubes suitable for nuclear weapons production." "The dictator of Iraq is not disarming. To the contrary; he is deceiving." "Year after year, Saddam Hussein has gone to elaborate lengths, spent enormous sums, taken great risks to build and keep weapons of mass destruction. But why? The only possible explanation, the only possible use he could have for those weapons, is to dominate, intimidate, or attack."

Toward the end of the speech, the president set the stage for one of the greatest acts of misinformation preceding the invasion of Iraq, Secretary of State Colin Powell's address to the United Nations. "The world has waited 12 years for Iraq to disarm. America will not accept a serious and mounting threat to our country, and our friends and allies. The United States will ask the U.N. Security Council to convene on February 5th to consider the facts of Iraq's ongoing defiance of the world. Secretary of State Powell will present information and intelligence about Iraq's legal—Iraq's illegal weapons programs, its attempt to hide those weapons from inspectors, and its links to terrorist groups. We will consult. But let there be no misunderstanding: If Saddam Hussein does not fully disarm, for the safety of our people and for the peace of the world, we will lead a coalition to disarm him."

On February 5, 2003, Powell made the UN presentation President Bush had referred to. This contained, apparently unknown to Powell, a number of false claims regarding Iraqi WMD, further preparing the way for the Bush administration's Iraq War, but also ultimately internationally damaging Powell's reputation once the bogus nature of the WMD claims was revealed.

Major Political Figures and Advisers

The administration's orientation toward Iraq was influenced by a highly educated cadre of hawkish advisers known as the neoconservatives (Cashman and Robinson 2007: 330–333). One of the most prominent was Paul Wolfowitz, the son of a Polish Jewish immigrant. Much of his extended family had perished during the Holocaust. He grew up mainly in Ithaca, New York, where his father was a statistics professor at Cornell University. He studied mathematics at Cornell but decided to pursue a graduate education in politics at the University of Chicago. As a teenager he had lived in Israel when his father taught briefly at the Israeli Institute of Technology. His older sister, a biologist, married an Israeli and moved to Israel.

Wolfowitz taught at Yale University in the Department of Political Science from 1970 to 1973. After being an aide for Washington state Democratic Senator Henry Jackson, he worked for Republicans, first for the Nixon administration, and then the Ford administration during 1973–1977 in the Arms Control and Disarmament Agency. During the Democratic Carter administration, Wolfowitz was deputy assistant secretary of defense for regional programs (1977–1980). During the Reagan administration, he was head of the State Department's planning staff (1981–1982), assistant secretary of state for Asia and Pacific affairs (1982–1986), and then US ambassador to Indonesia (1986–1989). In the George H. W. Bush administration he served as under secretary of defense for policy (1989–1993). During the Clinton administration, Wolfowitz served as dean of the Paul H. Nitze School of Advanced International Studies at Johns Hopkins University (1993–2001). When George W. Bush became president in 2001, Wolfowitz was appointed deputy secretary of defense, where he reportedly played a major role in promoting regime change in Iraq.

Richard Perle, born in 1941 in New York, earned a bachelor's degree in international politics from the University of California–Los Angeles and later a master's degree in political science from Princeton University. From 1969 to 1980 he served on the staff of Democratic Senator Henry Jackson. Perle worked on the amendment to the 1972 International Grain Agreement that permitted Soviet Jews to leave the USSR. Like other neoconservatives, Perle supported a stronger US military, a hard line on dealing with troublesome states, pro-Israel policies, and the spread of capitalism around the world. He served as

Ronald Reagan's assistant secretary of defense from 1981 to 1987 and from 2001 to 2003 as chairman of the Defense Policy Advisory Board of the Pentagon. Perle advocated Iraqi regime change and was one of the neoconservatives who signed a letter to President Clinton in 1998 calling for the overthrow of Saddam's government.

Douglas Feith was born in Philadelphia in 1953. His father's parents and other family members had perished during the Nazi Holocaust. Feith earned a bachelor's degree from Harvard University and a law degree from Georgetown University. He served as under secretary of defense for policy from 2001 to 2005 during the George W. Bush administration. According to Ricks (2006: 53–54), Feith and his associates may have believed that they were better at analyzing intelligence data on Iraq than the CIA and the Pentagon's Defense Intelligence Agency (DIA). But critics suggested that Feith's Pentagon group of analysts relied too uncritically on "murky intelligence" from various sources.

Following 9/11, Feith, Wolfowitz, and Vice President Dick Cheney, who predicted that US forces would likely "be greeted as liberators" (Fallows 2006: 79), were among those supporting the notion that Saddam's regime was an immediate danger to the security of the United States and should be removed (Draper 2007: 174). A Pentagon investigation of Feith's Pentagon group published in early 2007 indicated that it developed and circulated to "senior decision-makers" intelligence assessments about a possible relationship between Iraq and Al Qaeda that "included some conclusions that were inconsistent with the consensus of the Intelligence Community" (Cloud and Mazzetti 2007).

Critics of the Bush administration suspect that some administration figures recognized the dubious quality of claims about WMD and Iraqi 9/11 links, and were sufficiently historically informed to anticipate that a prolonged war of resistance would follow the invasion. But once US forces had invaded and destroyed the Iraqi regime, the altered context could provide new arguments for remaining in Iraq indefinitely: to prevent a new hostile government from controlling Iraq's oil and to suppress sectarian violence, foreign terrorist fighters, or the influence of Iran (all of which had in fact been brought about or made much worse because of the invasion). In other words, critics suggest that some in the administration understood that the invasion itself would create problems that could be used to justify a prolonged occupation.

Fallows (2006: 47) claims that a number of the difficulties the United States encountered in occupying Iraq were anticipated in various analyses and "laid out in detail and in writing long before the U.S. government made the final decision to attack" and that "it appears that the very people who were most insistent on the need to invade Iraq were most negligent about what would happen next" (2006: 222). He suggests that the ignoring of the preparatory work and warnings might have occurred because planning for the postinvasion situation would likely have slowed down the invasion process. Opponents of the war speculate that avoiding serious consideration of occupation issues was part of the strategy to go to war since this facilitated claims that only a relatively low number of US troops would be needed and that most of them would be in Iraq for only a short time. More realistic estimates might have delayed the invasion long enough for the US public's emotional reaction to 9/11 to moderate to the point where the Bush administration's arguments for attacking Iraq were no longer widely accepted.

Influential Iraqi Exiles

A number of defectors and other exiles played important roles in reinforcing Bush administration arguments for war. An Iraqi known to US intelligence by the code name "Curveball" was a key source for the false but highly circulated story that Saddam's regime had a number of mobile biological weapons labs. According to a CBS *60 Minutes* report (2007) that revealed the identity of Curveball, the CIA delivered this fabricated biological weapons claim to Secretary of State Powell for inclusion in his February 5, 2003, address to the UN.

Of all the Iraqi exiles who sought to overthrow Saddam's regime, three secular Iraqi Shia were particularly important: Ayad Allawi, Ahmed Chalabi, and Kanan Makiya. Allawi was born in 1945 into a prominent family. His father was a doctor and his Lebanese mother was a school administrator. He joined the Baath Party in the 1950s and is thought to have participated in the suppression of leftists following the overthrow of Qasim in 1963, but denied taking part in torturing or killing any of the hundreds of communists who perished at the time (Anderson 2005). After General Abd al-Salam Arif seized control in November 1963, ousting most Baathists from positions of power, both Allawi and Saddam were imprisoned for plotting against the government. Allawi's influential family helped get his release, while Saddam escaped. Allawi participated in the 1968 Baath coup, but he claimed that the brutality of some people he believed were associated with Saddam led him to leave the party while on a visit to Lebanon in 1971. Saddam reportedly tried to get him to return to Iraq but when Allawi, who was working on a medical degree in London, continued to refuse and was suspected of working with British intelligence, he was the target of an ax-wielding assassin in 1978 and spent about a year recovering from his wounds. According to sources cited by Anderson (2005), in the early 1990s British intelligence introduced Allawi to the CIA, which provided assistance to his anti-Saddam Iraqi National Accord (INA). Allawi's approach had been to try to organize a coup against the regime from within. If successful, this could have preserved a unified and stable Iraq, avoided the loss of life caused by the 2003 invasion, and prevented the sectarian violence and anti-US insurgency. But, as noted in chapter 5, the INA failed.

In contrast, Ahmed Chalabi supported the invasion. Born in 1944, Chalabi, a cousin of his political rival Ayad Allawi, was from a prominent Shia banking family that had lost much of its wealth inside the country after the 1958 anti-monarchy revolution and moved to Lebanon. He was charged in 1992 with defrauding Jordan's Petra Bank of about $215 million during the 1980s. He was found guilty in absentia and sentenced to twenty-two years of hard labor (Packer 2006: 76).

With CIA aid, Chalabi established bases for his Iraqi National Congress (INC) army in Iraqi Kurdistan. He anticipated that INC victories over Iraq's forces in the north would provoke large-scale uprisings and military defections, which would bring down the regime. But as described in chapter 5, his approach also failed and after 1996 the CIA appeared to temporarily lose faith in him. Neoconservatives, however, embraced Chalabi and his INC. A number of totally false accounts of WMD in Iraq were provided by Iraqi defectors reportedly connected to the INC, such as Adnan Saeed al-Haideri, whose claims of Iraqi WMD were published in the *New York Times*, as described in the US News Media section on pages 144–146 (Isikoff and Corn 2006: 55–59).

Kanan Makiya, a professor of Islamic and Middle Eastern studies at Brandeis University, raised awareness of the Iraqi regime's brutality. His *The Republic of Fear*, originally published in 1989, described Saddam's Iraq as a repressive totalitarian state. In his 1994 book, *Cruelty and Silence: War, Tyranny, Uprising and the Arab World*, Makiya criticized many Arab intellectuals for allowing their anti-Americanism to cause them to be relatively silent about the brutalities of Saddam's regime.

Makiya's father was an Iraqi architect and his mother was British. After attending Baghdad College, a Jesuit-run high school, he studied architecture at the Massachusetts Institute of Technology. Makiya supported the US-led invasion on the humanitarian grounds that it would replace the Baathist regime with one far more beneficial for the large majority of Iraqis. He reportedly predicted to President Bush two months before the start of the war that US troops would be greeted by Iraqis with "sweets and flowers" (Filkins 2007: 2). He later said he believed that the majority of Shia did initially welcome the Americans, but many were soon alienated by American policies that seemed to display more concern for seizing and securing Iraq's oil facilities than for the physical well-being and cultural heritage of the Iraqi people.

According to Filkins (2007: 4), Makiya believed that the biggest mistake the Americans committed "was the decision to occupy Iraq and govern the country themselves." This made Iraqis suspicious of US intentions. Failure to provide security for the general population also disillusioned many (NPR 2007), and he felt another serious American mistake was disbanding the Iraqi army (described later in this chapter) instead of preserving it after removing unacceptable personnel (Filkins 2007: 4). But according to Makiya, Iraqis also made mistakes. Political stability after the ouster of Saddam depended on the leaders of the Shia majority providing a sense of security for the Sunni Arab minority. Instead, Shia leaders, such as those in the US-approved twenty-five-person Iraq Governing Council (IGC), engaged in sectarian political tactics. When car bombs detonated in predominantly Shia neighborhoods, Shia leaders responded excessively and, as Makiya saw it, counterproductively, by arming Shia death squads that kidnapped and killed Sunni Arabs suspected of being insurgents or terrorists.

US Intelligence Agencies

Because of its help to Afghan Islamic fighters against Soviet forces in the 1980s, the CIA had extensive contacts in Afghanistan. In contrast, the agency had relatively few sources inside Iraq. This made it and other US intelligence organizations dependent on Iraqi exiles and defectors for information. Another factor apparently contributing to Bush administration representations concerning Iraq was the existence of a special intelligence investigatory and analysis group in the Pentagon associated with Under Secretary of Defense for Policy Douglas Feith that reportedly came into existence shortly after 9/11. Its ties to top-ranking officials in the Bush administration, such as Vice President Cheney and Secretary of Defense Donald Rumsfeld, key neoconservatives in addition to Feith such as Wolfowitz, and influential Iraqi exiles, such as Ahmed Chalabi, allowed Feith's group to compete with and, according to some observers, out-maneuver or intimidate the CIA and the DIA (Cloud and Mazzetti 2007; Hersh 2003, 2; Isikoff and Corn 2006: 100–114; Ricks 2006: 53–55). Critics believed that Feith's associates, who became known as the Policy Counterterrorism Evaluation Group (PCEG), also called "the Iraq intelligence cell," too often utilized flawed and unconfirmed reports they found among the CIA's raw data or offered by Iraqi defectors or other exiles. Some Iraqi expatriates had personal interests in providing false information, such as fabricated ties between Iraq and Al Qaeda or concocted accounts of WMD, ranging from the desire to get rid of Saddam's regime to gaining legal immigration status and a job or financial aid. The PCEG members reportedly appeared to believe they were better than others at finding connections between international terrorist groups and Iraq, although CIA and DIA analysts often questioned their conclusions (Isikoff and Corn 2006: 114).

One notorious story forwarded to US government officials was a supposed meeting of Mohammad Atta, a leader of the 9/11 attackers, with an Iraqi agent in Prague on April 9, 2001. Investigators found no evidence of any such meeting. Instead surveillance photos and cell phone records showed Atta was in Virginia and Florida during April. Yet the story was widely circulated in the US media and was cited by some government officials as evidence of cooperation between 9/11 terrorists and Iraq. Other highly publicized falsehoods that helped justify the Iraq War were those told by the mysterious Iraqi defector Curveball and the African-uranium story.

Curveball

Iraqi defector Rafid Ahmed Alwan, known for years as Curveball, left Iraq and made his way to a German refugee center in November 1999. He claimed to be an Iraqi chemical engineer who because of his high university grades had been made director of a facility in Djerf, Iraq. Alwan claimed the facility was a production center for mobile biological weapons and said he had witnessed an accident there in 1998 in which biological agents had killed twelve workers (CBS News 2007). He was hidden at secret locations and interrogated by German intelligence but refused to meet with American intelligence officers, forcing the CIA to rely on interrogation transcripts.

Alwan had actually worked at the facility until 1995, which was in reality a seed purification plant, and so could provide some convincing information about its physical layout. But his description of how the supposed biological weapons trucks entered what he described as the arming building appeared impossible according to satellite photos. The reason was that in 1997, when Alwan said he still worked there, new construction had occurred, of which he was not aware. Alwan also claimed that a certain Iraqi scientist worked in the biological weapons program. But unknown to Alwan, Saddam had allowed the scientist to emigrate in 1999 and when he was interviewed by British intelligence, he denied Alwan's story, also indicating that Alwan's university grades tended to be low. German agents became doubtful about Alwan's credibility and passed this warning on to the CIA (Risen 2006: 117). According to Risen (2006: 117–119), at least one CIA official tried to convince his superiors that the Curveball story was suspect and should not be presented to the UN as evidence of Iraqi WMD.

According to the November 4, 2007, CBS *60 Minutes* program on Alwan, CIA Director George Tenet sent a message to the director of German intelligence on December 18, 2002, saying that he was going to meet with President Bush in three days to discuss Iraq and wanted a US intelligence expert to speak to Curveball or have Curveball interviewed on television. Forty-eight hours later, the head of German intelligence replied in a letter that neither option was possible, adding that attempts to verify Curveball's information had not been successful. According to *60 Minutes*, Tenet, through a spokesperson, claimed that he never saw the letter and on December 21 met with President Bush and told him that making a public case that Saddam had WMD was "a slam dunk" (Woodward 2006: 90). Secretary of State Powell would make the claim of Iraqi mobile biological weapons before the UN on February 5, 2003 (Ricks 2006: 90–94). Before the presentation, Powell's chief of staff, Colonel Larry Wilkerson, reportedly went to the CIA and says he was told the information on biological weapons was accurate.

Powell included the claim of Iraqi mobile biological weapons as what many viewed as a central feature of his UN address. Three days later, UN inspectors visited the site Alwan described and found the ends of the building where Alwan said the weapons vehicles entered and exited lacked doors for vehicles to pass through and were also blocked by stone walls. Twenty days later, UN inspectors returned to the facility to test for traces of biological weapons agents and found nothing, but this did not stop the invasion. Alwan apparently concocted the biological weapons story so that he would be given political asylum and receive assistance from Western intelligence agencies.

African Uranium

Another false WMD claim the Bush administration used to justify the Iraq War was that Iraq had sought five hundred tons of milled uranium oxide ("yellowcake," derived from uranium ore by removing impurities) from the African country of Niger for use in developing nuclear weapons. The origin of the forged documents indicating such an event is not clear. Italian military intelligence, apparently believing they had come from the Niger embassy in Rome, shared the information with both US and British intelligence (Isikoff and Corn 2006: 86–92). When the forged documents reached Washington, a State Department analyst expressed doubt. First, five hundred tons of yellowcake represented about one-sixth of Niger's annual output, requiring thousands of barrels and many trucks, an amount almost impossible to conceal. Second, the French corporation overseeing the mining companies would have been unlikely to approve such a sale. Finally, it was unbelievable that Niger, a poor landlocked country of about 12 million people with uranium as virtually its only marketable resource, would have agreed to such a deal because it would have provoked retaliation from the United States and Britain and almost certainly cost more in foreign aid and trade than Iraq could pay for the yellowcake. Nonetheless, the Pentagon's DIA distributed a report on the alleged Niger documents on February 12, 2002, with the alarming title "Niamey (capital of Niger) signed an agreement to sell 500 tons of uranium a year to Baghdad" (Isikoff and Corn 2006: 91). Vice President Chaney reportedly ordered the CIA to investigate the matter further. A retired State Department official working in international finance, Joseph Wilson IV, who was married to Valerie Plame Wilson, the CIA's head of operations of the Counterproliferation Division's Joint Task Force on Iraq, was asked to go to Niger to investigate. Wilson spoke French, had served in Niger, and was familiar with the uranium industry. Wilson's investigation led him to doubt the Niger yellowcake story. And French intelligence concluded the documents were forged. In response, the CIA temporarily blocked the story from presidential speeches. But then on September 25, 2002, Britain indicated it had evidence that Iraq had tried to acquire African uranium. When President Bush gave his January 28, 2003, State of the Union address, he included the false assertion, citing British intelligence, that "Saddam Hussein recently sought significant quantities of uranium from Africa" (Bush 2003a).

The US Congress

On October 10, 2002, the US House of Representatives voted 296 to 133 in favor of the "Joint Resolution to Authorize the Use of United States Armed Forces Against Iraq" (US House of Representatives 2003). The bill stated, in part, that "Iraq both poses a continuing threat to the national security of the United States and international peace and security in the Persian Gulf region and remains in material and unacceptable breach of its international obligations by, among other things, *continuing to possess and develop a significant chemical and biological weapons capability, actively seeking a nuclear weapons capability, and supporting and harboring terrorist organizations*" (CBS 2002; emphasis added). The resolution continued: "The president is authorized to use the Armed Forces of the United States as he determines to be necessary and appropriate in order to (1) defend the national security of the United States against the continuing threat posed by Iraq; and (2) enforce all relevant United Nations Resolutions regarding Iraq." About 97 percent of Republican representatives and 39 percent of Democratic representatives approved the war resolution. The next day the US Senate voted 77 to 23 in favor (US Senate 2003), with 98 percent of Republican senators and 57 percent of Democratic senators voting for the bill.

All three of the Democratic senators who ran for president in 2004 voted in favor of the resolution, as did all four of the Democratic candidates for president in 2008 who had been senators in 2002: Joe Biden of Delaware, Hillary Clinton of New York, Christopher Dodd of Connecticut, and John Edwards of North Carolina. Since the majority of Americans seemed to favor a US attack on Iraq at the time of the vote, it is likely that some senators contemplating running for president believed it was politically beneficial to support the war authorization resolution.

The affirmative vote of Democratic Senator John Kerry, a former member of Vietnam Veterans Against the War, surprised many since the bill seemed to parallel the Gulf of Tonkin Resolution, which gave President Lyndon Johnson the authority to wage the Vietnam War. Although Kerry later opposed the Iraq War, his behavior seemed at times confusing. In accepting the presidential nomination at the 2004 Democratic Convention, Kerry described himself as reporting for duty as he had once volunteered to serve in Vietnam. This seemed somewhat strange to some previously attracted by his membership in a major anti–Vietnam War group. His attempt to simultaneously appeal to one segment of voters by publicizing his heroic war record and another by criticizing the Iraq War, which he had helped bring about by voting for the October 2002 resolution, probably contributed to President Bush's reelection.

The US Military

Many US war planners believed that victory in Iraq would be quick and relatively easy since the US armed forces were immensely superior to the Iraqi military, especially after it had been significantly weakened by not being able to upgrade equipment after the 1991 Gulf War due to UN sanctions. That there was no countervailing superpower that might come to the aid of an invaded Iraq also likely contributed to US war advocates' feeling relatively uninhibited and optimistic about the war. These circumstances undoubtedly played a role in the Defense Department's decision to use significantly fewer troops than several major military leaders believed were necessary to secure Iraq, apparently intending to compensate for limited ground forces through airpower and advanced weapons technology. US officials who dissented from Bush administration war plans and predictions risked retribution (Fallows 2006: 115). Another innovation was to rely on far more private contractors for tasks previously carried out by the armed forces. By the fall of 2007 there were tens of thousands of private contractors, many with their own weapons, vehicles, and aircraft, in Iraq. Many were former soldiers who could earn as much as three or four times their military salaries by working in private firms. Unlike US military personnel, private contractors seemed generally immune from punishment for any abuses in Iraq.

Although the invasion force of approximately 120,000 US ground soldiers was capable of defeating the Iraqi military, it was insufficient to accomplish a number of important tasks, such as providing security for much of the population or preventing the removal of weapons from unguarded arsenals.

The US News Media

News media coverage appeared decidedly prowar. The press seemed to uncritically accept claims that an elementary knowledge of Middle East history would call into question, such as the supposed link between Saddam and Al Qaeda. It tended to ignore internationally renowned moral critics of the coming war, such as Pope John Paul II and Nelson Mandela, and the enormous gap between US and international public opinion. Reporting on the opposition to the war among most people around the world would logically have required the uncomfortable task of explaining why they were opposed. In the view of many observers, the US news media served as cheerleaders for the war (Ricks 2006: 433).

There were several reasons for what some reporters later came to view as a serious lapse in objective journalism in the months leading up to the war. First, US media personnel were emotionally overwhelmed by 9/11 and reacted with the same patriotism and rage that gripped most Americans. Second, they were probably influenced by President Bush's 90 percent approval rating following 9/11 and subsequent opinion polls showing a high level of support for invading Iraq. Networks or newspapers reporting criticisms of the administration's arguments for war or that provided what some viewed as too prominent coverage of civilian casualties in Afghanistan received many hostile e-mails making accusations of anti-Americanism. Some also experienced complaints from advertisers or government officials (Moyers 2007: 4). News media executives understood that if they resisted public, business, or government pressures, they could suffer damaging consequences. Viewers, readers, or advertisers could turn to competitors who fell more completely into step with the Bush war policy, and access to prominent government officials might be denied. Individual reporters were also concerned about negative consequences if they did their jobs properly.

Those journalists who investigated the administration's war justifications by accessing easily available information found plentiful evidence to raise serious doubts, such as UN weapons inspectors' reports indicating no evidence of WMD. Others consulted Middle East experts who explained the absurdity of Saddam and Al Qaeda working together.

Cohen (2006) states that three weeks before the Iraq invasion, MSNBC terminated Phil Donahue's popular show, whose content had often been critical of Bush policies. Cohen's own debate segments on the approaching war, which he warned would hinder the fight against Al Qaeda and lead to a "quagmire" in Iraq, had been terminated in October 2002. "Myth and misinformation went unchallenged" as the military experts often expressed their views unopposed. Bush administration assertions were often parroted and its neoconservative officials and advisers, and approved Iraqi exiles, were often provided with a relatively exclusive national forum.

The US military, believing that relatively unregulated press coverage of the Vietnam War, including accounts of civilian and military casualties, had helped undermine support for that war, sought to deal with news coverage of the Iraq War differently. Reporters were provided with news briefings and some were allowed to be "embedded," a term referring to traveling with a military unit. According to Lindner (2009: 32–45), embedded reporters, compared to others in his study, tended to report soldiers' experiences rather than those of Iraqis. As the invasion proceeded, some news organizations were apparently so committed to the existence of Iraqi WMD that they eagerly reported encounters with innocuous factories, mobile health clinics, or old, rusted artillery shells as evidence that the Bush administration's elusive WMD were about to be uncovered.

Evidence also indicates that some news agencies did a better job of accurately informing their viewers or listeners than others. The World Public Opinion group (2003) reports that a study of polls conducted from June through September 2003 by the Program on International Policy at the University of Maryland and Knowledge Networks indicated that 60 percent of US adults had one or more significant misperceptions about Iraq and that these were strongly related to support for the war. About 48 percent of Americans incorrectly believed that a connection between Saddam's regime and Al Qaeda had been found, while 25 percent mistakenly believed that world public opinion had supported the US invasion, and 22 percent thought that WMD had been found. Of those with none of the misperceptions, only 23 percent supported the war, while 53 percent were prowar among those with one misperception, 78 percent with two misperceptions, and 86 percent with all three misperceptions. Furthermore, the study indicated that accuracy of information about Iraq was related to the self-reported primary news source. Among those whose primary news source was National Public Radio or the Public Broadcasting Service, about 77 percent had none of the three misperceptions, while the percentage for those whose primary news source was print media was 53 percent, CNN 45 percent, NBC 45 percent, ABC 39 percent, CBS 30 percent, and Fox 20 percent.

US Public Opinion

In stark contrast to international public opinion, US public opinion initially supported the invasion. A Gallup poll conducted between February 17 and 19, 2003, found that 57 percent of respondents favored invading Iraq with US ground forces to remove Saddam's regime (Curtin 2003: 2). Support increased in the weeks following the invasion as US troops engaged in combat and seemed to be winning a quick victory. A BBC survey conducted in May and June 2003 found that public support for the war in the United States had increased to about 74 percent (BBC 2003).

However, when no WMD were found and when investigations indicated Iraq had no role in carrying out the 9/11 attacks, support declined. The anti-occupation insurgency and Iraqi sectarian violence also likely reduced support after 2003. A series of surveys conducted by different polling organizations in late September or October 2007 all found that a majority of the US public opposed the Iraq War, although the percentage varied in relation to the specific wording of survey questions. The Pew Research Center poll of 2,007 adults conducted October 17 through 23, 2007, asked, "Thinking about Iraq: Do you think the U.S. made the right decision or the wrong decision in using military force against Iraq?" Fifty-four percent responded "wrong decision," 39 percent "right decision," and 7 percent "unsure" (Pollingreport.com 2007). A CBS News poll of 1,282 adults conducted October 12 through 16, 2007, asked, "Looking back, do you think the United States did the right thing in taking military action against Iraq, or should the U.S. have stayed out?" Fifty-one percent answered "stayed out," 45 percent "right thing," and 4 percent "unsure." In comparison, an ABC News/*Washington Post* poll of 1,114 adults conducted September 27 through 30, 2007, asked, "All in all, considering the costs to the

United States versus the benefits to the United States, do you think the war with Iraq was worth fighting, or not?" Fifty-nine percent answered "not worth it," 38 percent "worth it," and 3 percent "unsure." And a CNN/Opinion Research Corporation poll of 1,212 adults conducted October 12 through 14, 2007, asked, "Do you favor or oppose the U.S. war in Iraq?" Sixty-five percent responded "oppose," 34 percent "favor," and 2 percent "unsure."

Surveys conducted during the Vietnam War also indicated initial public support followed by majority opposition. The many Americans eventually opposing the Vietnam War, though, did so for different reasons. Some were against it because they felt the war was unjustified and immoral, some because they were disappointed by the human and financial costs and length of the war, and others because they thought the military was not allowed to fight the war with the appropriate resources and under the proper conditions. Similar differences probably existed to some extent among those indicating they opposed the Iraq War in response to the shortest and most simply worded questions.

International Public Opinion

Immediately after the 9/11 attacks, public opinion polls in a number of countries indicated that majorities sympathized with the United States. However, condolences of leaders in some nations contrasted with the opinions of citizens, who, while appalled at the horror and tragic loss of life in the United States, believed that the 9/11 casualties were in part victims of their own government's policies around the world. In certain Islamic nations many reacted as if the United States had reaped the results of past unjust actions, and Osama became a popular name for newborn boys.

Large majorities in many nations opposed the US-led invasion of Iraq. As best can be determined, the majority of people in most countries viewed the invasion as a seizure of Iraq's oil. The United States was seen as falsifying justifications for war against a nation that had not attacked it, and violating international law by invading it, an action for which Iraq in the early 1990s had been severely punished. The prolonged occupation indicated to many that the United States had no intention of allowing the Iraqis genuine sovereignty or a truly democratic political system. The Bush administration appeared willing to employ, but not admit to, torture and to deliver captives to other countries for more extreme abuse. The invasion of Iraq constituted one of the most damaging events ever to US international moral standing.

Hostility toward the United States in nations where it already existed deepened and much of the goodwill the United States had enjoyed after 9/11 in other countries, such as Germany, Spain, and France, dissipated. In some nations in the coalition force, a wide gulf existed between the conservative governments that committed their armed forces to the occupation and the majority of the people. For example, despite the fact that in January 2003 about 80 percent of Spaniards interviewed in an *El Mundo* poll and about 73 percent of Italians questioned by the Survey Working Group opposed a US invasion of Iraq, the conservative governments in both countries ordered their militaries to participate in the postinvasion occupation (Curtin 2003: 1–3). Similarly, in

February 2003, a *Kyoto News* survey indicated that about 79 percent of Japanese opposed the Iraq War even though Japan's military participated in the occupation. Surveys in Britain and Australia also indicated that majorities opposed attacking Iraq without UN approval, although troops from those countries participated in the invasion. Eventually lack of popular support for the war led to the downfall of prowar governments in some democracies, such as Spain, Italy, and Australia.

Pope John Paul II, who had played a significant role in the democratization of Eastern Europe, opposed the invasion. This may have contributed to lower levels of support for the war in US states with large proportions of Catholics as well as lower than average military enlistment rates in those states for at least two years after 9/11 (DeFronzo and Gill 2008: 6–11; see also chapter 9, section on the US Volunteer Army). Nelson Mandela and others in the struggle for democracy in South Africa also condemned the invasion.

The United Nations

The Bush administration claimed the right to take military action because Iraq violated UN Resolution 687 by not fully cooperating with UN inspectors and by continuing to possess WMD. However, British Prime Minister Tony Blair and US Secretary of State Powell suggested working through the UN. But nations on the Security Council, including permanent members Russia, France, and China with the power to veto UN actions, refused to approve new resolutions that Iraq was resisting UN inspection efforts enough to justify military action. Secretary-General Kofi Annan denied that any nation had the legal right to invade Iraq without specific UN approval and stated in 2004 that the US-led invasion of Iraq in 2003 had been "outside the UN Charter" and "illegal" (Williams 2006: 264).

Intense US pressure led to UN Security Council Resolution 1441 on November 8, 2002, which identified the situation in Iraq as perhaps the greatest threat to the world's security but, to the dismay of some prowar neoconservatives, appeared to provide Iraq an opportunity to avoid war if it cooperated with the UN Monitoring, Verification and Inspection Commission (UNMOVIC) and the International Atomic Energy Agency (IAEA). According to Williams (2006: 260), "The resolution also avoided giving the United States the automatic right to attack that the hawks had originally insisted on." In response to Resolution 1441 and warnings from the Russians that compliance with the resolution was almost certainly the last opportunity to avoid war, Iraq began cooperating with the new UN inspectors to a greater degree than ever before. The Iraqis also delivered a 12,000-page account of WMD and related topics to the inspectors. Since the Iraqis seemed to be fulfilling their disclosure and cooperation obligations, many governments concluded that only the discovery of WMD by inspectors could lead to a new UN resolution permitting an invasion of Iraq.

According to Williams (2006: 261–262), Hans Blix, the head of UNMOVIC, was dissatisfied with US intelligence. If US claims about Iraqi WMD were correct, then why, despite increased levels of Iraqi cooperation, were the inspectors finding no trace of WMD where the Americans told UNMOVIC to look? Blix began to suspect that the Iraqis were telling the truth and there were no WMD.

But the Bush administration continued to insist that the Iraqis were lying. According to Woodward (2006: 107), President Bush informed Secretary of State Powell on January 13, 2003, that the United States was going to war. As noted earlier, Powell was sent before the UN on February 5 to make the case for war (CNN 2003a). Powell claimed that Iraq had seven mobile biological agent factories and "between 100 and 500 tons of chemical weapons agents," none of which were found after the invasion. The address asserted that "most U.S. experts" thought that thousands of aluminum tubes sought by Iraq were for centrifuges to enrich uranium for an Iraqi nuclear program. The tubes were in reality components of short-range rockets, as Iraq claimed, which were permitted by the UN for defensive purposes. Powell also referred to "numerous intelligence reports over the past decade" indicating Saddam had retained "a covert force of up to a few dozen" UN-banned Scud long-range missiles, but none were found.

Powell, one of the few members of the Bush administration to push for UN approval of US actions regarding Iraq, later seemed to feel betrayed by being given questionable and in reality incorrect information for a historic presentation to the world community only weeks before the invasion. The multiple falsehoods in Powell's speech appeared to doom the political career of a person many thought might become the first African-American president. In May 2004, Powell apologized for "misleading the Security Council and the American public" (Polk 2005: 169).

After the invasion, Secretary-General Kofi Annan was eager to establish an important role for the UN in the "administration and relief of Iraq" (Williams 2006: 265). On March 28 the Security Council unanimously passed Resolution 1472, stating that "those causing the war should meet the humanitarian needs of the civilian population," including "food and medical supplies" (United Nations 2003a). Resolution 1483 on May 22, 2003, gave the United States and the United Kingdom collectively the "authority" to govern Iraq (United Nations 2003b) and the legal authority to sell Iraqi oil and use the resulting revenue. The UN intended to oversee expenditure of much of these funds, but according to Williams (2006: 265–266), lack of US cooperation made this ineffective and US courts decided that companies accused of looting the Iraqi development fund could not be prosecuted since no US Treasury money was alleged to have been stolen. In reality, these UN resolutions "provided a legal framework for the functioning of an occupation that resulted from an invasion that most of its members considered illegal."

Annan sent Human Rights Commissioner Sergio Vieira de Mello to be the UN's chief representative in Iraq. Although international leaders may have intended to monitor US and British actions and promote the welfare of the Iraqi people, the postinvasion UN resolutions and presence outraged many Iraqis. From their point of view, the UN had engaged in monumental hypocrisy. Iraq had been severely punished for invading Kuwait, whose policies posed an extreme threat to Iraq's security and the well-being of its people. But despite Iraq's ridding itself of all WMD, the UN refused to lift the trade sanctions that contributed to hundreds of thousands of deaths. Then after the United States, without UN authorization and under false justifications, led an invasion of Iraq in which thousands of young Iraqis died defending their country, as well as thousands of civilians, the UN leadership seemed to capitulate to US power by in effect legalizing the occupation. And while Iraq was prevented from freely selling its own oil after invading Kuwait, the United States not only did not suffer UN economic sanctions or even a UN vote of condemnation, but instead was allowed to sell Iraq's oil.

Almost certainly as a result of the UN's perceived hypocritical behavior, de Mello and much of his staff were killed in a bomb attack on the UN Iraqi headquarters in one of the first major acts of the Iraqi antioccupation insurgency on August 19, 2003. Following a second bombing near the UN compound on September 22, many surviving UN staff members were withdrawn (Allawi 2006: 171).

US-Based Corporations

The benefits of controlling Iraqi oil and using Iraq as a new super military base to protect or intimidate the already dependent Persian Gulf states was undoubtedly of interest to many in the US oil industry as well as to the former executives of such companies who served in the Bush administration. By occupying Iraq and putting in place a government that owed its existence and physical safety to US military forces and private security firms, the Bush administration was dealing with Iraqi officials who generally were in no position to object to its requests regarding Iraqi oil or anything else.

Control of Middle East oil, enhanced by domination of Iraq's energy resources, provided the United States with a major advantage against economic competitors heavily dependent on the region's oil. By influencing how Gulf states spent their oil revenues, the United States and many of its corporations could actually benefit from higher oil prices because the high prices could drain the surpluses of the European Union and Japan into the Middle East. When Middle Eastern governments purchase vast amounts of US technology, military equipment, and training services, the oil money is in effect redirected to the United States

US corporations also benefited more directly because occupation authorities initially restricted reconstruction contracts in Iraq almost totally to nations that supported the invasion. And as noted earlier in this chapter, there was extensive interest in the prospect that a new Iraqi government could be convinced or pressured to permit the privatization of the country's oil assets, which American corporations could then purchase.

The Decision for War

UN Security Council Resolution 1441, drafted primarily by the United States and Britain in consultation with China, France, and Russia, was unanimously approved fifteen to zero on November 8, 2002. The resolution stated that Iraq was "in material breach of its obligations" in particular because of its "failure to cooperate with United Nations inspectors and the IAEA" (United Nations 2002). Provision 5 required Iraq to give unrestricted cooperation to UNMOVIC and the IAEA. Inspectors were to be allowed to interview any Iraqis who had worked on WMD with no Iraqi government supervision and outside the country with their families if inspectors chose this option. UNMOVIC and the IAEA were to resume inspections within "45 days following adoption of this resolution and to update the Council 60 days thereafter" and to immediately report any interference with inspections.

The Bush administration apparently hoped Resolution 1441 would gain UN support for an invasion as soon as the Iraqis refused to cooperate. The Iraqi National Assembly considered rejecting the resolution, which seemed to require Iraqi scientists and their families to leave Iraq for interviews even if they did not want to, but Saddam was apparently convinced that any show of resistance would lead to a rapid US invasion, perhaps with UN consent. Therefore, Iraq accepted the resolution and began providing an unprecedented level of cooperation to UNMOVIC and IAEA inspectors.

The new inspectors found no evidence of WMD at any site suggested to them by US intelligence. The Iraqis, aware of the preinvasion buildup of US and British forces in neighboring countries, tried to find a new way to stop the attack. According to Polk (2005: 168), Vincent Cannistraro, former head of the CIA's office of counterterrorism, was contacted by the Iraqis with an offer to allow several thousand US troops or FBI agents to search Iraq for WMD. The Iraqis knew they would find nothing since, as Bush administration arms inspector Charles Duelfer's report of October 6, 2004, concluded, Iraq did not possess or produce any WMD "for more than a decade before the U.S. led invasion" (Polk 2005: 168). According to Polk (2005: 168), Cannistraro indicated that the Bush administration rejected the Iraqi proposal.

William Polk, an Arabic-speaking history professor and director of the Center for Middle Eastern Studies of the University of Chicago, traveled to Baghdad on February 1, 2003, to talk with Iraqi Deputy Prime Minister Tariq Aziz. Polk asked whether Iraq had any plans for how to prevent an invasion, but Aziz said, "America has long since decided to attack Iraq and nothing Iraq could do would prevent it" (Polk 2005: 169).

When the United States and Britain claimed that Iraq was still not sufficiently in compliance with Resolutions 687 and 1441 and requested a new Security Council resolution to provide a semblance of international legality for their impending invasion, it soon became clear that the Council would not supply the necessary votes. Rather than risk a humiliating defeat and a clear UN stamp of illegality on their actions, they abandoned the effort.

Many observers concluded that the Bush administration did not invade primarily out of concern for WMD, but instead to gain control of Iraq's oil. This would prevent Saddam's regime from recovering economically and militarily as the effects of sanctions continued to erode and Iraq was able to generate more oil revenue. A revived Iraq could have undermined American influence by reducing the economic dependency of a number of nations on the United States in the way that Venezuela under Hugo Chavez attempted to do. Another reason to attack was that Iraq was militarily weak. Its armed forces were one-third the size they had been in 1991, and more poorly armed because of the inability to purchase new equipment. Further, domestically the time was right to incorporate an attack on Iraq as part of the war on terrorism since in the wake of 9/11, alarmed Americans were receptive to striking hastily at potential threats. Finally, the president's commitment to destroying Saddam's regime seemed to stem in part from personal motivations: to rectify what some viewed as his father's failure to eradicate the Iraqi regime at the conclusion of the 1991 Gulf War, and to avenge the allegedly Iraqi-assisted attempt to assassinate his father.

The claims about Iraqi WMD helped steamroll Congress into giving Bush the authority to invade, similar to how the deceptive representation of North Vietnamese naval attacks against US destroyers in August 1964 caused Congress to quickly pass the Gulf of Tonkin Resolution, allowing President Johnson to wage the Vietnam War. The administration succeeded in redirecting US retaliation for an attack by the terrorist group Al Qaeda against a nation that had nothing to do with 9/11.

Planning for War

Military planning for war may be divided into four phases: Phase I, preparations for combat; Phase II, initial operations; Phase III, combat; and Phase IV, postcombat operations (Ricks 2004). Some Bush administration neoconservatives apparently believed that Phase IV of the Iraq War, the occupation phase, would require fewer troops than Phase III. Others disagreed. Garfield (2006) asserts that "the requirements of Phase IV, not Phases I–III, should determine the size of the intervention force. The U.S. military will assuredly defeat any conventional adversary with a relatively small force. However, the demands of an occupation necessitate a much larger garrison."

Iraq War military planning was influenced by the anticipated response of the Iraqi people, the estimated level of military resistance, and the goals of the invading force (e.g., to seize only specific targets, such as oil fields and key cities, versus occupying the entire country). A concern with minimizing the cost of the invasion financially and politically may also have affected planning.

Many believed the Iraqi people in general would welcome the invaders, depriving Saddam's forces of popular support and the will to resist either the invasion or the occupation. In any case, Iraq's weapons were markedly inferior and, lacking air support, Iraqi forces were vulnerable to US tank-killing A-10 jets and missile-firing helicopters. And since primarily only targets of great economic, political, or military value were to be attacked, it was thought that a relatively small, well-armed force would suffice.

General Eric Shinseki, however, feared that foreign Islamic volunteers might enter Iraq to fight US and British forces. Shinseki had participated in US military operations in Bosnia, where the formula was one soldier for every fifty Bosnians (Ricks 2006: 96). After subtracting the relatively friendly Kurds from the Iraqi population, that meant an occupation force of 300,000. Shinseki believed that the real outcome of the war would be determined in the postinvasion period and that victory required enough soldiers to control the relevant environments, including all areas capable of providing significant resources for resistance fighters. Ricks (2006: 97) cites sources claiming that Deputy Secretary of Defense Wolfowitz criticized General Shinseki's estimate and predicted that the US force in Iraq would be down to about 30,000 to 40,000 well before the end of 2003. Some war advocates speculated that Shinseki's forecast of 300,000 troops, which might strain US resources, was in reality an expression of opposition to the war because of concern that negative consequences of an invasion would be much worse than expected.

Administration neoconservatives repeatedly countered recommendations from experienced military commanders that the invasion force or occupation force or both should be much larger than planned. Some speculated that it was part of neoconservatives' strategy to lowball the cost of the war in troops and money to remove potential obstructions from their central goal of getting into Iraq, because US troops fighting and dying there, coupled with the impact of the occupation on Iraqis, would provide a whole new set of justifications for staying indefinitely.

Secretary of Defense Rumsfeld and the commander of the invasion, General Tommy Franks, believed a relatively small force would be adequate. The invasion, called Operation Iraqi Freedom, was to include combat forces composed of some 120,000 US Army soldiers and Marines, 45,000 UK troops, 2,000 Australians, and 200 Polish commandos. In northern Iraq tens of thousands of KDP and PUK peshmergas would participate, and an additional 128,000 US military personnel would be involved in intelligence, logistic, naval, or air operations.

The Coalition for Operation Iraqi Freedom

The Bush administration announced that a total of forty-nine nations were involved in the "Coalition of the Willing." Their contributions ranged from "direct military participation, logistical and intelligence support, specialized chemical/biological response teams, over-flight rights, humanitarian and construction aid, to political support" (White House 2003). Coalition members in March 2003, beyond the United States and United Kingdom, included Afghanistan, Albania, Angola, Australia, Azerbaijan, Bulgaria, Colombia, Costa Rica, Czech Republic, Denmark, Dominican Republic, El Salvador, Eritrea, Estonia, Ethiopia, Georgia, Honduras, Hungary, Iceland, Italy, Japan, Kuwait, Latvia, Lithuania, Macedonia, Marshall Islands, Micronesia, Mongolia, Netherlands, Nicaragua, Palau, Panama, Philippines, Poland, Portugal, Romania, Rwanda, Singapore, Slovakia, Solomon Islands, South Korea, Spain, Tonga, Turkey, Uganda, Ukraine, and Uzbekistan.

Many of these governments indicated their decisions to support the invasion were influenced by claims of Iraqi WMD in Colin Powell's UN presentation. Although in some cases 70 percent to 80 percent of their populations were opposed, the governing elites in these countries believed supporting the invasion was appropriate for a number of reasons. Japan, for example, is very dependent on Middle Eastern oil for its economy (Miyagi 2006: 106–107). Japanese leaders believed that assisting the United States would help protect their energy supply. Furthermore, Japan relied on US military protection and so felt obligated to deploy its forces to Iraq and pledge $5 billion for Iraqi reconstruction aid (Miyagi 2006: 105). Once Japan's troops were there, Japanese public opposition to the invasion fell from about 78 percent to 54 percent in May 2004 (Miyagi 2006: 110).

The Spanish and Italian governments joined with their fellow conservatives in the Bush administration, but since large majorities in both countries opposed the war, they lost power and their forces were withdrawn from Iraq. Many other countries in the coalition were developing nations in great need of US assistance. Their governments may have felt that for the well-being of their peoples it was wise to at least politically support the invasion or send a few troops to participate in the occupation. Moldova, for example, which first sent personnel in September 2003, had about eleven bomb disposal experts still in Iraq in October 2007 and Albania approximately 120 soldiers (Cohen 2007).

Fawn (2006: 83–101) suggests four major reasons why Central and Eastern European nations supported the invasion: pragmatism, obligations to the United States, opposition to authoritarianism, and fear of WMD. Pragmatically, these states looked to benefit from new or continued economic aid and trade with the United States and perhaps access to reconstruction contracts and Iraqi oil. They also often relied on US military assistance. Poland, the Czech Republic, and Hungary had joined the North Atlantic Treaty Organization (NATO) in 1999, and Bulgaria, Estonia, Latvia, Lithuania, Romania, Slovakia, and Slovenia were admitted in March 2004. Leaders in Georgia and Ukraine also expressed interest in joining NATO (Kamp 2006).

Many in Central and Eastern Europe were grateful for the United States' role in helping to liberate their countries from Russian domination and Communist Party rule. Supporting the United States was a way to repay America. Fawn also believes moral considerations influenced Central and Eastern European support. People who had struggled against authoritarian communist regimes felt obligated to help liberate the Iraqi people from a repressive government.

As noted earlier, 200 Polish commandos participated in invasion combat operations. Later, 2,500 Polish troops joined the occupation (Synovitz 2003). A Polish officer, Major General Andrzej Tyszkiewicz, was put in command of a multinational force in south central Iraq, the Multinational Division South Central, covering three of Iraq's eighteen provinces and sections of two others.

The Invasion

On March 17, 2003, President Bush addressed the American people and the world (Bush 2003b). The rationale for the invasion that dominated the speech was that Iraq still had WMD. Bush claimed, "Intelligence gathered by this and other governments leaves no doubts that the Iraq regime continues to possess and conceal some of the most lethal weapons ever devised." He continued, "Today no nation can possibly claim that Iraq has disarmed. . . . Yet some members of the Security Council have publicly announced they will veto any resolution that compels the disarmament of Iraq." The president expressed his disappointment by saying, "The United Nations Security Council has not lived up to its responsibilities, so we will rise to ours." He went on to announce that

"Saddam Hussein and his sons must leave Iraq within 48 hours. Their refusal to do so will result in military conflict, commenced at a time of our choosing."

Major Aspects of the Invasion

Unlike the 1991 Gulf War, in which weeks of aerial bombardment preceded the ground assault, air attacks and the ground invasion occurred nearly simultaneously in the 2003 Iraq War. The general approach was to identify concentrations of Iraq's military equipment or personnel, direct aircraft or missiles to destroy the targets, and then send ground forces, accompanied by supporting aircraft, for combat against surviving units.

Ground attacks were to be launched from Kuwait with the British heading for Basra and US Army and Marine units driving toward Baghdad, bypassing some Iraqi forces and cities to minimize casualties. The belief was that once Baghdad was taken and top Iraqi leaders killed, captured, or dispersed, the remaining commanders would surrender. Originally, a major US ground attack was to come from Iraqi Kurdistan. However, since Turkey refused to allow the passage of US troops, the revised plan called for hundreds of US paratroopers to fight alongside KDP and PUK soldiers who would make up the majority of anti-Saddam forces in the north.

Trying to Eliminate Saddam

War planners believed the removal of Saddam might precipitate an immediate collapse of Iraqi resistance. According to an October 28, 2007, CBS *60 Minutes* program, the use of bombing attacks to kill Saddam and other key leaders was preceded by US authorities estimating how many civilians were likely to die. The report indicated that the planners could proceed if the number of estimated civilians deaths was twenty-nine or fewer, but that if the prediction was thirty or more, special permission would be required from a higher authority such as the president or the secretary of defense (CBS *60 Minutes* 2007). The report stated that none of the high-priority targets were killed in leadership attacks but that hundreds of civilians perished.

On March 19, the day before the invasion began, an attempt was made to kill Saddam at a compound near Baghdad called Dora Farms. According to Gordon and Trainor (2006: 188–207), the CIA informed Lieutenant General T. Michael Moseley, the Operation Iraqi Freedom combined forces air component commander, that it was 99.9 percent sure that Saddam and his sons were at Dora Farms. Two F-117 stealth bombers were sent to drop two 2,000-pound bunker-busting EGBU-27 satellite-guided bombs each on the target. At the same time the US Navy was to attack Dora Farms with forty-five Tomahawk missiles. The mission failed since neither Saddam nor his family were there.

The Invasion Begins

The next day the drive toward Baghdad, called Cobra II, began (although special operations units almost certainly had already entered Iraq). The title Cobra II was reportedly selected by Lieutenant General David McKiernan, commander of the US 3rd Infantry Division, to be reminiscent of World War II General Omar Bradley's Operation Cobra to liberate France (Gordon and Trainor 2006: vii). The US Army's 3rd Division, equipped with many tanks, headed north toward Baghdad while the 1st Marine Expeditionary Force pushed to the Rumaila oil field. US Marines also entered the port city of Umm Qasr while British forces seized the Faw Peninsula.

One priority was to annihilate what was considered one of Iraq's best units, the Medina Republican Guard Division, which was stationed to the southwest of Baghdad near the city of Karbala. A bombardment reportedly destroyed hundreds of the division's tanks and other vehicles and many soldiers, although survivors were able to damage almost all of the thirty-two Apache helicopters of the 11th Attack Helicopter Regiment used in an attempted deep raid on the division (Gordon and Trainor 2006: 296–320; Ricks 2006: 119).

By March 23, the US 3rd Division was some 150 miles inside Iraq, about halfway to Baghdad. There were weapons arsenals throughout southern Iraq originally intended by the regime to counter any repetition of the 1991 Shia uprising. But as the 2003 invasion proceeded, Iraqis used the weapons to attack US and British supply lines. In some areas groups of Republican Guard soldiers and Iraqi paramilitary forces adopted mobile hit-and-run tactics. Some engaged in suicidal attacks, firing machine guns from pickup trucks or attempting to drive trucks or cars filled with explosives up to coalition units and detonate them.

Advancing US forces discovered a problem they could not adequately solve. They repeatedly encountered arsenals of AK-47 assault rifles, ammunition, and various types of artillery and mortar shells. Theoretically a US commander had three choices: leave a detachment of troops to guard the arsenal; blow it up; or simply abandon it. The choice was reportedly often number three. US commanders lacked sufficient personnel to guard all the arsenals and since they had been told that the Iraqis had WMD that might be stored in the arsenals, they were sometimes afraid to blow them up for fear of contaminating soldiers and civilians (Ricks 2006: 145–146). Thus arsenals were often abandoned. Thousands of Iraqis removed the weapons and explosives to sell or give away to friends and relatives or move to new secret locations for use in the anti-occupation insurgency.

A three-day sandstorm and rainstorm, which began on March 24, temporarily halted the drive toward Baghdad. But US aircraft using special sensors and radar were still able to continue destroying hidden Republican Guard vehicles, missile launchers, and personnel with pulverizing high-explosive bombs. The inability of Iraqi forces to effectively conceal heavy weapons or concentrations of personnel from high-tech US air attacks undermined morale and convinced some to adopt mobile small-unit tactics and others to just give up and go home.

Capturing Baghdad

After Qusay Hussein ordered three Republican Guard divisions to the southwest of Baghdad to block the American drive, they were decimated by coalition airpower long before they could engage US ground forces (Ricks 2006: 125). The United States' plan for Baghdad had been to encircle it and destroy concentrations of Iraqi armor and artillery from the air before actually commencing a ground assault into the city. However, the defeat of Republican Guard and Iraqi army divisions outside the city raised the possibility that Baghdad might be captured more swiftly and with much less fighting than anticipated. To assess this option, on early April 5, two days after the US 3rd Division captured Baghdad International Airport, the first of two high-speed armored penetrations (called "Thunder Runs") deep into the city took place. The first incursion included a column of twenty-nine tanks that moved north up Highway 8 and then turned west on the road to the airport. The armored column entered the city with its tanks and Bradley fighting vehicles continuously hit by rocket-propelled grenades and rifle fire. During the eight-hour foray, the 3rd Division believed about 2,000 Iraqi combatants were killed, but Iraqis claimed many civilians also perished (Ricks 2006: 126). The second armored incursion occurred on April 7, beginning like the first with a push north on Highway 8 but then turning east into central Baghdad, past Baath Party Headquarters to the Republican Palace (Gordon and Trainor 2006: xxv; Ricks 2006: 127). Many of those captured were Syrians who had recently arrived to help defend Baghdad. The two Thunder Runs demonstrated that US armored columns could move anywhere in the capital and strike at will. Some US tanks reportedly endured as many as seven rocket-propelled grenade hits, demoralizing Baghdad's defenders (Ferris 2003).

Regime officials, including Saddam and his sons, went into hiding while fighting continued in parts of the capital. A number of Iraqi military and government leaders were persuaded to cease organized resistance. General Tommy Franks stated in a May 2003 interview in *Defense Week* that US Special Operations Forces had contacted and bribed a number of senior Iraqi officers not to resist coalition forces: "The Pentagon said that bribing senior officers was a cost-effective method of fighting and one that led to fewer casualties" (Buncombe 2003). Another tactic was e-mailing Iraqi officers messages to convince them not to fight for Saddam (Ferris 2003). Even those officers who were loyal to the regime had to worry about the level of information the Americans had about them personally and how many of their fellow officers would respond favorably to the e-mails.

On April 9 a US Marine colonel decided to bring down the giant Saddam statue in central Baghdad's Firdos Square. "And it was a quick-thinking Army PSYOP (Psychological Operations) team that made it appear to be a spontaneous Iraqi undertaking" (Zucchino 2004). It was hoped that the sight of civilians participating in bringing down the statue would convince regime supporters to give up. The psyops team reportedly appealed on loudspeakers for Iraqis to assist in toppling the statue. Then a chain was fastened to the statue and a marine recovery vehicle, which pulled the statue down.

On the same day his statue fell, Saddam made his last public appearance in Baghdad in the northwestern district of Al-Adhamiya. He promised the crowd of supporters that he would continue the resistance against the invaders and then quickly disappeared. Within a few days he left the city, arriving in Ramadi on April 11 and then the town of Hit on April 12 (Gordon and Trainor 2006:

xxix). Qusay and Uday accompanied their father to Ramadi but continued west into Syria, where they stayed April 13 through 18. However, they were asked to leave the country, apparently arriving back in Iraq on April 19. They made their way to Mosul, where they were killed by US forces on July 22.

Action Elsewhere

In Iraqi Kurdistan, tens of thousands of Kurdish soldiers of the PUK and KDP, accompanied by US Special Operations Forces, drove from central Kurdistan toward Halabjah in the southeast of Kurdistan and west toward Mosul (Gordon and Trainor 2006: xxvii). By April 4 Kurdish peshmergas and Special Operations Forces had driven the fundamentalist Ansar al-Islam from Halabjah.

When Baghdad fell on April 9, many Iraqi soldiers in Kirkuk and Mosul abandoned their bases and went home. Kurdish peshmergas then seized Kirkuk on April 10 in violation of a previous understanding. Fearing a negative Turkish reaction, Marine General Pete Osman convinced Kurdish units to leave and by April 11 US forces controlled Kirkuk and its three hundred oil fields (Gordon and Trainor 2006: 525).

To prevent the Kurds from seizing Mosul, elements of the 26th Marine Expeditionary Unit were rushed from their ships in the Mediterranean to reinforce about thirty Special Operations Force soldiers. On April 22, 1,600 US troops, including elements of General David Petraeus's 101st Airborne Division, entered the city. Petraeus began negotiating with leaders of local ethnic groups and tribes to restore order and organize a new city government.

British commander General Robin Brims attempted to adapt to local circumstances in predominantly Shia Basra, and the British tried to facilitate an anti-Baathist Shia seizure of the city. British forces remained largely outside the city and, believing that most Iraqi soldiers in Basra wanted to give up the fight, allowed them an escape route. Brims employed more restrictive rules of engagement than some US commanders so as to limit civilian casualties (Gordon and Trainor 2006: 521). On April 6, British Challenger tanks entered Basra and accepted the mayor's surrender of the city.

Although some predominantly Sunni cities, such as Fallujah and Ramadi, were bypassed, the coalition command believed that the war could not truly be declared won until US forces seized Tikrit, Saddam's hometown. After limited fighting, Tikrit was occupied on April 14 by elements of the 1st Marine Division under Brigadier General John Kelly (Gordon and Trainor 2006: 510), and on April 16 President Bush announced that Iraq had been "liberated" (Polk 2005: 170).

On May 1, 2003, Bush flew to the *Abraham Lincoln*, a 1,092-foot-long aircraft carrier returning from almost ten months of operations in the wars in Afghanistan and Iraq (Battle Fleet 2003). In front of thousands of cheering sailors and a large banner with the words "Mission Accomplished," he declared that the war against Iraq had been won, although he anticipated that some fighting would continue. The official tally for US fatalities between the beginning of the war on March 20 and May 1 was 139, while 33 British personnel had died (Kinsella 2007: 26). Polk (2005, 169) estimates that during this period approximately 10,000 civilians and tens of thousands of Iraq's soldiers were killed.

Many top figures in the Baathist regime, however, had not been captured. To help US soldiers become familiar with the faces of these individuals and to publicize their "wanted" status more broadly, US Army psyops developed the famous "most wanted" deck of fifty-five playing cards, each with the face and title of a wanted Iraqi official. The decks included the fifty-two normal cards plus three extra. There were also two jokers, one showing Iraqi military ranks and the other displaying Arab tribal titles (Defend America 2009; Friedman 2004; Zucco 2003). Saddam appeared on the ace of spades, while Qusay was on the ace of clubs and Uday on the ace of hearts. Presidential secretary Abid Hamid Mahmud al-Tikriti was on the ace of diamonds. The large majority in the deck were captured or killed.

Occupation

Shortly after US forces captured Baghdad, a wave of looting began targeting government buildings, some businesses, and the national museum. One factor causing looting was the population's desperation. Another was that in October 2002, Saddam had granted amnesty to tens of thousands of prisoners, many political prisoners, but others common criminals (Polk 2005: 170–171). The collapse of regime law enforcement capabilities presented a huge opportunity made worse by the inability or lack of interest of US commanders to use their forces for the security of the general population or cultural institutions. The hundreds of unguarded weapons arsenals provided arms for criminals, civilians needing to protect themselves from lawless conditions, and the developing insurrection.

Polk (2005: 178) notes that the chaos following the invasion appeared "almost deliberate." US troops initially failed to stop looting (Fallows 2006: 102). Polk (2005: 178) claims that the US State Department's relatively comprehensive plan for Iraq was replaced by a tougher approach favored by some Bush administration personnel, apparently intended to more radically transform Iraqi society. One implication is that the more desperate Iraqis became regarding obtaining the basic necessities of life and safeguarding personal security, the more willing they would be to follow orders and cooperate with the restructuring set forth by the occupying powers.

President Bush selected retired three-star Army General Jay Garner as chief US authority in Iraq. Garner's official title was director of the Office for Reconstruction and Humanitarian Assistance for Iraq. He arrived in Iraq on April 21 and brought with him members of an advisory committee that included Ahmed Chalabi. Fearing that the United States was replacing Saddam's nationalist regime with a neocolonial apparatus to assist in America's exploitation of Iraq's oil, more Iraqis became supportive of the emerging antioccupation insurgency.

Garner faced difficulties from his neoconservative associates in the Defense Department. First, he sought to maintain much of Iraq's armed forces and use them for reconstruction and to help maintain order. Second, he wanted to hold rapid elections to give Iraq a democratic government. Both of these measures were opposed by many of the returning Iraqi exiles, some of whom were virtually unknown in the country, and by powerful neoconservative US officials. Exile leaders believed the Iraqi army was an instrument of repression that could not be trusted and could inhibit major reforms.

According to Ricks (2006: 154), Chalabi campaigned for radical de-Baathification, which seemed to mean removing all Baathists from significant positions of authority in the government or its institutions, including the educational system. Neoconservatives tended to argue that such a cleansing of government was necessary to build a democratic Iraq since, in their view, the Baath Party was similar to the German Nazi Party. Others suggested that many Baathists were misguided nationalists or careerists who had joined the party to gain access to higher-paying positions and should be judged on an individual basis rather than dismissed because of party affiliation. Removing Baathists would provide those with power in postinvasion Iraq the opportunity to fill the vacated positions with people loyal to them. Since turmoil was increasing and Garner seemed to be defying Washington neoconservatives, he was forced to turn control over to L. Paul Bremer III, the new presidential envoy.

Occupation Policies and the Insurgency

Secretary of Defense Rumsfeld called General Garner on April 24 to inform him that Bremer, a retired State Department official and diplomat, would be sent as presidential envoy to Iraq to control the US occupation as chief of the Coalition Provisional Authority (CPA) (Ricks 2006: 135). Garner declined to serve under Bremer, a darling of the US neoconservatives. Bremer's background appears similar to many who rose to high political office, State Department positions, or top jobs in the CIA. Born in 1941, he grew up in one of the wealthiest US towns, New Canaan, Connecticut, where he went to the private New Canaan Country School. Later he attended elite Phillips Academy in Andover, Massachusetts, whose alumni included Presidents George H. W. Bush and George W. Bush, and Jeb Bush, former governor of Florida. Bremer graduated from Yale in 1963 and then earned a certificate of political studies from the Institut D'Etudes Politiques of the University of Paris and later an MBA from the Harvard Graduate School of Business Administration (World Biography 2007). He entered the diplomatic corps in 1966, serving as deputy ambassador to Norway from 1976 to 1979 and as ambassador to the Netherlands from 1983 to 1986. He was President Reagan's ambassador-at-large for counterterrorism from 1986 to 1989. From 1989 to 2000, Bremer worked for former Secretary of State Henry Kissinger's consulting firm, Kissinger Associates. Speaker of the House Dennis Hastert appointed Bremer chairman of the National Commission on Terrorism in 1999. President Bush selected him to serve on the post-9/11 Homeland Security Advisory Council in June 2002. Bremer also oversaw a Heritage Foundation Study called "Defending the Homeland" and served on the National Academy of Science commission on combating terrorism. Since invading Iraq was partly justified as a component in the war on terrorism, appointing Bremer might have been viewed as a way to reinforce that argument.

According to Risen (2006: 136–137), the CIA believed that before the invasion members of Saddam's regime, including former intelligence officers, prepared to engage in guerrilla warfare against occupation forces by hiding weapons. But critics of Bremer believe he made three mistakes that helped bring about or significantly increase armed resistance to the occupation: launching an excessive de-Baathification program, disbanding the Iraqi armed forces, and postponing the implementation of a new sovereign Iraqi government (Ricks 2006: 158–166). When he flew into Baghdad on May 12, 2003, the day after General Franks dissolved Iraq's Baath Party (CNN 2003c), Bremer said he was shocked by the number of fires burning in the city (PBS 2006; Tyler 2003). He stated that one of his first goals was to restore law and order and stop widespread looting. He noted that giving the US military the authority to shoot looters had helped quickly end looting in Haiti in the mid-1990s. But this created a problem when the comment was leaked to the press (PBS 2006).

On May 16, Bremer issued CPA Order Number 1, the de-Baathification directive (Allawi 2006: 150). He claimed that this policy had been determined in Washington and presented to him the day before he left for Baghdad (PBS 2006). It required that all senior Baathist Party members be removed from government institutions and banned from any positions in the public sector (Ricks 2006: 158–159). According to the order, any party member employed in the upper three levels of any government entity, whether a ministry, educational institution, or corporation, was to be considered a senior party member and removed. Bremer estimated the number to be expelled from their jobs at about 20,000 (Cockburn 2007: 132; PBS 2006), but critics figured that 30,000 to 50,000 people would be affected and likely become strong opponents of the occupation (Ricks 2006: 159). Total Baath Party membership at the time of the invasion was estimated at 600,000 to 700,000.

According to Ricks (2006: 159–161), who describes Bremer's momentous May actions in his chapter titled "How to Create an Insurgency (I)," members of the CPA staff were greatly concerned when shown the order, because they believed that government ministries would lose their most qualified personnel when the country needed them most. Bremer claimed that he hoped distinctions could be made between those who belonged to the party because of its ideology and those who had joined simply because they thought membership would help them get a good position.

Implementation of the order was turned over to the successor to General Garner's Iraqi advisory committee, which Bremer named on July 13 the Iraq Governing Council (IGC) with twenty-five members. According to Polk (2005: 180), Bremer appointed thirteen Shia Arabs to the IGC, five Sunni Arabs, five from the Kurdish factions, one Turkoman, and one Assyrian Christian. Of the twenty-five, the Turkoman and two of the Shia were women and another of the Shia was the head of the Iraqi Communist Party. The IGC included Chalabi of the INC, Allawi of the INA, Talabani of the PUK, and Mahmoud Barzani of the KDP. The IGC, according to Bremer (PBS 2006), allowed Chalabi to disproportionately influence de-Baathification, which led to the council's implementing the policy more broadly.

Bremer's explanation for de-Baathifcation was that the party was one of the main mechanisms of repression and had been modeled to some extent after the German Nazi Party (NRO 2006; PBS 2006). Therefore, de-Baathification was part of providing the context for establishing a democratic political system. Others, however, believed the correspondence of the Baath Party, whose ideology appeared to shift over time, to either the German Nazi Party or the Russian Communist Party of Stalin's era appears to have been primarily in terms of structural characteristics, such as one-party rule, state control of the economy, and party control over the military and the media. Ricks (2006: 160) reported that as many as 85,000 Baath Party members were removed from their jobs, although later about 9,000 sought and were granted permission to return to government service.

On May 23 Bremer issued CPA Order Number 2, the Dissolution of Iraqi Entities (Allawi 2006: 155; Gordon and Trainor 2006: 554–555), which eliminated the Iraqi military, about 385,000 people; the Ministry of the Interior, including the police and internal security forces totaling approximately 285,000; and the 50,000-member presidential security force (Ricks 2006: 162). Order Number 2 has been viewed as possibly the most damaging action of the CPA contributing to the growth of the antioccupation insurgency. Fallows (2006: 102–104) reports that the Army War College, the Center for Strategic Studies, the Future of Iraq Project, and others "had all warned strongly against disbanding the Iraqi Army" and that the Army War College had observed that the Iraqi army was one of the few unifying institutions in Iraqi society.

According to Ricks (2006: 163), CPA Orders 1 and 2 together threw more than half a million people out of work, antagonizing not only them but also people dependent on their incomes. Furthermore, although there were generally disproportionately more Sunnis compared to Shia in the upper ranks of the Baath Party and the armed forces, these were organizations in which Sunnis and Shia worked together. The existence of these integrated institutions was thought to have limited sectarian conflict. When President Bush was described in the book *Dead Certain* by Robert Draper (2007: 211) as unaware that the Iraqi armed forces were going to be disbanded, Bremer made it clear that he had informed both the Pentagon and Bush of his CPA Order Number 2 ahead of time (Andrews 2007).

Many dismissed Iraqi soldiers had been convinced by American propaganda not to fight and that their welfare would be protected after the war. Following CPA Order Number 2 they felt bitterly betrayed. Furthermore, many Iraqis believed that liquidating the Iraqi armed forces, which had fought much larger Iran to a stalemate, and a number of whose units had fought courageously against overwhelming odds in the 1991 Gulf War and the 2003 invasion, was an extreme, intentionally humiliating act on the part of the Americans. In public protests, veterans threatened suicide attacks or to use their military skills against the occupation.

One reason Bremer offered for Order Number 2 was that the Iraqi armed forces had been used to repress the Shia (NRO 2006; PBS 2006). But opponents argued that the situation was more complex in that many in the armed forces were Shia and, in any case, many Shia were relatively secular and had not sympathized with fundamentalist militants or Iranian-assisted Shia who took up arms against the government. The Iraqi military had, of course, also suppressed Kurdish nationalists, and Bremer claimed in an NRO (2006) interview that Kurdish leaders had informed him that they would secede from Iraq if he resurrected the old armed forces.

Summary and Analysis

In the years following the 1991 Gulf War, the United States appeared oriented toward limiting Iraq's capabilities and deterring Iraqi attacks against other nations, rather than overthrowing the regime. Preserving the Baath government was seen as necessary to avoid the country's disintegration and Iranian domination of oil-rich, Shia-populated southern Iraq. Although after Iraq expelled UN inspectors in 1998, the US Congress passed the Iraq Liberation Act, which technically committed the United States to working for regime change, real abandonment of the containment policy occurred with the George W. Bush presidency, which had the will to oust Saddam, and the 9/11 attacks, which provided the public support necessary to act.

The Bush administration gave three main arguments for war: that Iraq was concealing WMD; that Iraq supported terrorism, was probably involved in the 9/11 attacks, and in the future could supply terrorists with WMD; and that the regime brutally repressed the Iraqi people. Opponents of the invasion doubted the existence of Iraqi WMD and rejected the idea that the relatively secular Baathist government had connections to Al Qaeda or 9/11. In addition, they questioned why, of all the repressive governments in the world, the United States was so concerned about ousting Saddam's regime while helping friendly monarchal dictatorships in oil-rich countries hold on to power. Their answer was that the real intention was to seize Iraq's oil and increase US domination of all Middle East energy resources upon which so much of the world, including America's economic rivals, depends.

A constellation of actors played significant roles leading up to the Iraq War. President Bush claimed Iraq had WMD and that the UN was ineffective. He also seemed personally motivated to avenge an alleged Iraqi assassination plot against his father. The administration was influenced by its neoconservative members, a number of whom were closely tied to Israel and reflected its hostility toward Saddam's regime. Several Iraqi exiles were also prominent in supplying invasion rationale. While some had been absent from Iraq for many years, recent defectors often provided false information about nonexistent WMD that the Bush administration and Britain used to justify war.

US intelligence agencies were accused of "getting it wrong" concerning Iraqi WMD. However, some CIA analysts had strong doubts. But their views appear to have been ignored or suppressed by government officials who favored what turned out to be fallacious reports. A special neoconservative-dominated unit within the Pentagon appeared able, with the support of powerful figures in the administration, to overcome opposition from the CIA or the DIA. Among the stories circulated to justify an invasion were tales of a meeting between an Al Qaeda operative and an Iraqi intelligence agent, mobile biological weapons, and African uranium oxide.

The US Congress failed to critically evaluate both the president's arguments for war and the questionable intelligence reports. Some observers were dismayed that members of Congress did not comprehend the parallel between their being stampeded into voting for war against Iraq based on nonexistent WMD, and how Congress in 1964 fell for the misrepresentation of events in the Gulf of Tonkin and voted to, in effect, authorize the Vietnam War. All the Democratic candidates for the 2004 and 2008 presidential elections who had been senators in 2002, when most Americans supported attacking Iraq, sided with the Republicans and voted to give Bush the authority to go to war. The US military assured the administration that it could carry out the rapid conquest of Iraq while continuing to wage war in Afghanistan. Certain generals, however, appeared to question the wisdom of shifting from containment to invasion of Iraq, and some favored employing larger numbers of ground troops, especially for the occupation.

The US news media, in the view of many, displayed a lapse of objective journalism in the lead-up to war and during the invasion. Some observers described the press as cheerleaders for war. Those who attempted to display more journalistic integrity by reporting criticisms of the rationale for war risked negative consequences from major news outlets, which feared repercussions from corporate advertisers, the administration, and the public.

US public opinion was understandably strongly affected by 9/11. President Bush, who had failed to win the popular vote in the 2000 election, saw his approval rating soar to an astronomical 90 percent in the wake of the attacks. In this context, his claims about Iraq convinced many Americans to support the invasion. In contrast, international public opinion was overwhelmingly opposed. The UN's behavior was inconsistent, reflecting intense US pressure in contention with nations opposing the approaching war. In the end, China, Russia, France, and other countries refused to support the invasion, forcing the United States, Britain, and their allies to attack Iraq without UN approval.

The war design called for fewer troops than some military experts thought necessary. War planners believed that factors such as an enormous advantage in military technology and airpower, and the expectation that most Iraqis supported the overthrow of the Baath regime, would compensate for the limited size of the invasion force. Air attacks devastated Republican Guard and regular Iraqi army divisions. The commanders of some Iraqi units chose not to fight against overwhelming odds. Much of the resistance to the invasion came in the form of ambushes by groups of Republican Guard soldiers, paramilitary militias, and foreign volunteers, including some suicide bombing attacks. These actions provided a preview of the antioccupation insurgency.

Many arsenals around the country were looted. Some Iraqis planned to use the weapons against the occupation and others simply for self-defense. Baghdad fell after two rapid armored incursions by US forces on April 5 and 7. A week later US Marines captured Saddam's hometown of Tikrit and on April 16

Bush declared that the war had been won. Later, on May 1, he made a more dramatic announcement of victory on the deck of the US aircraft carrier *Abraham Lincoln*. As it turned out, both the war and the suffering continued.

CPA decisions to remove many Baath Party members from government ministries and to disband the defeated regime's armed forces deprived Iraq of experienced administrators and technically skilled professionals and threw as many as 500,000 out of work, some of whom joined insurgent groups or criminal gangs. For many Iraqis, in a pattern reminiscent of colonial or neocolonial situations, the only available employment was to go to work for the occupiers' military or corporations operating in Iraq, or to join the new CPA-organized police or army. Economic desperation served as an asset to the US-led coalition's effort to reshape Iraqi society by tying physical survival to cooperation with the occupying powers.

References and Further Readings

Allawi, Ali A. 2007. *The Occupation of Iraq: Winning the War, Losing the Peace.* New Haven, CT: Yale University Press.

Ali, Tariq. 2003. *Bush in Babylon: The Recolonisation of Iraq.* New York: W. W. Norton and Company.

Anderson, Jon Lee. 2005. "A Man of the Shadows." *New Yorker*, January 24. www.newyorker.com/archive/2005/01/24/050124fa_fact1?printable=true (accessed November 1, 2007).

Andrews, Edmund L. 2007. "Envoy's Letter Counters Bush on Dismantling Iraq Army." *New York Times*, September 4. www.nytimes.com/2007/09/04/washington/04bremer.html.

Arnove, Anthony. 2007. *Iraq: The Logic of Withdrawal.* New York: Henry Holt.

Battle Fleet. 2003. "U.S. S. Abraham Lincoln CVN72." www.battle-fleet.com/pw/his/lincoln.htm (accessed November 14, 2007).

BBC. 2000. "Pope's Prayer for Iraq." March 19. http://news.bbc.co.uk/2/hi/middle_east/682407.stm (accessed September 16, 2007).

———. 2002. "Profile: Ahmed Chalabi." *BBC News*, October 3. http://news.bbc.co.uk.

———. 2003. "World Opposed to Bush and Iraq War, BC Poll Says." June 18. http://english.people.com.cn/200306/18/print20030618_118439.html.

———. 2004. "Who's Who in Iraq: Iyad Allawi." May 28. http://news.bbc.co.uk/2/hi/middle_east/3757923.stm (accessed September 16, 2007).

BP Statistical Review of World Energy June 2007. www.bp.com/statisticalreview.

Bremer, L. Paul III. 2006. *My Year in Iraq: The Struggle to Build a Future of Hope.* New York: Simon & Schuster.

Buncombe, Andrew. 2003. "US Army Chief Says Iraqi Troops Took Bribes to Surrender." *The Independent*, May 24. http://news.independent.co.uk/world/middle_east/article105987.ece.

Bush, George W. 2001. "Freedom at War With Fear." Presidential address to a joint session of Congress and the nation, September 20. http://georgewbush-whitehouse.archives.gov/news/releases/2001/09/20010920-8.html.

———. 2002a. "President Delivers State of the Union Address." January 29. http://georgewbush-whitehouse.archives.gov/news/releases/2002/01/20020129-11.html.

———. 2002b. "President Bush Outlines Iraqi Threat." Cincinnati Museum Center, October 7. http://georgewbush-whitehouse.archives.gov/news/releases/2002/10/20021007-8.html.

———. 2003a. "President Delivers State of the Union Address." January 28. http://georgewbush-whitehouse.archives.gov/news/releases/2003/01/20030128-19.html.

———. 2003b. "President Says Saddam Hussein Must Leave Iraq Within 48 Hours." March 17. http://georgewbush-whitehouse.archives.gov/news/releases/2003/03/20030317-7.htm.

Cashman, Greg, and Leonard C. Robinson. 2007. *An Introduction to the Causes of War: Patterns of Interstate Conflict from World War I to Iraq.* Lanham, MD: Rowman & Littlefield.

CBS *60 Minutes.* 2007. "Bombing Afghanistan." October 28. www.cbsnews.com/stories/2007/10/25/60minutes/main3411230.shtml.

———. 2008. "Interrogator Shares Saddam's Confessions." January 27. www.cbsnews.com/stories/2008/01/24/60minutes/printable3749494.shtml.

CBS News. 2002. "House Resolution Against Iraq." October 10. www.cbsnews.com/stories/2002/10/10/attack/main525165.shtml.

———. 2007. "Faulty Intel Source 'Curve Ball' Revealed." November 4. www.cbsnews.com/stories/2007/11/01/60minutes/main3440577.shtml.

Cheney, Dick. 2004. "Full Text of Dick Cheney's Speech at the Institute of Petroleum Autumn Lunch, 1999." *Energy Bulletin,* June 8. www.energybulletin.net/node/559.

CIA World Factbook: Iran. www.cia.gov/library/publications/the-world-factbook/geos/ir.html.

CIA World Factbook: Iraq. www.cia.gov/library/publications/the-world-factbook/geos/iz.html.

CIA World Factbook: Kuwait. www.cia.gov/library/publications/the-world-factbook/geos/ku.html.

Cloud, David S., and Mark Mazzetti. 2007. "Prewar Intelligence Unit at Pentagon Is Criticized." *New York Times,* February 9. www.nytimes.com/2007/02/09/washington/09feith.html?_r=1.

CNN. 2002. "Senate Approves Iraq War Resolution." CNN.com, October 11. http://archives.cnn.com/2002/ALLPOLITICS/10/11/iraq.us.

———. 2003a. "Transcript of Powell's U.N. presentation." CNN.com, February 6. www.cnn.com/2003/US/02/05/sprj.irq.powell.transcript.

———. 2003b. "Bush: Iraq Is One Victory in War on Terror." CNN.com, May 2. www.cnn.com/2003/ALLPOLITICS/05/01/sprj.irq.bush.speech/index.html.

———. 2003c. "Franks: Baath Party Dissolved." May 11. http://transcripts.cnn.com/TRANSCRIPTS/0305/11/sm.17.html.

———. 2007. "Poll: War Opposition Reaches High Despite Reports of Less Violence." CNN.com, November 8 (accessed November 8, 2007).

Cockburn, Andrew. 2004. "The Truth About Ahmed Chalabi." *Counterpunch,* May 20. www.counterpunch.org/chalabi05202004.html (accessed November 1, 2007).

Cockburn, Patrick. 2007. *The Occupation: War and Resistance in Iraq*. London: Verso.

Cohen, Jeff. 2006. "Inside TV News: We Were Silenced by the Drums of War." December 26. www.truthout.org/article/jeff-cohen-inside-tv-news-we-were -silenced-drums-war.

Cohen, Roger. 2007. "Coalition of the Reluctant." *New York Times*, October 15. www.nytimes.com/2007/10/15/opinion/15cohen.html?hp.

Curtin, J. Sean. 2003. "Japanese Anti-War Sentiment on Iraq in Accord with Global Opinion." *Japanese Institute of Global Communications Social Trends* 28 (February 24). www.glocom.org/special_topics/social_trends/20030224 _trends_s28/index.html.

Defend America. 2009. "Iraq's Most Wanted." March 12. www.defendamerica .mil/iraq/iraqi55.

DeFronzo, James, and Jungyun Gill. 2008. "Religious Adherence and Military En- listment Before and After the 9/11 Attacks." *Interdisciplinary Journal of Research on Religion*. www.religjournal.com/articles/article_view.php?id=24.

Draper, Robert. 2007. *Dead Certain: The Presidency of George W. Bush*. New York: Simon & Schuster.

Drogin, Bob. *Curveball: Spies, Lies, and the Con Man Who Caused a War*. New York: Random House.

Fallows, James. 2006. *Blind into Baghdad*. New York: Vintage Books.

Fawn, Rick. 2006. "Central and Eastern Europe: Independent Actors or Supplicant States." In Rick Fawn and Raymond Hinnebusch, eds., *The Iraq War: Causes and Consequences*, 83–101. Boulder, CO: Lynne Rienner.

Ferraro, Vincent. 2003. "Another Motive for Iraq War: Stabilizing Oil Market." *Hartford Courant*, August 12. www.mtholyoke.edu/offices/comm/oped/ Motive.shtml.

Ferris, John. 2003. "A New American Way of War? C4ISR in Operation Iraqi Freedom, a Provisional Assessment." *Journal of Military and Strategic Studies* (Spring– Summer). www.jmss.org/2003/spring-summer/documents/ferris-infops.pdf.

Filkins, Dexter. 2007. "Regrets Only?" *New York Times*, October 7. www.nytimes .com/2007/10/07/magazine/07MAKIYA-t.html?_r=1.

Friedman, Herbert A. 2004. "Operation Iraqi Freedom." April 29. www.psywarrior .com/OpnIraqiFreedomcont2.html.

Garfield, Andrew. 2006. *Succeeding in Phase IV: British Perspectives on the U.S. Effort to Stabilize and Reconstruct Iraq*. Philadelphia: Foreign Policy Research Institute. www.fpri.org/enotes/20060908.military.garfield.britishperspective iraq.html.

Goldenberg, Suzanne. 2007. "Bremer Refutes Bush's Accusations Over Iraqi Army." *Guardian Unlimited*, September 4. www.guardian.co.uk/world/ 2007/sep/04/iraq.usa1.

Gordon, Michael, and Bernard E. Trainor. 2006. *Cobra II: The Inside Story of the Invasion and Occupation of Iraq*. New York: Knopf Publishing Group.

Greenwald, Robert. 2006. *Iraq for Sale: The War Profiteers*. www.robertgreenwald .org/docs.php and http://iraqforsale.org.

Hersch, Seymour M. 2003. "Annals of National Security: Selective Intelligence." *New Yorker*, May 12. www.newyorker.com/archive/2003/05/12/030512fa _fact?printable=true.

Hiro, Dilip. 2007. *Blood of the Earth: The Battle for the World's Vanishing Oil Resources*. New York: Nation Books.

Isikoff, Michael, and David Corn. 2006. *Hubris: The Inside Story of Spin, Scandal, and the Selling of the Iraq War*. New York: Crown.

Judicial Watch. 2003. "Cheney Energy Task Force Documents Feature Map of Iraqi Oilfields." July 17. www.judicialwatch.org/printer_iraqi-oilfield-pr.shtml.

Kamp, Karl-Heinz. 2006. "Ukraine: Not Ready for NATO." *International Herald Tribune*, July 10. www.iht.com/articles/2006/07/10/opinion/edkamp.php.

Kinsella, David. 2007. *Regime Change: Origins, Execution and Aftermath of the Iraq War*. Belmont, CA: Thomson Wadsworth.

Kinsley, Michael. 2003. "Unauthorized Entry—The Bush Doctrine: War Without Anyone's Permission." *Slate*, March 20. www.slate.com/id/2080455.

Klare, Michael T. 2005. "Mapping the Oil Motive." *TomPaine.Common Sense*, March 18: 1–5. www.tompaine.com/print/mapping_the_oil_motive.php.

Kubursi, Atif. 2006. "Oil and the Global Economy." In Rick Fawn and Raymond Hinnebusch, eds., *The Iraq War: Causes and Consequences*, 247–256. Boulder, CO: Lynne Rienner.

Lindner, Andrew M. 2009. "Among the Troops: Seeing the Iraq War Through Three Journalistic Vantage Points." *Social Problems* 56, 1 (February): 21–48.

Makiya, Kanan (Al-Khalil, Samir). 1994. *Cruelty and Silence: War, Tyranny, Uprising, and the Arab World*. New York: W. W. Norton.

———. 1998. *Republic of Fear: Saddam's Iraq*. Berkeley: University of California Press.

Mann, James. 2004. *Rise of the Vulcans: The History of Bush's War Cabinet*. New York: Viking.

Maugeri, Leonardo. 2006. *The Age of Oil: The Mythology, History, and Future of the World's Most Controversial Resource*. Westport, CT: Greenwood.

Miyagi, Yukiko. 2006. "Japan: A Bandwagoning 'Lopsided Power.'" In Rick Fawn and Raymond Hinnebusch, eds., *The Iraq War: Causes and Consequences*, 103–114.

Moyers, Bill. 2007. "Buying the War." *Bill Moyers Journal*, April 25. www.truthout.org/docs_2006/042707H.shtml; www.pbs.org/moyers/journal/btw/watch.html.

National Public Radio (NPR). 2007. "Kanan Makiya: Changing Assumptions On Iraq." April 18. www.npr.org/templates/story/story.php?storyId=9635035.

NBC Nightly News. 2007. October 25.

NRO (National Review Online). 2006. "Interrogatory: An American in Baghdad, L. Paul Bremer III on his *Year in Iraq*." January 10. www.nationalreview.com/interrogatory/bremer200601100900.asp (accessed November 16, 2007).

Officers. 2007. "Officers: Ex-CIA Chief Tenet a 'Failed' Leader." April 29. www.cnn.com/2007/US/04/29/tenet.letter/index.html.

Olbermann, Keith. 2007a. *Countdown with Keith Olbermann*. MSNBC, September 11. www.msnbc.msn.com/id/20742066.

———. 2007b. "Olbermann to Bush: 'Your Hypocrisy Is So Vast.'" MSNBC, September 20. www.msnbc.msn.com/id/20896378.

"Osama bin Laden: In the Name of Allah." 2001. *Biography*. http://store.aetv.com/html/product/index.jhtml?id=70644.

Packer, George. 2006. *The Assassin's Gate*. New York: Farrar, Straus, and Giroux.

Paterson, Graham. 2007. "Alan Greenspan Claims Iraq War Was Really for Oil." *Times Online*, September 16. www.timesonline.co.uk/tol/news/world/article 2461214.ece.

Paul, James A. 2002. "Great Power Conflict Over Iraqi Oil: The World War I Era." *Global Policy Forum* (October): 1–4. www.globalpolicy.org/security/oil/ 2002/1000history.htm.

PBS (Public Broadcasting Service). 2004. "The Invasion of Iraq: Operation Iraqi Freedom." *Frontline*. February 26. www.pbs.org/wgbh/pages/frontline/shows/ invasion/cron.

———. 2006. "The Lost Year in Iraq: Interviews: L. Paul Bremer." *Frontline*. www.pbs.org/wgbh/pages/frontline/yeariniraq/interviews/bremer.html (accessed November 16, 2007).

Polk, William R. 2005. *Understanding Iraq*. New York: Harper Perennial.

Pollingreport.com. 2007. www.pollingreport.com/iraq.htm (accessed November 3, 2007).

Ricks, Thomas E. 2004. "Army Historian Cites Lack of Postwar Plan." *Washington Post*, December 25. www.washingtonpost.com.

———. 2006. *Fiasco: The American Military Adventure in Iraq*. New York: Penguin Press.

———. 2007. "Bush wants $50 Billion More for Iraq War." *Washington Post*, August 29. www.washingtonpost.com.

Risen, James. 2006. *State of War: The Secret History of the CIA and the Bush Administration*. New York: Free Press.

Suskind, Ron. 2008. *The Way of the World: A Story of Truth and Hope in An Age of Extremism*. New York: Harper Collins.

Synovitz, Ron. 2003. "Iraq: Polish Role Relieves Some of the U.S. Burden." Global Security.org. www.globalsecurity.org/wmd/library/news/iraq/2003/09/iraq -030904-04092003193821.htm.

Tyler, Patrick E. 2003. "Aftereffects: Law and Order: American Troops Step Up Efforts to Curb Crime in Iraqi Capital." *New York Times*, May 16. www .nytimes.com.

United Nations. 1991. Resolution 687. April 3. www.fas.org/news/un/iraq/sres/ sres0687.htm.

———. 2002. Security Council Resolution 1441. November 8. www.un.org/docs/ scres/2002/sc2002.htm.

———. 2003a. Security Council Resolution 1472. March 28. http://daccessdds .un.org/doc/UNDOC/GEN/N03/302/09/PDF/N0330209.pdf?OpenElement.

———. 2003b. Security Council Resolution 1483. May 22. http://daccessdds .un.org/doc/UNDOC/GEN/N03/368/53/PDF/N0336853.pdf?OpenElement.

US House of Representatives. 2002. "'To Authorize the Use of the United States Armed Forces Against Iraq' Passed 296–133." October 10. http://projects .washingtonpost.com/congress/107/house/2/votes/455/.

US Senate. 2002. "US Senate Roll Call Votes 107th Congress—2nd Session: A Joint Resolution to Authorize the Use of United States Armed Forces Against Iraq, Yeas 77, Nays 23." October 11. www.senate.gov/legislative/LIS/roll_call _lists/roll_call_vote_cfm.cfm?congress=107&vote=00237&session=2.

Vest, Jason. 2002. "The Men from JINSA and CSP." *The Nation,* September 2. www.thenation.com/docprint.mhtml?i=20020902&s=vest.

Walgrave, Stefaan, and Joris Verhulst. 2009. "Government Stance and Internal Diversity of Protest: A Comparative Study of Protest Against the War in Iraq in Eight Countries." *Social Forces* 87, 3 (March): 1355–1388.

White House. 2003. "Operation Iraqi Freedom: Coalition Members." http://georgewbush-whitehouse.archives.gov/news/releases/2003/03/20030327-10.html.

Williams, Ian. 2006. "The Role of the United Nations." In Rick Fawn and Raymond Hinnebusch, eds., *The Iraq War: Causes and Consequences,* 257–268.

Woodward, Bob. 2004. *Plan of Attack.* New York: Simon & Schuster.

———. 2006. *State of Denial: Bush at War, Part III.* New York: Simon & Schuster.

World Biography. 2007. "Louis Paul Bremer III." www.worldbiography.net/bremer_paul.html (accessed November 16, 2007).

World Public Opinion. 2003. "Misperceptions, the Media and the Iraq War: Study Finds Widespread Misperceptions on Iraq Highly Related to Support for War." www.worldpublicopinion.org.

Wyden, Peter. 1979. *Bay of Pigs: The Untold Story.* New York: Simon & Schuster.

Zucchino, David. 2004. "Army Stage Managed Fall of Hussein Statue." *Los Angeles Times,* July 3. http://articles.latimes.com/2004/jul/03/nation/na-statue3.

Zucco, Tom. 2003. "Troops Dealt Old Tool." *St. Petersburg Times,* April 12. www.sptimes.com/2003/04/12/Worldandnation/Troops_dealt_an_old_t.shtml.

Zunes, Stephen. 2006. "The United States: Belligerent Hegemon." In Rick Fawn and Raymond Hinnebusch, eds., *The Iraq War: Causes and Consequences,* 21–36.

7

||||||||||||||||||||||||||||||||||||||||||||||||||||||||||||||||||||||||||||||||||||||||||||||||||||||||||

Iraq in the
Context of Previous
US Interventions
and the Vietnam War

In *Overthrow*, Stephen Kinzer (2006: 1) argues that the 2003 invasion of Iraq is best understood within the context of previous US foreign interventions. He suggests that a more powerful country attacks a less powerful one typically to "impose its ideology, increase its power, and/or gain control of valuable resources." He believes that American corporations came to expect that the United States would protect their investments and profit-making activities in other nations even if this meant interfering in foreign political systems or, in some cases, ousting uncooperative governments.

Kinzer claims that before World War II, US leaders often admitted their intentions, as in the case of President William Howard Taft's successful effort to remove President Jose Santos Zelaya of Nicaragua in 1909 (Kinzer 2006: 5). But that pattern of intervention changed after the war and the USSR's detonation of an atomic bomb on August 29, 1949, because an open US attack on another country could potentially provoke the Soviets to move against a US ally or even precipitate nuclear war. Therefore, intervention tended to become more covert, typically combining economic pressure with support for pro-US elements within a targeted country such as occurred in the overthrows of the governments of Mohammad Mossadeq in Iran, Jacobo Arbenz in Guatemala, and Salvador Allende in Chile. Since these three governments had come to power through democratic elections, it was all the more necessary for US agents to try to conceal their involvement. However, Kinzer believes that the demise of the Soviet Union in 1991 permitted a return to direct military interventions. This chapter describes several US foreign interventions, focusing mainly on the three most relevant to Iraq: Iran in 1953, Vietnam from 1964 to 1973, and Afghanistan from 1980 to 1989.

Iran 1953: Britain and the United States Inadvertently Help Revive Islamic Fundamentalism

When the Bolshevik Revolution threatened to spread to Iran, Britain backed the tough and charismatic Reza Khan, commander of the British-advised Iranian Cossack Brigade, to oust the Qajar dynasty and establish his own stronger Pahlavi dynasty, capable of preventing a socialist revolution that would endanger British interests. During World War II, Britain and the USSR jointly occupied Iran. The British forced Reza, who was thought to be sympathetic to Germany, to abdicate in favor of his European-educated son, Mohammad Pahlavi. After the war, the National Front alliance of parties in the Iranian parliament led by Mohammad Mossadeq opposed the monarchy and its perceived subservience to British interests.

Mossadeq enjoyed the support of Ayatollah Abul Qassem Kashani's Islamic fundamentalists, who backed the National Front's anti-imperialist orientation in the hope of cleansing Iraq of un-Islamic foreign influences. The National Front moved to place Iran's armed forces under the control of the parliament, rather than the shah. The royal budget was reduced and savings used to benefit the poor through subsidizing medical services.

The parliament, dissatisfied with Iran's share of oil profits from the Anglo-Iranian Oil Company, expropriated the company in 1951. Outraged, the British responded by organizing an international boycott of Iran's oil (Hiro 2007: 92–98). Although Mossadeq looked to America for support in asserting Iran's independence from Britain and moving toward greater democracy, the British convinced the US government that Mossadeq's National Front was a threat not only to Britain but also to US security interests. Devastated by the inability to sell oil, Iran's economy deteriorated, playing into the hands of the British. When Mossadeq enacted regulatory measures to cope with shortages, members of the religiously oriented traditional middle class complained to Kashani, and he withdrew his support for the National Front. As the nationalist coalition fragmented, British and US intelligence agents worked to set the stage for a coup with pro-shah military leaders.

The shah attempted to dismiss Mossadeq as prime minister on August 12, 1953, but failed when the soldiers sent to arrest Mossadeq were themselves arrested by forces loyal to the prime minister. The shah fled the country, sparking celebrations by National Front supporters. But counterdemonstrations supporting the shah were organized by businessmen who benefited from the shah's policies. As rival groups poured into the streets, civil conflict prompted Mossadeq to ask the military to restore order. Pro-shah General Fazlollah Zahedi took advantage of the troop mobilization to launch the coup and attacked the prime minister's headquarters, defended by loyal troops. The pro-shah forces won after about nine hours of fighting, and Mossadeq and other members of his government were arrested. The shah returned to Iran, outlawed the National Front, and ruled like an absolute monarch. With the help of the CIA, in 1957 the shah's regime established the SAVAK (Organization of National Security and Intelligence), which would be accused of torturing and murdering thousands of people.

After Kashani's death in 1961, another fundamentalist leader emerged, Ayatollah Ruhollah Khomeini. In 1963 and 1964 he accused the shah of corruption and of being a tool of foreign powers. Khomeini was expelled from the country in 1964 and took up residence in Shia southern Iraq, where he communicated his ideas about Islamic government, a political system dominated by clerics and acting in accordance with Islamic law, not only to visiting Iranian students and clergy, but also to Shia Iraqis. Khomeini's ideas helped revitalize Shia fundamentalism.

The shah used oil revenues to purchase billions of dollars of modern military equipment, including aircraft, missiles, tanks, and naval vessels, from the United States and Britain, along with technology and machinery. New schools and hospitals were built. As the population became more educated, people became increasingly discontented with the inability to participate in government and the enormous wealth flowing to the shah's family and friends. Iranian clergy were alarmed that Western cultural influences were undermining moral standards. The tens of thousands of foreign military advisers and technicians who came to train Iranians to use new weapons and technology were viewed as a source of moral contamination.

A number of religious and secular revolutionary movements developed. Temporarily bound together by their hatred of the shah's regime, they succeeded in overthrowing it in January 1979. Soon, however, the Islamic fundamentalist branch of the anti-shah coalition, which enjoyed the most popular support and was led by the widely revered leader Ayatollah Khomeini, overcame other groups in the revolutionary alliance and brought to life Khomeini's dream of an Iranian Islamic Republic.

In effect, the covert US–British intervention in Iran in 1953 contributed to the resurgence of Islamic fundamentalism because many Iranians turned to their traditional culture, religious organizations, and leaders in search of the means to free Iran from foreign domination and humiliation. Fundamentalism had the capacity to boost people's sense of self-worth. "The process of modernization in Muslim countries had exposed many educated persons . . . to foreign values and norms and relatively nonreligious lifestyles. But the largely secular ideologies . . . appeared to offer little to the middle and lower classes except a perpetual sense of cultural and technological inferiority and the threat of the progressive erosion of cherished moral values. In contrast, the fundamentalists put forward the appealing notion of a value and belief system ordained by God and, thus, immeasurably superior to all other cultures" (DeFronzo 2007 [1991]: 313). The Anglo-American intervention to reinstate the shah was one of the earliest in the post–World War II pattern of covert measures to destroy governments whose policies were perceived to threaten the freedom of action or profitability of US corporations or perceived American security interests.

The ability of US and British intelligence agents to recruit members of the Iranian armed forces showed that a government attempting to bring about sweeping political and/or socioeconomic change must secure the loyalty of its military. In Iraq after the Baathist revolution of 1968, for example, no officer or soldier was allowed to belong to any political party except the Baath Party.

The Iranian Islamic Revolution of 1979, which succeeded in removing the monarchy widely perceived to have been an instrument of US and British imperialism, had enormous consequences for Iraq, as well as for a number of other nations, Islamic and non-Islamic, including the United States and the USSR. Many Iraqi Shia, alienated by the Baathist regime, were inspired to mount their own revolutionary movement, and Khomeini encouraged them. As noted earlier, Saddam Hussein responded by launching what he thought would be a short war to undermine the Iranian Islamic regime so that internal enemies could overthrow it and set up a new government friendly toward Iraq. His decision to invade was influenced by his perception that Iran's military had been significantly weakened because the United States and Britain had responded to Khomeini's regime and attempts to spread fundamentalist revolution by cutting off weapons sales to Iran.

Instead the Iraqi invasion set in motion the eight-year Iran–Iraq War, in which tens of thousands of Iraqis perished. To avoid defeat, Iraq turned to other oil-rich Arab states for billions in financial assistance, including Saudi Arabia, Kuwait, and the United Arab Emirates, whose ruling monarchs also feared Iran and the threat of Islamic fundamentalist revolution. Many Iraqis came to view their nation as the barrier to Persian aggression and "a shield against Islamic fundamentalism for much of the Arab world" (DeFronzo 2006: 422). They felt bitterly betrayed when Kuwait demanded repayment of the billions in aid it had provided Iraq and actually appeared to overproduce oil, lowering Iraq's badly needed postwar revenues. Thus many Iraqis tended to support their leaders' decision to invade Kuwait and, in their view, reunite it with Iraq. But this in turn resulted in the 1991 Persian Gulf War, in which a US-led coalition forced Iraq to withdraw from Kuwait, and in UN economic sanctions, restrictions on Iraq's sovereignty, the destruction of Iraqi WMD and long-range missiles, and years of UN weapons inspections. As described in chapter 6, this situation set the stage for the US-led invasion of Iraq in 2003.

But the Iranian Islamic Revolution also helped bring about the invasion of Iraq in other ways. The success of Shia Islamic fundamentalists in overthrowing Iran's US-supported monarchy encouraged Sunni Arabs from many countries to go to Afghanistan during the 1980s to join in the struggle against the pro-Soviet Afghan government and Soviet forces occupying the country. The Soviets were eventually defeated and forced to withdraw from Afghanistan, contributing to the fall of the Soviet communist government and the disintegration of the USSR at the end of 1991.

Turmoil and political change in the Soviet Union meant that it could not deter the US-led attack on Iraq's forces in 1991. And the new Russia that emerged from the dismantling of the USSR was less supportive of Iraq's Baathist government and significantly weaker in military strength than America. This meant the United States and Britain had little concern that Russia would attempt to use its armed forces to counter the 2003 invasion. The Islamic victory in the Afghan War also led to events that provided the political opportunity for the Bush administration to invade Iraq. As is described in more detail on pages 190–191 in the section on US intervention in Afghanistan, many of the Islamic volunteers who fought the Soviets there were organized by Osama bin Laden and his associates into Al Qaeda. Objecting to the United States' establishment of a huge military presence in Saudi Arabia after Iraq's invasion of Kuwait, bin Laden turned Al Qaeda against the United States, launching a series of terrorist attacks culminating in 9/11. As noted in chapter 6, this event, which provoked rage, fear, and a desire for revenge among the American people, provided the mass psychological condition the Bush administration could take advantage of to attack Iraq as part of the war on terrorism. Thus British–US intervention in Iran to overthrow a government in 1953 helped give birth to modern political Islamic fundamentalism and set in motion a series of interrelated events that had enormous impacts, including on the Iraqi people.

Guatemala and Cuba

Following its success in getting rid of Mossadeq and installing the far more co-operative shah, the CIA set its sights on newly democratic Guatemala, where a left-leaning government had been elected following many years of right-wing authoritarian rule. A group of young military officers declared the establishment of a democratic political system in 1944. The new constitution set up a public educational system and guaranteed freedom of speech and the right of workers to form labor unions. In late 1944 a reformist former university professor, Juan Jose Arevalo, was elected president and served from March 15, 1945, until March 15, 1951 (Streeter 2006: 325–326, 328). During his presidency, he established a social security system and built new health clinics. By encouraging the formation of labor unions and thereby increasing the cost of labor, he angered the country's upper class and the US-based United Fruit Company (UFCO).

Arevalo's Defense Minister Jacobo Arbenz was elected president in November 1950. His 1952 Decree 900 land reform program was the most sweeping in Guatemalan history. Streeter (2006: 328) describes Decree 900 as breaking "the hold of the agrarian elite by redistributing 1.4 million acres of land to more than 500,000 individual campesinos (peasants)." The Arbenz government extended the land reform to UFCO, which held approximately 550,000 acres in Guatemala, of which 15 percent to 20 percent were planted annually. Arbenz expropriated about 300,000 of UFCO's acres for distribution to the poor and offered to pay in compensation the amount that UFCO said the land was worth when paying taxes to the Guatemalan government.

UFCO executives complained to the Eisenhower administration. The example that Guatemala was setting for other countries in taking significant actions to reclaim its resources, place limitations on corporations' freedom of action, and potentially reduce their profitability contributed to US officials' devising a plan to get rid of the Arbenz government. The CIA provided weapons and financing for an estimated 150 Guatemalan exiles in Honduras headed by Castillo Armas, a former Guatemalan colonel (Streeter 2006: 328) and a small air force of World War II–era fighter-bombers flown by US pilots. According to Streeter, the CIA bribed officials in the Guatemalan armed forces to support the coup. As a result, the government fell within ten days of the invasion and Arbenz was forced to leave the country. Armas reversed the Decree 900 land reform and crushed the labor movement. The Armas dictatorship and later right-wing Guatemalan regimes were accused of killing many opponents.

Survivors of the democratic reform era and some dissident military officers launched a rebellion in 1962. Following a 1996 peace agreement between leftist rebels and the government, the Guatemalan Commission for Historical Clarification (CEH) report in 1999 stated that more than 200,000 Guatemalans had perished in the civil war, 90 percent killed by the Guatemalan military or its paramilitary auxiliaries in service to the country's wealthy oligarchy.

The CIA Guatemalan operation's tactics of arming and providing financial assistance to exiles to wage war against a targeted government would be used against Cuba and later against Saddam's regime. Both the CIA Iranian operation and the Guatemalan coup constituted a warning to revolutionaries about the vulnerability of democratic governments attempting to free themselves from foreign domination. Cuba would provide one model of how to resist foreign intervention.

Although the United States intervened in the 1895–1898 Second War of Cuban Independence on Cuba's side, it imposed the Platt Amendment in 1902, severely limiting Cuban sovereignty and permitting the United States to militarily intervene as it proceeded to do in 1906, 1912, and 1917. Many Cubans believed that despite two long, brutal independence wars, Cuba had simply passed from Spanish to US control. The Revolution of 1933 brought limited reforms, but the economy remained foreign dominated and Havana became a hemispheric center for gambling and prostitution.

Promising to fight corruption and foreign exploitation, Cuban Senator Eduardo Chibas organized the reformist Orthodox Party in 1947. One of its members was Fidel Castro, a student at Havana University Law School and a candidate for the Cuban legislature in 1952. But rather than allow the election, former president and army commander Fulgencio Batista seized control of the government and established a US-supported dictatorship. In response Fidel Castro; his brother Raul; a young Argentine medical doctor, Ernesto "Che" Guevara; and others organized the revolutionary Movement of the 26th of July, or M-26-7, named after Castro's failed July 26, 1953, attack on the Moncada army barracks in Santiago de Cuba.

Guevara, who had personally witnessed the US-supported suppression of Guatemala's democratic government, emphatically summarized what he considered the painful lessons of Guatemala: US administrations would betray democracy in lesser developed countries and support fascist-type regimes if doing so benefited US economic interests; only an armed revolutionary movement had a chance of winning; successful revolutionaries must construct a postrevolution army that was absolutely loyal to the new revolutionary government and its goals of social transformation; and instead of an open democratic political system that had proved vulnerable to foreign manipulation elsewhere, only a one-party revolutionary state could liberate Cuba from foreign domination and swiftly improve the well-being of the poor.

The Cuban model impressed revolutionaries around the world because unlike Iran or Guatemala, it was able to withstand US intervention. Cuba sent representatives to General Abd al-Karim Qasim's revolutionary government and eventually developed good relations with the Iraqi Baathist regime. During the Iran–Iraq War, Cuba remained relatively neutral. It objected to Iraq's invasion of Kuwait but opposed US military actions against Iraq, including the 2003 invasion.

Vietnam:
Comparison to the Iraq War

Of all US interventions, it is the war in Vietnam to which most people compared the Iraq War, either to demonstrate similarities or contrasts. US involvement in Vietnam was an overt intervention because the American goal was not to overthrow but to preserve the South Vietnamese government.

Following the victory of the Viet Minh, the communist-led Vietnamese nationalists, at the Battle of Dien Bien Phu in 1954, the French left after nearly one hundred years of colonial rule and the brutal eight-year French Indochina War. Hundreds of thousands of Vietnamese who were allied with the French moved south of the seventeenth parallel. The Geneva Accords of 1954, which formally ended the war, stated that no new foreign troops could be introduced into Vietnam and that an election would be held in 1956 throughout Vietnam for a single government for the entire country. The expectation internationally was that such an election would result in an overwhelming victory for communist leader Ho Chi Minh and his Viet Minh.

As the French pulled out, the Eisenhower administration decided to preserve the southern half of Vietnam as a separate non-communist state called South Vietnam (officially the Republic of Vietnam) and recognized the French puppet ruler of Vietnam, Emperor Bao Dai, as its leader. Bao Dai was asked to appoint a Catholic from a wealthy Vietnamese family, Ngo Dinh Diem, as his prime minister in 1954 although Diem had been living in New Jersey for some time. North Vietnam (the Democratic Republic of Vietnam) was controlled by the Vietnamese communists. In 1955 Bao Dai was ousted and Diem assumed total control. American military advisers began to train Diem's US-supplied Army of the Republic of Vietnam (ARVN), initially made up of many of the anti-communist Vietnamese who had fought for the French. Diem used the ARVN to repress Vietnamese communists and Viet Minh supporters in the south who were relatively unprotected since southern Viet Minh soldiers had gone north of the seventeenth parallel in line with the Geneva Accords, planning to return after the 1956 unity election.

Diem's supporters burned down the offices of the Geneva Accord representatives from India, Canada, and Poland and refused to hold the 1956 election. In response, the Vietnamese communists in 1960 organized a new armed nationalist movement in the south, the National Liberation Front (called the Vietnamese communists or Viet Cong by Diem), which by 1963 was winning the war. Since American officials by then believed that Diem's autocratic ways and mistakes were contributing to a Viet Cong victory, the United States permitted high-ranking ARVN officers to overthrow him on November 1, 1963. He was captured and executed the next day. President John Kennedy was shocked by Diem's murder, although he reportedly knew of the coup plot. Some of Kennedy's associates believed he was going to withdraw US forces from Vietnam, but about three weeks after Diem's murder, Kennedy was assassinated on November 22 in Dallas, Texas. The new president, Lyndon Johnson, was informed by his military advisers that without greatly increased US intervention, the Viet Cong would win. Johnson then made the decision to commence large-scale US military action involving over 500,000 American soldiers on the ground in South Vietnam in 1968 and 1969 (Nagl 2005: 173). US involvement in Vietnam from 1964 through 1972 caused at least 55,750 American deaths. The Vietnamese communists claimed that the conflict with the Americans resulted in their forces losing 1.1 million dead and an estimated 2 million civilians being killed (Record and Terrill 2004: 11–13). After a negotiated withdrawal of remaining US ground units in 1973, South Vietnam quickly succumbed to a general offensive by North Vietnamese and National Front Liberation forces in the spring of 1975, ending the war.

In comparing Iraq and Vietnam, Record and Terrill (2004: 54) argue that the historical knowledge of policy-makers is often poor, and that in appealing to the public they are inclined to propose analogies that best fit the policies they advocate. Policy-makers supporting the Iraq War tend to see it as similar to the US-led World War II occupations of Germany and Japan, which led to both nations becoming thriving capitalist democracies, while war opponents think the Vietnam War is the more appropriate analogy. Record and Terrill contend that neither analogy adequately corresponds to the circumstances in Iraq. They describe what they believe are more differences than similarities between the Iraq and Vietnam wars, but also argue that Vietnam showed that in order to succeed, the Iraq intervention must build a new popularly supported state, which was not achieved in South Vietnam, and must maintain sufficient US domestic support for the intervention (Record and Terrill 2004: 54). Kagan (2006) also describes more differences than similarities but notes that people are prone to think about Vietnam when the United States becomes involved in a major foreign intervention because the United States lost the Vietnam War. It is clear from the comparisons of the Iraq and Vietnam wars below that there are many differences. But the issues on which similarities do exist between the two interventions may outweigh the differences in total significance.

Justification for War

There are similarities in the ways the Iraq War and the Vietnam War were justified to the American people and to Congress. The conflict in Vietnam was not portrayed as a civil war or the continuation of an anticolonial war, but rather as international communist aggression whose origin was in Moscow. North Vietnam was depicted as a repressive dictatorship and the south as a developing democracy despite the fact that a key reason for the conflict was the refusal of the US-backed Diem regime to allow the nationwide election called for in the 1954 Geneva Accords. Following Diem's murder and replacement by a South Vietnamese military council, President Johnson told the American people in August 1964 that North Vietnamese naval vessels had attacked US ships in international waters in the Gulf of Tonkin. Amazingly few questioned the seeming irrationality of unprovoked North Vietnamese patrol boats attacking much larger and more powerful US destroyers. To get Congress and the American people to back war, North Vietnam was depicted as the aggressor so that the expanded US occupation of Vietnam could be accepted in the United States as a purely defensive move. The resulting Gulf of Tonkin Resolution allowed President Johnson to take whatever measures necessary to protect US service personnel in Southeast Asia. All US offensive actions, including subjecting Vietnam to more bomb tonnage than dropped by American planes in all of World War II, were justified as defending against communist aggression.

In reality the North Vietnamese patrol boat attack on August 2 seems to have been in response to a military operation against North Vietnam. The alleged second attack on August 4 probably did not happen. Referring to the Gulf of Tonkin Resolution, Olbermann (2006) describes the overwhelming vote of the Senate in favor of President Johnson's request as approving "the blank check with which Lyndon Johnson paid for our trip into hell." Similarly, to convince Congress in 2002 to approve a war against Iraq, it was Iraq, not the United States, the invading nation, that had to be depicted as the aggressor through claims that it continued to possess WMD and was likely involved in the 9/11 attacks.

Nature of the Resistance

The Iraqi insurgency contrasted significantly with that in Vietnam. Differences included the ecological contexts and levels of population homogeneity. Vietnam's varied natural environment—including mountains and large areas that are heavily forested—was much more favorable for resistance fighters. In contrast, Iraq's deserts and farmland provided little cover for resistance fighters and instead gave a major advantage to occupation forces with airpower and heavy weapons. Iraqi insurgents also faced superior armament than what was available to US forces in Vietnam, including many more precision-guided weapons and unmanned armed surveillance aircraft. Since opportunities were less frequent for traditional guerrilla warfare techniques, Iraqi insurgents were prone to using Improvised Explosive Devices (IEDs), which could be remotely detonated. Vietnamese insurgents were also advantaged by receiving material assistance and military units from North Vietnam, which was not occupied by US ground forces.

About 85 percent of the people in Vietnam are ethnically Vietnamese, while 15 percent are Chinese, Cambodian, or members of other ethnic minorities. In central Vietnam the French called highland minorities *montagnards* (mountain people). Both the French and later the Americans tried to arm montagnards as allies against the Vietnamese resistance. About 10 percent of Vietnamese are Catholic, who tended to be disproportionately first pro-French and later pro-American, and 6 percent to 8 percent are members of the Cao Dai or Hoa Hao religious sects. Eighty percent or more belong to a dozen or so Buddhist sects. In comparison, the Iraqi population is about 15 percent to 20 percent ethnic Kurds (overwhelmingly Sunni), 60 percent Shia Arabs, and 20 percent Sunni Arabs. It was estimated that about 90 percent of all insurgents in Iraq were Sunni Arabs, providing a much narrower population base for the Iraqi resistance than was the case in Vietnam.

Another distinction is that in Vietnam the antioccupation resistance was highly unified, with a relatively uniform leftist nationalist ideology. In contrast, Iraq appeared to have many separate resistance groups, characterized by two broad ideologies with further subdivisions: Iraqi nationalism, with Baathist and non-Baathist varieties, and Islamic fundamentalism (DeFronzo 2007: 342–344). Most fundamentalists were indigenous Iraqis, but others were foreign volunteers from Saudi Arabia, Syria, Jordan, or elsewhere. Many were associated with Al Qaeda in Mesopotamia. Armed conflict developed between the nationalists and Al Qaeda, whose extreme violence and mass casualty bombings many nationalist insurgents considered unacceptable and counterproductive since such tactics often killed innocent people, alienated large numbers of Iraqis, and lowered world opinion of the insurgency.

Beyond contrasting ideologies, Record and Terrill (2004: 17–18) believe different Iraqi resistance organizations may have employed distinct strategies. Some tried to kill as many American soldiers as possible to undermine US domestic support, while others may have hoped that bringing about a civil war between Sunni and Shia Arabs would end the occupation. Many insurgents attacked Iraqis who collaborated with Americans to interfere with reorganizing the country according to US plans.

In general, the Iraqi nationalist resistance targeted occupation forces by using firearms or IEDs. In comparison, Al Qaeda and foreign fighters were believed responsible for the bulk of suicide bombing attacks that killed large numbers of Shia (considered religious apostates by some Sunnis). In contrast, the Vietnamese resistance generally used more discriminate violence (Record and Terrill 2004: 26).

Kagan (2006) argues that the ideologies of Iraqi insurgents were less internationally attractive than the Marxist-oriented anti-imperialism of the Vietnamese resistance. He, along with Record and Terrill (2004: 8, 14–18), also notes that members of the Iraqi resistance received much less foreign support and were less experienced resistance fighters than the Vietnamese, who had fought the French before confronting US forces. Another difference was that while the Vietnamese resistance benefited from internationally known charismatic leaders, such as Ho Chi Minh politically and Vo Nguyen Giap militarily, no such widely respected or dominant figures were known to exist among the Iraqi resistance movements (Record and Terrill 2004:15).

Roles of Other Nations

Several countries, such as Australia, New Zealand, the Philippines, South Korea, and Thailand, sent troops to assist US forces in Vietnam. But other foreigners entered Vietnam to aid the resistance against the Americans, such as thousands of Russians who trained the Vietnamese in using Russian military equipment. And according to Record and Terrill (2004: 29–30), some 300,000 Chinese engineering and antiaircraft personnel helped operate air defense systems and maintain North Vietnam's transportation system, especially its railroads. In contrast, the number of foreigners who entered Iraq to fight the occupation was much lower.

The Soviet Union and China delivered enormous amounts of military equipment to Vietnam to use against US forces, including antiaircraft missiles, fighter planes, tanks, trucks, and hundreds of thousands of AK-47 assault rifles. Neither of these nuclear powers expected the United States to militarily retaliate against them. Their goals were similar: to aid a communist-led movement in a struggle against what they viewed as American imperialism, anticipating that defeat in Vietnam would weaken the United States and discourage its military intervention elsewhere. In comparison, no country admitted to aiding the Iraqi resistance, in part out of fear of a reprisal attack or even an invasion from the United States. Foreign assistance was far more limited, with much of the external aid coming from nonstate groups or individuals. While the United States accused Iran of training and arming some Iraqi Shia militias, Iran denied actively participating in the resistance, which, in any case, was overwhelmingly based among Sunni Arabs. Finally, foreign assistance was limited by the divided and ideologically more diverse nature of the Iraqi insurgency in comparison with the Vietnamese resistance forces.

Military Strategy and Tactics

Military "strategy" refers to a plan for configuring and deploying armed forces to achieve victory and other policy goals, while "tactics" refers to the ways in which personnel, weapons, and resources are used to carry out strategy. Military strategy and tactics in Iraq and Vietnam manifested both similarities and differences. One important factor affecting US military planning and operations in Vietnam was the constraint imposed by concern over potential massive military intervention by Russia and China, which could have proved catastrophic for US forces. This contributed to the gradualistic application of US military force so that each potential escalation could be weighed against anticipated Russian and Chinese reaction before actually being implemented. But by the time of the Iraq War, the United States, the only remaining superpower, while concerned to some degree with international opinion, had no fear of military retaliation from any major nation as a result of its actions in Iraq.

However, another factor affecting US gradualism in the use of military force in Vietnam, while perhaps not as readily acknowledged by some military historians, and obviously also affecting the US war strategy in Iraq, was an underestimation of popular opposition to US forces. The hostility of South Vietnamese and Iraqis came as a shock to US commanders and soldiers alike. Their expectation was that the Vietnamese would welcome Americans as saviors from communist aggression, and Iraqis would view them as liberators from Saddam's dictatorship. In both cases underestimating popular resistance led to an initial anticipation that a limited troop deployment could achieve victory. In the case of Iraq, the strategy of destroying key military units, largely from the air, the taking of Baghdad and several other politically significant cities, and perhaps the killing of Saddam and his close associates, was to have essentially ended the war. The actual level of popular resistance in both wars called into question the moral basis for US intervention as well as the soundness of strategy.

In both the Vietnam and Iraq wars the US military initially relied on mainly conventional warfare tactics but later expanded the role of counterinsurgency techniques. An aspect of the US counterinsurgency efforts in Vietnam was the notorious Phoenix Program, in which US Special Forces targeted persons in the National Liberation Front's organizational and political infrastructure. Phoenix operations between 1968 and 1972 were estimated to have claimed about 20,000 victims, according to US officials, and as many as 41,000, according to the South Vietnamese government (Hersh 2003: 2). US Special Forces, using information from captured prisoners or other sources, may have attempted similar operations in Iraq once it was clear that a significant insurgency was under way. However, Shia death squads, including those within Shia militias or even Iraq's new military and police, seemed to have carried out this type of activity against Sunni Arabs and suspected Baathist sympathizers.

US freelance reporter Steven Vincent found evidence in Basra, the largest Iraqi city of the predominantly Shia south, that many members of the new British-trained police force were tied to Shia religious fundamentalists and that some were responsible for assassinations, mostly of former Baath Party members. In his July 31, 2005, *New York Times* op-ed article on the subject, he argued that the British should be training the Basra police force in democracy and respect for human rights, not simply in weapons use and police techniques (Vincent 2005). On August 2, Vincent and his translator were kidnapped in Basra by men reportedly wearing police uniforms and using a car with police markings. Vincent was shot and killed, while his wounded female translator survived.

Shia militia death squad killings of Sunni Arabs surged in sections of Baghdad and elsewhere following the February 22, 2006, bombing of the sacred Shia al-Askari mosque in the city of Samarra. Death squads reportedly even operated within some hospitals, where Sunni patients were dragged away and executed (CBS 2006).

Counterinsurgency techniques, which rely heavily on gathering useful information about individuals and their activities, also included employing anthropologists in both Vietnam and Iraq to help soldiers understand local culture and communicate more effectively with indigenous people.

Another similarity between Vietnam and Iraq was the extremely large insurgent-to-counterinsurgent casualty ratios. According to the data cited in Record and Terrill (2004: 11–13), the ratio of killed Vietnamese enemy soldiers to US soldiers was 1.1 million to 55,750, almost 20 to 1. If the estimate of Vietnamese civilians killed is included, the ratio climbs to 3.1 million to 55,750, or more than 55 to 1. In the Iraq War, estimates of fatalities caused by the war and the occupation vary greatly. From the beginning of the invasion, March 20, to the supposed end of the combat phase, May 1, 2003, somewhere between approximately 7,000 to more than 20,000 Iraqi troops and armed paramilitary fighters may have been killed (Conetta 2003; Steele 2003). If the lower figure is used, then the ratio of Iraqi military fatalities to those of the United States was 7,000 to 139, or about 50 to 1. If the low estimate of 7,000 for combat-phase

Iraqi military fatalities is added to the estimated number of insurgents killed, 19,000, up through about September 2007 (Michaels 2007), the ratio of total Iraqi military or insurgent deaths to US military fatalities from the start of the war through September 2007 would be about 26,000 to 3,800, or 7 to 1 (the lowered ratio is undoubtedly due to the insurgents' use of the lower-risk IED [improvised explosive device] weapon). The ratio of all Iraqi deaths caused by the war, military and civilian, to US deaths is of course much higher. Estimates of total Iraqi war deaths run to over half a million. Adding the lower limit of a more moderate assessment of the range of Iraqi civilian deaths from the beginning of the war through October 2007—78,071 to 85,055 (IBC 2007)—to the previous calculation of Iraqi military and insurgent fatalities results in a relatively conservative estimate of total Iraqi war-related deaths of about 104,071. Using this figure, the ratio of total Iraqi war deaths to US military fatalities would be 104,071 to 3,800, or about 27 to 1.

The relatively high ratios of Vietnamese and Iraqi war deaths to US military killed raises a question of morality for both wars. Such extreme ratios of suffering between the occupied and the occupier are reminiscent of brutal European colonial conquests and implicitly question whether such wars should ever be permitted from a human rights standpoint. Demonizing the enemy during times of war is a typical method of justifying lethal violence. But it is hard to imagine that the Vietnam War would have persisted for so long and taken the lives of some 3 million Vietnamese if the American people had greater familiarity with the biographies of individual casualties, such as the moving diary of the young medical doctor Dang Thuy Tram (2007), who had volunteered to work at a concealed forest hospital in Quang Ngai Province in South Vietnam caring for wounded National Liberation Front and North Vietnamese soldiers. Her diary, filled with descriptions of her experiences, her dreams for peace and independence for her country, and her longings to feel her mother's touch, fell into American hands after she was shot and killed by soldiers of the Americal Division close to her forest hospital on June 22, 1970. Instead of destroying it according to regulations, a US soldier kept it for some thirty-five years and then sought out Thuy's family in Vietnam, leading to the diary's publication as an international best-seller.

An additional similarity regarding military operations in Vietnam and Iraq was the construction of big base camps in an attempt to maintain high morale. These large bases had many of the pleasures of home, such as good food, movie theaters, swimming pools, and baseball fields. While providing a sense of security for the soldiers by isolating them from the indigenous population, they were also seen as preventing the level of interaction between US personnel and local people that might lead to obtaining useful information for counterinsurgency efforts. Record and Terrill (2004: 21) claim that constructing, maintaining, and guarding the huge camps, along with airfields, ports, and other facilities in Vietnam, absorbed about 85 percent of the 536,000 US military personnel in South Vietnam in 1968, leaving only about 80,000 US soldiers available for protracted ground combat.

Both the Vietnam and Iraq conflicts also involved civil wars. In Vietnam a civil war already existed when the Americans arrived. US assistance allowed the ultimately losing side to survive many years longer than it probably would have. In the case of Iraq, the invasion and occupation led to the outbreak of a Shia versus Sunni civil war (Rosen 2007: 412–413). Shia fundamentalist-oriented religious-political organizations came to dominate the government and the new US-equipped army and police, while the insurgency was largely Sunni Arab. By the end of 2007, the United States was backing the Shia-controlled Iraqi regime while also supporting Sunni militias and encouraging them to attack Al Qaeda groups. Rosen describes this situation as helping to ensure that Iraq never again exists as a unified state. He compares American support for both the Shia-dominated government and the Sunni militias as similar to the US backing of both Iran and Iraq during the Iran–Iraq War, which helped perpetuate the conflict and ensure that there would be no decisive winner.

Finally, military differences between the two wars included that the Iraq War was fought on a smaller scale and resulted in considerably lower daily casualty rates. This was partly because US forces had more advanced weapons in Iraq that both reduced the vulnerability of US personnel and reduced the potential for killings of noncombatants (lower "collateral damage"). Because the US military was a totally volunteer force in the Iraq War, its personnel were on average better trained than those in Vietnam. Another contrast was that whereas the Vietnam conflict was often characterized by rivalries between the branches of the US armed forces, contributing to inefficiency, US operations in Iraq were significantly better coordinated (Record and Terrill 2004: 20). Still another difference was that in Vietnam the United States inherited a large anti-communist Vietnamese army from the French as an ally in anti-insurgent operations. But in Iraq, the United States had to organize a new Iraqi force for this purpose.

Political Legitimacy of US-Supported Governments

Record and Terrill (2004: 40) argue that two essential requirements for success in both Vietnam and Iraq were the creation of an indigenous government considered legitimate by a large majority of the population, and the establishment of armed forces capable of protecting the political system. The United States failed to accomplish either of these goals in Vietnam. The US project in South Vietnam began with the imposition of an American-selected leader, Diem, from a wealthy family of the country's 10 percent Catholic minority. Ruling as an autocrat accused of favoring his coreligionists while repressing Buddhist critics, he was overthrown and murdered by members of his own army. General Nguyen Van Thieu, who had served in the French-sponsored Vietnamese National Army during the French Indochina War, soon assumed control. The South Vietnamese government and armed forces were saturated with corrupt officials, further undermining their legitimacy. According to Record and Terrill (2004: 34), South Vietnam was "crippled from the start by three main weaknesses that no amount of American intervention could offset: professional military inferiority, rampant corruption, and lack of political legitimacy."

Although the United States sponsored Iraqi elections in December 2005, many Iraqis lacked faith in the new Shia-dominated government and feared its armed forces and police. The new constitution "stipulated that Islam is the religion of state and that civil parliament could pass no legislation that contravened established Islamic laws" (Cole 2006: 21). To many, this represented achieving the fundamentalist goal of integrating church and state, the triumph of the Iranian Ayatollah Khomeini's ideas in Iraq. Such a state was not acceptable to many Sunni Arabs or secular Shia Arabs.

In effect, the Kurds established an independent state in Iraqi Kurdistan with its own army, flag, and president. The Iraqi army and flag were banned there (Galbraith 2007: 405). Many observers concluded that Iraq as a unified country ceased to exist. Sectarian conflict forced the emigration of hundreds of thousands of Iraqis, including many of the best educated and most talented, over 7 percent of the population (Rosen 2007: 410–413). Many of those unable or unwilling to emigrate were also forced to leave their homes and relocate within the country as rival Shia and Sunni militias created an increasingly religiously segregated Iraq.

Iraq was designated sovereign on June 28, 2004. But many questioned what this meant when its government could not control much of its own armed forces, which often responded more directly to tribal, religious, or sectarian militia leaders or in some cases to US occupation officials. The new Iraqi government also apparently had no ability to immediately ban a private US security firm, Blackwater, accused of killing innocent Iraqi civilians on September 16, 2007.

The US invasion and occupation policies seemed to create the very conditions that negated the possibility of real Iraqi sovereignty or a unified state and instead provided self-serving rationale for perpetual US military occupation. Rosen (2007: 412) raises the question of whether allowing immediate sovereignty and elections and the rapid withdrawal of US troops after removing Saddam's regime would have resulted in a genuinely legitimate, popularly supported government. To some observers, the United States created neither a truly democratic nor sovereign Iraq but rather a colonial-like entity paralleling British-controlled Iraq of the 1920s and 1930s run by political figureheads kept in power mainly by the gun muzzles of a permanent US occupation force.

US Policy Goals

In both Vietnam and Iraq, the United States claimed to be countering a transnational threat: for Vietnam the spread of communism and for Iraq international terrorism. And apart from the false claims of WMD in Iraq, the stated purposes of US interventions in both Vietnam and Iraq included building stable democratic governments. Record and Terrill (2004: 6) describe the Vietnam mission as counterrevolutionary in aiming to preserve a regime threatened by a revolutionary movement, while they view the Iraq mission as revolutionary in seeking to replace a dictatorship with a democratic political system.

Critics argued, however, that in Vietnam the United States was in fact using violence to crush the aspirations of most Vietnamese for independence and a unified country, which explained why so many Vietnamese were willing to risk death in pursuit of these goals. The United States left Vietnam in part because the country really wasn't of vital interest, economically or militarily. In contrast, because many in Washington view Iraq's huge energy resources as of great importance to the US economy and international power, they may decide that real Iraqi democracy and sovereignty are too risky.

Arguments to Stay

After the initial occupations of both Vietnam and Iraq, US policy-makers found that important assumptions on which the interventions were based were false. In the case of Vietnam, the revolutionary forces and the level of popular support those forces enjoyed in southern Vietnam were much greater than anticipated. Further, the North Vietnamese countered the deployment of US forces and resources in the south. Just as had happened earlier to the French, the United States found itself locked into an indefinite war.

In Iraq the primary justification given for the invasion, WMD, did not exist. Neither did Iraq play a role in the 9/11 attacks. And, as was the case in Vietnam, popular resistance to the US occupation proved far greater than anticipated. The response of US policy-makers in both cases was to develop a new set of arguments to continue the wars. One was that a US pullout would quickly lead to large-scale massacres. In Vietnam this did not occur, though it did happen in the nearby country of Cambodia, where the extremist faction of the Khmer Rouge came to power largely as a result of rural rage at US bombings and military interventions carried out as part of an effort to destroy Vietnamese National Liberation Front sanctuaries there.

In Iraq it is difficult to predict whether a US withdrawal would worsen the sectarian conflict that the invasion helped bring about. But Rosen (2007: 410) points out that the "division of Iraq into homogeneous ethnic or sectarian zones has been nearly completed." The new level of residential segregation would seem to make an increase in sectarian or interethnic killings after a US pullout less likely.

With Vietnam, some argued that if the United States left, other countries in Southeast Asia would fall like dominos to communism. But outside of the other former components of French Indochina, Laos and Cambodia, this did not happen. The analogous prediction for Iraq is that a US withdrawal could lead to Iraq's becoming a new international base for terrorism. But Al Qaeda did not exist in Iraq before the war except in a small corner of Kurdistan far beyond the control of the Iraqi state. It was the US invasion that attracted Al Qaeda and foreign volunteers to fight the Americans.

President Bush stated that the United States made a mistake in withdrawing from Vietnam (BBC 2007) because of negative consequences for the Vietnamese who were allied with the United States, many of whom left the country.

But the Iraqi refugee problem became enormous because of sectarian violence during the occupation. Opponents of the Iraq War claimed that Bush repeatedly shifted reasons for occupying Iraq and that, in reality, the only constant argument for keeping US troops there is often the least mentioned by the US government: oil.

US Public Opinion (Domestic Sustainability)

A parallel between the Vietnam and Iraq wars was the shift in public opinion. In the case of Vietnam the decline in support for the war was referred to as losing the war back home or the loss of domestic sustainability (Record and Terrill 2004: 47–54). Betts (1980: 523) states that "the Vietnamese Communists were fighting for their country as well as their principles, while the Americans had only their principles at stake—and as the anti-war case became steadily more persuasive, even those principles were discredited. . . . Hanoi bent but never broke because it preferred endless war to defeat; Washington bent and finally did break because the public preferred defeat to endless war."

At the beginning of both the Vietnam and Iraq wars, most of the US public, including some prominent liberal politicians, supported war. But eventually a majority opposed continuing US involvement. General David Petraeus (1987: 127–133), who became the third commander of US forces in Iraq in February 2007, states in his Princeton University international affairs dissertation that having and maintaining popular domestic support was important for an extended US military intervention. He argues that one of the important lessons of Vietnam was that the US "public must be made aware of the costs up front." Petraeus (1987: 132) advises any future US president not to commit American troops to a war unless "1) you really have to (. . . vital U.S. interests are at stake); 2) you have established clear-cut, attainable military objectives. . . . 3) You provide the military commander sufficient forces and the freedom necessary to accomplish his mission swiftly. . . . 4) You can ensure sufficient public support to permit carrying the commitment through to its conclusion."

According to Record and Terrill (2004: 50–53), research has indicated that in limited inconclusive wars, mounting casualties tended to undermine public support. But decline in support was probably partly due to a type of educational process for large sectors of the public who previously had little or no knowledge of the society in which the war occurred. Limited prewar information likely contributed to widespread initial acceptance of government justification for war. But once a war was an important element of national life, a motive existed to learn more about the background of the conflict, leading a number of people to alter their earlier opinions. In the case of Iraq, loss of public support was rapid and so likely due not just to growing casualties, but also to the realization that the major reason for going to war, to eliminate WMD, was false. In both wars the US public became concerned about the costs in terms of lives, money, internal conflict, and international isolation. However, the fact that the United States deployed a volunteer military force to Iraq supplemented by contracted soldiers from private military firms meant that, unlike during the Vietnam War, young people who had not chosen to join the armed forces did not fear being drafted. This factor almost certainly limited anti–Iraq War protests on college campuses and prevented a more militant antiwar movement from developing.

US public opinion played a significant role in the outcome of the Vietnam conflict and may do the same regarding the Iraq War. Nagl (2005: 23) notes that Chinese revolutionary leader Mao Zedong envisioned three phases of protracted revolutionary wars of national liberation. At the beginning the immediate aims are to politically mobilize the population, and to organize the revolutionary army and preserve its existence by mobility and by engaging in battle only in limited circumstances. In the second phase, the revolutionary movement gains strength and its army expands to the point where it engages in more aggressive military activity, attacking regime patrols or vulnerable isolated bases to gather weapons and ammunition. The increased successful revolutionary military activity helps destroy the population's belief in the power of the regime's armed forces and creates the impression of the revolution's growing strength and inevitable victory. In the final phase, during which many in the insurgent army reorganize into conventional military formations while others continue guerrilla warfare tactics, the greatly strengthened revolutionary forces confront and decisively defeat the old regime's military in sustained battles.

The problem with Mao's model is that it has limited relevance to an insurgent or revolutionary situation in which the enemy is the armed forces of the world's superpower, the United States. The Vietnamese revolutionaries demonstrated that in this case the new decisive phase is not the impossible task of defeating US military power in open battle, but in convincing the American public of the immorality and/or futility of the war effort.

Chile 1973: A Latin American Democracy's 9/11

As the Vietnam War continued, the Nixon administration confronted a new threat when a medical doctor from the Socialist Party, Salvador Allende, was elected president of Chile in 1970 by winning a majority of the vote in Chile's national legislature. The legislature overwhelmingly approved Allende's bill nationalizing US-owned copper mines. Allende claimed Chile would democratically carry out a social revolution to lift up the poor and secure the independence of its economy through nationalizations of large economic enterprises. But his nationalization policy distressed the country's upper class and sectors of the middle class. The Nixon administration helped undermine Chile's economy by restricting aid and international credit (Oppenheim 1993: 106).

After prodemocracy military leaders were killed by right-wing officers or forced out of the armed forces, conservative generals overthrew Chile's democratic system and imposed military rule. On September 11, 1973, the coup plotters attacked the presidential palace, and President Allende apparently committed suicide rather than surrender. The military dictatorship created favorable conditions for domestic and foreign business operations. The brutal takeover and the seventeen years of dictatorship that followed caused the deaths of more than 3,000 people while thousands more were imprisoned and tortured (Sigmund 2006: 109).

When Chile returned to civilian rule, it had a constitution written under the supervision of the dictatorship that gave the military a strong role in government. The destruction of Chilean democracy seemed to again indicate that American commitment to democracy was contingent on elected governments' maintaining US-approved policies. The US role in toppling democracy in Chile was largely concealed from the American public and Congress at the time, reminiscent of covert actions against Iran and Guatemala and prefiguring those regarding Nicaragua and Iraq.

Nicaragua: Low-Intensity Warfare

Nicaragua has experienced both US occupation and covert intervention. Marine Major General Smedley Butler, awarded the Congressional Medal of Honor twice, participated in US military action in Nicaragua in the early twentieth century and ultimately concluded the motive was primarily economic. General Butler (1933) stated, "I helped in the raping of half a dozen Central American republics for the benefits of Wall Street. . . . I helped purify Nicaragua for the international banking house of Brown Brothers in 1909–1912. . . . [U]ntil I left the service . . . my mental faculties remained in suspended animation while I obeyed the orders of higher-ups. . . . I spent most of my life being a high class muscle-man for Big Business. . . . In short I was a racketeer, a gangster for capitalism."

The US intervention in which General Butler participated led to the establishment of what came to be viewed as a neocolonial political system in which local government leaders served foreign interests while enriching themselves and leaving many Nicaraguans oppressed and impoverished. In 1961 student activists led by Carlos Fonseca formed the Sandinista Front for National Liberation (FSLN). The goals of the FSLN, inspired by both the Cuban Revolution and the nationalism of Augusto Sandino, who had fought US military intervention in the 1920s and 1930s, were to end Somoza family rule, assert Nicaraguan independence, and provide opportunities for the poor. After many setbacks, the Sandinistas succeeded in July 1979.

The Reagan administration accused the Sandinistas of supporting terrorism by aiding leftist revolutionaries in El Salvador and of failing to establish democracy. But after achieving about 67 percent of the vote in the 1984 Nicaraguan elections, the Sandinistas claimed to be an internationally certified, democratically elected government (Stahler-Sholk 2006: 610–611). However, while the Sandinistas allowed other political parties to contest elections and in fact allowed themselves to be voted out of power in 1990, not regaining the presidency until 2007, from the 1979 victory of the revolution through the 1980s only the FSLN controlled the new armed forces. Sandinista control of the military, ostensibly to ensure the fulfillment of the revolutionary program, was criticized as preventing a fully democratic system.

The Reagan administration banned trade with Nicaragua, placed underwater mines in Nicaragua's harbors, and armed and provided bases for Nicaraguan exiles to launch attacks into Nicaragua. These counterrevolutionaries, or contras, were accused of destroying schools and clinics the revolutionary government had constructed and executing local officials and Sandinista soldiers. Over the years, economic hardship, the contra war, the destruction of many health care and educational gains of the revolution, and the ever-present fear of direct US military intervention shattered Nicaraguan morale. This slow torture on a societywide scale was called "low intensity warfare" (DeFronzo 2007: 257). The post–1991 Gulf War sanctions and support for attacks by the Iraqi exiles paralleled aspects of the low-intensity war against Nicaragua.

Afghanistan: Al Qaeda Blowback

The USSR, after helping defeat the United States in Vietnam, made its own tragic mistake intervening in Afghanistan to support a pro-Soviet regime. Witnessing the triumph of Shia fundamentalists in the Iranian Revolution, Sunni Islamists were encouraged to fight the Soviets. The United States provided them with shoulder-fired Stinger missiles that shot down or drove off low-flying helicopter gunships and jets, neutralizing Soviet airpower and helping Islamists win the Afghan War.

Abdallah Azzam, a Palestinian-born professor of Islamic law, taught international volunteers, including Osama bin Laden, that Muslims had lost their power because they no longer waged jihad against imperialist nations or corrupt regimes in Muslim countries that cooperated with them. During the Afghan conflict, bin Laden met Egyptian Ayman al-Zawahiri, who believed the United States should be attacked since it provided crucial support to Israel and pro-US regimes in Islamic countries. In 1988 bin Laden organized a communication network, Al Qaeda, for the thousands of foreign volunteers who fought in Afghanistan. He returned to Saudi Arabia as a hero shortly before Iraq invaded Kuwait in 1990. Bin Laden offered to bring as many as 35,000 Al Qaeda fighters to defend Saudi Arabia against a potential Iraqi invasion. Instead the royal family allowed the deployment of American forces. Neither the monarchy nor the United States wanted to see tens of thousands of battle-hardened fundamentalist fighters in Saudi Arabia where they could potentially turn against the pro-US regime. Bin Laden objected, believing the United States was establishing permanent military domination of Middle East oil and the religious-cultural core of Islam, and he was forced to leave the country.

In 1993 Al Qaeda attacked the New York World Trade Center with a truck bomb. In February 1998, bin Laden, al-Zawahiri, and leaders of a number of Islamist extremist organizations announced the formation of the Islamic World Front for the Struggle Against the Jews and the Crusaders, a global jihad alliance. Al Qaeda bombed US embassies in Kenya and Tanzania in August 1998, carried out a suicide attack on the USS *Cole* in 2000, and then on September 11, 2001, used hijacked airliners to destroy the World Trade Center and attack the Pentagon.

The Afghan War against the Soviets, from 1980 to 1989, spawned Al Qaeda, whose September 11 attack incited US public and congressional support for invading Iraq. The anti-Soviet struggle, however, also provided a model for new insurgents. Young people from Islamic countries came to Iraq to fight the occupation as once volunteers had gone to Afghanistan to oust Soviet soldiers. But the US invasion of Iraq under false justifications and its lengthy occupation also almost certainly increased the motivation of many young people to fight

US forces in Afghanistan, where ecological and strategic conditions (such as the proximity of supporters and bases in parts of neighboring Pakistan) were more favorable than in Iraq.

Summary and Analysis

The 2003 Iraq invasion is one of many foreign interventions. In 1953 the United States helped overthrow the Mossadeq government in Iran and install the pro-US monarch as essentially an absolute ruler. This had enormous consequences for Iran and Iraq. It prevented Iranians from using democracy as a means to achieve true national independence. Many concluded that imperialism could be defeated only through reviving Shia fundamentalism and establishing an Iranian Islamic Republic. The victory of fundamentalism over the US-supported Iranian monarchy in 1979 helped inspire a broad revival of political Islam, contributing to the creation of Al Qaeda during the war against Soviet forces in Afghanistan and motivating Saddam's government to launch the Iran–Iraq War, which in turn led to the Iraqi invasion of Kuwait and the 1991 Gulf War, and ultimately to the US invasion of Iraq in 2003.

The intervention most often compared to the invasion of Iraq is the Vietnam War. Analyzing the two interventions reveals many differences and some striking similarities. In Vietnam the resistance had a wider base of popular support, was much more unified organizationally and ideologically, and received far more international assistance.

In both the Vietnam and Iraq wars, US soldiers believed they would be welcomed by most of the people but then were shocked at the level of popular resistance. In both cases the United States initially relied on conventional warfare techniques and heavy weapons in the expectation that well-placed devastating blows would bring quick victory. Lack of success led to a counterinsurgency focus of gathering useful intelligence through communicating and working with locals and trying to win them over with effective incentives.

Both interventions began with false justifications for war. Another similarity was the shift in public opinion from initial support to opposition after casualties mounted, the justifications for war were exposed as false, and the conflicts appeared to have no end. However, without the threat of the draft, student opposition to the Iraq War was less militant than during the Vietnam era. A further similarity was that US administrations tended to add new arguments to justify continuing the wars in the face of mounting opposition, such as predictions that violence would get worse if US forces left.

Apart from the unique policy goals in each war, stopping the spread of communism in Vietnam and getting rid of WMD and combating terrorism in the case of Iraq, US leaders stated the intention of building popularly supported democratic governments in both South Vietnam and Iraq. Both wars were characterized by very high casualty ratios between the indigenous populations and the occupying forces, paralleling European colonial wars in Africa and Asia. For the Iraq War, the major possible redeeming factor capable of distinguishing it from the Vietnam tragedy on a moral basis would be the establishment of a truly sovereign and democratic state. But if this is blocked by American desire to control Iraq's oil and enhance domination of the Middle East, most Iraqis will likely view the US occupation as another manifestation of imperialism.

References and Further Readings

BBC. 2007. "Bush in Vietnam Warning Over Iraq." August 22. http://news.bbc.co .uk/2/hi/middle_east/6958824.stm.

Betts, Richard K. 1980. "Interests, Burdens, and Persistence: Asymmetries Between Washington and Hanoi." *International Studies Quarterly (*December): 523.

Blum, William. 2004. *Killing Hope: US Military and CIA Interventions Since World War II*. Monroe, ME: Common Courage Press.

Butler, General Smedley. 1933. "On War, by General Smedley Butler." http://co .quaker.org/Writings/SmedleyButler.htm.

Buttinger, Joseph. 1977. *Vietnam: The Unforgettable Tragedy*. New York: Horizon.

CBS News. October 4, 2006. "Death Squads in Iraqi Hospitals." www.cbsnews .com/stories/2006/10/04/eveningnews/printable2064668.shtml.

Cole, Juan. 2006. "A Shiite Crescent? The Regional Impact of the Iraq War." *Current History* 105 (January): 20–26.

Coll, Steve. 2004. *Ghost Wars: The Secret History of the CIA, Afghanistan, and Bin Laden, from the Soviet Invasion to September 10, 2001*. New York: Penguin Books.

Conroy, Michael E. 1987. "Economic Aggression as an Instrument of Low-Intensity Warfare." In Thomas W. Walker, ed., *Reagan Versus the Sandinistas*. Boulder, CO: Westview.

Conetta, Carl. 2003. "The Wages of War: Iraqi Combatant and Noncombatant Fatalities in the 2003 Conflict." *Project on Defense Alternatives*, October 20. www.comw.org/pda/0310rm8.html.

DeFronzo, James. 2006. "Iranian Revolution." In James DeFronzo, ed., *Revolutionary Movements in World History: From 1750 to the Present*, 412–427. Santa Barbara, CA: ABC-CLIO.

———. 2007. *Revolutions and Revolutionary Movements*. Boulder, CO: Westview.

Duiker, William J. 2000. *Ho Chi Minh*. New York: Hyperion.

Galbraith, Peter W. 2007. "After Iraq: Picking up the Pieces." *Current History* 106 (December): 403–408.

Gott, Richard. 2005. *Cuba: A New History*. New Haven, CT: Yale University Press.

Hersh, Seymour M. 2003. "Annals of National Security: Moving Targets, Will the Counter-Insurgency Plan in Iraq Repeat the Mistakes of Vietnam?" *New Yorker*, December 13. www.newyorker.com/archive/2003/12/15/031215fa_ fact?printable=true.

Hiro, Dilip. 2007. *Blood of the Earth: The Battle for the World's Vanishing Oil Resources*. New York: Nation Books.

IBC (Iraq Body Count). 2007. "Documented Civilian Deaths From Violence." www.iraqbodycount.org (accessed December 7, 2007).

Kagan, Frederick. 2006. "Iraq Is Not Vietnam: A Pernicious Equivalence." *Policy Review (*January). www.hoover.org/publications/policyreview/2920091.html.

Karnow, Stanley, 1983. *Vietnam: A History*. New York: Viking.

Kinzer, Stephen. 1982. *Bitter Fruit: The Untold Story of the American Coup in Guatemala.* New York: Doubleday.

———. 2003. *All the Shah's Men: An American Coup and the Roots of Middle East Terror.* Indianapolis: Wiley.

———. 2006. *Overthrow: America's Century of Regime Change From Hawaii to Iraq.* New York: Time Books.

Michaels, Jim. 2007. "19,000 Insurgents Killed in Iraq Since '03." *USA Today,* September 27. www.usatoday.com/news/world/iraq/2007-09-26-insurgents_N.htm (accessed December 7, 2007).

Milani, Mohsen M. 1994. *The Making of Iran's Islamic Revolution.* Boulder: Westview.

Nagl, John A. 2005. *Learning to Eat Soup with a Knife: Counterinsurgency Lessons from Malaya and Vietnam.* Chicago: University of Chicago Press.

Olbermann, Keith. 2006. "Lessons from the Vietnam War." MSNBC *Countdown,* November 20. www.msnbc.msn.com/id/15821138.

Oppenheim, Lois Hecht. 1993. *Politics in Chile.* Boulder, CO: Westview.

Petraeus, David Howell. 1987. *The American Military and the Lessons of Vietnam: A Study of Military Influence and the Use of Force in the Post-Vietnam Era.* Ann Arbor, MI: UMI.

PBS (Public Broadcasting Service). 1987. "War on Nicaragua." *Frontline.*

———. 1988. "Guns, Drugs, and the CIA." *Frontline.*

Record, Jeffrey, and W. Andrew Terrill. 2004. *Iraq and Vietnam: Differences, Similarities, and Insights.* Carlisle, PA: Strategic Studies Institute, US Army War College. www.strategicstudiesinstitute.army.mil/pubs/display.cfm?pubID=377.

Ricks, Thomas E. 2007. "War Called Riskier than Vietnam: Military Experts Fretful Over Long-Term Consequences." *Washington Post,* April 29. www.washingtonpost.com.

Rosen, Nir. 2007. "The Death of Iraq." *Current History* 106 (December): 409–413.

Sigmund, Paul. 2006. "Chilean Socialist Revolution, Counter-Revolution, and the Restoration of Democracy." In James DeFronzo, ed., *Revolutionary Movements in World History,* 107–117.

Stahler-Sholk, Richard. 2006. "Nicaraguan Revolution." In James DeFronzo, ed., *Revolutionary Movements in World History,* 609–622.

Steele, Jonathan. 2003. "Body Counts." *Guardian,* May 28. www.guardian.co.uk/world/2003/may/28/usa.iraq.

Streeter, Stephen M. 2000a. "Interpreting the 1954 US Intervention in Guatemala: Realist, Revisionist, and Postrevisionist Perspectives." *History Teacher* 34 (1): 61–74.

———. 2000b. *Managing the Counterrevolution: The United States and Guatemala, 1954–1961.* Athens: Ohio University Press.

———. 2006. "The Guatemalan Deomocratic Revolution, Counter-Revolution, and Restoration of Democracy." In James DeFronzo, ed., *Revolutionary Movements in World History,* 325–335.

Tram, Dang Thuy. 2007. *Last Night I Dreamed of Peace: The Diary of Dang Thuy Tram.* New York: Harmony Books.

Turley, William S. 1986. *The Second Indochina War.* Boulder, CO: Westview.

Vincent, Steven. 2005. "Switched Off in Basra." *New York Times,* July 31, 2005. www.nytimes.com/2005/07/31/opinion/31vincent.html?pagewanted=print.

Walker, Thomas. 1987. *Reagan Versus the Sandinistas.* Boulder, CO: Westview.

Wyden, Peter. 1979. *Bay of Pigs: The Untold Story.* New York: Simon & Schuster.

8

‖‖‖

Postinvasion Iraq

Occupation and Insurgency

The Iraqi people's reaction to the invasion varied by social group. Most Kurds supported it, though they were concerned about maintaining the autonomy they had enjoyed from 1992 to 2003. In contrast, Sunni Arabs overwhelmingly condemned the invasion and feared Iraqi Shia fundamentalist and Iranian domination, and the permanent loss of Iraq's sovereignty. Many Shia Arabs welcomed the overthrow of Saddam's regime, but some questioned whether America's intention was to liberate them or gain control of their country's resources.

When elections were held in 2005 for a constitutional assembly and then a parliament, Shia political-religious groups dominated the vote. They and other political parties attempted to combine Islamic and democratic concepts in a new constitution. After boycotting the first election, Sunni Arabs began to participate. The government resulting from the December 2005 election was accused of sectarian bias, corruption, and an inability to deal effectively with such pressing issues as reconstructing the country and enacting a national oil law.

While the new regime faced an insurgency, the Kurdish region was relatively calm. Many Kurds favored secession but endured continuing federation with Iraq for pragmatic reasons. Central Iraq experienced the highest levels of insurgent activity. Mass bombings by Al Qaeda in Mesopotamia weakened the insurgency by provoking the animosity of the nationalist branch of the resistance, alienating much of the public, and causing a number of Sunni tribal leaders to desert the insurgency and accept American money and weapons to fight Islamic extremists.

The Occupation

In May 2003 there were about 142,500 US ground troops in Iraq (GlobalSecurity .org 2007), supplemented by about 45,000 from the UK, 2,000 Australians, and 200 Poles (more Polish troops would soon arrive to participate in the occupation). US forces occupied Baghdad and all or large parts of four other central, mainly Sunni Arab provinces (the Central Zone), as well as the five northern provinces, including Mosul and the Kurdish areas (the Northern Zone). The predominantly Shia South Central Zone, composed of three provinces and parts of two others, was held by a multinational division under Polish command. Basra and three other largely Shia provinces, the Southern Zone, were occupied by a multinational division under British control. Occupation policies varied somewhat among the zones and even among commanders within particular zones. In Mosul, for example, General David Petraeus, commander of the 101st Airborne Division, began in the spring of 2003 to employ some aspects of the counterinsurgency approach he advocated, which would not be more widely used in Iraq until much later.

Reactions to the Fall of the Baathist Regime

Shia Arabs

Most Iraqi Shia appeared to welcome the fall of Saddam's regime, though many were not happy that this was brought by a foreign invasion rather than solely by the Iraqi people. Suspicions over US motives were in part due to the American failure to assist Shia rebels in the south of Iraq in 1991. As a result, coalition troops received only a lukewarm reception in some Shia areas.

Internal Divisions. Iraqi Shia were far from unified. While some adopted the Iranian Shia concept of vilayat-e faqih, or clerical domination of government, others did not. Historically, the Shia clergy were either "quietist" (focusing mainly on religious matters) or "activist" (attempting to influence society through a direct role in politics). Unlike Iran's Ayatollah Khomeini, Ayatollah Ali Husseini al-Sistani, Iraq's major Shia religious leader, disapproved of the clergy's playing any executive or administrative role in government (Allawi 2006: 168, 210). In reality, though, some top Iraqi clerical leaders with reputations as quietists, including Sistani, became activists during special periods. For example, after the invasion Sistani pushed the CPA (Coalition Provisional Authority) to hold elections and grant sovereignty to Iraq quickly (Allawi 2006: 168–169). In addition, many Shia were secularly oriented and a large number had been members of the Baath Party. Shia were also divided by economic class. While some were affluent businessmen, more lived in poverty, like many among the 2 million residents of the Saddam City section of Baghdad, renamed Sadr City after the invasion.

Shia leaders and political organizations were also differentiated by either having ties to foreign powers such as Iran or the United States or being relatively independent. For example, a number of the leaders of two major Shia political-religious organizations, the Dawa and the Supreme Council for the Islamic Revolution in Iraq (SCIRI), led by Ayatollah Muhammad Baqir al-Hakim, had lived in Iran from about 1980 until the removal of the Baathist regime and had received Iranian support. SCIRI was established on November 17, 1982, as an umbrella confederation of Shia groups opposing Saddam's government. SCIRI (renamed the Islamic Supreme Council of Iraq, ISCI, in May 2007, also known as the Supreme Islamic Iraqi Council, SIIC) and Dawa emerged as major Shia political parties and dominant members of the governing coalition following US-sponsored elections in 2005. Unlike Dawa, however, SCIRI originally supported the vilayat-e faqih concept.

In contrast to US-sponsored secular Shia exiles Ayad Allawi and Ahmed Chalabi, and such Iranian-oriented groups as SCIRI and Dawa, the Mahdi Army was more nationalist and opposed both US and Iranian domination of Iraq. The leader of the Mahdi Army, Moqtada al-Sadr, is the second cousin of executed Ayatollah Muhammad Baqir al-Sadr and the son of the Grand Ayatollah Muhammad Sadiq al-Sadr, the most influential religious leader in Iraq until his murder in 1999. The grand ayatollah had used religious taxes to organize an extensive welfare assistance network for the hundreds of thousands of poor in Sadr City, and Moqtada would inherit many of his supporters (Hashim 2006: 250). Moqtada criticized SCIRI for being too pro-Iranian and questioned the leadership of Iraq's top Shia cleric, Iranian-born Ayatollah Sistani (Galbraith 2008: 84).

Unlike SCIRI, which was run by senior clerics and had support among many middle-class Shia, Moqtada's Sadrist movement, the Jaish al-Mahdi, or Mahdi Army (named for the Shia twelfth imam, who will one day return to establish a just Islamic society), drew much of its support from the vast numbers of young Iraqis in impoverished Shia areas of central and southern Iraq, especially Sadr City. While Moqtada claimed his movement was oriented mainly toward peaceful community assistance work, many of his supporters reportedly looted weapons from military arsenals. When Ayatollah Hakim and almost a hundred other people were killed by a powerful car bomb on August 29, 2003, in Najaf, shocking SCIRI, some thought Moqtada's supporters were responsible (Allawi 2006: 171–173; MacFarquhar and Oppel 2003). But suspicion also fell on Baathists and Al Qaeda associates. Following his brother's assassination, Abdul Aziz al-Hakim, the last of the eight Hakim brothers, assumed leadership of SCIRI. Moqtada demanded a withdrawal of coalition forces and the establishment of a government that embraced Islamic law, but claimed he did not favor the creation of a theocratic state, as existed in Iran (Hashim 2006: 251).

Moqtada's weakness was his youth (he was about twenty-nine at the time of the invasion). He lacked the long years of training for high clerical rank, which provides recognition as a legitimate Islamic authority with the right to issue religious rulings. His youth and limited religious education divided the Sadrist movement in 2003 when Ayatollah Muhammad al-Yacoubi founded the Islamic Fadhila (Virtue) Party, which, like the Mahdi Army, was strongly nationalist. Following the invasion, thousands of young men joined militias organized by local clerical leaders, who along with their followers attempted to reestablish basic services and provide for the needy.

Issues and Orientations. The major differences among the Shia political-religious groups were exemplified by the contrasts between SCIRI, led by the Hakims, and Moqtada's Mahdi Army. SCIRI was formed by Shia from Iraq's business class who were often able to leave Iraq and oppose the regime from Iran. In comparison, Moqtada's supporters were typically too poor to leave the country and had to endure regime repression and the effects of UN sanctions. The

Sadrists viewed SCIRI not only as overly cooperative with occupation authorities but also as representing Iranian interests. This suspicion was reinforced in August 2005 when SCIRI advocated a federalist system for Iraq (Hashim 2006: 267–268), which would give local governments in the Shia southern provinces greater control over their oil resources. Sadrists claimed that this was part of a plan to place the oil-rich south, with as much as 80 percent of the country's oil reserves, under Iranian influence, disadvantaging Iraqis in the center of the country, including the 2 million Shia in Sadr City, Moqtada's central base of support.

Kurds

The removal of Saddam's regime was simultaneously a cause for celebration and anxiety for Iraqi Kurds. Since the end of the Kurdish civil war, Kurdistan had enjoyed a relatively peaceful state of de facto independence from the central government and reportedly benefited from collaborating with Baghdad to circumvent UN sanctions by smuggling oil to foreign markets (Anderson and Stansfield 2004: 178).

The removal of international sanctions seemed to mean the end of lucrative smuggling operations through Kurdistan. Would the new Iraqi government provide alternate economic benefits to make up for those about to be lost? Would Kurdistan be allowed to maintain the independence it had enjoyed before the invasion? Further, if the Shia religious parties took power in Baghdad, would they attempt to impose a fundamentalist religious state system, which the relatively secularly oriented Kurds oppose?

Internal Divisions. The major political division within Kurdistan was between the Kurdistan Democratic Party (KDP) and the Patriotic Union of Kurdistan (PUK), whose militias fought a civil war against each other from 1994 to 1996. The KDP was formed in 1946 as a result of the growth of the Kurdish national movement following World War I. The party included a strained alliance between rural-based tribal groups whose leaders' wealth and power derived from traditional land ownership patterns and urban-based left-leaning intellectuals. The leftists advocated reforms to bring about greater economic equality, which threatened the interests of tribal chiefs. The KDP was led by members of the powerful Barzani tribe, originally Mullah Mustafa Barzani. Jalal al-Talabani eventually emerged as the leader of the KDP leftists.

The ideological division within the KDP worsened after the 1958 anti-monarchal revolution when General Abd al-Karim Qasim carried out agricultural reforms to redistribute some of the lands previously controlled by tribal elites. While tribal leaders opposed the reforms, the leftists within the KDP and urban professionals, workers, and small farmers tended to support them. In reaction to Baghdad's actions and rejection of his demands for expanded Kurdish rights, Mullah Mustafa called on Kurds to take up arms against the Iraqi government on September 11, 1961, launching the Kurdish rebellion.

The fighting temporarily subsided when the Baathist government promised a greater level of Kurdish autonomy. However, Baghdad's failure to live up to

Mullah Mustafa's demands led him to resume fighting in 1974. But when Baghdad and Iran signed a treaty in March 1975 in which Iraq granted Iran the international boundary it desired, Iran in return closed its border to Kurdish fighters and stopped aiding them. This forced an end to the rebellion.

The rebellion's failure caused the left wing of the KDP to break away and form the PUK on June 1, 1975, under Talabani's leadership. The PUK had many supporters in Sulaimaniyya and Arbil and among the Kurdish populations of Kirkuk and Baghdad. As noted earlier, the aftermath of the 1991 Gulf War allowed the Kurds to establish a de facto independent state, which was later torn by the 1994–1996 Kurdish civil war between the KDP and PUK. By the end of 1996, a relative balance of power was restored and with US prodding, the Kurdish parties agreed to cooperate with each other again in a reunified Kurdish Regional Government (KRG).

Issues and Orientations. The Kurds' major concerns included preserving autonomy, replacing income lost because of the reduction of smuggling, maintaining the peshmergas of the KDP and PUK, and expanding Kurdistan by including Kirkuk and other Kurdish-populated areas. Kurdish leaders supported creating a multiparty democracy and transforming Iraq's international identity from that of an Arab state to a multiethnic one. Although most Kurds seemed to favor total independence, Kurdish leaders appeared willing to remain part of a federated Iraq, periodically using the threat of secession as leverage to bring about concessions from Iraq's Arab majority.

Forgoing independence was motivated primarily by pragmatic considerations. One was opposition from Turkey and Iran, which feared their Kurdish populations might want to join an independent Kurdish homeland. Many Iraqis also opposed secession, especially if the Kurds tried to incorporate Kirkuk into their state. A trade blockade by Turkey, Iran, and Iraq could economically devastate landlocked Kurdistan. As long as Kurdistan stayed federated with Iraq, Kurdish leaders believed they could count on US protection and could help safeguard the well-being of the many Kurds who lived in Iraq but outside of Kurdistan.

Sunni Arabs

Many Sunni Arabs feared that the invasion would destroy Iraq, which in their view had bravely fought fundamentalist extremism and imperialism. They were appalled to see their armed forces, which had valiantly withstood much larger Iran during the Iran–Iraq War, overwhelmed by the airpower and technology of the invaders and then disbanded by occupation authorities.

Hashim (2006: 67–70) notes that the conquest of Iraq traumatized many Sunni Arabs, who believed they had played a disproportionately important role in building the nation. They found themselves out of power, often unemployed, and portrayed by the CPA as oppressors of Shia and Kurdish Iraqis. They watched angrily as people who had been out of the country for many years and had received aid from Iran or the United States were installed as leaders of Iraq, and the Badr Brigade, the SCIRI militia that had fought on Iran's side in the

Iran–Iraq War, operated openly with its personnel reportedly allowed to join the new Iraqi army and police (Galbraith 2008: 66).

Internal Divisions. Sunni Arabs who opposed Saddam but were military officers occasionally took advantage of their unique opportunities to try to overthrow the regime and as a result suffered severe repression. Whenever Saddam's regime cleansed the military of opponents, the largest percentage of officers killed were Sunni Arabs (Anderson and Stansfield 2004: 141). It appeared, however, that even those Sunni Arabs whose extended-family members had been persecuted by the regime tended to oppose the invasion, especially after the CPA carried out de-Baathification of government institutions and liquidated the Iraqi armed forces and it became clear that what had been publicized as a war of liberation was resulting in a long-term foreign occupation.

As with the Shia, Sunni Arabs were also differentiated along the religious dimension, with the totally secular at one end and religious fundamentalists at the other. Sunni Arabs, as other Iraqis, were also divided tribally. During the difficulties caused by UN sanctions and the resulting reduction of state resources, many Iraqis were forced to rely on tribal ties for assistance.

Issues and Orientations. Sunni Arabs believed the country was experiencing two occupations: that of the US-led coalition and a more covert one by Iranian intelligence agents supporting pro-Iranian Shia groups in persecuting Baathists (Hashim 2006: 84). They were concerned about their physical safety and families' well-being. Many also believed that a purpose of the invasion was to destroy an opponent of Israel and supporter of the Palestinians. As long as the occupation continued, Iraq was prevented from playing these roles to anywhere near the degree of the preinvasion regime.

The New Iraqi Government

When the United States, after removing the Baath regime and finding no WMD, failed to leave, many Iraqis concluded that the Americans were there not to liberate them but to seize their resources. General Jay Garner had apparently planned to hold elections to put Iraqis in charge of their country as soon as possible, although he indicated that they would be guided and helped by the United States (Garner 2004). But the CPA stopped local elections and all self-rule in the provinces in June 2003 in favor of appointing administrators and mayors (GlobalSecurity.org 2008). On July 13, 2003, CPA head Paul Bremer appointed the Iraq Governing Council (IGC) with twenty-five members: thirteen Shia Arabs (including Chalabi and Allawi), five Kurds, five Sunni Arabs, one Turkoman, and one Assyrian Christian (Polk 2005: 180). Instead of promoting a sense of security and inclusiveness for all Iraqis, Shia leaders began voting as a majority block in the IGC, indicating they would give priority to Shia interests.

The dissolution of the Baath Party and the armed forces contributed to undermining Iraq's unity. Both of these institutions, although disproportionately Sunni Arab at the highest levels of leadership, included many Shia. Their continued existence might have not only limited discontent but also served as barriers against developing sectarian violence.

The IGC, which designated April 9, the day Baghdad was captured by US forces in 2003, as Iraqi Freedom Day, was given the task of developing a temporary constitution, the Transitional Administrative Law (TAL) (Allawi 2006, 220–225). This would come into effect when the CPA declared that Iraq was again a sovereign nation in June 2004. The TAL stated that Islam was Iraq's "official religion" and "a source of Iraqi law," but supported "freedom of religious practice" (Kinsella 2007: 42). It stated that when sovereignty was returned to Iraq, an interim government would assume the CPA's and IGC's previous administrative and political powers. The TAL also called for an election to select the Transitional National Assembly (TNA), whose primary function would be to formulate a permanent constitution, which would then be subject to approval by the people through a national referendum. Election rules required that every third candidate on each party's or coalition of parties' list of candidates be a woman. And at least 25 percent of TNA members were required to be women (White House 2005).

UN Security Council Resolution 1546, adopted on June 8, 2004, gave unanimous support to the transfer of sovereignty from the CPA to the new Iraqi government and for the January 2005 election of the TNA (al-Marashi 2005). The resolution stated, in part, that the Security Council "welcomes that, also by 30 June 2004, the occupation will end and the Coalition Provisional Authority will cease to exist, and that Iraq will reassert its full sovereignty" (USIP 2004). All Iraqi citizens born before January 1, 1987, including those residing in other countries, were eligible to vote. The TNA election was held on January 30, 2005, with a reported 58.3 percent voter turnout (IFES 2005). Most Sunni Arabs boycotted this election (Cockburn 2007: 187). A Zogby International poll showed an 80 percent Shia Arab turnout, and 57 percent for Kurds, but only 9 percent for Sunni Arabs. The results gave 140 of 275 assembly seats to the Shia United Iraqi Alliance (50.9 percent of the vote), thought to be supported by Ayatollah Sistani (composed of mainly SCIRI and Dawa). The Democratic Patriotic Alliance of Kurdistan (which included the KDP and the PUK) received 25.7 percent, and interim Prime Minister Ayad Allawi's Iraqi List (which included the relatively secular Iraqi National Accord) got about 13.8 percent. Sunni Arabs were nearly absent from the assembly. Following the election, Ibrahim Jaafari, a fifty-eight-year-old physician and leader of the Islamic Dawa Party, replaced Allawi as prime minister. Like other prominent postinvasion Iraqi leaders, Jaafari had lived outside of Iraq for many years, in both Iran and the UK (Asser 2005), and Cole (2005) describes him as "an old time Muslim fundamentalist" who wanted to implement Islamic law as much as possible in Iraq.

Following the election, the TNA oversaw the drafting of a permanent constitution, whose Article 1 declared Iraq a republic with a parliamentary democracy form of government. Article 2 stated that "Islam is the official religion of the State and is a foundation source of legislation." "No law may be enacted that contradicts the established provisions of Islam." "No law may be enacted that contradicts the principles of democracy." "This Constitution guarantees the Islamic identity of the majority of the Iraqi people and guarantees the full religious rights to freedom of religious belief and practice of all individuals such as Christians, Yazidis, and Mandean Sabeans." The document provided for an elected parliament, the Council of Representatives, with a four-year term, which would specialize (Article 61) in "enacting federal laws," "monitoring the performance of the executive authority," electing the republic's president, and approving the appointment of the members and head of the Federal Court of Cassation, the chief public prosecutor, ambassadors, and "the Iraqi Army Chief of Staff, his assistants," and those officers with ranks of division commander or higher, as well as the head of the Iraqi intelligence service (Iraqi Constitution 2005). The constitution's Article 49 also stated that "the elections law shall aim to achieve a percentage of representation for women not less than one-quarter of the members of the Council of Representatives."

The executive branch is composed of a prime minister and a cabinet of ministers, and there are provisions for an independent judiciary and a presidency. The structure of government is federal with significant levels of autonomy for the individual governorates (provinces). Galbraith (2008: 31–32) notes that Article 110 gives the central government exclusive control of only a relatively short list of functions, such as foreign policy and national security, while Article 115 gives regional or governorate laws priority over national laws on all issues other than those covered in Article 110. Furthermore, Article 121 gives regional governments the authority for "the establishment and organization of the internal security forces for the region" and guarantees regions diplomatic representation in other countries (Iraqi Constitution 2005). The right of governorates to form regions is described in Articles 117–120.

Adoption of the constitution required that the majority of the country's voters approve it and that people in no more than two of Iraq's governorates could reject it by more than two-thirds of the governorate vote (Kinsella 2007: 43). Many Sunni Arabs rejected the constitution because they believed that it provided a foundation for transforming Iraq into a Shia Islamic state and set the stage for future Kurdish secession. Another concern was that its federal system could lead to the Shia-dominated southern governorates' depriving the central provinces of a sufficient share of oil revenues. Although many Sunni Arabs voted in the October 15, 2005, popular referendum on the constitution, the majority in the estimated 64.6 percent voter turnout (IFES 2005) approved the new constitution. Since it was rejected by more than two-thirds of the voters in only two governorates, the constitution went into effect.

The first Council of Representatives election was held on December 15, 2005. The Shia United Iraqi Alliance, composed of some seventeen parties, of which the largest were SCIRI and its associated Badr Organization (formerly the Badr Brigade); Dawa; Moqtada al-Sadr's movement; and the Islamic Fadhila Party, won 128 council seats (BBC 2006a). The Kurdistan Alliance of eight parties, including the KDP and the PUK, won 53 seats while Allawi's new coalition, the Iraqi National List of fourteen relatively secular parties, won 25 seats. Sunni Arabs voted in greater numbers in this election and the overall voter turnout rose to 79.6 percent. The Sunni Arab Iraqi Accord Front coalition of three parties won 44 seats and the Sunni Arab Iraqi Front for National Dialogue won 11 seats. Since Jaafari had become unacceptable to both the Kurds and Sunni Arabs, and, reportedly, to the United States (*New York Times* 2007), Nouri al-Maliki, a member of Dawa, was appointed prime minister when the Council of Representatives convened on April 22, 2006 (Parline 2008).

Maliki had fled Iraq in 1980, eventually residing in Syria (BBC 2006b). He was characterized in August 2007 as being highly sectarian (*New York Times* 2007), and his government was accused of molding Iraq's new security forces "into an instrument of Shiite domination and revenge" and "leaving Sunni Arab civilians unprotected from sectarian terrorism."

Top government posts were apportioned to the various major political coalitions. A deputy prime minister position and the largely symbolic presidency went to the Kurdistan Alliance. President Talabani's deputy presidents were from the Iraqi Accord Front and the United Iraqi Alliance. Twelve government ministries went to the United Iraqi Alliance and others to the Kurdistan Alliance, the Iraqi National List, the Iraqi Accord Front, and other coalitions or parties.

The government, despite a shortage of capable administrators, was slow to allow former Baathists access to government jobs. It also delayed enacting the crucial oil law to ensure an equitable share of the country's oil revenues to all sectors of the population. Many US officials seemed to believe that if the Iraqi government could effectively deal with these and other significant issues, the war in Iraq would end and US forces there could be significantly reduced.

The September 2007 US Government Accountability Office report on Iraq (GAO 2007: 3) indicates that Iraq's security forces were failing to administer laws fairly and were often incapable of acting without the support of the US military. These assessments were similar to findings in the *Iraq Study Group Report*, or ISGR (Baker and Hamilton 2006: 20–21), which had been released on December 6, 2006. For example, the ISGR claimed that the Iraqi government tended toward sectarian bias in the provision of services such as electricity, drinking water, health care, education, sewage treatment, and trash removal and that the country was plagued by corruption costing Iraq as much as $5–$7 billion annually. A report in May 2007 also indicated that $5 million to $15 million worth of oil production per day over the previous four years was unaccounted for (Glanz 2007c). Allawi (2006: 356–361) indicates that oil theft was facilitated in part by a general lack of effective metering (measurement) of Iraq's oil exports at loading terminals. The ISGR also indicated that many government positions were awarded as political patronage to people who lacked the ability to adequately perform their jobs. In some cases only 15–20 percent of ministry budgets were being spent, little more than the allocation to pay officials' salaries.

Modifying De-Baathification

Since the 2003 de-Baathification policy had contributed to depriving the country of desperately needed skilled personnel, sectarian hostility, and motivating thousands to support the antioccupation insurgency, the Bush administration

pushed the Iraqi parliament to allow many former Baath Party members to return to government jobs. This was partly intended to bring about sectarian
reconciliation and weaken the nationalist branch of the insurgency.

On January 12, 2008, the parliament passed a modified de-Baathification
law that would potentially allow anywhere from 13,000 to 31,000 former low-
level Baath Party members to reenter government service (Oppel and Myers
2008; Rubin 2008b). Galbraith (2008: 27–28), however, states that many Sunnis opposed the law revising de-Baathification because they feared it would
worsen, not improve, their situation. He says the law did not require that
people be given back the same government jobs from which they had been dismissed and it forced the retirement of other former Baath Party members from
"security-related ministries."

Provincial Elections Law

On September 24, 2008, after months of contentious negotiations, Iraq's national legislature passed a long-awaited elections law for province governments
(Goode 2008). However, this was accomplished in great part by setting aside
and delaying resolution of the divisive issue of the status of Kirkuk. While the
leaders of the Kurdish Regional Government demanded that Kirkuk be included in the autonomous region, the Arab and Turkoman residents of Kirkuk
generally opposed this option. So the province's future status would undergo
further study and the election in this province would be postponed. The new
law stated that elections should be held in fourteen of Iraq's eighteen provinces
by January 31, 2009. As in the case of Kirkuk province, elections in the three
provinces that compose the Kurdish autonomous region were also delayed until
later in 2009 (Yaphe 2008: 405). The provincial elections were held on January
31, 2009, in the fourteen predominantly Arab provinces with dozens of parties
and thousands of candidates competing for 440 provincial council seats. Voter
turnout was estimated at about 51 percent (Daniel 2009), down significantly
from 79.6 percent for the December 2005 Council of Representatives election.
In nine provinces Prime Minister Nouri al-Maliki's Coalition of the State and
Law, which included Dawa, won more votes than any other party or coalition
and strongly outpolled the more sectarian ISCI slate. Throughout the fourteen
provinces Maliki's coalition won about 29 percent of the seats, compared to
only about 12 percent for ISCI (Boston.com 2009). Moqtada al-Sadr's supporters appeared to win a little over 9 percent of the seats, though Moqtada did not
officially put forth his own slate of candidates. In general the results seemed to
indicate that in both the majority Shia and Sunni Arab provinces, voters rejected the more fundamentalist religious parties and also more often supported
candidates favoring a relatively strong central government. Despite his previous
reputation as a highly sectarian Shia, Maliki during the year leading up to the
provincial elections publicly adopted a more moderate and pragmatic stance,
and increased his personal popularity by reining in extremist Shia militias in
Baghdad and Basra (Susman 2009) and improving people's sense of physical
security.

Economy: Reconstruction and Oil

The United States reportedly spent tens of billions of dollars attempting to improve Iraq's petroleum, electricity, transportation, water, and sewage sectors, often with unsatisfactory results (Glanz 2007b; Glanz 2008). By December 2006 it had become clear that Iraq was failing to spend billions of dollars of its own oil revenue that had been designated for reconstruction. The January 2008 GAO report indicated that in reality Iraq had spent only 4.4 percent of its reconstruction budget by August 2007, only about half the percentage of its infrastructure reconstruction budget spent during the same period in 2006, suggesting that the problem had gotten worse rather than improving (Glanz 2008). The reasons offered by US and Iraqi officials included the lack of skilled personnel, lack of security in certain areas, and new anticorruption efforts, which some thought inhibited the productivity of Iraqi officials accustomed to accepting bribes or receiving other illegal favors for initiating reconstruction projects.

In addition, Iraq's economic recovery was hindered by its debt. Following the 2003 invasion, Iraq was estimated to owe about $140 billion to Saudi Arabia, Kuwait, the United Arab Emirates (UAE), and a number of other nations (Mufson and Wright 2007). But in 2004, the Paris Club of nineteen relatively rich lender nations, including Australia, Britain, Canada, France, Germany, Italy, Japan, Russia, Spain, and the United States, decided to gradually reduce by 80 percent the approximately $42 billion Iraq owed them (Smith 2004; Weiss 2004). And Saudi Arabia indicated that it would waive about 80 percent of Iraq's debt. Then in 2008 the UAE stated that it would forgive almost $7 billion Iraq owed (Ibrahim 2008).

One important goal of the CPA and then the new Iraqi government was to increase oil production. The ISGR (Baker and Hamilton 2006: 23) indicated that Iraq's hydrocarbon production and marketing represented 70 percent of Iraq's GDP and over 95 percent of government revenue. But for years after the invasion, Iraqi oil production was generally below prewar levels (Hiro 2007: 146–148). In 2006 oil production averaged about 2.2 million barrels a day. This was less than Iraq's highest level of oil production in 1979, 3.7 million barrels a day, and the preinvasion rate of 2.6 million barrels a day (Wong 2007a). The US State Department (Bureau of Near Eastern Affairs 2008) reported that Iraqi oil production was 2.46 million barrels per day during August 18–24, 2008. Although oil production had not changed much from its preinvasion level, Iraq's government benefited from increases in oil prices on the international market.

As Shia political-religious groups dominated the central government, Iran came to play a major role in Iraq's economy (Wong 2007b). By 2007 Iranian-made Peugeot cars and air conditioners were popular. The two economies became more integrated, and many Iraqis looked to Iran not only for manufactured goods, but also to supply certain food items and electricity for parts of southern Iraq, including Basra. Iraq's reliance on Iran was in part due to deterioration of its own industrial infrastructure during the 1992–2003 sanctions period and inadequate postinvasion reconstruction.

The Oil Law

In theory, a national oil law placing ultimate control of the nation's energy resources in the hands of the central government, agreed to by all major ethnic and religious groups, could be an economic mechanism for maintaining a unified Iraq. Such a law would also establish a stable legal framework for international oil companies (IOCs) to invest in bringing unexploited oil fields into production. The goal was to eventually produce as much as 6 million barrels per day.

Many Iraqis suspected, however, that the national oil law would serve as a means for the United States to take over Iraq's energy resources, most likely through a process of privatization. Drafts of the oil law permitted any region producing at least 150,000 barrels of oil per day to create its own local oil company. These companies would be allowed great independence from the central government to produce and export oil, potentially leading to private ownership (Glanz 2007a). Once privatized, Iraq's energy resources could pass into foreign ownership. In June and July 2007, a survey of 2,200 Iraqis in all eighteen provinces indicated that 63 percent preferred "Iraq's oil to be developed and produced by Iraqi state-owned companies" rather than foreign companies (Angus Reid Global Monitor 2007).

Difficulties in establishing a national oil law distributing revenues proportionately to different social groups included conflicting estimates of their size. Although many claim that Sunni Arabs are only about 20 percent of the population, members of this group often assert that they are a much larger percentage of Iraq's people. Also, while many Arabs believe that only about 13 percent of Iraqis are Kurds, Kurdish leaders think that as many as 23 percent are Kurds (Rubin 2008a). Lack of a recent census made it hard to evaluate conflicting claims. Another major delay in passing the national oil law was the conflict between the KRG and the central government over control of regional energy resources (Lando 2008). The KRG demanded the right to establish its own contracts with IOCs. In contrast, Sunni Arabs favored strict central government control over energy resources and contracts with foreign companies. Shiite Arabs appeared divided, with the Sadrists preferring central government control and other Shia Arabs, including some in SCIRI (ISCI), favoring a strong local government role in making contracts with foreign companies. The KRG proceeded to pass its own Kurdish Oil Law on August 6, 2007, and, without the approval of the central government, negotiated at least twenty production-sharing agreements with relatively small IOCs by January 2008 (Chalabi 2008).

Army and Police

The new Iraqi armed forces recruited heavily among Shia Arabs. In social surveys the vast majority of Sunni Arabs expressed almost no confidence in the new army, viewing it more as a US-equipped super Shia militia meant to dominate them. The army, like the country's National Police, seemed focused inward on counterinsurgency rather than on protecting Iraq from foreign threats. The ISGR observed that the Iraqi army tended to lack effective leadership and equipment. Some soldiers wanted to serve only in certain parts of the country and many were often on leave for one week per month to bring their pay home to their families. Soldiers seemed to face no penalties for being absent without leave. The ISGR indicated that the police were in a substantially worse state. They were described as infiltrated by militias and accused of engaging in sectarian violence, including killing civilians (Baker and Hamilton 2006: 9–10).

According to the US State Department's August 27, 2008, Iraq Weekly Status Report (Bureau of Near Eastern Affairs 2008), the Iraqi Ministry of Defense "currently authorized personnel" (army, air force, navy and support forces) numbered 189,728, while the Ministry of the Interior (police service, national police, border enforcement) totaled 363,876. The Counter Terrorism Bureau's special operations was 4,733.

Women's Rights

The Iraqi government decided in December 2007 to order policewomen to hand in their weapons so that only male police could carry guns (Susman 2007). The decision appeared to reflect the entrenchment of Islamic fundamentalism. The absence of female police officers made it easier for female suicide bombers to operate since male security personnel often neglected to search women to detect explosive belts (Farrell and Al-Husaini 2008). But the measure also impacted women's rights. The lack of policewomen interfered with effective investigation and prosecution of rape and domestic abuse. Women were reluctant to serve as unarmed police officers since many officers and police administrative workers had been killed for working for the new government or collaborating with occupying forces. Like men, they felt they needed guns both on the job and at home to protect themselves. The Iraqi government also prevented women from rising to police command positions. Hundreds of thousands of women in Iraq were widowed by wars and by postinvasion conflict and had been drawn to police jobs, which paid $600 to $700 per month, about twice the salary of most civil servants (Susman 2007). US General David Phillips, who had supported the concept of recruiting female officers, was quoted as saying that because Iraq was a sovereign nation, the United States could not interfere with Iraqi government decisions regarding female police (Susman 2007).

The discrimination against female police reflected other restrictions on women. In once secularly oriented cities women were pressured to wear head scarves in public (Ahmed 2006). In Shia-dominated Basra dozens of women were reportedly murdered during 2007 for allegedly acting in immoral ways (Hamdani and Hider 2007; Mahmoud, O'Kane, and Black 2007).

Whereas General Qasim's Law of Personal Status gave women similar rights to divorce and inheritance as men and the Baath regime provided women with more educational and occupational opportunities than most countries in the Middle East, the actual freedom and rights of women, secular women in particular, appeared to decline under the new government. Some Iraqi women working for women's rights were killed in postinvasion Iraq while others fled the country or attempted to protect themselves by operating in secret.

While the 2005 Iraqi constitution in Article 14 banned discrimination based on gender, it contained the potentially contradictory statement in Article 2, as noted earlier, that "no law may be enacted that contradicts the established provisions of Islam." Women's rights were endangered by changes in family legal procedures. During the Baath regime, civil courts typically dealt with divorce, marriage, and inheritance. But under the new regime, these issues were often handled by religious courts whose judges could differ in their interpretation and strictness in the application of Islamic law.

Sovereignty

Iraq seemed to lack real sovereignty when it came to the occupation, oil, and the presence of US private military firms. In reality, to many observers the US-led invasion resulted in only a limited autonomy for Iraq in which the Shia political-religious parties were allowed to pursue their vision of an Islamist state and the Kurds to retain their independence from the central government. Iraqi parliamentarians' requests for a timetable for the departure of US forces appeared to have little effect until late 2008 when US and Iraqi leaders negotiated the Iraq–US Status of Forces Agreement (SOFA), which required in Article 24, Paragraph 8, that "all the United States Forces shall be withdrawn from all Iraqi territory no later than December 31, 2011" (White House 2008).

The Kurdish Government

The KRG was unified by an agreement that went into effect on January 21, 2006. Until then, the Arbil and Dohuk governorates were under KDP-led administrations while the Sulaimaniyya governorate had a PUK-led administration (KRG 2006). On May 7, 2006, a broad coalition government under Prime Minister Nechirvan Barzani, including the KDP, PUK, Kurdistan Toilers Party, the Kurdistan Socialist Party, Kurdistan Islamic Union, Kurdistan Communist Party, Islamic Group, and Turkoman Brotherhood, assumed office. The relative political stability and low level of postinvasion violence or flight of administrative and technical personnel contributed to a flood of investment into Iraqi Kurdistan from the United States, Europe, Turkey, Iran, the Persian Gulf states, and some wealthy Iraqis. As a result, reconstruction and economic development occurred more rapidly in Kurdistan than in other parts of Iraq (Semple 2007).

The Kurdish government wanted to maintain the peshmerga force as the KRG's regional army, the right of return for Kurds who had been removed from Kirkuk during the Baath regime, and a referendum in Kirkuk so that local residents could determine whether to join the Kurdish region. In a January 28, 2008, speech KRG Prime Minister Barzani said, "Stability, security and prosperity in the Kurdistan Region is dependent to a great extent on stability and security in Iraq" (KRG 2008). He recalled the many betrayals the Kurdish people had experienced internationally and as citizens of Iraq, and stated, "We must always be strong and united" and maintain the "capability to protect our own people whatever the cost."

Iraqi Kurds faced potential threats because rebel Turkish and Iranian Kurds set up bases in their territory. Parts of the Iraqi Kurdish region were used by Kurdish Workers Party (PKK) guerrillas, a rebellious leftist-oriented movement among Turkey's estimated 20 percent Kurdish minority. On February 21, 2008, thousands of Turkish soldiers invaded Iraqi Kurdistan to attack PKK forces (BBC 2008). In addition, a leftist Iranian Kurdish guerrilla group, the Party for Free Life in Kurdistan, used parts of Iraqi Kurdistan to launch attacks into Iran (Oppel 2007a).

Iraqi Public Opinion

While social surveys can provide important information on people's attitudes on important topics, findings should be viewed with caution. In face-to-face interviews there is a danger that interviewees will tend to respond more in terms of what they think the interviewer wants to hear or considers socially acceptable. In an occupied country this methodological problem can be much more serious. Even when Iraqis are hired to do the interviews, rather than Arabic-speaking foreigners, many respondents may be concerned that surveys are a covert form of gathering intelligence.

Nevertheless, a number of surveys may provide approximations of Iraqi attitudes toward crucial issues. One of the more extensive and widely cited was carried out during August 17–24, 2007, for the BBC, ABC, and NHK (Japan Broadcasting Corporation) involving a sample of 2,212 randomly selected Iraqi adults (including Iraqi Kurds). Of those surveyed, 79 percent opposed the presence of coalition forces in Iraq, and 72 percent said their presence was making the security situation worse. About 63 percent stated that the US-led coalition was wrong to invade Iraq, up from about 50 percent in a November 2005 survey. The poll indicated that 47 percent wanted occupation forces to leave Iraq immediately, while the other 53 percent indicated that they should leave after "Iraqi security forces can operate independently" or some other goal, such as greater security, was achieved. However, there was considerable variation among social groups, with about 72 percent of Sunni Arabs calling for immediate withdrawal, compared with 44 percent of Shia Arabs, and only about 10 percent of Iraqi Kurds (Greenwell and Cohen 2007). Almost all Sunni Arabs disapproved of the performance of the Shia-led central government, compared with about 53 percent of Kurds and 47 percent of Shia Arabs. Approximately 62 percent stated that there should be "one unified Iraq with a central government in Baghdad." But whereas about 97 percent of Sunni Arabs and 56 percent of Shia Arabs supported this position, only about 9 percent of the Kurdish respondents did (Greenwell and Cohen 2007). Of the Kurds, 42 percent wanted Iraq to be "a group of regional states with their own regional governments and a federal government in Baghdad" and 49 percent preferred that Iraq be "divided into separate independent states." In the August 2007 poll only 29 percent thought their lives would get better in the coming year, down from the 64 percent in the November 2005 poll.

Comparisons of Shia and Sunni Opinion

High Similarity: Opposition to Sectarian Segregation and Violence Against Civilians. The August 2007 survey revealed some topics about which Shia

Arabs and Sunni Arabs displayed almost identical opinions. In both groups, 98 percent indicated that the "separation of people on sectarian lines" was "a bad thing" for Iraq. In addition, 100 percent of both groups stated that attacks by Al Qaeda against Iraqi civilians were "not acceptable," 98 percent of both opposed Al Qaeda "attempts to gain control of local areas," and 96 percent of Sunni Arabs and 97 percent of Shia Arabs opposed Al Qaeda's "recruitment of foreign fighters to come to Iraq" (Global Policy Forum 2007). Both groups were roughly evenly split on whether a US withdrawal "from Iraq before civil order is fully restored" would result in "parts of Iraq becoming a base of operation for international terrorists." Large majorities of both Sunni Arabs (82 percent) and Shia Arabs (98 percent) considered attacks on Iraqi government forces unacceptable (Global Policy Forum 2007).

Moderate Similarity: Opposition to US-Led Coalition Forces. There was also a relatively high level of agreement among Sunni Arabs and Shia Arabs regarding the US-led occupation. For example, 98 percent of Sunni Arabs and 91 percent of Shia Arabs stated that they had "not very much confidence" or "none at all" in US and UK occupation forces, and 98 percent of Sunni Arabs and 82 percent of Shia Arabs stated that "the United States and other Coalition forces did a 'quite bad' or 'very bad job'" in carrying out their responsibilities in Iraq. Similarly large majorities of both groups, 98 percent of Sunni Arabs and 84 percent of Shia Arabs, "somewhat" or "strongly" opposed "the presence of Coalition forces in Iraq." That large majorities of both Iraqi Sunni and Shia Arabs were critical of the US-led coalition indicated that if Iraq achieved genuine sovereignty and democracy, one key issue capable of uniting the Sunni and Shia Arabs was their attitudes toward those who had occupied Iraq.

Moderate Dissimilarity: Greater Sunni Arab Problems Regarding Jobs, Services, Security, and Recovery. There were larger differences between the Sunni and Shia Arabs with regard to "the availability of jobs," "the availability of medical care," freedom "to go where you wish safely," "your freedom to live where you wish without persecution," and "the security situation." Majorities in both groups were discontented about these issues, but the gap between the more distressed Sunni Arabs and the Shia Arabs ranged from 22 percent to 27 percent. In addition, 89 percent of Sunni Arabs and 68 percent of Shia Arabs stated that reconstruction efforts in their local areas since the invasion were quite or very ineffective. Further, 80 percent of Shia Arabs believed that a US withdrawal from Iraq "before civil order is fully restored" would make the probability of a full-scale civil war in Iraq less likely or would have no effect, but the figure for Sunni Arabs was lower, at 59 percent.

High Dissimilarity: Sunni Arabs' Greater Willingness to Support Violence Against Coalition Forces and Express Discontent. While 93 percent of Sunni Arabs considered attacks on coalition forces acceptable, only 50 percent of Shia Arabs did. Another wide gap was in regard to whether it was right or wrong for coalition forces to invade: 97 percent of Sunni Arabs considered the invasion wrong, while only 52 percent of Shia Arabs did.

Other large differences between Sunni and Shia Arabs concerned attitudes toward the postinvasion Shia-dominated government, army, and police. The percentage expressing confidence in the postinvasion government was only 4 percent for Sunni Arabs, compared with 58 percent for Shia Arabs, and only 34 percent of Sunni Arabs had confidence in the new army, compared with 83 percent of Shia Arabs. Confidence in the police was 37 percent for Sunni Arabs but 83 percent for Shia Arabs.

Finally, Sunni Arabs were more pessimistic: 87 percent said things were going quite badly or very badly in their lives, compared with 45 percent of Shia Arabs, and only 7 percent of Sunni Arabs believed their children would have better lives than they did, while 55 percent of Shia Arabs believed this to be true. Thus, while majorities of both Shia and Sunni Arabs opposed foreign occupation, they differed greatly regarding acceptance of the government the occupation authorities had helped come to power and how its policies and actions affected their lives.

Saddam's Trial and Execution

Among the major politically significant events of postinvasion Iraq were the capture of Saddam Hussein on December 13, 2003 (Allawi 2006: 242), and his trial, conviction, and death sentence for executions following a July 8, 1982, assassination attempt. Since at the time Iraq was at war with Iran, the assassination attempt against the president while he was visiting Dujail, a community with a mixed Sunni and Shia Arab population about sixty kilometers north of Baghdad (Menendez 2005), was viewed as treason. However, the execution of scores of people appeared an unjustifiable act of collective punishment.

There were other charges against Saddam for which he could have conceivably received the death penalty, such as the Anfal campaign against the Kurds or the March 16, 1988, chemical attack against the Kurdish city of Halabja. Some also suggested the possibility of trying Saddam for starting the Iran–Iraq War or for invading Kuwait. However, these options were potentially problematic. For example, a trial on the Iran–Iraq War likely would have led to defense attorneys' bringing up American support provided to both Iraq and Iran indicating that the United States had helped prolong the war, costing great additional loss of life and property. The attorneys would have argued that Saddam intended a short, punitive war, not a long war, to stop Iran from shelling Iraqi territory and fomenting a Shia religious rebellion. The Kuwait invasion presented other problems, such as why the United States did not provide a clearer warning against an attack on Kuwait. In addition, defense attorneys would almost certainly have brought up the instances in which US military forces invaded other countries that posed far less of a threat to the United States than Kuwait's policies did to Iraq. The problem with trying Saddam for the Anfal campaign or for the chemical attack on Halabja was that there seemed to be less evidence directly linking him to those events, compared with the Dujail executions. The "Dujail Massacre" had the best chance of resulting in swift conviction and execution of the former Iraqi president, since he was accused of signing the execution order.

In court appearances Saddam was often defiant, rejecting the court's legitimacy and charging that the proceeding was simply a mechanism for the American invaders to put him to death to demoralize the antioccupation insurgency. Three defense attorneys representing codefendants were assassinated, resulting in protests from surviving defense attorneys that lack of security made a fair trial impossible.

Saddam was convicted, sentenced to death, and rushed to execution on December 30, 2006. He was brought by helicopter from a US base to the Shia-dominated Baghdad suburb of Khadimiya, where he was turned over to government soldiers, who appeared to be mainly members of Moqtada al-Sadr's militia, for execution. He exchanged insults with some in the crowd in the concrete-lined execution room and refused to wear a hood for the hanging. As he stood on the gallows, his last words were reported as "Down with the traitors, the Americans, the spies and the Persians" (Santora 2006). Saddam's defiance in court and bravery at the execution seemed to, in effect, resurrect his reputation as an opponent of imperialism. Many in Iraq and elsewhere saw his trial and execution as little more than a thinly disguised lynching orchestrated by the occupying authorities and carried out by vengeful Shia militants. Many concluded that the impact would be not to reduce but to spur more resistance to the occupation.

Insurgents and Militias

Occupation Policies and the Rise of Resistance

The key reason for the rise of the resistance insurgency was the perception that the United States and its partners had launched an unprovoked and unjustified invasion of Iraq for the purpose of seizing control of its energy resources and removing an opponent of US and Israeli policies. As noted in chapter 6, the CIA believed that former intelligence officers and others from the defeated Baathist regime had prepared before the invasion to conduct guerrilla warfare against the occupying forces by hiding stores of weapons (Risen 2006: 136–137). But the sweeping de-Baathification program and the disbanding of the Iraqi armed forces collectively punished hundreds of thousands, providing many more vengeful recruits and supporters for armed resistance.

Insurgents

Insurgent activity became most intense in the provinces of Baghdad, Diyala, Anbar, and Salah ad-Din, where about 40 percent of the country's population lived. The resistance was composed of many networks, varying in motives, ideology, and tactics with at least eleven major insurgent organizations or alliances. As many as forty or more smaller insurgent groups also operated. Estimates of active insurgents ranged "from a few thousand to more than 50,000" (Finer 2006), and approximately 90 percent were thought to be Iraqi Sunni Arabs. According to documents and computers found by US forces on September 11, 2007, near Sinjar, Iraq, close to the Syrian border at the desert camp of the insurgent cell considered responsible for smuggling the large majority of foreign fighters into Iraq, 301 of the more than 700 entering the country in the previous year were from Saudi Arabia (Oppel 2007b). An additional 137 were from Libya. Of the foreign fighters, 291 came from North Africa, including Libya; 56 were from Syria; and 14 were from Jordan. US officials reported that most foreign fighters entered Iraq to be suicide bombers, snipers, or bomb makers, or to carry out logistics or financial functions (Cooper 2007). Saudi authorities were concerned that some Saudi volunteers could get training in Iraq and then return home to launch an insurgency against the rule of the royal family. But of the approximately 25,000 persons imprisoned in US detention centers in Iraq, only about 290 (approximately 1.2 percent) were foreigners. The primary motivations of Sunni Arab insurgents appeared to be either "patriotism or Salafi . . . religious fervour" (Guidère and Harling 2006). Hashim (2006: 71) describes Sunni Arab nationalists as fighting to force the Americans to leave Iraq and to prevent the Shia exiles that the coalition allowed back into the country from establishing an Iraqi version of the Iranian theocratic political system. Some Sunni Arab nationalists believed that thousands of Iranian intelligence agents, some of whose function was to eliminate former Baath Party members and certain Shia Iraqi nationalists, had infiltrated occupied Iraq (Hashim 2006: 84). One of the leaders of the Baathist insurgents was believed to be Izzat Ibrahim al-Douri, who had been a close associate of Saddam, a former vice president of Iraq, and a member of the Revolutionary Command Council.

As noted above, the CPA decision to disband the Iraqi army and security forces, likely intended in part to remove a threat to the returning US-supported Iraqi exiles (Hashim 2006: 93), motivated thousands to join the insurgency. Responding to the danger, the CPA decided to provide monthly stipends of $50 to $150 to almost 250,000 of the dismissed soldiers (Allawi 2006: 158) and to continue pensions to former members of the Iraqi armed forces to reduce their motivation to join resistance groups (Hashim 2006: 93). But many members of the Iraqi military felt betrayed and humiliated by the US decision to disband the armed forces. From their point of view the armed forces had defended the Arab world against the Persian fundamentalist threat and then, unlike all the other Arab states that voiced opposition to Western imperialism, actually took on the immensely more powerful United States in the 1991 Gulf War and the 2003 invasion. For many of these former Iraqi soldiers, joining the resistance was a matter of honor (Hashim 2006: 98–99).

Hashim (2006: 99) suggests that in addition to honor, Iraqis were compelled to fight the occupation because of feelings of pride, nationalism, and revenge, aroused by the collective national humiliation of being invaded, conquered, and occupied. Revenge was especially strong among those whose relatives or friends had been killed by coalition forces. But many Iraqis did not at first violently resist the occupation until the economically and psychologically devastating CPA de-Baathification and military dissolution orders, and the abuse of Iraqi prisoners at Abu Ghraib prison in Iraq, provoked them into taking up arms.

Religion emerged as another major motivation for resistance fighters. Many Sunni Arabs came to the conclusion that Iraq had become vulnerable to conquest and occupation because its people had fallen away from the true teachings of Islam. In response they were drawn to the Salafi version of Islam. Sunni Salafi Islam ("Salafi" here refers to "predecessors," or the early generations of Islam) held that believers must embrace the form of Islam that existed at the time of the Prophet Muhammad and during the period immediately after his death when Islam was led by the first four caliphs, the so-called Rightly Guided Caliphs, who had actually known Muhammad. Many of the Iraqi Salafi fundamentalists became members of Al Qaeda in Mesopotamia (AQM), also called Al Qaeda in Iraq.

Hashim (2006: 104–108) explains that many tribal leaders resisted the occupation because they opposed domination by non-Islamic occupation forces. Lack of sufficient resources from the coalition also contributed to their discontent because they needed material benefits, such as money and jobs, to distribute to tribal members. In addition, tribal members were offended by coalition forces' treating Iraqis in what they considered unjustifiably harsh ways, humiliating them, and violating tribal customs. This included many searches of individuals and homes and the long-term detainment of suspects.

Resistance networks were composed of different types of organizational structures (Hashim 2006: 158–170). Combat cells had four to seven members, depending on specific operational requirements. Noncombat cells specialized in IEDs, logistics, support for suicide bomber operations, reconnaissance, propaganda, communications, Internet recruiting, funding, procurement of weapons, training, or security for the operations of other cells. Individual cells, even operating in the same area, often had no knowledge of each other for security reasons. Financial support for both nationalist and Islamic insurgents came in part from outside Iraq, and former Baathist regime officials were thought to have access to funds for insurgent support. Before the invasion, large quantities of money were reportedly hidden in various locations for use in the nationalist insurgency. Individual Saudi Arabians were also suspected of channeling assistance to insurgents. And some insurgents were thought to have gotten funding through activities such as oil smuggling and ransoms for kidnap victims (Burns and Semple 2006).

Insurgents detonated IEDs in various ways, including cell phones and remote garage door openers. When coalition forces used jammers to block detonation signals, some insurgents responded by using a signal to keep an IED from detonating so that the jammer's breaking of the signal would detonate the device. As coalition forces employed more heavily armored vehicles for IED protection, insurgents used shaped charges capable of propelling a partially molten copper projectile through armor (Gordon 2007).

The insurgency was limited mainly to Sunni Arabs and was not unified with regard to ideology, goals, or leadership for coordinating efforts. The lack of forests in much of the country meant only very limited physical cover for resistance fighters. US counterinsurgency capabilities, including surveillance of suspected insurgents' communications, biometric identification methods (photographs, fingerprints, or retinal scans) of individual Iraqis to control the population, and remotely controlled planes that could stay aloft for long periods and deliver lethal attacks on insurgents, became more effective in hampering the insurgency.

Another counterinsurgency technology used in Iraq was the Human Terrain System (HTS), which uses cultural and sociological approaches advocated by counterinsurgency authorities to influence and gather information from indigenous people. HTS involves the embedding of Human Terrain Teams (HTTs) with forward military units to provide commanders with advice and intelligence about local culture, social structure, economics, and leadership (Kipp, Grau, Prinslow, and Smith 2006). An HTT typically has five members, including three military personnel: one in command of the team, who acts as an adviser to the commander of the combat unit to which the HTT is attached; the HT analyst, who gathers intelligence by debriefing soldiers returning from operations; and the HT research manager. The other two members of the team are cultural anthropologists or sociologists, ideally fluent in the local language, one designated the cultural analyst who carries out or manages ethnographic or other related research, and the other, titled the regional studies analyst, who specializes in gaining knowledge of how local people interpret events and information and who runs focus groups with them. Unlike the Vietnam War Civil Operations and Revolutionary Development Support program, which generally relied on only its own social research and intelligence gathering, the HTS is tied to larger "reachback research cells" and "subject-matter expert networks" in the United States or elsewhere that can both advise the embedded HTTs and provide them with previously collected cultural or social information about the team's area of operation. They also receive, systematically archive, and/or further analyze data received from HTTs. Advocates of HTS hoped that the system would increase understanding and allow anticipation of the behavior of resistance fighters and indigenous noncombatants. A central goal was to gain local population support for the counterinsurgency or, at minimum, reduce the population's assistance to the resistance and achieve victory mainly through nonviolent means.

Nationalist Insurgents. Many of the initial insurgents were Baathists, including former military and intelligence officers, who either participated in the fighting or trained younger volunteers. Following Saddam's capture on December 13, 2003, Baathists tended to lose hope that the Baath Party could regain power and shifted primarily to the nationalist goals of driving out the occupiers and establishing a government that was the product of Iraqi self-determination rather than a puppet of the invaders. Nationalist insurgents targeted mainly coalition forces or non-Iraqi contractors.

Some former Baathists, however, joined one of several Islamic resistance movements. The nationalist and Islamic Sunni resistance groups both opposed the Shia political religious parties, SCIRI and Dawa, for collaborating with the occupation forces, but also for other reasons. The nationalist insurgents viewed SCIRI and Dawa as representatives of Iran's interests, which they believed included destroying Iraq as a unified nation, while the Sunni Islamist insurgents opposed the Shia parties because they viewed them as traitors to Islam (Hashim 2007: 7).

Some of the nationalist resistance groups included religious themes in their titles, such as the expression "Islamic," despite their mainly secular orientation.

The Islamic Front of Iraqi Resistance (Cordesman 2007: 5) claimed to avoid targeting Iraqi government or military personnel. Other nationalist-oriented resistance groups were the General Command of the Armed Forces, Resistance and Liberation in Iraq (thought to include former members of the Special Republican Guard), the Al 'Awdah ("the Return"), and the Iraqi Resistance and Liberation Command (Hashim 2006: 170–171).

Sunni Islamic Insurgents. Some Sunni Arabs were associated with the Iraqi branch of the Muslim Brotherhood, which aimed at creating an Iraq free from non-Islamic influences, called for the Iraqi people to adopt the authentic form of Islam that they believed existed early in Islam's history, and favored Iraq's becoming an Islamic republic. In addition to the indigenous Salafi Sunni insurgents, hundreds of foreign Islamic volunteers crossed into Iraq from Saudi Arabia and elsewhere. Many of the Saudi fighters had been schooled in the Wahhabi version of Islam, whose founder, Muhammad al Wahhab (1703–1791), held "that no doctrine or practice originating after the end of the third Islamic century would be acceptable" (Joffé 2006: 455). Despite the influx of foreign volunteers, 90 percent to 95 percent of Al-Qaeda in Mesopotamia's membership was estimated to be Iraqis (Cordesman 2007: 3).

Whereas nationalist insurgents tended to attack occupation forces by means of roadside bombs, ambushes, snipers, mortars, and rocket-propelled grenades, Islamic fighters were more prone to engaging in suicide bombings ("martyrdom missions") than other fighters. Jordanian Abu Musab al-Zarqawi's AQM was accused of brutal acts of violence, including bombing attacks that killed many civilians, and gruesome executions. In particular, Zarqawi was suspected to have been behind the highly organized February 22, 2006, bombing and destruction of the Shia's sacred golden-domed al-Askari mosque in Samarra, which ignited Shia reprisal killings and increased the intensity of sectarian conflict (Woodward 2008: 35). Some believed that Zarqawi targeted Shia civilians and mosques in an attempt to provoke a civil war between Sunni and Shia Iraqis, anticipating that this would somehow force the United States to abandon Iraq. Others rejected this idea, believing instead that sectarian conflict would in fact provide an excuse for the occupation to continue until some level of stability acceptable to the US administration was achieved.

Many nationalist and some Islamic insurgents condemned the bombings of civilians and the brutal beheadings of captured hostages as immoral and counterproductive. Even Al Qaeda leaders outside of Iraq criticized some of these actions. In July 2005 Ayman al-Zawahiri, considered the second-ranking leader of Al Qaeda after Osama bin Laden, sent a letter to AQM leader Zarqawi, warning against such extreme actions as mass bombings targeting Shia civilians that provoked opposition from the majority of Muslims (Hashim 2007: 4). (The letter also contained Al Qaeda goals: First, force the United States out of Iraq; second, create an Islamic government in Iraq; third, spread jihad to nearby countries, including Israel; and, finally, establish the caliphate or unified worldwide political-religious authority for all Muslims.) Despite earlier criticisms of Zarqawi's methods, bin Laden and Zawahiri made audio recordings praising him as a martyr after he was killed by a US air strike on June 7, 2006.

Another resistance group was the Islamic Resistance Movement–1920 Revolution Brigades, named after the 1920 uprising against British occupation. This confederation of more than a dozen groups, reportedly organized and led by former Iraqi military officers, aimed to create a nationalist government based on Islam. It targeted US and pro-US Iraqi forces and their employees, claiming to carry out 5,000 attacks in 2006 (Cordesman 2007: 5). Yon (2008: 123, 135) reports that members of the 1920 Revolution Brigade developed a hatred for Al Qaeda's brutality and eventually joined US forces in fighting Al Qaeda forces in Baqubah.

Militias

Following the invasion, Shia men joined militias, often under the authority of one of the four main Shia political-religious organizations: SCIRI, Dawa, the Mahdi Army, or Islamic Fadhila. Moqtada's Mahdi Army drew much of its support from poor young Iraqis and accused SCIRI and Dawa of being too closely tied to Iran. In March 2004, after Moqtada's preaching was interpreted as calling for violent resistance to the occupation, the CPA ordered Moqtada's newspaper shut down and one of his assistants arrested in connection with the April 10, 2003, murder of Sayyid Abd Majid al-Khoei, a member of a prominent Shia family who had reportedly been working with the US CIA to establish a relationship between coalition authorities and religious leaders in Najaf (Allawi 2006: 91–93, 271–273). Fighting temporarily broke out between the Mahdi Army and US forces. Moqtada repeatedly demanded an end to the occupation but tended to avoid renewed conflict with the overwhelmingly more powerful US forces. He called on Shia, Sunnis, and Christians to unite against the occupation, and for a timetable for the withdrawal of US forces (Burns 2007; Wong 2007c). Members of the Mahdi Army, however, were suspected in the August 2007 assassinations of the ISCI (SCIRI) governors of the southern Iraqi provinces of Qadisiya and Muthanna (Farrell 2007; Oppel and al-Saiedi 2007).

The United States was able to hire tens of thousands of Arab tribesmen, many of whom had previously fought against the occupation, in what was called the Awakening movement, to combat Al Qaeda. (The Awakening movement groups that include many former Baathists are often known as "the Sons of Iraq" [Galbraith 2008: 120].) West (2008: 365) notes that the formation of the Awakening militias originated in western Iraq in Anbar province when Sunni Arab tribesmen turned against Al Qaeda and sought the help of US marines. This shift in tribal orientation, West explains, was facilitated because the marines had a policy of deploying the same units to the same locations over a long period of time, leading to the development of acquaintanceships between marine battalion commanders and some local leaders. This provided channels of communication used to develop an alliance with the marines once tribal leaders were ready to turn against Al Qaeda. Local people provided valuable information on AQM and its supporters.

The success of the Awakening in Anbar led General David Petraeus, commander of all US forces in Iraq, in 2007 to authorize army battalion commanders across the country, including in Baghdad, to also recruit and pay Iraqis to guard neighborhoods and otherwise assist in combating Al Qaeda. In 2008 the Awakening groups had some 90,000 members nationally, about 80 percent of whom were Sunnis. The Awakening movement, Moqtada al-Sadr's August 2007 cease-fire order for his Mahdi Army, the 2007 surge in US troop strength, and advanced US counterinsurgency technology were considered responsible for the dramatic decline in both military and civilian deaths after July 2007. Woodward (2008: 380) also claims that starting around May 2006, US intelligence agencies and military personnel conducted secret operations to identify and kill central figures in Al Qaeda groups, other Sunni insurgent organizations, and rebellious Shia militias. Eliminating these individuals was thought to deprive their groups of essential leadership and skills, as well as weakening the morale of surviving resistance fighters.

Summary and Analysis

Sunni Arabs were overwhelmingly opposed to the invasion and feared persecution by the postinvasion Shia-dominated government. Most Shia Arabs supported the overthrow of the Baathist regime but were otherwise divided. The Shia SCIRI and Dawa were favorable toward Iran, while the Sadrists were more nationalistic. In addition, other Shia were secularly oriented and many had been Baath Party members.

The decision to postpone elections and impose a long-term occupation raised doubts about whether the intention of the occupying forces was to liberate Iraq or replace an authoritarian nationalist government with a puppet regime. Most Sunni Arabs boycotted the January 2005 election for a national assembly to write a new constitution. A Shia alliance won the majority of votes and played a major role in shaping the constitution, which extolled democracy at the same time that it declared that Islam would be a major source for laws. While the new political system guaranteed women a large minority of seats in parliament, secularly oriented women were pressured to adopt the Islamic style of dress and began to fear violence from strangers for violating Islamic tradition. A major concern was to enact a national law to ensure that oil revenue was distributed fairly to all Iraqis and provide a legal framework for increased foreign investment. The oil law was potentially crucial in determining whether Iraq would remain a unified nation.

The central Iraqi provinces, which were disproportionately Sunni Arab, experienced the highest levels of insurgent activity and sectarian violence, while Basra was characterized by conflict among Shia militias. Among the many insurgent networks, the two major types were nationalist and Islamic. Mass bombings by AQM damaged the insurgency by provoking sectarian conflict and motivating major Sunni tribes to drop out of the insurgency and, through the Awakening movement, work with occupation forces in fighting Islamic extremists. The Awakening groups, Moqtada al-Sadr's long-term truce, the 2007 US troop surge, and advanced counterinsurgency technology combined to reduce insurgent attacks, US casualties, and sectarian violence after the summer of 2007.

The Kurdish region experienced far less violence and significantly more economic development than the rest of Iraq. The KRG ran the autonomous area as almost an independent nation with its own flag and armed forces, formulating its own oil law, and negotiating its own contracts with international oil companies. Many Kurds favored secession but for pragmatic reasons agreed to maintain a federal relationship with Baghdad.

Social surveys of the Iraqi people revealed that discontent with the occupation was extremely high among Sunni Arabs and seemed to increase among Shia Arabs over time. But Sunni Arabs expressed more support for violent resistance and had much lower confidence in the Shia-dominated central government, military, and police. Shia and Sunni Arab opposition to sectarian strife, violence against civilians, and the occupation suggested a future basis for renewed trust and cooperation between these groups.

The Iraq–US Status of Forces Agreement, which was approved by branches of the Iraqi government in November and December 2008 and will be discussed in more detail in chapter 9, was viewed by some as finally setting a deadline for the withdrawal of US forces from Iraq. But others, both in Iraq and the United States, feared that it was mainly a ploy intended to maintain US military occupation of Iraq not only until the agreement's December 31, 2011, deadline for US withdrawal but far beyond.

References and Further Readings

Ahmed, Huda. 2006. "Women in the Shadows of Democracy." *Middle East Report* 239 (Summer). www.merip.org/mer/mer239/mer239.html.

Allawi, Ali A. 2007. *The Occupation of Iraq: Winning the War, Losing the Peace.* New Haven, CT: Yale University Press.

Al-Marashi, Ibrahim. 2005. "Boycotts, Coalitions and the Threat of Violence: The Run-Up to the January 2005 Iraqi Elections." *Middle East Review of International Affairs,* January. http://meria.idc.ac.il/news/2005/05news1.html.

Anderson, Liam, and Gareth Stansfield. 2004. *The Future of Iraq: Dictatorship, Democracy, or Division?* New York: Palgrave MacMillan.

Angus-Reid Global Monitor: Polls & Research. 2007. "Iraqis Call for State-Owned Oil Company." www.angus-reid.com/polls/view/iraqis_call_for_state_owned_oil_company/; www.angus-reid.com/uppdf/Iraq_oil.pdf.

Asser, Martin. 2005. "Profile: Ibrahim Jaafari." BBC. http://newsvote.bbc.co.uk.

Associated Press. 2005. "Full Text of Iraqi Constitution, Draft Document, to Be Presented to Voters Saturday." October 12. www.washingtonpost.com.

Baker, James A., and Lee H. Hamilton. 2006. *The Iraq Study Group Report.* New York: Vintage Books.

BBC. 2006a. "Guide to Iraqi Political Parties." http://newsvote.bbc.co.uk.

———. 2006b. "Profile: Nouri Maliki." May 20. http://newsvote.bbc.co.uk.

———. 2008. "Turkish Troops Enter North Iraq." February 22. http://newsvote.bbc.co.uk.

Boston.com. 2009. "Iraqi Provincial Election Results." February 19. www.boston.com/news/world/middleeast/articles/2009/02/19/iraqi_provincial_election_results.

Bureau of Near Eastern Affairs, US Department of State. 2008. *Iraq Weekly Status Report.* August 27. www.state.gov/documents/organization/109093.pdf.

Burns, John F. 2005. "Ambush of Defense Lawyers in Hussein Trial Kills One." *New York Times,* November 9. www.nytimes.com.

———.2007. "Shiite Cleric Ends Absence From Iraq with Fiery Speech." *New York Times,* May 26. www.nytimes.com.

Burns, John F., and Kirk Semple. 2006. "US Finds Insurgency Has Funds to Sustain Itself." *New York Times,* November 26. www.nytimes.com.

Cave, Damien. 2007. "Militant Group Is Out of Baghdad, US Says." *New York Times,* November 8. www.nytimes.com.

Chalabi, Munir. 2008. "The Internal Struggle for the Iraqi Oil Law Continues." *Z Magazine,* January 1. www.zmag.org/znet/viewArticle/16075.

Cole, Juan. 2005. "Juan Cole on Ibrahim al-Jaafari, the Iraqi Elections and the Future of Islamic Law in Iraq." *Democracy Now!* www.democracynow.org/2005/2/23/juan_cole_on_ibrahim_al_jaafari.

Cooper, Helene. 2007. "Saudis' Role in Iraq Frustrates US Officials." *New York Times,* July 27. www.nytimes.com/2007/07/27/world/middleeast/27saudi.html.

Cordesman, Anthony H. 2007. "Iraq's Sunni Insurgents: Looking Beyond Al Qa'ida." Washington, DC: *Center for Strategic and International Studies.*

Daniel, Trenton. 2009. "Iraq's Final Election Results Secure Victory for Maliki." www.mcclatchydc.com/251/story/62512.html.

Fallows, James. 2008. *Blind into Baghdad.* New York: Vintage Books.

Farrell, Stephen. 2007. "Governor of Iraqi Province Assassinated." *New York Times,* August 21. www.nytimes.com.

Farrell, Stephen, and Mudhafer Al-Husaini. 2008. "Two Bombings Wreak Carnage in Iraqi Capital." *New York Times,* February 2. www.nytimes.com.

Fattah, Hassan M. 2007. "Images of Hanging Make Hussein into a Martyr to Many." *New York Times,* January 6. www.nytimes.com.

Finer, Jonathan. 2006. "Iraq's Insurgents: Who's Who." Washington Post Foreign Service, March 19. www.washingtonpost.com.

Galbraith, Peter W. 2008. *Unintended Consequences: How the War in Iraq Strengthened America's Enemies.* New York: Simon & Schuster.

Gallu, Joshua. 2006. "The Race for Iraq's Resources: Will Iraq's Oil Blessing Become a Curse?" *Spiegel Online,* December 22. www.spiegel.de/international/0,1518,druck-456212,00.html.

Galula, David. 2006 (1964). *Counterinsurgency Warfare: Theory and Practice.* Westport, CT: Praeger Security International.

Gamel, Kim. 2008. "Iraq: Muqtada Al-Sadr Extends Cease-Fire." Associated Press, February 22. http://abcnews.go.com/print?id=4328471.

GAO. 2007. *Securing, Stabilizing, and Rebuilding Iraq: Iraqi Government Has Not Met Most Legislative, Security, and Economic Benchmarks.* GAO report to congressional committees. www.GAO.gov/new.items/d071195.pdf (accessed February 20, 2008).

Garner, Jay. 2004. "General Jay Garner." BBC, March 22. http://newsvote.bbc.co.uk.

Glanz, James. 2006. "Iraq Is Failing to Spend Billions in Oil Revenues." *New York Times,* December 11. www.nytimes.com.

———. 2007a. "Draft Law Keeps Central Control Over Oil in Iraq." *New York Times*, January 20. www.nytimes.com.

———. 2007b. "Rebuilt Iraq Projects Found Crumbling." *New York Times*, April 29. www.nytimes.com.

———. 2007c. "Billions in Oil Missing in Iraq, US Study Says." *New York Times*, May 12. www.nytimes.com/2007/05/12/world/middleeast/12oil.html.

———. 2008. "Iraqi Spending to Rebuild Has Slowed, Report Says." *New York Times*, January 16. www.nytimes.com.

Global Policy Forum. 2007. "Iraq Poll September 2007." www.globalpolicy.org/security/issues/iraq/resist/2007/09bbciraqipoll.pdf.

Global Security.org. 2007. "U.S. Ground Forces End Strength." www.globalsecurity.org/military/ops/iraq_orbat_es.htm.

———. 2008. "Iraqi Governing Council." www.globalsecurity.org/military/world/iraq/igc.htm.

Goode, Erica. 2008. "Iraq Passes Election Law, Setting Aside Kirkuk Status." *New York Times*, September 25. www.nytimes.com.

Gordon, Michael R. 2007. "US Says Iran-Supplied Bomb Kills More Troops." *New York Times*, August 8.

Greenwell, Megan, and Jon Cohen. 2007. "Poll Highlights Disconnect Between US Commanders, Iraqis." *Washington Post*, September 10. www.washingtonpost.com.

Guidère, Mathieu, and Peter Harling. 2006. "'Withdraw, Move On, Rampage:' Iraq's Resistance Evolves." *Le Monde Diplomatique*, May. http://mondediplo.com/2006/05/02irak.

Hamdani, Ali, and James Hider. "Basra's Murderous Militias Tell Christian Women to Cover Up or Face Death." Timesonline, December 8. www.timesonline.co.uk/tol/news/world/iraq/article3018766.ece.

Hashim, Ahmed S. 2006. *Insurgency and Counter-Insurgency in Iraq*. Ithaca, NY: Cornell University Press.

———. 2007. "Iraq's Civil War." *Current History* 106 (January): 3–10.

Hiro, Dilip. 2007. *Blood of the Earth: The Battle for the World's Vanishing Oil Resources*. New York: Nation Books.

Ibrahim, Waleed. 2008. "Kuwait to Discuss War Payment in Historic Iraq Visit." *International Herald Tribune*, September 7. www.iht.com.

IFES (International Foundation for Election Systems). 2005. "Election Guide." www.electionguide.org/voter-turnout.php?search_year=2005.

Iraqi Constitution. 2005. www.uniraq.org/documents/iraqi_constitution.pdf.

Joffé, E. G. H. 2006. "Islamic Fundamentalist Revolutionary Movement." In James DeFronzo, ed., *Revolutionary Movements in World History: From 1750 to the Present*, 452–464. Santa Barbara, CA: ABC-CLIO.

Kinsella, David. 2007. *Regime Change: Origins, Execution and Aftermath of the Iraq War*. Belmont, CA: Thomson Wadsworth.

Kipp, Jacob, Lester Grau, Karl Prinslow, and Captain Don Smith. 2006. "The Human Terrain System: A CORDS for the 21st Century." *Military Review* (September–October): 8–15. www.army.mil/professionalwriting/volumes/volume4/december_2006/12_06_2.html.

KRG (Kurdish Regional Government). 2006. "Structure of the KRG." www.krg
.org/articles/print.asp?anr=48&lngnr=12&rnr=93.

————. 2008. "Speech by KRG Prime Minister Nechirvan Barzani: We Call for International Recognition of Anfal Genocide." January 28. www.krg.org/articles/print.asp?anr=22516&lngnr=12&rnr=268.

Lando, Ben. 2008. "Top Iraqi in US: Oil Law Progress a Must." United Press International, February 5. www.upi.com/international.

MacFarquhar, Neil, and Richard A. Oppel Jr. 2003. "After the War: Attack at Shrine; Car Bomb in Iraq Kills 95 at Shiite Mosque." *New York Times*, August 30. http://query.nytimes.com.

Mahmoud, Mona, Maggie O'Kane, and Ian Black. 2007. "UK Has Left Behind Murder and Chaos, Says Basra Police Chief." *Guardian*, December 17. www.guardian.co.uk/Iraq/Story/0,,2228690,00.html.

Menendez, James. 2005. "Seeking Justice in Dujail." BBC News, November 25. http://newsvote.bbc.co.uk.

Mufson, Steven, and Robin Wright. 2007. "In a Major Step, Saudi Arabia Agrees to Write Off 80 Percent of Iraqi Debt." *Washington Post*, April 18, p. A18. www.washingtonpost.com.

New York Times. 2007. "The Problem Isn't Mr. Maliki." *New York Times*, August 24. www.nytimes.com/2007/08/24/opinion/24fri1.html.

Oppel, Richard A. Jr. 2007a. "In Iraq, Conflict Simmers on a 2nd Kurdish Front." *New York Times*, October 23. www.nytimes.com.

————. 2007b. "Foreign Fighters in Iraq Are Tied to Allies of U.S." *New York Times*, November 22.

Oppel, Richard A. Jr., and Mudhafer Al-Husaini. 2008. "Suicide Bomber Kills Key Sunni Leader." *New York Times*, January 8. www.nytimes.com.

Oppel, Richard A. Jr., and Abdul Razzaq al-Saiedi. 2007. "Road Bomb in Iraq Kills 5, Including a Governor." *New York Times*, August 12. www.nytimes.com.

Oppel, Richard A. Jr., and Steven Lee Myers. 2008. "Iraq Eases Curb for Former Officials of Hussein's Party." *New York Times*, January 13. www.nytimes.com.

Parline. 2008. "Iraq." www.ipu.org/parline-e/reports/2151.htm.

PBS. 2006a. "The Lost Year in Iraq: Interviews: L. Paul Bremer." *Frontline*. www.pbs.org/wgbh/pages/frontline/yeariniraq/interviews/bremer.html (accessed November 16, 2007).

————. 2006b. "The Insurgency." *Frontline*. www.pbs.org/wgbh/pages/frontline/insurgency.

Petraeus, David H., and James F. Amos. 2006. *Counterinsurgency.* Army Field Manual No. 3–24; Marine Corps Warfighting Publication No. 3–33.5, December. Washington, DC: Department of the Army.

Polk, William R. 2005. *Understanding Iraq.* New York: Harper Perennial.

Ricks, Thomas E. 2006. *Fiasco: The American Military Adventure in Iraq.* New York: Penguin Press.

Risen, James. 2006. *State of War: the Secret History of the CIA and the Bush Administration.* New York: Free Press.

Rubin, Alissa J. 2008a. "Kurds' Power Wanes as Arab Anger Rises." *New York Times*, February 1. www.nytimes.com.

————. 2008b. "Sunnis Say Law Opening Jobs to Ex-Baathists Would Do More Harm than Good." *New York Times*, February 3. www.nytimes.com.

Rubin, Alissa J., and Damien Cave. 2007. "In a Force for Iraqi Calm, Seeds of Conflict." *New York Times*, December 23. www.nytimes.com.

Santora, Marc. 2006. "On the Gallows, Curses for U.S. and 'Traitors.'" *New York Times*, December 31. www.nytimes.com.

Santora, Marc, James Glanz, and Sabrina Tavernise. 2006. "Dictator Who Ruled Iraq with Violence Is Hanged for Crimes Against Humanity." *New York Times*, December 30. www.nytimes.com/2006/12/30/world/middleeast/30hussein.html.

Semple, Kirk. 2007. "Pointing to Stability, Kurds in Iraq Lure Investors." *New York Times*, June 27. www.nytimes.com.

Smith, Craig S. 2004. "Major Creditors in Accord to Waive 80% of Iraq Debt." *New York Times*, November 22.

Susman, Tina. 2007. "Iraqi Policewomen Are Told to Surrender Their Weapons." *Los Angeles Times*, December 11. www.latimes.com.

————. 2009. "Maliki's Bloc Prevails in Iraqi Elections." *Los Angeles Times*, February 6. www.latimes.com/news/nationworld/world/la-fg-iraq-elections 6-2009feb06,0,2550359.story.

United Nations. 2004. Security Council Resolution 1546. June 8. www.un.org/Docs/sc/unsc_resolutions04.html.

USIP (United States Institute of Peace). 2004. "United Nations Security Council Resolution 1546 (2004)." www.usip.org/library/pa/iraq/adddoc/iraq_unsc 1546.html.

Weiss, Martin A. 2004. "Iraq: Paris Club Debt Relief." *Congressional Research Service—The Library of Congress*. www.fpc.state.gov/documents/organization/44019.pdf.

West, Bing. 2008. *The Strongest Tribe*. New York: Random House.

White House. 2005. "Iraqi Women Prepare for Democratic Election." January 13. http://georgewbush-whitehouse.archives.gov/news/releases/2005/01/20050113 -1.html.

White House. 2008. "Agreement Between the United States of America and the Republic of Iraq on the Withdrawal of United States Forces from Iraq and the Organization of Their Activities During Their Temporary Presence in Iraq." November 17. www.mnf-iraq.com/images/CGs_Messages/security_agreement.pdf.

Wong, Edward. 2007a. "Iraqis Reach Accord on Oil Revenues." *New York Times*, February 27. www.nytimes.com.

————. 2007b. "Iran Is Playing a Growing Role in Iraq Economy." *New York Times*, March 17. www.nytimes.com.

————. 2007c. "Radical Shiite Cleric Calls on Iraqi Forces to Unite Against the U.S. Military." *New York Times*, April 9. www.nytimes.com.

Woodward, Bob. 2008. *The War Within: A Secret White House History, 2006–2008*. New York: Simon & Schuster.

Yaphe, Judith S. 2008. "Iraq: Are We There Yet?" *Current History* 107 (713): 403–409.

Yon, Michael. 2008. *Moment of Truth in Iraq*. Minneapolis, MN: Richard Vigilante Books.

9

Counterinsurgency and US Corporate Presence

US forces invaded Iraq, seizing or destroying important political and military targets on the assumption that once these were removed, the overwhelming majority of Iraqis would welcome them as liberators. Instead a multifaceted antioccupation resistance emerged, requiring more US troops. US National Guard units were activated, tours of duty were extended, financial incentives for enlistment were increased, and private contractors were hired to perform tasks previously carried out by military personnel.

The antioccupation resistance also resulted in a shift toward greater reliance on counterinsurgency methods, the January 2007 appointment of General David Petraeus as commander of US forces in Iraq, the surge in the number of US troops in early 2007, and the funding of Sunni Arab militias to combat Al Qaeda. Although 2007 was the deadliest year of the Iraq War for US forces, losses peaked in May and then tended to decline. Observers cited this trend as evidence that the innovations were at least partially successful.

US corporations benefited from reconstruction, supply, and service contracts in Iraq. Support for the war appeared to decline within the US military, as it did among the general public. Despite the lower level of approval of the war, Iraq and the United States agreed to the so-called Status of Forces Agreement in late 2008 that permitted the US military to remain in Iraq until December 31, 2011.

Antioccupation Resistance

The antioccupation resistance, as noted in chapter 8, was composed of dozens of groups varying in size, motives, ideology, and tactics. It was spurred not only by the invasion, but also by the Coalition Provisional Authority's decisions to remove thousands of Baath Party members from their jobs and disband the Iraqi armed forces, throwing hundreds of thousands out of work, and further by US abuse of Iraqi prisoners at Abu Ghraib prison. The insurgents were estimated to be about 90 percent Sunni Arab and at least 90 percent Iraqis. Motivations for resistance were mainly patriotism or Islamic fundamentalist fervor

(Guidière and Harling 2006). Many nationalist resistance fighters were former officers and soldiers in the preinvasion armed forces and fought to drive foreign forces out and structure conditions for a government that was the product of Iraqi self-determination rather than the creation of the occupying forces.

Modern Principles
of Counterinsurgency

Galula's Counterinsurgency Classic

French Colonel David Galula wrote his widely regarded classic, originally published in 1964, *Counterinsurgency Warfare: Theory and Practice* (2006), while at Harvard University's Center for International Affairs. Galula fought during World War II and later served in China and as a UN observer in Greece. Much of his thinking about counterinsurgency was derived from the Chinese Communist Revolution, the Greek civil war, the Malayan insurgency, the Vietnamese Revolution, and the French effort to defeat the Algerian Revolution. Though Galula provides unique analyses, he at times makes statements that seem contradictory or overly generalized, such as stating (2006: 9) that the insurgent is "free to use every trick . . . lie, cheat . . . he is judged by what he promises, not by what he does." This assertion appears inconsistent with what Galula emphasizes as the insurgent's, as well as the counterinsurgent's, goal of winning and maintaining popular support. Mao Zedong, recognized by Galula as a major authority on revolutionary warfare, emphasized the importance of the insurgent's winning popular support precisely by what he does, not just says, by acting respectfully and kindly toward the majority of the people as essential to expanding and holding popular support. Lieutenant Colonel John Nagl (2002: 22) points this out in his description of Mao's Three Rules and Eight Remarks to the Chinese Communist Eighth Route Army.

Another indication of Galula's fallibility was his underestimation in the early 1960s of the favorable conditions for the Viet Cong in South Vietnam (2006: 71). Nonetheless, Galula is credited with significant contributions on counterinsurgency, and his concepts are reflected in the US Army and Marine Corps 2006 Counterinsurgency Field Manual, authored by Generals David H. Petraeus and James F. Amos.

Galula (2006: 3–4) observes that insurgents and counterinsurgents compete for the population's allegiance in *asymmetrical warfare*. The insurgent force is at first weak and must use only methods appropriate to its limited capabilities. The counterinsurgents must not attempt to copy insurgent methods, but use tactics that take full advantage of counterinsurgent strength. For example, although the insurgent force can be highly mobile and choose when and where to strike, the population on which the insurgents depend for support is generally not mobile and therefore much more vulnerable. Galula asserts that it is typically more effective for the counterinsurgent force to target the population on which the insurgents rely, rather than focus mainly on physically destroying the insurgents. He argues that putting pressure on the population is a major way the counterinsurgent force could use its strength advantage to seize the initiative.

Galula (2006: 43–47) first discusses dealing with a "cold revolutionary war . . . when the insurgent's activity remains on the whole legal and non-violent." In this context he describes "direct action against the insurgent" as potentially including arrests or banning organizations or publications, and indirect action such as solving the issue the insurgent champions, or, if this threatens the counterinsurgent's interests, "alleviating weaknesses in the counterinsurgent's rule" that provide opportunities for the insurgent. He also suggests methods such as infiltrating and subverting the insurgent movement from within. One or more of these approaches might also be used in "hot revolutionary war" when the "insurgent's activity becomes openly illegal and violent" (2006: 43).

Further, Galula (2006: 49–60) defines victory for the counterinsurgent in "hot revolutionary war" as not only the destruction of insurgent armed forces and/or their political organizational infrastructure, but also "the permanent isolation of insurgent from the population, isolation not enforced upon the population but maintained by and with the population." His four laws of counterinsurgency warfare are (1) the counterinsurgent needs the support of the population; (2) support is gained through an "active minority" (most of the population is "neutral" with activist minorities of insurgent and counterinsurgent supporters trying to win over the majority to their side); (3) gaining support from the population within a given area is contingent on successful military actions against the insurgent force and its political organization in that area because, in Galula's view, people would otherwise be afraid to cooperate with the counterinsurgent for fear of insurgent reprisals; and (4) counterinsurgency operations must be intensive, involve large numbers of personnel and resources, and be of long duration.

In addition, Galula (2006: 71–72) argues that counterinsurgent efforts must be carried out under one commander with total control, must continually adapt to changes in circumstances, and must show the insurgent has no valid cause, or adopt the insurgent's cause, negating the reason for the insurgency, or use coercive methods such as withholding jobs, food, or other resources until the population in a targeted area cooperates. He also asserts that the insurgent must be denied "safe havens" and that counterinsurgent troops should live among the population and protect it until the population is able to protect itself.

Galula (2006: 70) emphasizes the importance of adjusting to objective and subjective characteristics of the indigenous population. Objective characteristics include its size and distribution (spatially concentrated or dispersed widely over the territory), and whether it is economically self-sufficient or dependent on trade that can be interrupted by the counterinsurgent. Galula viewed subjective characteristics as even more important. These include how people view the opposing forces, what proportions are friendly to the insurgents, friendly to the counterinsurgents, or are neutral, and what economic or social characteristics can be used to identify these tendencies. The counterinsurgent is also interested in divisive factors within the population, such as those of an economic or ethnic or religious nature, that can be used to the advantage of either the insurgent or the counterinsurgent. Galula (2006: 70) explains, "This sort of political analysis is as important in counterinsurgency warfare as map study is in conventional warfare, for it will determine, however roughly, whether the area considered will be easy or difficult to work on."

The "strategy of the counterinsurgency," according to Galula (2006: 55–56, 75–94), involves carrying out eight steps in successive selected areas with specific types of "propaganda" directed at counterinsurgent forces, the population, and the insurgents at each stage. First, in a selected area, use sufficient armed forces to expel or destroy the insurgent combatants. Second, once the area has been cleared, station enough troops there to protect counterinsurgent supporters and prevent insurgents from returning in significant strength. Galula recommends putting the counterinsurgent troops in direct contact with the people by placing them in villages and towns rather than in detached bases. He states that step three is the most critical. In this phase, the counterinsurgent tries to establish control over the population, separate it from the insurgents by physical means, limit people's movements so they cannot assist the insurgents, and obtain information to exterminate insurgent political cells. Galula asserts that achieving control should begin with a census of the territory's population and issuing "foolproof" identity cards to its inhabitants (2006: 82). He also recommends arresting a large number of "minor suspects" (2006: 88) to obtain useful information. Fourth, demolish local insurgent political organizations. Fifth, select new provisional authorities through elections. Galula believes the counterinsurgent would not have to worry about election results because people in the cleansed area would be unlikely to elect people they perceived to be disapproved by counterinsurgent authorities. Sixth, Galula says, the counterinsurgents should "test" the new leaders in the controlled areas by giving them tasks to carry out and then remove "the softs and incompetents" (2006: 56). The counterinsurgent should organize "self-defense units" among the area's population to help fight the insurgency. Seventh, "educate" and organize the new local leaders into a national counterinsurgency political movement. And eighth, suppress or convert the remaining insurgents.

Counterinsurgency (Army Field Manual No. 3–24; Marine Corps Warfighting Publication No. 3–33.5, 2006)

Many of Galula's ideas are reflected in Petraeus and Amos's (2006) Counterinsurgency Field Manual for the US Army and Marines. These include viewing the indigenous population as composed of a "neutral or passive majority" and two "active minorities," one insurgent and the other counterinsurgent, competing to win over the majority (2006: 1-20). The manual stresses the need for intelligence (2006: 1-23) and for isolating insurgents from their supporters and resources and/or from their cause by effectively dealing with their economic, political, or social issues. Petraeus and Amos state that protecting the civilian population is the central element of counterinsurgency because this is a prerequisite for implementing lasting reforms. Similar to Galula, they state that counterinsurgent forces should maintain close contact with the population because without it they risk putting their local allies in danger of insurgent retaliation, losing important sources of information, and losing the initiative.

Petraeus and Amos also emphasize the importance of unity of command (2006: 2-2) and of neutralizing the insurgent political infrastructure (2006: 5-5). Their "clear-hold-build" approach (2006: 5-18–23) expands on Galula's (2006: 55–56, 75–94) eight steps for successively clearing and taking control of selected areas. Like Galula, Petraeus and Amos (2006: 5-20) describe messages (Galula's "propaganda") to be directed in clear-hold-build operations toward the population, the insurgents, and the counterinsurgent forces, but add a fourth message target, the "regional and international audiences."

Petraeus and Amos stress sociological issues such as understanding local cultures and social networks to facilitate productive interaction with the population and obtaining information. They also emphasize social psychological factors such as fostering a "realistic set of expectations" among the indigenous population, the allied forces, and international audiences (2006: 1-24–25, 5-9) to avoid creating discontent. They (2006: 1-29) describe successful counterinsurgency practices, including intelligence gathering, providing the population with security and other benefits, creating and expanding secure areas, and denying the insurgent any sanctuaries. They also describe the importance of learning the insurgents' narratives and messages to develop effective counternarratives and messages (2006: 5-9–10).

Petraeus and Amos advocate "population control measures," such as administering a census (2006: 5-21), requiring people to carry pass cards, and limiting their movement. They also emphasize limits on interrogation and state that no one "under the physical control of the United States Government" should be "subject to cruel, inhuman, or degrading treatment or punishment." They assert that to "lose moral legitimacy" is to "lose the war," and cite the French decision to permit torture against Algerian rebels as an example of defeat through loss of moral legitimacy. Commenting on the Petraeus and Amos manual, Williams (2007) raises the question of whether its emphasis on moral legitimacy implies the ultimate failure of the US intervention in Iraq.

Counterinsurgency in Iraq

Denial of Sanctuary

US forces attacked cities and other locations thought to be insurgent sanctuaries to deprive them of secure areas where they could recruit, organize, train, manufacture IEDs or car bombs, and plan attacks. A major assault occurred after the March 31, 2004, killings of four Blackwater private security contractors in the largely Sunni Arab city of Fallujah (Scahill 2007: 101–104). On April 5 about 2,500 US Marines supported by tanks, Cobra attack helicopters, and AC-130 gunships began an offensive into the city (Ricks 2006: 333–334).

After several weeks of fierce fighting, US authorities stopped the assault, apparently fearing a large number of civilian casualties would cause some countries to desert the coalition. The insurgents viewed the First Battle of Fallujah as a victory and seemed to gain strength. With the first postwar Iraqi elections scheduled for January 2005, US authorities decided on a much larger assault (Allawi 2006: 338–339). The city's 250,000 civilians were told to leave and US authorities estimated that only about 400 noninsurgents remained. Approximately 6,500 marines, 1,500 army soldiers, and 2,000 members of the new Iraqi army attacked Fallujah on November 8, 2004 (Ricks 2006: 399), with the Iraqi interim government endorsing the offensive. The battle, involving air and artillery strikes and ground assaults, lasted about ten days. Though it was estimated that at least one thousand resistance fighters were killed, compared with fifty-four US soldiers and eight Iraqi soldiers, most insurgents apparently escaped the city. Other cities considered havens for insurgents became targets of similar operations. In 2007, the surge in American troop strength allowed for the deployment of many US soldiers to locations in the "belts" around Baghdad to eliminate Al Qaeda staging areas and reduce suicide bombing attacks in the capital (West 2008: 250, 365).

Surge-Clear-Hold-Build

Since American officials initially tended to underestimate the size and likely duration of the insurgency, US forces were slow to adopt counterinsurgency methods until the summer of 2006, when they attempted to implement the clear-hold-build approach. But a crucial fault in this operation was that the hold-and-protect function was quickly turned over to US-trained Iraqi forces who often failed. The Democratic victory in the 2006 congressional election, coupled with the ongoing war, the flaws of the clear-hold-build strategy, the troublesome findings of the Iraq Study Group Report (Baker and Hamilton 2006), and the shift in public opinion against the war, led to the resignation in early November 2006 of Secretary of Defense Donald Rumsfeld, whom many blamed for helping to bring about the war and for misunderstanding the difficulties it would involve. Further consequences of these developments included the installation of General David Petraeus on January 5, 2007, as commander of US forces in Iraq and implementing the so-called surge in US forces by sending in an additional 30,000 troops. This allowed the clear-hold-build strategy to be carried out more successfully in Baghdad with US forces doing both the clearing and holding, creating an opportunity for those willing to provide information. The modified effort appeared to increase the flow of intelligence, permitting a new approach against the IED threat, the form of attack that had been responsible for an estimated 60 percent of coalition combat deaths (Eisler, Morrison, and Vanden Brook 2007). Previously US forces had attempted to avoid IEDs, destroy them, or use electronic jamming equipment to prevent the detonation signals from being transmitted. But increased information from informants permitted occupation forces to go after key people in IED networks, including those providing financial support, smuggling bomb components, making the devices, placing them, or controlling the equipment for transmitting detonation signals. This appeared to be one of the reasons why deaths from IEDs declined significantly in the second half of 2007 (Vanden Brook and Morrison 2007).

Another measure employed in connection with the clear-hold-build approach was the use of biometric methods, including photographs, fingerprints, or retinal scans, to identify and keep track of thousands of Iraqis for potential use in controlling their movements or locating or investigating suspects. US troops were issued $6,500 handheld units for taking fingerprints and eye scans and inputting names and other personal data (Frank 2007; Shachtman 2007).

Death Squads

Sectarian violence in 2005 and 2006 diverted some Iraqis from resisting occupation forces, and Shia and Sunni death squads took many victims. Scahill (2007: 281–290) also notes the possibility that a death squad counterinsurgency strategy had been considered or even employed in Iraq. Hirsh and Barry discuss "the Salvador Option" in a January 8, 2005, *Newsweek* article. This term referred to the killings of tens of thousands of suspected leftist rebels or their sympathizers by US-supported El Salvadoran military or allied right-wing paramilitary groups during El Salvador's 1980–1992 civil war. The Iraq plan was alleged to have involved the concept of training teams of Iraqi Kurds and Shia Arabs to eliminate Sunni Arab resistance fighters and possibly some of their supporters.

Allying Sunni Militias Against Al Qaeda

One of the major counterinsurgency innovations was the creation of the Awakening movement (Yon 2008: 85–101). The Awakening movement reportedly began in the summer of 2005 when a Sunni tribe, the Abu Mahals, allegedly involved in smuggling across the border with Syria, found itself at a disadvantage after a competing tribe gained strength through an alliance with Al Qaeda in Mesopotamia (AQM; Rubin and Cave 2007). The threat from their rivals and AQM motivated the tribe to propose an alliance with occupation forces, which US officials decided to accept. With American aid, the Abu Mahals effectively resisted their enemies. Pressure from Al Qaeda and the lure of financial incentives led other Sunni Anbar tribes to join the Awakening movement, whose members received salaries, training, and weapons from the United States. By mid-2007, the Awakening had become an important force against AQM and helped reduce insurgent attacks on US forces in Anbar province to about 10 percent of what they had been in 2006. By the end of 2007, with new Awakening groups in the Baghdad area and elsewhere, total membership was estimated at as many as 90,000 (West 2008: 365). Tribal leaders' rewards for cooperating with Americans included being allowed to recommend people to be hired as Anbar province police officers, a force that grew from about 5,200 in June 2006 to 24,000 in late 2007. Sunni tribes might also have been motivated to accept help from the Americans because of the Democratic victory in the November 2006 US congressional elections, which increased the possibility of a US withdrawal. Some sheiks might have concluded that, for the sake of survival, it was best to stop fighting the Americans and instead accept their money and weapons as a way of building strength against both the Shia-dominated government and AQM. Some observers believe that the alliance between Sunni groups formerly involved in the antioccupation insurgency and US forces against Al Qaeda was more important than the 2007 surge in US troop strength in significantly reducing Iraqi and US casualties in Iraq after mid-2007 (Galbraith 2008).

The Awakening movement included two major components: the Anbar tribally based groups and those in Baghdad province that were often former members of Saddam's security forces drawn together by their common Baathist past, relative secularism, dislike of the new Iraqi regime, and the American money and construction projects for their neighborhoods. Some observers speculated that the United States' arming and financing of Sunni Awakening groups could set the stage for a future civil war between them and government forces. Others noted a resemblance between the US Awakening movement and Britain's buying the support of tribal leaders in the 1920s. Awakening members reportedly received about $300 per month. There was concern about what would happen if the United States cut funding and the Shia-dominated government refused to hire them.

British Zone of Occupation

The British followed relatively restrictive guidelines for the use of violence in the heavily Shia region of southern Iraq they controlled, and they disapproved of the US reliance on armored patrols, which tended to alienate the population (Dagher 2007b; Gordon and Trainor 2006: 521). They preferred the counterinsurgency approach they had used in Northern Ireland, which involved lightly armed foot patrols to increase interaction with the people and encourage cooperation. Although they originally deployed about 46,000 troops to southern Iraq (Graff 2007), they reduced their contingent to 9,000 by early 2005 (DeYoung and Ricks 2007). The British concentrated on quickly training and arming some 13,000 new Iraqi soldiers (Dagher 2007b) but in the process allowed many to enlist who appeared more loyal to Shia political-religious movements than to the new central government. Weapons the British provided were often diverted to Shia militias so that, according to Basra's police chief in late 2007, they tended to be better armed than the police (Mahmoud, O'Kane, and Black 2007), many of whose members below the top leadership were themselves affiliated with or sympathetic to the militias.

Three major Shia groups contended for power in Basra. The largest in 2007, estimated at about 17,000 (Dagher 2007b), was Moqtada al-Sadr's Mahdi Army. It had significant influence in the city's police force, university, board of education, oil terminals, and port facilities. The Mahdi Army, which followed the teachings of Ayatollah Muhammad Baqir al-Sadr, the cousin of Moqtada's father, was believed responsible for most attacks on British forces and took credit for the British phased withdrawal from Basra. As noted earlier, the movement had an Iraqi nationalist orientation and staunchly opposed any foreign control of Iraq.

A second armed Shia political-religious organization was the Islamic Fadhila (Virtue) Party, whose spiritual authority was Ayatollah Muhammad al-Yacoubi, who had split from Moqtada in 2003. The Fadhila also followed the ideas of Ayatollah Baqir al-Sadr but did not accept the leadership of young Moqtada. Like the Mahdi Army, the Fadhila was strongly nationalist and rejected the proposal some Shia advocated to create a nine-province predominantly Shia region in southern Iraq, which could potentially come under Iranian influence. In 2007 Fadhila members held the governorship of Basra province and twelve seats on the forty-seat Basra provincial council (Dagher 2007b). Fadhila, like the Mahdi Army, also opposed the more pro-Iranian Iraqi Shia organization, the Islamic Supreme Council of Iraq (ISCI) (until May 2007 called the Supreme Council for Islamic Revolution in Iraq, SCIRI).

ISCI played a major role in the central government as a main component of the United Iraqi Alliance, which also included Iraqi Prime Minister Nouri al-Maliki's Dawa Party. In Basra the ISCI was associated with four other parties, the Badr Organization (formerly the SCIRI militia, the Badr Brigade), the Shaheed Al-Mihrab Organization, the Sayed Al-Shuhada Movement, and the Hezbollah Movement in Iraq (different from the Hezbollah of Lebanon). The ISCI and its four affiliated parties, known as the Bayet al-Khumasi (the Pentacle House), held twenty-one seats in the Basra provincial council. All five of these groups had been headquartered in Iran during Saddam's regime, had close ties to the Iranian government, and favored the creation of a nine-province Shia region. The Shia political groupings periodically engaged in conflict, sometimes violent.

During the period from September 2006 to March 2007, British and Iraqi military forces carried out Operation Sinbad, their own clear-hold-build operations in selected districts of Basra (DeYoung and Ricks 2007), which contributed to reducing political assassinations and crime. However, by early September, forty-two British soldiers had been killed, compared with twenty-nine for all of 2006, and the last five hundred were withdrawn from their base in central Basra. They joined some 5,000 British troops at the Shaibah air base about ten miles to the southwest, which was subjected to almost six hundred mortar and rocket attacks from April to early August 2007 (DeYoung and Ricks 2007). Britain officially handed control of Basra over to the Iraqi government on December 16, 2007, and its contingent overseeing southern Iraq was reduced to about 4,500 (Mahmoud, O'Kane, and Black 2007).

Many Basra residents associated with the Baathist regime were killed or forced to leave the city, and secular-oriented people were pressured to adopt fundamentalist patterns of behavior. Women, including Christians, who had worn Western-style clothing, were forced to adopt the Muslim *hijab* (head scarf) to conceal their hair (Hamdani and Hider 2007). According to Mahmoud, O'Kane, and Black (2007), forty-five women were killed in the Basra area from September to mid-December 2007 for reasons such as giving birth while not married or going out in public while not fully covered.

US Corporations in Iraq

Reconstruction, Supply, and Service

The Bush administration created a reconstruction agency for Iraq, the Office of Reconstruction and Humanitarian Assistance, on January 20, 2003 (Miller 2006: xiii–xiv). In March 2003 KBR (Kellogg, Brown & Root), an engineering and construction company then a subsidiary of Halliburton, was selected for a US contract paying as much as $7 billion for tasks such as rebuilding Iraqi oil facilities and providing logistical support services such as delivering fuel. The army was accused of awarding this contract without competitive bidding, but army officials indicated that KBR was unique in its capabilities and ability to deploy quickly and that the classified circumstances of the contract ruled out public bidding (CPI 2007). The reconstruction of Iraq's industries and electrical, water, sewage, and transportation systems was intended, in part, to win more support for the occupation by improving Iraqis' living conditions. Upgrading the oil industry was intended to dramatically expand revenues, allowing Iraq to pay for its own reconstruction.

Bechtel, a major engineering and construction company, was selected on April 17, 2003, for a $680 million project to reconstruct electricity, sewage treatment and water facilities, and schools (Miller 2006: xiv–xvi). On March 4, 2004, reconstruction contracts worth billions were awarded to other US multinational corporations. CH2M Hill was contracted for the Iraq Public Works and Water Sector program (CPI 2007), Lucent Technologies for repair and modernization of Iraq's communications systems, and Parsons Corporation to destroy captured weapons and to supply engineering and technical services.

Some contracts stipulated a fixed price but others were "cost plus award fee," which was theoretically to be used in circumstances of extreme uncertainty to encourage companies to carry out projects they probably would have refused on a fixed-price basis. The cost plus award fee system guaranteed that the government would pay all the contractor's costs plus provide a guaranteed profit margin. Critics claimed that without tight government oversight, these types of contracts had a great potential for abuse (Miller 2006: 78, 211).

The US State Department also hired private security contractors to provide services such as guarding State Department personnel and training members of the new Iraqi police force. DynCorp of El Segundo, California, won a contract in April 2003 that included organizing Iraqi judicial and correctional agencies (CPI 2007). From March 20, 2003, to October 2007, State Department payments to private security and law enforcement companies reportedly climbed from about $1 billion to $4 billion per year.

Reconstruction Problems

A number of factors interfered with reconstruction. The sanctions between 1991 and 2003 prevented Iraq from acquiring modern machinery, and therefore Iraqi engineers were limited to maintaining increasingly outmoded technologies and had little opportunity to update their skills. Replacing old machinery was easier than locating Iraqi personnel with knowledge to operate new equipment. The scarcity of qualified Iraqis was also due to the de-Baathification policy and the flight of many highly educated Iraqis from the country. Dissolving Iraq's armed forces also impeded reconstruction by transforming thousands of men who might have been used to rebuild infrastructure into embittered insurgents bent on frustrating occupation goals.

Insurgents repeatedly sabotaged pipelines and targeted electricity transmission towers, toppling 623 of Iraq's 2,554 by September 2003 (Miller 2006: 275). Lack of security due to inadequate numbers of troops to guard construction projects often kept construction personnel from reporting to job sites, slowing down projects and contributing to increasing costs. By May 19, 2007, at least 917 contractors had been killed in Iraq (Broder and Risen 2007a).

Some problems appeared to stem from poor staffing decisions. Miller (2006: 38–39) reports that a number of those selected for the US mission were recent college graduates with conservative political leanings, sometimes political science majors with limited understanding of accounting or overseeing the finances of reconstruction projects. He indicates (2006: 39) that in one instance the Pentagon requested a list of job applicants on file with the conservative Heritage Foundation. The headquarters of the US occupation was the so-called fortified Green Zone in Baghdad, the site of the Iraq Republican Palace, symbolic of the revolution against the British-sponsored monarchy, but which after the invasion, as Miller (2006: 39) points out, became the temporary home of many American Republicans. Within the Green Zone the Bush administration commenced building what reportedly would be the largest American embassy in the world.

Cheap Labor

Contractors supplying goods or services to US bases often considered it too dangerous to employ Iraqis, even though many were desperate for work. To save money some sought cheap labor from Nepal, the Philippines, Somalia, or Pakistan. A labor broker would recruit a worker who would often borrow money to pay for travel to Iraq and then would use earnings to pay back the loan. The minimum salary for a KBR US employee was around $60,000 per year, while that for some foreign workers might be as low as $3,000 (Miller 2006: 245). Miller (2006: 244) states that 25,000 to 35,000 of KBR's approximately 50,000 employees in Iraq were neither US citizens nor Iraqis. Third-country employees of private security companies came from nations including Chile, Colombia, Fiji, South Africa, and Ukraine (Miller 2006: 244; Scahill 2007: 199–200).

Spending Iraq's Oil Money

UN Resolution 1483 (United Nations 2003) called for humanitarian assistance and reconstruction, and looked forward to the establishment of a new sovereign Iraqi government. Provision 12 of the resolution "notes the establishment of a Development Fund for Iraq to be held by the Central Bank of Iraq" with oversight by the UN secretary-general and representatives of the International Monetary Fund and the World Bank. Provision 13, however, allowed the Development Fund, which Provision 20 stated would be funded by export sales of Iraq's oil, natural gas, and petroleum products, to be "disbursed at the direction" of the CPA. However, CPA Memorandum Number 4 appeared to make it easier to spend Development Fund money than US funds. This directive covering contracting guidelines did not require competitive bidding and permitted contract proposals to be posted and awarded in one day. Critics suggested that the CPA appeared to award a majority of the large contracts to US corporations such as Halliburton (Miller 2006: 188–189) and that the fund was victimized by fraud or overcharging. Since US courts were likely to rule that misuse of Iraqi money was beyond their jurisdiction and because the feeble Iraqi government appeared to lack effective enforcement power under coalition occupation, war profiteers and perpetrators of outright fraud seemed to have little fear of punishment. Miller (2006: 181) describes the apparent more than doubling of the loss of some items provided by one company to the coalition. In another case workers told of being ordered to destroy large shipments of brand-new equipment of the wrong type in "burn pits" (Greenwald 2007).

Poor decision-making also contributed to waste and failure to achieve goals. For example, American planners decided to spend hundreds of millions of dollars for twenty-six electricity-generating natural gas turbines to take advantage of Iraq's large supply of this resource. But most of the gas pipelines were not constructed because both the new Iraqi government and American officials were more interested in exporting oil. As a result, only seven of the turbines were fueled by natural gas (Miller 2006: 270–271). Converting the other turbines to other fuels, including in some cases heavy fuel oil, reportedly increased maintenance requirements, decreased electric generation capacity, and seemed likely to shorten generator life.

Attempts to Reduce Waste and Fraud

Some officials displayed concern for the misuse of US and Iraqi funds. One was Texas-born Colonel Theodore Westhusing, whose PhD dissertation in philosophy at Emory University evaluated the behavior of famous soldiers. His study described the difficulties confronting military personnel in maintaining a commitment to honor and attempted to provide a vision of the ideals that American soldiers should display during war. Westhusing became one the US Army's top experts on military ethics in modern warfare.

In January 2005 Westhusing was sent to Iraq, where he supervised private security contractors training new Iraqi police in guarding top officials and in carrying out US SWAT (Special Weapons and Tactics)–type operations. He hoped his mission would contribute to the creation of an Iraqi police force imbued with ideals suitable for a democratic Iraq. At first he embraced the mission enthusiastically, but by April 2005 he began to express disappointment with the lack of sufficient progress, the corrupt behavior of some recruits, weapons disappearances, the religious hatred that characterized many Iraqi police, and their mistreatment of captured suspected insurgents (Bryce 2007; Miller 2006: 279–286). He was also disgusted with the level of profit motivation among some private US security personnel and the reported involvement of a number of private contractors in killing Iraqis. What further distressed Westhusing was that the corruption, abuse, and mercenary behavior that he found so objectionable seemed to be widely tolerated.

In May 2005 Westhusing received an anonymous letter that appeared to be from a private military contractor describing how other contractors had engaged in human rights abuses and corruption (Bryce 2007; Miller 2006: 280). On June 5, after a morning meeting with contractors, Colonel Westhusing became one of the twenty-two American soldiers to commit suicide in Iraq in 2005, apparently shooting himself with his own service pistol (Bryce 2007). He left behind a note indicating that he had lost trust in those with whom he was supposed to work to fulfill the mission, that he felt dishonored by his experiences in Iraq, and that he had not come there to support money-motivated, corrupt contractors or human rights abuses (Miller 2006: 279–286).

Republican lawyer Stuart Bowen, whom the Bush administration appointed in January 2004 as special inspector general for Iraq reconstruction in response to congressional demands that something be done about reports of fraud and other criminal activities in the reconstruction program, also objected to corruption (Glanz 2006; Miller 2006: 186–206). Bowen investigated the flow of money out of the Iraq Development Fund and soon concluded that, far from the intent and guidelines of UN Resolution 1483, enormous sums were being drained from the fund with little accountability. The head of the CPA, Bremer, objected to what he regarded as Bowen's application of "unrealistic" accounting standards in turbulent Iraq (Miller 2006: 198). Others opposed Bowen's use of the news media to publicize his findings of waste and crime. But Bowen argued that it was effective to publicize the results of "successful investigations" in order to deter "other potential wrongdoers" (Glanz 2006). Bowen and his staff went on to discover and expose "disastrously poor construction work by well-connected companies." Perhaps not surprisingly, Republicans on the House Armed Services Committee managed to insert a clause into the October 2006 military authorization bill that set October 1, 2007, as the date for the elimination of Bowen's oversight activities in Iraq.

Private Military Firms

The practice of employing mercenary soldiers began thousands of years ago (Singer 2008: 20). But use of hired soldiers by governments appeared to decline significantly by the beginning of the twentieth century as many nations attempted to ensure that military forces were exclusively under state control. During the Cold War, US and Soviet provision of financing and military trainers for armies in developing nations limited their need to hire mercenaries. The United States employed about one civilian in military-related activity for every seven soldiers in World War II and one civilian for every six soldiers in the Vietnam conflict (Miller 2006: 75). But as the US armed forces were reduced in size after the end of the Cold War, reliance on private contractors increased. The number of private contractors supporting US troops in Iraq during 2006 was estimated at about 1 per 2.6 American soldiers (Miller 2006: 76). Singer (2008: 8–18) notes that privatized military firms (PMFs) were active in virtually every part of the world and that the state's control of military violence has declined.

Several major reasons have been offered for the growth of PMFs. One is that relatively weak states may lack the capacity to deal with military crises, such as attacks by other nations or destabilizing internal conflicts, and may seek to hire temporary assistance, rather than expend scarce funds for large permanent armed forces. Another type of PMF customer is corporations or international humanitarian organizations operating in dangerous or unstable areas or in locations where the police are too few, too corrupt, or too incompetent to provide protection. The US volunteer armed forces have attempted to maximize the use of enlistees in combat-type roles and hire private contractors to carry out essential noncombat functions, such as the marines' privatizing 1,100 cook jobs in 2001 (Singer 2008, 15).

Another PMF function is carrying out covert, semicovert, or other missions in which the use of uniformed US troops might constitute a political provocation. For example, Scahill (2007: 172–179) describes how the Pentagon hired the PMF Blackwater to train an elite Azeri force to help protect American oil interests in Azerbaijan because using US troops might cause a hostile reaction from either neighboring Russia or Iran. Still another argument for PMFs is that through their elevated pay levels they constitute a mechanism for maintaining the skill levels of highly and expensively trained special operations or technical military personnel who might otherwise lose their proficiencies when they leave government military service and no longer be competent when their skills are needed. PMFs also theoretically reduce individual nations' military budgets by allowing them to downsize their armed forces with the knowledge that they can access a ready pool of military specialists to supplement their standing forces when temporary needs arise.

The end of the Cold War increased the demand for PMF services because in some places ethnic or religious strife or cross-border conflicts, previously inhibited by Communist Party governments and ideologies or by the threat of external economic pressure or military intervention, increased. Post–Cold War demobilization of armed forces caused a surge in the availability of weapons and trained military personnel in search of employment. In addition, globalization of capitalist market forces appeared to have only limited or no benefits for hundreds of millions of people whose extreme poverty drove them into armed conflict or crime (Singer 2008: 51). Individuals or institutions hired PMFs to protect them from nonstate entities with the ability to use violence, including leftist revolutionary groups, such as the Revolutionary Armed Forces of Colombia (FARC), various revolutionary or ethnically or religiosly based militias in Africa, Al Qaeda–associated groups, and major criminal networks.

Twenty-first-century PMFs tend to be relatively permanent, hierarchically structured businesses that compete globally, often proffering specific skill sets for particular market sectors (Singer 2008: 45–48). They pursue corporate profit and, compared with earlier mercenary-type operations, the modern organizations have a wider range of potential clients for a greater variety of services, ranging from training through material support to resolving conflicts once the fighting is over. As corporations, modern PMFs can openly screen and recruit applicants. They vary in their structure, with some being independent organizations while others are components of larger, multifaceted corporations. While the role of PMFs increased significantly in the 1990s, the 2003 Iraq War provided an unprecedented opportunity.

Singer (2008: 91–148) describes three types of PMFs, all of which were active in the Iraq War: the military provider firm, whose employees engage in combat in roles such as soldier or helicopter gunship pilot or control those in combat; military consultant firms, which mainly provide training and advising for a customer's armed forces; and military support firms, which provide support services such as fuel, food, technical assistance, or transportation. PMFs played roles in training exercises in Kuwait before the war and were especially important in providing logistics in the buildup to the attack. During the invasion, Singer notes, private employees participated in fueling, arming, and maintaining advanced weapons systems such as the F-117 (stealth fighter) and attack helicopters.

US occupation troops in Iraq were supplemented by PMFs. A census of contractors working in Iraq described in the *Washington Post* in December 2006 indicated that about 25,000 were security contractors (Merle 2006). The PMF Blackwater USA reportedly had about 1,000 employees in Iraq, while Dyncorp International was reported to have had more than 1,500.

Blackwater

One of the most highly publicized PMFs operating in postinvasion Iraq was Blackwater, estimated to have had as much as $678 million worth of contracts for providing protection services (Engelhardt 2007). Blackwater was founded by Erik Prince, whose wealthy father had established a manufacturing company, the Prince Corporation, in Holland, Michigan. He grew up in the Dutch Reform Church but later converted to Catholicism.

Erik enrolled in the US Naval Academy but left after three semesters for Hillsdale College, a Michigan Christian liberal arts college (Scahill 2007: 12). He did a six-month internship at George H. W. Bush's White House but in 1992 decided to attend Officer Candidate School and join Navy Seal Team 8. Erik served in Bosnia, Haiti, and the Middle East. After his father died in 1995, he left the navy, and the family decided to sell the Prince Corporation for about $1.35 billion.

Erik returned to civilian life while the military was undergoing a historic process of downsizing begun during the 1989–1993 tenure of Secretary of Defense Dick Cheney, oversaw the reduction of the armed forces from about 2.2 to 1.6 million. Cheney proposed that many of the noncombat tasks formerly performed by military personnel be taken over by private companies.

The initial concept for what became Blackwater may have come from a navy firearms trainer Erik met while with Seal Team 8, Al Clark (Scahill 2007: 25–27). Instructors like Clark were concerned about a lack of comprehensive training facilities. If a private company could develop such a facility, it could become a vital and profitable enterprise by serving the training needs of the armed forces and specialized law enforcement units around the country. Prince founded Blackwater in 1997 and purchased thousands of acres of the North Carolina Great Dismal Swamp area, a gigantic peat bog. The company reportedly took its name from the swamp's black water. This location was conveniently near the Norfolk Naval Station and the national centers of US intelligence and federal law enforcement.

By 1999 the site featured a variety of weapons ranges, including the facade of an urban street, and an approximately 9,000-square-foot lodge with class and conference rooms and a dining facility. In 2008 the Blackwater Web site offered "advanced training," "mobility and logistics," "technology and innovation," and "human and material resources" and described its personnel as including many experts who had previously been members of the US military or law enforcement agencies. The company's "contract opportunities" dated December 19, 2007 (accessed on January 24, 2008), indicated that Blackwater was interested in applicants with eight years of active military experience with a Special Forces background. It banned people with a history of mental illness or convictions for violent or felony crimes or child or spousal abuse.

Several traumatic events spurred the company's growth. The first was the April 20, 1999, Columbine High School mass murder by two students, which took thirteen lives. After the Columbine tragedy Blackwater used a mock high school building, R U Ready High School, complete with sound effects of screaming students, for training hundreds of SWAT police officers (Scahill 2007: 36–37). The National Tactical Officers Association decided to hold part of its 1999 sixteenth annual conference at the Blackwater training center. These developments not only spread Blackwater's name among law enforcement officials nationally, but also led to the company's getting its first contract from the US General Services Administration. Scahill (2007: 37) states that this contract established an approved set of goods and services with associated price levels and constituted a basis and precedent for future federal Blackwater contracts.

The next major boost for Blackwater came after the October 12, 2000, suicide boat attack on the USS *Cole*, a guided-missile destroyer, at the port of Aden in Yemen. Seventeen sailors were killed by the bomb, which blew a forty-foot hole in the ship. As a result, Blackwater received a contract worth about $35.7 million to train navy personnel to more effectively protect ships and naval facilities. By the end of 2005, Blackwater was thought to have trained 30,000 or more sailors in how to identify, engage, and defeat attempted attacks on naval assets in ports or at sea.

But the September 11, 2001, attacks caused a much greater surge in Blackwater business contracts, and soon it was training personnel from almost every branch of government including the FBI, the Department of Energy's National Nuclear Security Administrative Service Center, and the Treasury Department's Financial Crime Enforcement Network.

As the United States' volunteer military prepared for offensive actions in the war on terrorism, it attempted to maximize the use of its personnel for combat by hiring private contractors for tasks such as guarding facilities. Blackwater created a new division, Blackwater Security Consulting, in 2002 to move beyond training to providing highly skilled armed personnel for protection services. The CIA awarded Blackwater its first guard contract in April of that year to provide twenty security guards to protect the CIA station in Kabul, Afghanistan (Pelton 2006: 37–38; Scahill 2007: 45–46). This contributed to Blackwater's getting probably the most highly publicized private security contract in post-invasion Iraq, guarding Louis Paul Bremer III, head of the CPA. Before long,

Blackwater had hundreds of contractors and its own helicopter force in Iraq guarding US civilian personnel.

Blackwater received worldwide notoriety when four employees were ambushed and killed on March 31, 2004, in Fallujah (Pelton 2006: 132–142; Scahill 2007: 1001–104). The killings alarmed contractors and may have contributed to the notorious September 16, 2007, Nisour Square shootings, in which Blackwater men were accused of killing seventeen Iraqis. Investigations indicated that after a bomb went off near a convoy of vehicles Blackwater was guarding, a single bullet struck and killed a young Iraqi man driving his mother on an errand (Glanz and Rubin 2007a). As the car rolled forward, Blackwater guards may have feared that the vehicle was carrying another bomb, leading them to open fire. According to Pelton (2006: 201), Blackwater had a policy of responding to a perceived assault with overwhelming firepower in order to escape the attacking force.

The Nisour Square tragedy focused attention on whether and how any abuses or crimes by private contractors in Iraq could be punished. Even members of the US-backed Iraqi government appeared outraged that private contractors seemed virtually immune from Iraqi law and from either the US military or civilian systems of justice (Broder and Risen 2007b). One reason appeared to be L. Paul Bremer's CPA Order Number 17 (Bremer 2004; Engelhardt 2007; Scahill 2007, xx, 150, 163, 359). Section 2, 1 of Order 17 declared that "unless provided otherwise herein, the MNF [Multinational Force], the CPA, Foreign Liaison Missions, their Personnel, property, funds and assets, and all International Consultants shall be immune from Iraqi legal process."

Further, Section 4, 3 stated that "contractors shall be immune from Iraqi legal process with respect to acts performed by them pursuant to the terms and conditions of a Contract or any sub-contract thereto." Sovereignty seemed little more than a sham because of the apparent inability of the Iraqi government to expel Blackwater from the country. Although in 2006 South Carolina Republican Senator Lindsey Graham, an Air Force Reserve lawyer (Singer 2008: 258–259; Witte 2007), had inserted a provision into the 2007 defense bill subjecting private contractors in Iraq accused of wrongdoing to the US Uniform Code of Military Justice, enforcement was in doubt (Broder and Risen 2007b).

The role of Blackwater and similar companies in Iraq, according to advocates of PMFs, presaged a future in which the United States, seeking to circumvent domestic opposition to intervention in other countries, could rely more heavily on hiring private contractors. Some also suggested that private contractors could deploy more quickly and/or more cheaply than UN, NATO, or African Union forces to deal with conflicts or humanitarian problems. While some governments with limited resources were attracted to PMFs to save the cost of maintaining large permanent military forces, critics saw a potential for great abuses, such as ruling elites' hiring foreign mercenaries to suppress domestic opposition or threaten war against neighbors.

With a reported contractor base of approximately 21,000 people, Blackwater seemed to be preparing the way for greater international reliance on PMFs (Scahill 2007: 365–369). On May 13, 2004, the company registered a new division, Greystone Limited, with the US Central Contracting Office. The Greystone Web site (Greystone Ltd. 2006), accessed March 16, 2009, indicated capabilities to deploy its employees for a number of tasks including security, humanitarian assistance, and peacekeeping. Its security workforce was characterized as coming "from the best militaries throughout the world" trained to "have the skills they need for a specific assignment." Drawn from a "diverse base of former special operations, defense, intelligence, and law enforcement professionals," Greystone's personnel were "ready on a moment's notice for global deployment."

Reacting to reports of contractor abuses and that thousands of South Africans, many white former members of South Africa's armed forces, were working for PMFs around the world, perhaps 2,000 to 4,000 in Iraq alone, the South African National Assembly on August 30, 2006, passed the Prohibition of Mercenary Activity and Regulation of Certain Activities in Areas of Armed Conflict Bill. The act stipulated that all South Africans wanting to work abroad in security- or military-type jobs had to register with an arms control committee (Nullis 2006). According to the BBC (2006), this would require South Africans to get their government's permission to work in security companies abroad or serve in foreign armies. Whether other countries would follow South Africa's lead was an open question. Possibly in response to the negative publicity it received concerning events in Iraq, Blackwater Worldwide, which includes the Blackwater subsidiary companies, announced in February 2009 that it was changing its name to Xe, pronounced like the letter "Z," and was going to focus on providing training services over private security (Associated Press 2009).

The Iraq and Afghan wars stretched US capabilities. If PMFs were not to be relied upon more heavily, policy-makers had to either reinstate conscription or provide greater incentives for people to join the volunteer armed forces.

The US Volunteer Armed Forces

As modern weapons technology gave relatively small numbers of military personnel increased destructive power and often offered them much greater protection from enemy fire than in past wars, reliance on volunteer armed forces became more feasible. All US military personnel in Iraq had volunteered to enlist, unlike Vietnam, in which many soldiers had been drafted. States vary greatly in military enlistment (DeFronzo and Gill 2008a: 1–2). For example, in fiscal year 2000 (FY2000, October 1999 through September 2000) the ratio of Massachusetts's enlistees to its share of the country's eighteen- to twenty-four-year-olds was about 0.53, meaning that its number of enlistees was about 47 percent below its share of people in that age group nationally, while Montana's ratio was 1.91, indicating that Montana provided enlistees about 91 percent above its share of the nation's eighteen- to twenty-four-year-olds.

Psychology and Sociology of Enlistment

Winkler (1993: 398–399) provides a review of research indicating that decisions to enlist are often based on seeking to improve economic and/or educational opportunities. Bachman, Segal, Freedman-Doan, and O'Malley (2000: 1–30), analyzing data from a sample of over 100,000 high school seniors for the years 1984 to 1991, find that people's attitudes toward the military affected enlistment. Young people who felt the military does a good job for the country, should have more influence, and should receive greater funding were more likely to enlist. In addition, those who expressed support for a "superior military force" or "willingness to use that force for protecting other countries, in pursuit of US economic interests, or both rather than only in reaction against attack" were also more likely to enlist.

The Rand Corporation (2001) reports research that found that the higher the local unemployment rate, the more likely high school seniors are to enlist, and that among high school graduates enlistment was more likely if the respondent had a parent serving in the military. Kleykamp (2006) finds that the percentage of male Texas students' county workforce employed in the military tends to be positively associated with their choosing to enlist. That is, she found that the higher the percentage of the local workforce employed in the military, the more likely male students were to join the armed forces.

DeFronzo and Gill (2007: 12–18; 2008a: 1–13; 2008b) analyze Defense Department data for all fifty states before and after 9/11 and find that cultural, social, and economic factors—including the percent of hunters in a state, church adherence, and divorce levels—and the unemployment rate influence the tendency to enlist. Controlling for relevant variables, those states with high levels of hunters, divorce, and unemployment, and relatively low levels of church adherence tend to have higher enlistment rates. It may be that where church adherence is low and a high percentage of families are disrupted by divorce, enlistment in the military has the attraction of providing the benefits of community and extended family. Interestingly, the effects of church adherence and divorce on enlistment rates seemed to become stronger after 9/11, while the influences of some variables appeared to weaken (at least temporarily).

Morgan (2001: 3) discusses military recruiting problems in terms of large-scale social and cultural characteristics and describes what he calls "the apparent sociological gap in civil-military relations." He suggests that this was due to factors such as the end of the draft, the resulting changes in the geographic origins of military personnel, the end of many college-based ROTC units, the banning of military recruiters from some college campuses, the "increase in service-members' children making the military a career," and "significantly greater average length of service," which was partly the result of offering incentives for soldiers to renew enlistment. Morgan claims that the institutional presence of the US military in the lives of most Americans declined in terms of social contact and morally in regard to people's priorities for the requirements of a good society. One important dimension of the increasing separateness of the military was the shrinking percentage of political leaders who have served in the armed forces. He notes that there were 320 military veterans in the House of Representatives in 1970 but only 130 in 1994 (Morgan 2001: 4). In addition, in 1997, for the first time in history, the secretaries of defense and state, the national security adviser, and their deputies had no military experience.

In addition, popular films often portrayed the military as out of touch with modern social values (Morgan 2001: 6). Cultural changes such as resistance to authority, more desire for personal self-expression, and greater hedonism were also thought linked to the "decline of mass armies in Western nations." Such cultural shifts meant that without the draft to randomly select recruits, only those young people with values most congruent with military service would be inclined to enlist, helping to account for why there are apparently far fewer liberals among military officers than among civilian leaders.

The US Military in Iraq

In 2007, about half of the US Army's combat brigades were in action, while the other half were recuperating from previous deployments or preparing to go into action (Thompson 2007). Since the United States had prioritized spending on weaponry that could destroy from long distances, the air force and the navy each received about twice the army's percentage of the Pentagon hardware budget between 1990 and 2005. This meant that behind the invasion's armored phalanxes, US trucks and transport vehicles tended to be only lightly protected, making personnel vulnerable to small-arms fire, roadside bombs, and portable mortars and rockets used by resisting Iraqi forces and later by the insurgents. As Galula (2006) and later Petraeus and Amos (2006) assert, a counterinsurgency is won by gaining the support or control of the population. But army patrols in sixty-eight-ton M1A Abrams tanks, while providing occupants with good protection, tended to alienate the people through whose neighborhoods the tanks crunched their way, while the option of using weakly shielded Humvees or trucks was far more dangerous. The army scrambled to obtain better-suited vehicles.

The army also faced personnel shortages since its limited size was premised on fighting quick wars rather than the lengthy insurgencies that developed in Iraq and Afghanistan. The response was new methods to expand enlistment rates and retain existing personnel, such as raising the maximum enlistment age from forty to forty-two, providing larger enlistment bonuses and postenlistment educational benefits, increasing the number of waivers, which permitted thousands more with criminal convictions (moral waivers) or lacking high school degrees (educational waivers) to enlist, and offering advantages for immigrants on the path to citizenship in exchange for military service (Stock 2006). Bender (2006) reports that about 30,000 noncitizens were serving in the US military and that approximately 100 had perished in Iraq or Afghanistan.

By November 2007 the Pentagon was offering up to $40,000 enlistment bonuses for those signing up for a four-year commitment (Carter and Flora 2007). Military personnel could enroll in the active-duty Montgomery GI Bill program, which could pay up to $38,700 for future vocational training or college while recruits who entered service with existing college loans could be eligible for $65,000 in loan repayment for a three-year tour of duty. Up to $10,000 bonuses were offered in 2007 for officers from other services to switch to the army, and $20,000 to $35,000 to army captains to commit to an additional three years. Gaps in the higher ranks were apparently sometimes filled by quicker promotions. Since some of the best special operations officers retired to work for PMFs for as much as $200,000 per year, the army reportedly offered retention bonuses of up to $150,000 to the most highly skilled Special Forces soldiers (Carter and Flora 2007).

The military had concluded that 90 percent or more of recruits should have at least a high school degree, since research indicated that more intelligent soldiers tended to perform better. But educational waivers brought the percentage of recruits with regular high school diplomas down to about 81 percent in FY2006 (US Defense Department 2006). The army's use of enlistment "moral waivers," also called "conduct waivers," for misdemeanors and felonies increased significantly from FY2006 to FY2007 (Alvarez 2008). In April 2007 a decision was announced to extend tours of duty in Iraq and Afghanistan from twelve to fifteen months (Cloud 2007). Other measures to deal with personnel limitations were so-called stop-loss and stop-move programs, designed to ensure the cohesion and effectiveness of units. "Stop-loss" referred to keeping soldiers in the military beyond the length of their enlistment contract, while "stop-move" referred to freezing people in a particular assignment. Carter and Flora (2007) report that the number affected by stop-move was not clear but that there may have been as many as 9,000 soldiers affected by stop-loss in 2007. Changes in enlistment policies may have contributed to the US armed forces' meeting or exceeding their recruitment goals for FY2007 (US Defense Department 2008).

The willingness of soldiers to continue their military service was likely influenced by their attitudes toward the war being fought. Polls of active-duty personnel indicated that their views shifted over time. In 2004, 83 percent responded that US success in Iraq was likely. This dropped to 50 percent in 2006 but rebounded to about 62 percent in the 2007 poll of 1,468 active-duty service people conducted during the week of December 10–17 after the level of US casualties dropped significantly in the second half of the year (Hodierne 2006; Naegele 2007). In the 2006 poll, in which almost half of the respondents were in the army, more than two-fifths in the navy or air force, and the rest in the marines or coast guard, approximately 47 percent felt that the war in Iraq was part of the war on terrorism, but 47 percent responded that it was a separate military action (the rest had no opinion or declined to answer). While two-thirds supported going to war in Iraq in the 2003 poll, in 2007 only 46 percent did. In contrast, 88 percent of the 2007 respondents stated that the United States should have gone to war in Afghanistan.

Charges of US Human Rights Abuses

Televised pictures in the spring of 2004 that showed naked Iraqis at Abu Ghraib prison being threatened and forced to perform humiliating acts by US soldiers instantly damaged America's reputation and enraged millions of Arabs, including Saudis, Syrians, Libyans, and Jordanians, many of whom would come to Iraq to seek revenge. The obscene images raised questions about how captured Iraqis were being treated elsewhere.

Ricks (2006: 147, 378–379) provides evidence suggesting that the Abu Ghraib abuses were at least partly due to the failure to send enough soldiers to

Iraq and to anticipate significant resistance to the occupation. Some abuse had apparently taken place in the summer of 2003. But in October, new military police (MPs) took over a section of the prison and mistreatment appeared to worsen. Beginning on October 17, one MP began photographing the abusive behavior. Later investigations revealed accounts of prisoners being sexually abused (Hersh 2007; Ricks 2006: 292). The extent of mistreatment is difficult to accurately gauge since many army soldiers and marines indicated they would not report another service member for injuring or killing an innocent Iraqi (Reuters 2007). Some soldiers, however, did state that abuse of Iraqi prisoners was a frequent occurrence and not limited to that depicted in the Abu Ghraib pictures (Arnove 2007: 27; Reuters 2006). Hersh (2007) reports that General Antonio Taguba, who was assigned the job of investigating some of the activities at Abu Ghraib, found evidence that the policies of higher authorities contributed to the abuse but that the response to his honesty and courage was apparently to pressure him to retire from the military.

The Status of Forces Agreement

UN Security Council Resolution 1790 (2007), passed on December 18, 2007, had permitted US and allied multinational forces to stay in Iraq until December 31, 2008. For US forces to remain "legally" beyond this deadline without UN approval was viewed as requiring a bilateral agreement, a so-called Status of Forces Agreement (SOFA), between the Iraqi and US governments. SOFA, which permits US forces to remain in Iraq until December 31, 2011, was approved by the Iraqi parliament on November 27, 2008, by a vote of 149 out of the 275 members of the national legislature. Seventy-seven members of the legislature were absent and of those who were present, 35 voted against approval and 14 abstained (Raghavan and Sarhan 2008). While a majority, about 54 percent, of Iraq's legislators voted for SOFA, the large number who were absent was somewhat reminiscent of the 1922 Iraqi Constituent Assembly, where many members did not attend the session at which the British-Iraq Treaty supporting Britain's continued presence in Iraq was approved (see chapter 1).

In his efforts to secure a parliamentary majority vote for SOFA, Iraqi Prime Minister Maliki consented to allow a national referendum on SOFA no later than July 30, 2009 (Myers 2008; Raghavan and Sarhan 2008). The influential Shia religious leader Ayatollah Sistani did not oppose SOFA, reportedly on the basis of its ultimately being subject to approval by Iraqi voters. Some believe that if US forces substantially fail to live up to their side of the agreement, the majority of Iraqi voters will choose to cancel SOFA, which either Iraq or the United States is allowed to do according to Article 24, Paragraph 4. However, SOFA Article 30, Paragraph 3 also states that "this Agreement shall terminate one year after a Party (either Iraq or the U.S.) provides written notification to the other Party to that effect" (White House 2008). This seems to mean that even if the majority of Iraqi voters reject SOFA in a July 2009 referendum, SOFA will allow US forces to remain in Iraq a minimum of about a year and a half beyond the UN December 31, 2008, deadline.

The preamble of SOFA describes Iraq and the United States as "two sovereign, independent, and coequal countries." In Article 4, "Missions," Paragraph 1, "The Government of Iraq requests the temporary assistance of the United States for the purposes of supporting Iraq in its efforts to maintain security and stability in Iraq, including cooperation in the conduct of operations against Al Qaeda and other terrorist groups, outlaw groups, and remnants of the former regime." Paragraph 2 indicates that "all such military operations that are carried out pursuant to this Agreement shall be conducted with the agreement of the government of Iraq" and coordinated with Iraqi authorities through the Joint Military Operations Coordination Committee (JMOCC), composed of both Americans and Iraqis. However, Paragraph 5 indicates that both Iraq and the United States "retain the right to legitimate self defense." Article 9, Paragraph 3 states that "surveillance and control of Iraqi airspace shall transfer to Iraqi authority immediately upon entry into force of this Agreement." Article 12 gives Iraq jurisdiction over members of US forces and civilians working for the US Defense Department for "grave premeditated felonies" committed outside facilities and areas used by the United States and "outside duty status"; otherwise, the United States has primary jurisdiction over such individuals. The "grave premeditated felonies" will be "enumerated" in the future. The expression "duty status" was not among the terms defined in Article 2.

SOFA states in Article 24, Paragraph 2, that US "combat forces" would "withdraw from Iraqi cities, villages, and localities" "no later than June 30, 2009." However, "combat forces" was another expression not included among those defined in Article 2. Critics feared that US soldiers designated as training personnel but granted the right of self-defense under SOFA would in reality continue to engage in combat operations alongside Iraqi troops. Some observers estimated that perhaps thousands of US troops, most likely designated as trainers or advisers, would remain in Iraqi cities after the June 30 deadline and that possibly tens of thousands would stay in Iraq even after December 31, 2011 (Bumiller 2008).

Article 27 of SOFA indicates that the United States, in agreement with Iraq, may take military or other action to defend Iraq, its "sovereignty," "democratic system," "elected institutions," territory, and so on against "any external or internal threat or aggression" and train and equip "Iraqi Security Forces." But Paragraph 3 states, "Iraqi land, sea, and air shall not be used as a launching or transit point for attacks against other countries." Although Article 28 states that after the enactment of SOFA, Iraq would have full responsibility for the Green Zone, the Iraqi government can request "temporary support" from the United States for Green Zone security.

While some believed SOFA achieved the goal of finally getting the United States to agree to a firm deadline to withdraw from Iraq, others, such as many of the supporters of Shia leader Moqtada al-Sadr as well as many Sunni Arab Iraqis, suspected that it was mainly a deception to ensure continued and perhaps indefinite US military occupation of Iraq. Criticisms of SOFA beyond those mentioned above included questioning the designation of Iraq as a "coequal" "sovereign" country or how its political leaders or representatives on

JMOCC could exercise power equivalent to that of their American counterparts while some 146,000 US military personnel were stationed on Iraq's territory.

Summary and Analysis

Invading Iraq under false justifications virtually ensured violent resistance to the occupation. The CPA's sweeping de-Baathification and dissolution of the Iraqi armed forces, coupled with the perverse abuse of Iraqi prisoners at Abu Ghraib, undoubtedly increased the extent and intensity of the insurgency. The numbers of US troops, their equipment, and their initial strategy and tactics were not well suited to coping with a large-scale insurgency.

Eventually US forces shifted toward a counterinsurgency approach theoretically aimed at winning the support of the population. This included denying insurgents safe havens in which to assemble weapons and plan attacks, and so-called clear-hold-build operations, which involved selecting a particular area, clearing it of insurgent forces, and holding it to provide security so that people could feel safe giving information on insurgents and their supporters to counterinsurgents. Delivering more services and beneficial construction projects was intended to reduce support for the insurgency. The early clear-hold-build operations appeared flawed by reliance on units of the new Iraqi military to carry out the hold function, but the 2007 surge in the number of American troops permitted US forces to be used more widely in holding the territories they cleared. This, along with other factors, seemed to improve results, contributing to success in defeating IED networks and to a significant drop in US casualties in the second half of 2007.

Another counterinsurgency innovation involved, in effect, hiring Sunni Arabs, many of whom had previously participated in the resistance against the occupation, to fight against a main fundamentalist branch of the insurgency, Al Qaeda in Mesopotamia, thought to have been responsible for many mass-casualty bombing attacks. Advanced counterinsurgency technology also played a role in reducing the level of the insurgency by providing more comprehensive control of the population and increased capacity to eliminate antioccupation resistance leaders and fighters.

US corporations profited from service or reconstruction contracts in Iraq worth billions of dollars. The occupation also benefited PMFs hired to provide security for US officials and to train elements of the new Iraqi armed services. The thousands of private military contractors helped compensate for the strain on US forces as the insurgency continued. Enlistments in America's volunteer armed forces tended to decline temporarily, possibly partly in reaction to a drop in public support for the Iraq War. To improve enlistment levels, Washington increased financial incentives for enlistees and reenlistees. Waivers were expanded to allow more people to enlist who previously would have been rejected on moral grounds or for failing to meet educational requirements. Some were forced to remain in the military beyond their enlistment termination points. After it became clear that Iraq had played no role in the 9/11 attacks and that it did not possess WMD, and as casualties from the insurgency mounted, surveys indicated that support for the Iraq War within the US armed forces declined significantly. Many soldiers did not view it as part of the war on terrorism.

As December 31, 2008, the date ending UN authorization for US forces to be in Iraq, approached, a Status of Forces Agreement between Iraq and the United States, which permitted US forces to remain until December 31, 2011, was approved. But some speculated that thousands of US military personnel, perhaps designated as advisers or trainers, would stay in Iraq beyond 2011.

References and Further Readings

Alvarez, Lizette. 2008. "Army and Marine Corps Grant More Felony Waivers." *New York Times*, April 22. www.nytimes.com.

Arnove, Anthony. 2007. *Iraq: The Logic of Withdrawal*. New York: Henry Holt.

Associated Press. 2009. "Blackwater Changes Its Name to Xe." *New York Times*, February 14. www.nytimes.com.

Bachman, J. G., D. R. Segal, P. Freedman-Doan. and P. M. O'Malley. 2000. "Who Chooses Military Service? Correlates of Propensity and Enlistment in the U.S. Armed Forces." *Military Psychology* 12 (1): 1–30.

Baker, James A., and Lee H. Hamilton. 2006. *The Iraq Study Group Report*. New York: Vintage Books.

BBC. 2006. "MPs Approve New SA Mercenary Bill." August 30. http://news.bbc.co.uk/2/hi/africa/5297704.stm.

Bender, Bryan. 2006. "Military Considers Recruiting Foreigners." *Boston Globe*, December 26. www.boston.com.

Blackwater Worldwide. 2008. www.blackwaterusa.com/company (accessed January 23, 2008).

Bremer, L. Paul III. 2004. *Coalition Provisional Authority Order Number 17 (Revised): Status of the Coalition Provisional Authority, MNF-IRAQ, Certain Missions and Personnel In Iraq*. Coalition Provisional Authority, June 27. www.cpa-iraq.org/regulations/20040627_CPAORD_17_Status_of_Coalition_Rev__with_Annex_A.pdf (accessed March 16, 2009).

Broder, John M., and James Risen. 2007a. "Contractor Deaths in Iraq Soar." *New York Times*, May 19. www.nytimes.com.

———. 2007b. "Armed Guards in Iraq Occupy A Legal Limbo." *New York Times*, September 20. www.nytimes.com.

Broder, John M., and David Rohde. 2007. "State Department Use of Contractors Leaps in 4 Years." *New York Times*, October 24. www.nytimes.com.

Bryce, Robert. 2007. "I Am Sullied No More." *Texas Observer*, March 9. www.texasobserver.org/article.php?aid=2440.

Bumiller, Elizabeth. 2008. "Redefining the Role of the U.S. Military in Iraq." *New York Times*, December 22. www.nytimes.com.

Buzenberg, Bill. 2006. "Baghdad Bonanza: The Top 100 Private Contractors in Iraq and Afghanistan." Windfalls of War II—Center for Public Integrity (CPI). www.globalpolicy.org/security/issues/iraq/contract/2007/1120tophundred.htm.

Carter, Phillip, and Brad Flora. 2007. "I Want You . . . Badly: A Complete Guide to Uncle Sam's Recruiting Incentives." *Slate*, November 7. www.slate.com/toolbar.aspx?action=print&id=2177426.

Chandrasekaran, Rajiv. 2006. *Imperial Life in the Emerald City: Inside Iraq's Green Zone*. New York: Knopf.

Cloud, David S. 2007. "US Is Extending Tours of Army." *New York Times*, April 12. www.nytimes.com.

Cordesman, Anthony H. 2007. "The British Defeat in the South and the Uncertain Bush 'Strategy' in Iraq: 'Oil Spots,' 'Ink Blots,' 'White Space,' or Pointless?" *Center for Strategic and International Studies*, February 21.

CPI (Center for Public Integrity). 2007. "Windfalls of War, Contractors: Iraq." www.publicintegrity.org/wow/bio.aspx2?act=pro&ddlC=6.

Dagher, Sam. 2007a. "As British Leave Basra, Militias Dig In." *Christian Science Monitor*, August 28. www.csmonitor.com/2007/0828/p01s03-wome.html.

———. 2007b. "Basra After the British." *Christian Science Monitor*, September 21. www.alternet.org/module/printversion/63220.

Debusmann, Bernd. 2007. "In Outsourced U.S. Wars, Contractor Deaths Top 1,000." *Reuters*, July 3. www.alertnet.org/thenews/newsdesk/N03186503.htm.

DeFronzo, James, and Jungyun Gill. 2007. "Hunting and Military Recruitment Before and After 9/11." *Rural Sociologist* 27 (December): 12–18.

———. 2008a. "Religious Adherence and Military Enlistment Before and After the 9/11 Attacks." *Interdisciplinary Journal of Research on Religion* 4: 1–13. www.religjournal.com.

———. 2008b. "Cultural and Structural Factors Affecting Interstate Variation in Military Enlistment Before and After 9/11." American Sociological Association Meetings, August 2, Boston.

DeYoung, Karen, and Thomas E. Ricks. 2007. "As British Leave, Basra Deteriorates." *Washington Post*, August 7. www.washingtonpost.com.

Eisler, Peyer, Blake Morrison, and Tom Vanden Brook. 2007. "Strategy that Is Making Iraq Safer After It Was Snubbed for Years." *USA Today*, December 18. www.usatoday.com/news/military/2007-12-18-iraqstrategy_N.htm (accessed December 24, 2007).

Engelhardt, Tom. 2007. "Order 17." *The Nation*, September 24. www.thenation.com/docprint.mhtml?i=20071008&s=engelhardt (accessed January 23, 2008).

Fallows, James. 2006. *Blind into Baghdad*. New York: Vintage Books.

Frank, Thomas. 2007. "US Building Database on Iraqis." *USA Today*, July 12. www.usatoday.com/news/world/iraq/2007-07-12-iraq-database_N.htm.

Galbraith, Peter W. 2008. *Unintended Consequences: How the War in Iraq Strengthened America's Enemies*. New York: Simon & Schuster.

Galula, David. 2006 (1964). *Counterinsurgency Warfare: Theory and Practice*. Westport, CT: Praeger Security International.

Glanz, James. 2006. "Congress Tells Auditor in Iraq to Close Office." *New York Times*, November 3. www.nytimes.com.

———. 2007. "Audit Finds US Hid Cost of Iraq Projects." *New York Times*, July 30. www.nytimes.com.

Glanz, James, and Alisa J. Rubin. 2007a. "From Errand to Fatal Shot to Hail of Fire to 17 Deaths." *New York Times*, October 3. www.nytimes.com.

———. 2007b. "Blackwater Shootings 'Murder,' Iraq Says." *New York Times*, October 8. www.nytimes.com.

Glanz, James, and Eric Schmitt. 2007. "Iraq Weapons Are a Focus of Criminal Investigations." *New York Times*, August 28. www.nytimes.com.

Gordon, Michael, and Bernard E. Trainor. 2006. *Cobra II: The Inside Story of the
Invasion and Occupation of Iraq*. New York: Knopf Publishing Group.

Graff, Peter. 2007. "Analysis—Britain's Iraq War Is Ending. Who Won?" *Reuters*,
December 9. www.reuters.com/article/latestCrisis/idUSL08668175.

Greenwald, Robert. 2007. *Iraq for Sale: The War Profiteers*. Culver City, CA: Brave
New Films. Also iraqforsale.org and www.robertgreenwald.org/docs.php.

Greystone Ltd. 2006. www.greystone-ltd.com/index.html (accessed March 16,
2009).

Guidière, Mathieu, and Peter Harling. 2006. "'Withdraw, Move On and Rampage':
Iraq's Resistance Evolves." *Le Monde Diplomatique*, May. http://monde
diplo.com/2006/05/02irak.

Hamdani, Ali, and James Hider. 2007. "Basra's Murderous Militias Tell Christian
Women to Cover Up or Face Death." Timesonline, December 8. www
.timesonline.co.uk/tol/news/world/iraq/article3018766.ece.

Hashim, Ahmed S. 2006. *Insurgency and Counter-Insurgency in Iraq*. Ithaca, NY:
Cornell University Press.

Hersh, Seymour M. 2007. "Annals of National Security: The General's Report."
New Yorker, June 25. www.newyorker.com/reporting/2007/06/25/070625fa
_fact_hersh?printable.

Hirsh, Michael, and John Barry. 2005. "The Pentagon May Put Special Forces–Led
Assassination Teams in Iraq." *Newsweek*, January 8. www.newsweek.com.

History Channel. 2004. "Soldiers for Hire." South Burlington, VT: A&E Home
Video.

Hodierne, Robert. 2006. "Poll: More Troops Unhappy with Bush's Course in Iraq."
Army Times, January 6. www.militarycity.com/polls/2006_main.php.

Kane, T. 2005. *Who Bears the Burden? Demographic Characteristics of U.S. Military Recruits Before and After 9/11*. Washington, DC: Heritage Foundation
Center for Data Analysis.

———. 2006. *Who are the Recruits? The Demographic Characteristics of U.S. Military Enlistment, 2003–2005*. Washington, DC: Heritage Foundation Center
for Data Analysis.

Kessler, Glenn. 2007. "Iraq Embassy Cost Rises $144 Million Amid Project De-
lays." *Washington Post*, October 7. www.washingtonpost.com.

Kleykamp, Meredith A. 2006. "College, Jobs, or the Military? Enlistment During a
Time of War." *Social Science Quarterly* 87 (2): 272–290.

Mahmoud, Mona, Maggie O'Kane, and Ian Black. 2007. "UK Has Left Behind
Murder and Chaos, Says Basra Police Chief." *Guardian*, December 17.
www.guardian.co.uk/Iraq/Story/0,,2228690,00.html.

McElroy, Damien. 2007. "Moqtada al-Sadr Announces Ceasefire in Iraq." *Tele-
graph*, August 31. www.telegraph.co.uk/news/main.jhtml?xml=/news/2007/
08/30/wiraq130.xml.

Merle, Renae. 2006. "Census Counts 100,000 Contractors in Iraq." *Washington
Post*, December 5. www.washingtonpost.com.

Miller, T. Christian. 2005. "Soldier's Journey Ends in Anguish." *Boston Globe*, December 4. www.boston.com.

————. 2006. *Blood Money*. New York: Little, Brown and Company.

————. 2007. "Private Contractors Outnumber US Troops in Iraq." *Los Angeles Times*, July 4. www.latimes.com.

Morgan, Matthew J. 2001. "Army Recruiting and the Civil-Military Gap." *Parameters, US Army War College Quarterly* (Summer): 101–117.

Myers, Steven Lee. 2008. "A Loosely Drawn American Victory." *New York Times*, November 29. www.nytimes.com.

Naegele, Tobias. 2007. "Positive Outlook—Poll: Despite Misgivings, Troops Optimistic on Iraq." www.militarycity.com/polls/2007_main.php.

Nagl, John A. 2002. *Learning to Eat Soup with a Knife: Counterinsurgency Lessons from Malaya and Vietnam*. Chicago: University of Chicago Press.

Nullis, Clare. 2006. "South African Assembly OKs Mercenary Bill." *News and Observer*, August 29. www.zimbabwesituation.com/aug30_2006.html#Z10.

PBS. 2005. "Private Warriors." *Frontline*. www.pbs.org/wgbh/pages/frontline/shows/warriors/view (accessed January 15, 2008).

Pelton, Robert Young. 2006. *Licensed to Kill: Hired Guns in the War on Terror*. New York: Three Rivers Press.

Petraeus, David Howell. 1987. *The American Military and the Lessons Of Vietnam: A Study of Military Influence and the Use of Force in the Post-Vietnam Era*. Ann Arbor, MI: UMI.

Petraeus, David H., and James F. Amos. 2006 (December). *Counterinsurgency*. Army Field Manual No. 3–24; Marine Corps Warfighting Publication No. 3–33.5, December. Washington, DC: Department of the Army.

Raghavan, Sudarsan, and Saad Sarhan. 2008. "Top Shiite Cleric in Iraq Raises Concerns About Security Pact." *Washington Post*, November 30. www.washingtonpost.com.

Rand Corporation. 2001. *Rand Research Brief: What Affects Decisions to Enlist in the Military*. Santa Monica, CA: Rand Corporation.

Reuters. 2006. "Iraqi Detainee Abuse Widespread: Report." *New York Times*, July 23. www.nytimes.com.

————. 2007. "Not All Troops Would Report Abuse, Study Says." *New York Times*, May 5. www.nytimes.com.

Ricks, Thomas E. 2006. *Fiasco: The American Military Adventure in Iraq*. New York: Penguin Press.

Risen, James. 2008. "2005 Use of Gas by Blackwater Leaves Questions." *New York Times*, January 10. www.nytimes.com.

Rohde, David. 2007. "Army Enlists Anthropology in War Zones." *New York Times*, October 5. www.nytimes.com.

Rubin, Alissa J., and Damien Cave. 2007. "In a Force for Iraqi Calm, Seeds of Conflict." *New York Times*, December 23. www.nytimes.com/2007/12/23/world/middleeast/23awakening.html.

Rubin, Alissa J., and Andrew E. Kramer. 2007. "Maliki Accuses Blackwater of Challenging Iraq's Sovereignty." *New York Times*, September 24. www.nytimes.com.

Sallinger, Rick. 2006. "CBS4 Investigates Army Recruits' 'Moral Waivers.'" November 20. http://cbs4denver.com/seenon/Colorado.News.Denver.2.554096.html.

Scahill, Jeremy. 2007. *Blackwater: The Rise of the World's Most Powerful Merce- nary Army*. New York: Nation Books.

Schmitt, Eric, and David Rohde. 2007. "Reports Assail State Department on Iraq Security." *New York Times*, October 23. www.nytimes.com.

Schmitt, Eric, and Ginger Thompson. 2007. "Broken Supply Channel Sent Arms for Iraq Astray." *New York Times*, November 11.

Shachtman, Noah. 2007. "Iraq's Biometric Database Could Become 'Hit List.'" *Wired*. http://blog.wired.com/defense/2007/08/also-two-thirds.html.

Singer, P. W. 2008. *Corporate Warriors: The Rise of the Privatized Military Industry* (updated edition). Ithaca, NY: Cornell University Press.

Stock, Margaret D. 2006. "Essential to the Fight: Immigrants in the Military, Five Years After 9/11." *Immigration Policy In Focus 5* (November). Washington, DC: American Immigration Law Foundation. www.immigrationline.org/ research.asp?pubid=967.

Thompson, Ginger, and Eric Schmitt. 2007. "Graft in Military Contracts Spread From Base." *New York Times*, September 24.

Thompson, Mark. 2007. "America's Broken-Down Army." *Time*, April 5. www .time.com/time/printout/0,8816,1606888,00.html.

United Nations. 2003. Security Council Resolution 1483. May 22. www.un.org/ Docs/journal/asp/ws.asp?m=s/res/1483(2003).

United Nations. 2007. Security Council Resolution 1790. December 18. www .iamb.info/pdf/unscr1790.pdf.

United States Department of Defense. 2006. "Recruitment Quality Over Time as Percent of Annual NPS (Non-Prior Service) Accessions." www.defense link.mil/prhome/docs/page.html (accessed September 2, 2008).

———. 2008. "DoD Announces Recruiting and Retention Numbers for FY 2007." www.defenselink.mil/releases.aspx?releaseid=11398.

Vanden Brook, Tom, and Blake Morrison. 2007. "Troop Patrols—Not Technology— Help Revive War-Torn Neighborhoods." *USA Today*, December 8. www .usatoday.com/news/military/2007-12-18-ied-side_N.htm.

West, Bing. 2008. *The Strongest Tribe*. New York: Random House.

White House. 2008. "Agreement Between the United States of America and the Re- public of Iraq on the Withdrawal of United States Forces from Iraq and the Organization of Their Activities During Their Temporary Presence in Iraq." November 17. http://georgewbush-whitehouse.archives.gov/news/releases/ 2008/11/print/20081127-2.html.

Williams, Kristian. 2007. "Counterinsurgency 101." *In These Times*, March 5. www.inthesetimes.com/article/3056/counterinsurgency_101.

Winkler, John. D. 1993. "Potential Effects on Military Recruitment and Retention." In National Defense Research Institute, *Sexual Orientation and US Military Personnel Policy: Options and Assessment*, 395–407. Santa Monica, CA: Rand Corporation.

Witte, Griff. 2007. "New Law Could Subject Civilians to Military Trial." *Washing- ton Post*, January 15. www.washingtonpost.com.

Yon, Michael. 2008. *Moment of Truth in Iraq*. Minneapolis, MN: Richard Vigi- lante Books.

10

||||||||||||||||||||||||||||||||||||||||||||||||||||||||||||||||||||||||||||||||||||||||||||||||||||

Impacts
of the
Iraq War

The Iraq War had profound impacts not only on Iraq, but on many other countries as well. Iraq's Kurdish region became a de facto independent state, and much of the rest of the country experienced a resistance insurgency, counterinsurgent military actions, and sectarian violence. The invasion was widely viewed as increasing motivation for terrorism. Minimum estimates indicated that many tens of thousands of Iraqis were killed and millions forced to leave their homes. Fighting the war diverted US resources from Afghanistan, where the Taliban and Al Qaeda reorganized.

The war also took the lives of thousands of American soldiers and wounded many more. Total economic cost, both direct and indirect, was estimated to be between $1 trillion and $3 trillion and may have exacerbated the US economic crisis that began in the fall of 2008. On the other hand, the war appeared to give the US government dominance over Iraqi energy resources and a potentially tremendous advantage relative to economic rivals. The decline in public support for the war after 2004 contributed to Democratic victory in the 2006 congressional elections and played a role in the 2008 presidential campaign and election. Election-day exit polls showed that the vast majority of those opposed to the war voted for Barack Obama. Internationally, the invasion and occupation severely damaged the moral status of the United States worldwide.

The American people confronted a range of issues including how to end the war, regain the world's trust, and more effectively combat terrorism. War advocates believed that American forces should remain in Iraq as long as necessary to defeat insurgents and terrorists and ensure the stability of Iraq's new government. Opponents of the war disagreed among themselves regarding whether some US forces should continue a long-term presence in Iraq. Central questions regarding Iraq's future included whether or to what degree Iraq should remain a unified country, and whether it or its successor states could be fully democratic and sovereign.

Impacts on Iraq

The invasion removed a brutal regime, freeing Iraq from a personality cult reflected in numerous statues and public portraits of the leader, and from a one-party political system that stressed Arab identity for a nation that in reality was multiethnic. In addition, economic sanctions against Iraq that had been in effect since the 1991 Gulf War were removed.

Loss of Life, Sectarian Violence, and Refugees

An estimated 7,000 to 20,000 Iraqi soldiers and paramilitary fighters died between March 20 and May 1, 2003, resisting coalition forces. Occupation authorities claimed an additional 19,000 Iraqi insurgents were killed by the end of September 2007. Estimates of civilian deaths from the invasion, insurgent and counterinsurgent actions, and sectarian violence varied widely from a minimum of 78,000 through the end of October 2007 to well over half a million (Parsons 2006).

The invasion led to sectarian violence, resulting in many thousands of Iraqis fleeing their homes to live among coreligionists in segregated neighborhoods. By September 2007 the Iraqi Red Crescent humanitarian organization indicated that in Baghdad alone almost 1 million people had relocated (Glanz and Rubin 2007). The total internal displacement was about 2.3 million in 2008 (Damon 2008). In addition, as many as 2 million left Iraq for other countries, mainly Syria and Jordan. The United States and the UN seemed slow to address the hardships refugees faced and the burdens endured by the nations where they took refuge (Libal and Harding 2007).

The exodus significantly reduced the country's middle class. The scope of the problem was reflected in Cave's (2007) interviews with more than thirty students from seven universities among Iraq's 2007 college graduates. All but four planned to leave the country immediately after graduation. Like other members of the middle class, they were at first hopeful that the Americans would bring democracy to Iraq and help it modernize. But hope gave way to despair, fear, growing hostility toward the occupiers, and distress that fundamentalism was enveloping Iraq. American mistakes were seen as leading to the highest level of sectarian violence and terrorism in Iraq's history, including the murder of over two hundred college professors and the emigration of many more.

Syria, a country of only 19 million, became the destination of about 1.2 million Iraqi refugees. Refugee families were often female-headed because husbands or brothers had been killed. Poverty forced thousands of young Iraqi women to turn to prostitution to support their mothers and siblings or their own children, attracting sex tourists from wealthy Middle Eastern countries, such as Saudi Arabia (Zoepf 2007).

Women's Rights

Another consequence of the Iraq War appeared to be reduced freedoms of secularly oriented women. CNN correspondent Arwa Damon (2008) observes that "a lot of women in Iraq will say this was a war that was meant to bring democracy. It was meant to bring freedom. It was meant to bring a better life and in fact, the bitter irony is that it brought exactly the opposite." She reports that prostitution was on the rise as desperate women attempted to care for their children. Yanar Mohammed of the Organization of Women's Freedom in Iraq noted that every woman in the streets was now veiled.

Family law was turned over to religious courts. A number of female activists or women considered immoral were murdered, and criminal justice authorities seemed unwilling or powerless to punish the perpetrators. Banning female police officers from carrying guns threatened to reduce the number of policewomen, making the investigation and punishment of rape and spousal abuse much more difficult (Susman 2007). The spread of conservative religious culture appeared to fatally undermine the constitutional ban against gender discrimination. Galbraith (2008: 6) describes some Shia areas of southern Iraq where girls do not attend school and where violation of clothing or conduct norms can result in death, resembling Afghanistan under the Taliban.

The imposition of fundamentalist views, along with sectarian violence, led many young Iraqis, both Shia and Sunni, to turn away from clerics and even from religion (Tavernise 2008). Although after the invasion there was a flood of support for Shia political-religious parties, many later said that when they voted for them in 2005, they were voting to affirm the identity and new political power of Shia Iraqis, not to support the domination of religion over society.

Children

Apart from children killed through coalition military action and those who perished in suicide bombings, hundreds of thousands suffered because only 30 percent of Iraqis had access to clean drinking water and because of the decline in medical care when many doctors were murdered or fled the country. The danger of being killed in fighting or bombings prevented many parents from bringing their children to hospitals or clinics, resulting in a decline in rates of immunization vaccinations (MacInnis 2007). Threats to security caused schools to close periodically and interfered with attendance when they were open. Children were also refugees, making up about half of Iraqis who had fled their homes since the invasion. UNICEF research indicated that only 28 percent of Iraqi seventeen-year-olds were able to take school leaving exams in 2007 and that only 40 percent received a passing grade in central or southern Iraq (*Times of India* 2007). The number of Iraqi primary school–age children not in school was estimated at more than 760,000 in 2007.

Many children were psychologically traumatized from the loss of loved ones or friends and/or from witnessing violence. Parents, doctors, and teachers described children suffering from nightmares or social withdrawal, or acting violently (Howard 2007). Children feared explosions or becoming kidnap victims to force their parents to pay ransom. Few were able to receive psychological counseling to help recover from trauma (MacInnis 2007). The Association of Iraqi Psychologists noted that violence was impacting millions of Iraqi children, raising fears that without treatment and adequate emotional support, many would develop personality disorders and/or become violence-prone adults (Howard 2007).

In 2008, captured videos showed young boys apparently being trained by Al Qaeda to carry out assassinations and kidnappings (Howard 2007), and criminals began using juveniles to commit murders. Nine hundred juveniles were in American detention in November 2007, a more than sevenfold increase since April (Tavernise 2008). Iraq's main prison for youth in Baghdad had about triple the number of prewar prisoners.

Government and Sovereignty

The invasion led to a new constitution that supported democracy but stated that laws could not violate Islamic principles. Apart from the potential contradictions this might cause, the fact that the country was under foreign military occupation, and that the Baath Party was not allowed to participate in elections left the designation of Iraq as a democracy open to question. Nevertheless, in December 2005 many political parties participated in a parliamentary election and in 2009 in provincial elections.

Despite the official restoration of Iraqi sovereignty in 2004, it was apparent that Iraq enjoyed nothing comparable to the level of sovereignty that it had before the 1991 Gulf War. The Iraqi government seemed to lack even the power to ban the PMF Blackwater from operating on its territory after the Nisour Square killings in September 2007.

Kurds

The invasion preserved the autonomy of the Kurdish region, and relative political stability brought economic development. Instead of losing skilled professionals and technicians, the Kurdish region saw a significant number of those fleeing the rest of Iraq, such as many Christians, seeking refuge there. The possibility of a future independent Kurdish state encouraged Kurdish rebels in Turkey and Iran. Galbraith (2008) states that the Kurdish region is the most democratic part of Iraq but that the majority of its people really favor becoming an independent nation. Of all Iraqis, the Kurds appear to have the most favorable orientation toward the United States. According to Galbraith, the Kurdish government offered the US military bases on Kurdish territory, which in part could serve to deter intervention from neighboring countries.

The War on Terrorism

Postinvasion investigations found no Iraqi assistance to Al Qaeda or role in 9/11. The invasion in which the United States retaliated for the loss of some 3,000 of its citizens by launching a war that took the lives of tens of thousands in a country that played no role in the attack on America appeared, not surprisingly, to increase terrorism. It led to the establishment of a major Al Qaeda network in Iraq, which carried out attacks on coalition forces and mass bombings that killed thousands of civilians. Iraq became a major training ground for a new generation of terrorists and a historic cause that could motivate attacks on Americans for many years to come. The invasion, which many Iraqis viewed as unprovoked aggression costing the lives of friends, relatives, and soldiers defending their country, created strong reasons for Iraqis to kill Americans and delivered numerous targets in the form of US military personnel. The occupation also led to an unprecedented level of sectarian terrorist violence, including the deaths of thousands by Shia or Sunni death squads.

Critics asked whether Bush administration policies were actually prolonging the war on terrorism. Failing to address the conditions and/or correct the policies that gave rise to motivations for terrorism could not but result in providing recruits for terrorist groups. But continuing the war on terrorism could serve the function that the post–World War II Cold War did in providing an excuse for US governments to intimidate other nations or interfere in their affairs. Defense against terrorist attacks, then, would rely not on alleviating the circumstances that gave rise to terrorists, but on improving the means to deter or destroy them and taking advantage of the ongoing war on terrorism to achieve domestic and international political goals.

Neglecting Afghanistan

Developments in Afghanistan raised further doubts about the Iraq War. The Afghan military campaign in late 2001 had driven many Al Qaeda and Taliban leaders across the border into Pakistan. Some American officials believed the Taliban had been so devastated that it could not recover (Rohde and Sanger 2007). In reality, while US forces strained to contain the situation in Iraq, the Taliban regrouped, grew stronger, and launched counterattacks (Barfield 2008). The US invasion of Iraq appeared to benefit both the Taliban and Al Qaeda, and the top Al Qaeda leaders remained free. It's likely that the invasion of Iraq under false justifications increased the motivation of many Afghans, Pakistanis, and others to fight Americans in Afghanistan, where conditions for resistance fighters were more favorable than in Iraq. In other words, the war in Iraq probably shifted in part to the mountains of Afghanistan.

The US reconstruction plan for Afghanistan was impeded as the war in Iraq diverted resources (Rashid 2007). New Predator remote-controlled surveillance planes with Hellfire missiles, which some considered effective weapons in Afghan mountains, were often sent to Iraq instead. While social needs in Afghanistan were inadequately addressed, Taliban activity increased. US officials there complained that Iraq was depriving their antiterrorism effort not only of sufficient Predators, but also of badly needed Special Operations Forces units. In 2006, suicide bombings in Afghanistan, often carried out by pro-Taliban Pakistanis, quintupled to 136, while roadside bombings doubled and casualty rates among US and NATO troops increased significantly. The heightened violence caused hundreds of schools to shut down (Rashid 2007). Some US allies were reluctant to commit more troops to Afghanistan while American forces were, in their view, involved in a mistaken enterprise in Iraq (Barfield 2008).

President George W. Bush stated that the United States had about 31,000 troops in Afghanistan in September 2008, while coalition forces including NATO had another 31,000 (White House 2008). As of early 2009, President Obama reportedly intended to send as many as 30,000 additional US soldiers to Afghanistan (DeYoung 2009).

Risen (2006: 153, 154, 157) states that after 9/11 the Bush administration did not seem greatly concerned about Afghan opium production, that the Pentagon worried that anti-opium efforts would force the US military to turn against Afghan warlords who were assisting them, and that US soldiers were instructed they "could" destroy drugs they discovered rather than being ordered that they "must" destroy them. Despite what was described as a $600 million US counternarcotics program, Afghanistan broke opium production records for two years in a row, producing an estimated 92 percent of the world supply of opium poppies (Rohde 2007). (Poppy prices were about ten times higher than for comparable amounts of wheat.) Both the Taliban and a number of Afghan officials were reportedly benefiting from opium revenue.

Impacts on the United States

War Justification and International Relations

In the end, the invasion justification was prevention. US forces were sent into action not to respond to an attack on America, or to defend an ally from aggression, or to protect the imminently threatened lives of US citizens, or even to demolish forces poised to attack the United States. Instead, when most other justifications proved false, the Baathist regime was defined as so hostile toward the United States and its allies that it was justifiable to destroy it because it might obtain the capability to become a threat in the future. It was this preventive-war Bush Doctrine that much of the world considered so dangerous because in theory its acceptance meant that either any nation in the world could employ it, leading to the outbreak of many wars, or that, as was surely the Bush administration's intention, preventive war would be solely a US prerogative, a manifestation of American exceptionalism (the belief that America's values and economic, social, and political systems were superior to those of other nations, providing the United States a unique God-given right to promote them around the world) (Unger 2007: 13, 15–34, 38).

The Iraq War also provided an object lesson of the new polarized international framework that President Bush had proclaimed on September 20, 2001, nine days after the Al Qaeda attacks. Reminiscent of the most intolerant periods of the Cold War, he warned that other nations had to choose either to be with us against terrorism or to be considered allied with the terrorists and eligible for American retribution. Furthermore, terrorists were portrayed as evil in essence, attacking America because of their desire to destroy its most cherished qualities, freedom and the democratic way of life. Therefore, terrorists could not be reasoned with or dissuaded by a change of US policy. The only option was to capture or destroy them.

Economic Costs

The Iraq War had varying economic effects on different groups of Americans. The US companies that received reconstruction or service contracts generally profited handsomely, as did thousands of US citizens who traveled to Iraq to work as contracted engineers, truck drivers, security personnel, or in other capacities. But the US population as a whole had to bear an enormous financial burden. By March 2008, the Iraq War had cost about $500 billion in direct spending, ten times the original estimate (CRS 2008; Lindsey 2008). The February 8, 2008, Congressional Research Service Report provided different projections of the costs of continued military operations depending on how many US troops were still committed to Iraq after fiscal year 2008. Estimates also varied because of differences among economists in the range of factors included under indirect costs, such as veterans' benefits, the ongoing expenses of treating the physical or psychological injuries of soldiers, and the billions that must be spent replacing military hardware. Also, some economists did not adjust for what the costs would have been for continuing the prewar containment deployments and operations. Leonhardt in January 2007 calculated that the war would cost $1.2 trillion (Leonhardt 2007). But in March 2008, Stiglitz and Bilmes (2008) estimated that it would cost $3 trillion.

The direct cost of the Iraq War was increasingly viewed as a major cause of the deterioration of the US economy. Because of Bush administration tax cuts that lowered revenue, the rise in fuel prices, and other increased expenses, the government borrowed to finance the war. Politicians debated whether the war would result in neglecting repairs to US infrastructure, or health care reform, or the need to invest in alternative energy sources, especially after massive mortgage losses created instability in major financial institutions (Andrews 2008). There was also concern that the cost of the war contributed to the economic crisis that began in the fall of 2008 that prompted the US government to try to bail out financial institutions with an infusion of hundreds of billions of dollars (Herszenhorn 2008; Landler 2008).

Control of Oil

Regardless of losses in US and Iraqi lives and hundreds of billions spent in fighting the war, the long-range benefits of the US conquest of Iraq might be viewed by some war supporters as significantly outweighing the costs. Increasing Iraqi oil production could help supply keep pace with growing demand. Control of Iraq was seen as enhancing US domination of the Middle East's estimated 61.5 percent of the world's known oil reserves. Through securing Middle Eastern nations as markets for American products and services, the United States could ensure its economic advantage over other oil-consuming nations. It was this strategic result that many war supporters almost certainly anticipated when pushing for the invasion. The war also allowed a redeployment of many US troops from Saudi Arabia to Iraq, lessening a potentially destabilizing problem for the Saudi royal family.

US Domestic Politics

Public opinion surveys indicated that in the wake of 9/11 a large majority of Americans, receptive to false stories that Iraq played a role in the terrorist attacks and continued to possess WMD, approved of the invasion. This public support facilitated the occupation and ongoing war, which in turn created new circumstances, such as sectarian violence and the onset of terrorist activity in Iraq, that fostered new rationales for continuing the conflict and preventing the withdrawal of US forces, regardless of changes in public attitudes regarding the war or government leadership.

US public opinion shifted quickly after no WMD were found, nor an Iraqi role in the 9/11 attacks, and the Iraqi resistance insurgency resulted in ongoing casualties for US forces. US Gallup polls (Gallup 2008a) indicated that when asked whether the US action in Iraq was "morally justified," 73 percent answered yes during March 29–30, 2003, but only 47 percent during March 10–12, 2006. In addition, while only 31 percent in June 2003 believed that the "Bush administration deliberately misled the American public about whether Iraq has weapons of mass destruction," that figure had risen to 51 percent in March 2006. These shifts played a major role in the November 2006 congressional elections, in which Democrats took control of the House of Representatives and achieved a majority in the US Senate (CNN 2007). National polls showed that in the last few months of 2005 the number saying that sending troops to Iraq was a mistake moved above 50 percent and later during 2007 and 2008 climbed to 55 percent to 60 percent (Jones 2008). The January 30–February 2, 2008, *USA Today*/Gallup poll showed that among liberal Democrats, 91 percent believed sending troops to Iraq was a mistake, moderate Democrats 81 percent, and conservative Democrats 74 percent, while 40 percent of moderate Republicans and only 20 percent of conservative Republicans believed it was a mistake. Among self-described independents, 53 percent believed it was a mistake while 40 percent did not.

Political candidates, however, had to take into account that 65 percent of those surveyed in a February 21–24, 2008, Gallup poll responded that the United States "has an obligation to remain in Iraq until a reasonable level of stability and security has been reached" (Newport 2008).

The Iraq War impacted the 2008 presidential campaign as well. Barack Obama's opposition to the war helped him defeat his main opponent for the Democratic nomination, Hillary Clinton, who had voted for Bush's war authorization bill. However, the Republican nominee, John McCain, seemed to benefit politically from his early support for the 2007 surge in US troop strength that Obama and many others opposed. By the 2008 nominating conventions, many observers believed that the surge, in combination with other factors, had played a significant role in reducing violence and casualties in Iraq. But it was unclear how much of the reduction in violence was due to underlying changes in social and political conditions in Iraq versus simply a deterrence effect of increased US counterinsurgency capabilities. General David Petraeus cautioned against removing significant numbers of US troops from Iraq too quickly because gains in security in Iraq were "not durable yet. It's not self-sustaining" (Filkins 2008).

Discontent over the Iraq War appeared to play a role in voters' delivering a devastating blow to the Republican Party in the 2008 election. The Democrats expanded their majority from 51 to 59 seats in the Senate and extended their dominance in the House of Representatives by 21 seats so that the resulting composition was 257 Democrats and 178 Republicans (*New York Times* 2008). Obama, who had opposed the Iraq War from before it was launched, won the presidency with 53 percent of the popular vote and 365 electoral votes to 46 percent and 173 electoral votes for prowar candidate McCain (CNN Election Center 2008, President 2008b). Election-day exit polls of 17,836 voters indicated that 63 percent opposed the Iraq War, and of those stating they opposed the war, 76 percent voted for Obama (CNN Election Center 2008, Exit Polls 2008a; Todd and Gawiser 2009: 39–40). The cost of the Iraq War in American lives appeared to influence the presidential vote. DeFronzo and Gill (2009) show that, controlling for other factors that affected voter choice, the number of state military fatalities per 100,000 state residents tended to independently increase the percent of the vote Obama received in a state over the percent received by the Democrats' 2004 presidential candidate, Senator John Kerry of Massachusetts. Obama had proposed steadily withdrawing US combat brigades from Iraq so the last would potentially leave around May 2010, but did not set a date for the withdrawal of all US forces (Rubin and Robertson 2008). Since the 2008 Status of Forces Agreement between Iraq and the United States permitted either nation to end the US military presence within one year of providing the other country a written notice to that effect, some hoped that President Obama would withdraw all US troops well before the SOFA deadline of December 31, 2011.

However, when President Obama gave a major speech on Iraq at the US Marine base at Camp Lejeune, North Carolina, on February 27, 2009, he did not announce a rapid withdrawal of US forces from Iraq. Instead he stated that "by August 31, 2010, our combat mission in Iraq will end" (Lalate 2009). And he said that after US combat brigades were withdrawn there would still be "a transitional American force" with an initial size of about 35,000 to 50,000 soldiers supporting the Iraqi government and its armed forces and carrying out three tasks: "training, equipping, and advising Iraqi Security Forces as long as they remain non-sectarian; conducting targeted counter-terrorism missions; and protecting our ongoing civilian and military efforts within Iraq." Obama continued by declaring that all US troops would be removed from Iraq by the end of 2011, in line with SOFA. Not surprisingly, some of those who opposed the Iraq War viewed his speech as describing a prolonged stay in Iraq more than a convincing plan for withdrawal.

Apart from its effects on elections, the invasion of Iraq provided a basis for appraising claims that Iran constituted a threat to the United States and its allies. Members of Congress seemed more wary of scare narratives and rationales for war against Iran than they had been in the case of Iraq.

News Media

The Iraq War also damaged the credibility of the US news media. Most major news personnel seemed to fall into step with the Bush administration's march to war. News programs were flooded with retired military officers providing often prowar commentary in place of critical news analysis. "Myth and misinformation went unchallenged," according to Jeff Cohen (2006), formerly of MSNBC, as former generals and colonels often expressed their views on-air unopposed. The forms of slanted or uncritical reporting included providing a national forum for prowar politicians, neoconservative officials and advisers, and Iraqi exiles. News agencies varied in how quickly they recovered from their prowar euphoria to return to a semblance of journalistic integrity.

Impact on the US Military

The most direct impact of the war on the US military was the number of soldiers killed or wounded. By January 31, 2009, 4,236 US military personnel had died in Iraq and more than 30,000 had been wounded (icasualties.org 2009). Of those killed by the end of 2007, 145 (118 army, 23 marines, and 4 navy) had taken their own lives. The overall army suicide rate rose from about 10 per 100,000 in 2002 to almost 19 per 100,000 in 2007 (Pessin 2008). The army suicide rate for 2008 was even higher at over 20 per 100,000 soldiers (CBS News 2009). Many returned from Iraq with emotional difficulties such as post-traumatic stress syndrome (Frosch 2007; Hodge et al. 2004), and veterans with either physical or mental injuries and their families often faced difficulties obtaining adequate treatment (Sontag and Alvarez 2007; Urbina and Nixon 2007).

The lengthy resistance insurgency forced the US military to shift toward General Petraeus's counterinsurgency approach, deploy many National Guard and reserve units, and rely more heavily than ever on help from PMFs. To maintain adequate enlistment levels, financial incentives, educational and moral waivers, and age limits for enlistees were increased. In exchange for military service, the path to citizenship was eased for immigrants. Like the general population, the support of military personnel for the war declined after 2004, although not to the same extent.

The Antiwar Movement

The Iraq War, like the Vietnam War, provoked an antiwar movement. But, due to several factors, it was less militant. One was the lower levels of civilian and military casualties in Iraq. Another was the relatively rapid shift of the majority of the US population to an antiwar view regarding the Iraq War compared with Vietnam. Also, the United States' reliance on a volunteer military force for the Iraq War, augmented by PMFs, meant that young people did not fear being drafted to serve in a war they opposed. The Iraq antiwar movement could campaign to get the largely antiwar Democrats elected to Congress and the presidency, which was conceivably a more efficient way to end the war than staging demonstrations (Luo 2007). As was the case with the Vietnam antiwar movement, some former soldiers formed their own antiwar organizations including Iraq Veterans Against the War and Veterans Against the Iraq War (IVAW 2008; Shane 2008; VAIW 2008).

International Political Developments

World Opinion

The Iraq War severely damaged US moral standing internationally as have few events in history. The majority of people in many countries appeared to believe the Bush administration had taken advantage of 9/11 to invade Iraq mainly to seize its oil. The invasion seemed to show that the US government would falsify evidence to justify going to war against a nation with valuable resources and act without UN consent, behavior for which other nations were punished. In the relatively moderate Islamic state of Turkey, for example, public approval of the United States declined drastically from 60 percent in 2000 to just 9 percent in 2007 (Galbraith 2008: 9).

United Nations

The Iraq War demonstrated the weakness of the UN in the face of the world's only superpower. The Bush administration was able to bypass the UN Security Council with ease once it was clear that the council would not approve the invasion. Secretary-General Kofi Annan denied that any nation had the legal right to invade and occupy Iraq without specific UN approval. But once Iraq was occupied, the UN attempted to ensure, through Resolution 1472, that "those causing the war should meet the humanitarian needs of the civilian population," including "food and medical supplies" (United Nations 2003a). But then Resolution 1483 recognized the authority of the United States and the UK to govern Iraq, sell its oil, and use the resulting revenue. However noble the UN's intentions, this resolution made it appear that the UN was hypocritically reversing itself and approving an invasion most members had considered illegal.

Effect on Nuclear Programs in Other Countries

Lindsey (2008) and Suskind (2008: 382) suggest that the invasion deterred Libya and possibly Iran from attempting to develop nuclear weapons. Shortly after the invasion, Libya abandoned its nuclear weapons program voluntarily. Furthermore, the US National Intelligence Estimate in December 2007 indicated that Iran had likely suspended a nuclear weapons program in 2003.

On the other hand, North Korea, which President Bush had categorized with Iraq as part of the so-called axis of evil in his January 29, 2002, State of the Union address, probably decided to construct and detonate its own nuclear weapon on October 9, 2006 (Sanger 2006), in part to deter the United States from invading it.

Developments in Other Countries

Regional

With the destruction of Saddam Hussein's government, Israel was freed from a once significant threat as well as a government that had provided support to the

Palestinian Arabs. On the other hand, outrage among most Arabs and Muslims over the invasion, which was widely believed to be due in part to the efforts of the Israelis, contributed to other developments: the increased strength of the militant Hamas Sunni Islamist movement among Palestinians and the Shia Hezbollah movement in Lebanon. In the January 2006 Palestinian elections Hamas won control of the Palestinian parliament and, specifically, of Gaza. In July violent conflict broke out between Hezbollah and Israel. Hezbollah launched hundreds of rockets against Israel and destroyed or badly damaged a number of Israeli tanks, killing about 150 Israelis, mainly soldiers. Invading Israeli forces and aircraft killed hundreds of Hezbollah fighters and Lebanese civilians and destroyed much of Lebanon's infrastructure before the conflict ended and Israeli forces withdrew.

Syria, Jordan, and Saudi Arabia all opposed the invasion of Iraq but were affected in different ways. Syria and Jordan endured the immense burdens of hundreds of thousands of Iraqi refugees. Saudi Arabia, while antagonistic to Saddam's regime, feared that its removal could open the door for an Iranian takeover of Iraq's largely Shia-populated, oil-rich south, and many Saudis reportedly contributed funds to Sunni insurgents.

Iran, although it had suffered greatly during the Iran–Iraq War, which it blamed on Saddam's government, opposed the US-led invasion of Iraq. Since Bush had included Iran as a member of the "axis of evil," many Iranians feared that once US troops and military bases were in place in Iraq, Iran could be the next target for a US invasion. The invasion and Bush's verbal assaults undermined Iran's moderate political movement and contributed to the election of the more fundamentalist-oriented Mahmoud Ahmadinejad as president in 2005 (Baktiari 2007). The occupation, though, allowed the Iranian-aided SCIRI and Dawa Shia Iraqi parties, many of whose leaders had resided in Iran before the invasion, to play major roles in the new Iraqi government, and in the view of some observers this constituted a "strategic victory" for Iran (Galbraith 2008: 67).

The World

Conservative governments in Spain, Italy, and Australia that supported the invasion and contributed troops to the occupation were voted out of power. In other countries pro-Bush conservative parties and candidates suffered losses likely in part because of what many of their citizens considered US aggression against Iraq. Leftist or moderate leftist presidents critical of the US-led invasion were elected or reelected in nine of the eleven Latin American countries holding national elections between December 2005 and December 2006 (Castañeda and Navia 2007). Then in October 2007, the left-leaning Cristina Kirchner was elected president of Argentina (Schamis 2008). BBC polls of adults in Chile and Brazil, conducted between May 29 and July 26, 2007, showed that 72 percent and 70 percent, respectively, wanted US forces withdrawn from Iraq immediately or within one year (BBC World Service Poll 2007). In Mexico, the third Latin American country the BBC surveyed, a total of 78 percent wanted US forces withdrawn, either immediately (68 percent) or within one year (10 percent). The entire BBC World Service Poll involved interviewing about 23,000 people, constituting national samples of the adult populations of twenty-two nations in North America, Latin America, Europe, the Middle East, Africa, and Asia. For all twenty-two nations, an average of 67 percent of the respondents wanted US troops withdrawn from Iraq either immediately (39 percent) or according to a one-year timetable (28 percent). Twenty-three percent responded that US troops should "remain until security improves." The remaining 10 percent gave other answers or responded "don't know." Although in the United States 61 percent supported withdrawal of US troops immediately or within one year, the average was about 70 percent for the European countries in the study, and 72 percent and 76 percent for Russia and China, respectively. In Islamic countries surveyed, the corresponding percentages were 79 percent in Turkey, 81 percent in Indonesia, and 93 percent in Egypt. Even 52 percent of Israelis responded that US forces should leave Iraq either immediately or within a year. The enormous level of international popular objection to continued US occupation of Iraq indicated that the war had seriously damaged what moral leadership the United States had enjoyed before the invasion, and that most people in the countries surveyed would tend to support indigenous governments that opposed America's military presence in Iraq.

In addition, since the UN seemed to, in effect, consent after the fact to the US-led seizure of Iraq, the Russian government apparently concluded that it could get away with defying the organization in nearby Georgia. Following Georgia's attack on one of its pro-Russian provinces, South Ossetia, in an attempt to crush separatists, Russia responded with a massive military intervention. Then it recognized the independence of both South Ossetia and another part of Georgia, Abkhazia, in August 2008 (Levy 2008).

Plans for Dealing with the War

Varying plans for ending the Iraq War and overcoming or reversing some of its negative effects were put forward during the 2008 US presidential campaign. Major Republican politicians, such as John McCain, proposed that there should be no timetable for US troop withdrawal and that American forces should continue to be involved in Iraq as long as necessary to defeat insurgents and Islamic extremists. McCain believed that there was no sound alternative to the Bush administration's military effort in Iraq and defended the 2007 surge in US troop strength (Gordon and Nagourney 2007). He stated that beating back Democrat demands for a deadline for US troop withdrawal from Iraq was a crucial historic event and that he would steadfastly resist any effort to, in his view, prematurely end the war (FOXNews.com 2008). He anticipated the continued presence of US troops in Iraq for possibly many years.

In contrast, Democrats proposed beginning significant troop withdrawals to force Iraqi political factions to make crucial political agreements that would bring about national reconciliation. Then the United States could devote more resources to hunting down the terrorists who had attacked the United States on 9/11. Barack Obama (Obama 2008) asserted that the Iraq War should never have taken place. He proposed to begin removing US combat brigades from Iraq, refocus on going after the Taliban and Al Qaeda in Afghanistan, increase

US foreign aid to drastically reduce extreme poverty around the world, invest in technological change to lessen US dependence on foreign oil, and attempt to deal with international issues by more readily negotiating with America's adversaries.

Hillary Clinton supported a bigger role for the UN in Iraq, providing aid more directly to the Iraqi people, and dealing with the needs of refugees (White 2007). Joe Biden proposed a "soft partition" of Iraq into three autonomous federal territories, with the Kurdish region in the north, a large Shia Arab–dominated area in the south, and a central area where Sunni Arabs would be the dominant population group, similar to a plan developed at the Saban Center of the Brookings Institution (Biden 2006; Joseph and O'Hanlon 2007). These plans seemed to assume that once each major group had its own designated territory within which it could feel secure, sectarian and ethnic conflict would decline significantly. Biden's plan stated that each autonomous region would have its own government in charge of education and other services, and its own security forces, but the central government would control border defense, foreign policy, and oil production and revenues. US troops would be "responsibly" gradually withdrawn, leaving a smaller force of maybe 20,000 in or near Iraq to fight "terrorists," deter intervention from Iraq's neighbors, and train Iraqi forces. Increased reconstruction and a program to provide jobs for tens of thousands of young Iraqis was to reduce the flow of recruits to militias or criminal gangs. Biden's plan suggested that without a federal system, the only two other ways to govern Iraq from its center were "a foreign occupation that the United States cannot sustain or the return of a dictator like Saddam Hussein."

John Edwards favored a total withdrawal of US combat forces over a period of twelve to eighteen months and no permanent US bases in Iraq to avoid the charge that the US invasion had resulted in an indefinite military occupation. He also advocated having direct talks with all nations in the region, including Iran and Syria (Edwards 2007). Bill Richardson advocated a complete removal of US troops as soon as possible (Richardson 2007) and called for deauthorization of the war.

Dennis Kucinich's plan included ideas similar to the Edwards and Richardson plans but called for stronger measures. It included closing US bases in Iraq and rapid withdrawal of all US forces. They would be replaced by a multinational peacekeeping force under UN control, half of whose troops would be from countries "with large Muslim populations," which would help keep the peace until a stable Iraqi government capable of providing security was in place. The plan also called for the removal of all US contractors from Iraq, US and British payment of reparations to the Iraqi people, and genuine economic and political sovereignty for Iraq (Kucinich 2007).

The Possibility of Democracy and Sovereignty in Iraq

Democracy in Muslim and Arab Societies

About two-thirds of the world's Muslims live in societies widely recognized as democracies. These include over 200 million in Indonesia, over 150 million in

India, more than 124 million in Bangladesh, and over 71 million in Turkey. But of the approximately one-third of Muslims who do not live in countries with democratically elected governments, most are Arabs (Ibrahim 2007: 6–7).

Saad Eddin Ibrahim (2007), an Egyptian professor of political sociology at American University in Cairo and a democratic activist, argued that historical events contributed significantly to the lack of democracies in Arab nations. Following Napoleon's invasion of Egypt in 1798, which demonstrated how European military technology could overwhelm local resistance, a process of modernization and democratization was set in motion in several Arab countries. But it was the very European countries whose democratic ideals and political systems modernizing Arabs most looked forward to emulating, Britain and France, whose occupation and colonial policies in the last quarter of the nineteenth century stymied progress toward democracy.

After World War I, a number of Arab countries achieved independence and resumed implementing some elements of democracy. But according to Ibrahim (2007), the creation of Israel in 1948 contributed to the establishment of military regimes. Many Arabs felt that Israel's existence had been achieved through dispossessing the Palestinians of their homes and homeland. When Arab leaders, pressured by their citizens to go to war against Israel, were badly defeated in the first Arab–Israeli War, they were blamed by many of their military officers for mismanaging the war and providing soldiers with inadequate weapons and supplies. In popularly supported military revolutions, ruling dynasties were overthrown in Egypt in 1952 and Iraq in 1958. During the cold war, authoritarian Arab leaders often turned to the Soviet Union for assistance since Western nations supported Israel. Following the 1979 Iranian Revolution, the emerging threat of Islamic fundamentalism brought Western support for Arab autocrats, including Saddam in his war against Ayatollah Khomeini's Iranian Islamic Republic from 1980 to 1988. After the Al Qaeda 9/11 attacks in 2001, the United States was inclined to provide assistance to Arab leaders, regardless of their lack of support for democracy, who pledged to fight Islamic extremism. Ibrahim argues that nothing in the Quran or other Islamic religious texts prevents the formation of a democratic political system. He suggests that Western nations could help the process of Arab democratization by reducing aid to authoritarian regimes.

Francis Fukuyama (1995: 7–8) writes that the consolidation of democracy must occur on four mutually interactive levels: ideology, institutions, civil society, and culture. Democratic ideology is essentially the belief that democracy is the most desirable type of political system. But people who draw this conclusion may initially lack institutions to support a democratic political system, such as a democratic constitution and corresponding forms of social organization including appropriate legal and political party systems. Civil society refers to forms of social organization separate from formal institutions, which arise relatively spontaneously as people seek to achieve goals or express positions on particular issues. Culture includes historic traditions passed on from one generation to another, such as the dominant type of family structure and its supporting ideology, and religious and moral systems and other beliefs, attitudes, or forms of knowledge that influence political activity. Ideally the underlying culture of a society should be the foundation for a democratic system, providing support for all the levels above; otherwise the transition to democracy may be incomplete, become stalled, or even recede. Ibrahim's analysis, however, suggests that the decision to shift to a democratic political system can foster institutional and cultural changes that can then strengthen and protect democratic political systems.

Can Democracy Succeed in Iraq?

There are a number of reasons why a democratic political system might not succeed in Iraq. These include the possibility that after achieving power, Islamic political parties might move Iraq away from anything recognizable as a democratic system. In other words, democratic voting for religious parties could mean a "one man, one vote, one time" temporary democracy that the elected religious politicians might soon effectively terminate (Ibrahim 2007: 12). Another possibility is that Sunni Arab resistance to the domination of Shia political religious parties could lead to civil war and then to an authoritarian central government to maintain order. Others believe, however, that the sustained operation of a democratic political system could strengthen support for democracy in Iraq.

Democratic Legacies in Iraq's Past?

Dawisha (2005c) believes that from 1921 to 1958, many Iraqis displayed enthusiasm for the concept of a democratic political system, even though they had been pressured in the 1920s into accepting a constitution that served British interests and gave the monarch authority that superseded that of elected government officials. He notes, however, that the system at least introduced Iraqis to the political institution of parliament. Some Iraqis organized political parties or operated independent newspapers, which were occasionally able to criticize British policies or those of the government (although opposition parties and newspapers were periodically banned). In addition, there were some episodes when opposition political parties were able to influence government policy through mobilizing mass protests, in particular against the proposed 1948 Portsmouth Treaty. This suggested that Iraqis could embrace democratic institutions despite decades of authoritarian rule.

Building Democracy Internally

Dawisha and Dawisha (2003) and Dawisha (2005b) describe ways to build a democratic Iraq. For example, they suggest that the more secularly oriented Kurds and the Sunni Arabs, together with a sizeable proportion of secular Shia, could limit any intentions of Shia political religious parties to establish an Iraqi Islamist state along the lines of Iran (Dawisha 2005a).

Dawisha and Dawisha (2003) and Dawisha (2005b) argue that democratizing Iraq would be facilitated by a prosperous, economically independent middle class whose well-being derived primarily from privately owned businesses rather than state employment. They note that during much of its history, Iraq lacked an adequately large self-sufficient middle class since many people maintained a middle-class lifestyle through employment in state-owned industries, government administrative or service jobs, or in the military or security forces. Since this sector of the middle class relied on the state economically, its capacity to challenge the government was limited. In addition, since the Iraqi government had derived most of its income through oil revenue rather than through taxing its citizens, many Iraqis lacked a motivation to demand the right to participate in government. If a large amount of government property was transferred to private ownership, the government could then tax the new owners, who would be motivated to participate or seek representation of their interests, including control of taxation rates, in local and national legislatures. Despite the theory behind this concept, there was significant fear among many Iraqis that privatizing government resources could soon lead to foreign ownership of much of Iraq's wealth.

Iraq Political Democracy and National Sovereignty

An assessment of the feasibility of a stable democratic Iraq and the ways in which such a goal might be achieved is incomplete without taking into account the interests, intentions, and actions not only of Iraq's neighbors but also of the powers that pledged to bring it democracy, mainly the United States and Great Britain. In the view of many observers, Britain from 1920 to 1958 delivered neither genuine democracy nor full sovereignty to Iraq because to do so might have damaged its own interests. The 1958 antimonarchy revolution resulted in Iraq's achieving true independence for the first time. When General Abd al-Karim Qasim considered whether to allow totally free elections in which the then-popular Iraqi Communist Party might have gained a significant number of seats in an Iraqi legislature, he had to take into account not only the potential response of Iraqi Arab nationalists but also the possible reactions of Britain and the United States, which had intervened in Iran in 1953 to reinstall the Iranian monarchy when Iranian nationalists defied Britain and appropriated its oil holdings. Later rulers of Republican Iraq would use the threat of intervention from perceived imperialist powers and their ally Israel to justify limiting dissent.

Will the United States repeat British mistakes? Will the greatest impediments to real democracy come from those who promised to liberate Iraq in 2003? It is difficult to believe that a US administration of the type that launched the invasion would genuinely carry through with allowing Iraq to attain full democracy or sovereignty. Arnove (2007: 70) suggests that in reality the US government opposed democracy in Middle Eastern countries because this would allow the people in these societies to give priority to using their energy wealth for their own welfare and economic development rather than to enhance the profit margins of foreign oil companies. Achieving Iraqi democracy seems to rely as much, if not more, on political change in the United States as on developments in Iraq.

Reviving America's International Moral Standing and Avoiding Similar Situations in the Future

Although the Iraq War differed from the Vietnam War in many ways, it had some key moral similarities. Both were based on false justifications and both were characterized by very high casualty ratios between the indigenous population and the occupying forces, paralleling European wars of colonial conquest in the Middle East, Asia, Africa, and the Americas. Since US counterinsurgency authorities recognize that losing moral legitimacy means ultimately losing the war, a central question is whether a war launched largely on false premises and viewed internationally as a violent seizure of another country's energy resources can achieve moral legitimacy. The only possibility of accomplishing this would seem to be an unqualified fulfillment of America's promise to bring real and unfettered democracy and sovereignty to the Iraqi people.

Besides fulfilling the democracy pledge, other steps that can be taken by future US administrations to revive America's moral reputation and avoid similar disastrous actions in the future might include banning reliance on any foreign intelligence services or domestic advisers or consultants, be they individuals or organizations, that promoted war by providing or funneling false information. Criminal investigations and punishment of all government officials and others suspected of deception or fraud in the decision to invade Iraq or any subsequent criminal activity related to Iraq should be pursued. Prosecutor Vincent Bugliosi (2008) has specifically described reasons for criminally prosecuting George W. Bush. If such prosecution is justified and feasible, it might extend beyond Bush to certain members of his administration.

The UN should assume responsibility for the exercise of all international authority in Iraq. All US bases and military personnel should be removed, except those troops necessary to protect the US embassy. If the UN determines that there is a need for a continued international military presence in Iraq for peacekeeping purposes and if that presence is approved by an Iraqi government elected under UN supervision, it should consist of forces from nations approved by the Iraqi people. All non-Iraqi personnel accused of criminal acts in Iraq should at minimum be investigated by the UN for possible prosecution.

Reconstruction projects should be carried out, as far as possible, by Iraqi construction companies and workers. After the 1991 Gulf War Iraqis were able to restore electrical service within a few months. Within six months, Iraqis on their own and burdened by UN sanctions were able to repair virtually all the damage done to Baghdad (Dawisha 2005b: 731). In comparison, coalition efforts to provide sufficient electricity lagged for years.

US administrations could also help rehabilitate America's international moral standing by displaying vigorous commitment to spreading democracy around the world, especially to the monarchies and other authoritarian regimes dependent on the United States for the training and supply of their military and security forces. Such assistance could be withheld unless these governments agreed to rapidly democratize. The United States can prove the sincerity of its commitment to democracy only if it is not providing the means for dictatorships to maintain power and repress freedom and human rights, including women's and children's rights, or movements for democracy.

The Future of Iraq

The 2003 US-led invasion can lead to any one of a range of futures for Iraq: the division of the country into two states, one Kurdish and one Arab, or three, including separate Sunni Arab and Shia Arab nations; the maintenance of a strained federal system; a US-dominated partial democracy or authoritarian state; continuous US military occupation of all or parts of the country; or a sovereign, democratic Iraq free of foreign occupation.

An independent Kurdish state would serve as an inspiration and possibly a base of operations for rebel Kurds in other countries and would likely request a prolonged US military presence to deter intervention from Turkey, Iran, or Iraq. An independent Shia nation in oil-rich southern Iraq would probably be closely allied with Iran and might attempt to establish a more comprehensive Islamic Republic form of government than would be possible if Iraq remained one country. Galbraith (2008) suggests that Iraq's post-Saddam constitution, which has a federalist orientation and allows for the possibility of forming regional administrations for groups of provinces similar to the Kurdish Regional Government, may lead to the breakup of Iraq into three separate states and possibly increase interstate antagonisms in the area. Others, however, feel it is more likely and in fact in the greater interest of Iran that Iraq remain a stable unified state politically dominated by a Shia coalition of parties friendly to Iran (Yaphe 2008: 406–407).

In a united Iraq, Sunni and Shia Arab resentment against foreign occupation has the potential to unify large numbers of the members of both groups. The possibility that a fully sovereign democratic Iraq could result in an elected government hostile to the United States likely generates a strong inclination among a number of US political leaders to maintain a permanent military occupation and allow only a US-dominated Iraqi government. In all likelihood, the option of permitting Iraq to become a sovereign democracy could not become a reality without, in effect, a political revolution in the United States both in terms of government leadership and popular sentiment. Fostering real democracy there and in the Middle East as a whole is a risk that those who launched the invasion of Iraq almost certainly were not willing to take, regardless of their prodemocracy rhetoric, for fear of allowing populations with long-repressed hostility toward US foreign policy the right to select their own governments.

Summary and Analysis

The Iraq War cost far more in lives and economic resources than most Americans anticipated. When the invasion, touted in part as a war of liberation from dictatorship, transformed into an ongoing occupation, Iraqi nationalism was inflamed. Many Sunni Arabs and some Shia Arabs formed organizations that waged a multifaceted antioccupation insurgency. By empowering Shia groups that had been aided by Iran, banning the Baath Party, removing thousands of Baathists from government jobs, and disbanding Iraq's armed forces, the occupation not only intensified the insurgency but also helped set the stage for the outbreak of sectarian violence on a level never before experienced in Iraq's history.

Although in some ways Iraq became more democratic, it failed, in the view of many observers, to regain the level of sovereignty it had before the invasion. The war, occupation policies, and ongoing fighting caused more than 4 million Iraqis to flee their homes, many seeking refuge outside the country. Millions of Iraqi children were traumatized by being the victims of or witnessing the effects of war-related violence. Instead of enjoying the full benefits of democracy, Iraqi women began conforming to traditional Islamic custom, many fearing violence from strangers if they did not appear in public veiled or if they were suspected of immoral behavior. Ironically, despite Iraq's cultural shift toward Islamic traditionalism, economic desperation forced many Iraqi women into prostitution both within Iraq and among the expatriate refugee population.

Rather than reducing terrorism, the invasion motivated many Iraqis, Saudis, North Africans, and others to join terrorist or insurgent groups and launch violent attacks not only against occupation forces, but also against Iraqis viewed as collaborating with them, including horrific mass suicide bombings. Although Al Qaeda did not exist in Iraq before the invasion, outside of a small part of autonomous Iraqi Kurdistan beyond Saddam's reach, the war led many Iraqis and foreign Muslims to organize or join Al Qaeda–linked groups inside Iraq. The invasion diverted US military personnel and resources to Iraq, while construction efforts in Afghanistan lagged, opium poppy production for the international market soared to new levels, and the Taliban and Al Qaeda, which had used Afghanistan as a base of operations, revived and carried out increased attacks.

The US economy deteriorated under the impact of war costs and other factors, contributing to the American and worldwide financial emergency that developed in the fall of 2008. The recognition that major reasons for launching the invasion were false and distress at the mounting costs of the occupation caused the majority of Americans to turn against the war, impacting US politics. The simultaneous prosecution of both the Iraq and Afghan wars appeared to dangerously stress the personnel and resources of the US volunteer military, leading to compensating policies such as extended tours of duty, multiple deployments, activation of National Guard and reserve units, increased financial incentives for enlistment and reenlistment together with lowered enlistment standards, and heavier reliance on PMFs to perform roles previously carried out by US forces. American corporations were awarded profitable contracts for work reconstructing Iraqi infrastructure or providing goods and services to coalition forces.

US leaders, who manipulated the public with claims of Iraqi WMD and ties to Al Qaeda's 9/11 attacks to launch the invasion, displayed less concern for popular opinion when it turned against the war. The false basis for the invasion revived public skepticism and mistrust, prevalent for many years after the Vietnam conflict, of government claims about alleged foreign threats.

The invasion and occupation of Iraq significantly eroded US moral standing worldwide. Majorities of the populations in many nations supported withdrawal of US forces from Iraq, and elections often resulted in the victory of leaders and parties opposing the US-led occupation. Much of the world was struck by what appeared to be transparent mercenary aspects of the American invasion. Once in possession of Iraq's energy resources, the United States seemed to have no intention of ending the occupation or giving up control. American and coalition corporations were awarded attractive contracts, US citizens working for American companies in Iraq earned high salaries, US military personnel received enlistment bonuses, and eventually American authorities even began paying Sunni militias to at least temporarily desert the insurgency and fight against Al Qaeda in Mesopotamia.

To some the spectacular growth of PMFs brought about by the Iraq War constituted a new weapon in the arsenal of aggressive nations and multinational corporations analogous to the introduction of machine gun–toting white mercenaries to the African continent many decades earlier, a relatively cheap way to achieve international goals, such as access to resources, through the combination of high-tech weaponry and small numbers of highly trained military personnel.

The question of what to do about the Iraq War predictably emerged as a major issue of political contention. Most Republicans advocated continuing the US occupation as long as necessary to achieve what they viewed as an acceptable level of political stability. The majority of Democrats supported the notion of commencing significant withdrawals of US troops, partly on the assumption that this would force competing Iraqi factions to compromise with each other over crucial matters such as a national law to fairly distribute oil revenues. In addition, proposals forwarded by some Democrats called for an increased UN role in overseeing Iraq. A longtime opponent of the Iraq War, Barack Obama, was elected president in 2008 and the Democrats increased their majorities in both the Senate and the House of Representatives. But it was unclear whether the United States would maintain some type of long-term military presence in Iraq despite the Iraq–US Status of Forces Agreement of November–December 2008, which seemed to require the withdrawal of all US military forces by the end of 2011.

Historically many Iraqis have been attracted to the concept of a democratic political system. But some observers questioned whether decades of authoritarian rule or the heightened intergroup violence and mistrust that followed the invasion would prevent the development and consolidation of a democratic government. Others doubted whether true democracy for Iraq was really a goal of those who had launched the war, but rather an Iraq subservient to US interests. Britain did not establish a truly democratic political system in Iraq when it had the opportunity after World War I. Its leaders drew Iraq's borders with the apparent intent of maintaining British control over Mesopotamia's oil. Instead of fostering democracy in the Middle East, Britain and the United States collaborated in overthrowing a nationalist government in Iraq's huge neighbor Iran in 1953 and reinstalled the Iranian shah as a virtual absolute monarch. Over time this antidemocratic intervention led to the development and success of the

Iranian Islamic Revolution in 1979, which had major effects on Iraq. Iraq's secular leaders attempted to neutralize the perceived threat of Islamic fundamentalist revolution from Iran by launching the Iran–Iraq War in 1980. The unexpectedly long and devastating conflict left Iraq in a difficult economic situation, which Saddam mistakenly tried to alleviate through seizing Kuwait. This blunder ultimately resulted in the 2003 US-led invasion and the removal of the Baathist government with the stated goals of eliminating WMD, combating terrorism, and finally bringing real democracy to Iraq. Somewhat inconsistently, however, the United States continued to support nondemocratic but cooperative oil-rich monarchies, casting doubt on its stated political intentions in Iraq. It is likely that achieving a genuinely democratic and sovereign Iraq is of necessity contingent on dramatic political and policy change within the United States.

References and Further Readings

Anderson, Liam, and Gareth Stansfield. 2004. *The Future of Iraq: Dictatorship, Democracy, or Division?* New York: Palgrave MacMillan.

Andrews, Edmund L. 2008. "Vast Bailout by U.S. Proposed in Bid to Stem Financial Crisis." *New York Times*, September 19. www.nytimes.com.

Arnove, Anthony. 2007. *Iraq: The Logic of Withdrawal.* New York: Henry Holt.

Baker, James A., and Lee H. Hamilton. 2006. *The Iraq Study Group Report.* New York: Vintage Books.

Baktiari, Bahman. 2007. "Iran's Conservative Revival." *Current History* 106, no. 696 (January): 11–16.

Barfield, Thomas. 2008. "The Roots of Failure in Afghanistan." *Current History* 107 (December): 410–417.

BBC World Service Poll. 2007. "Global Poll: Majority Wants Troops Out of Iraq Within a Year." www.worldpublicopinion.org/pipa/articles/international_security_bt/394.php?lb=btis&pnt=394&nid=&id=.

Biden, Joseph R. 2006. "Iraq: A Way Forward." October 6. www.israpundit.com/2008/wp-content/uploads/2008/08/pfi.pdf.

Bugliosi, Vincent. 2008. *The Prosecution of George W. Bush for Murder.* New York: Vanguard Press–Perseus Books.

Castañeda, Jorge, and Patricio Navia. 2007. "The Year of the Ballot." *Current History* 106, no. 697 (February): 51–57.

Cave, Damien. 2007. "Cheated of Future, Iraqi Graduates Want to Flee." *New York Times*, June 5. www.nytimes.com.

CBS News. 2009. "U.S. Army Suicides Highest in Three Decades." January 29. www.cbsnews.com/stories/2009/01/29/nation/printable4762268.shtml.

CNN Election Center 2008, Exit Polls. 2008a. "President National Exit Poll." www.cnn.com/ELECTION/2008/results/polls/#USP00p1.

CNN Election Center 2008, President. 2008b. "President, Full Results." www.cnn.com/ELECTION/2008/results/president.

CNN.com. 2007. "America Votes 2006: Democrats Retake Congress." www.cnn.com/ELECTION/2006.

Cohen, Jeff. 2006. "Inside TV News: We Were Silenced by the Drums of War." Truthout, December 26. www.truthout.org/docs_2006/printer_122606M.shtml.

Crossette, Barbara. 1995. "Iraq Sanctions Kill Children, U.N. Reports." *New York Times*, December 1. http://query.nytimes.com.

CRS (Congressional Research Service). 2008. "The Cost of Iraq, Afghanistan, and Other Global War on Terror Operations Since 9/11." CRS Report for Congress, February 8. www.fas.org/sgp/crs/natsec/RL33110.pdf.

Damon, Arwa. 2008. "On Deadly Ground: Women of Iraq." CNN Special Investigations Unit (SIU), March 16. www.cnn.com.

Dawisha, Adeed. 2005a. "Democratic Institutions and Performance." *Journal of Democracy* 16, no. 3 (July): 35–49.

———. 2005b. "The Prospects for Democracy in Iraq: Challenges and Opportunities." *Third World Quarterly* 26, no. 4–5: 723–737.

———. 2005c. "Democratic Attitudes and Practices in Iraq, 1921–1958." *Middle East Journal* 59, no. 1: 11–20.

Dawisha, Adeed, and Karen Dawisha. 2003. "How to Build a Democratic Iraq." *Foreign Affairs* 82, no. 3: 36–50.

Dawisha, Adeed, and Larry Diamond. 2006. "Iraq's Year of Voting Dangerously." *Journal of Democracy* 17, no. 2 (April): 89–103.

DeFronzo, James, and Jungyun Gill. 2009. "Iraq War Costs and the 2008 Presidential Election." American Sociological Association Meetings, August. San Francisco, CA.

DeYoung, Karen. 2009. "Afghan Conflict Will Be Reviewed." *Washington Post*, January 13. www.washingtonpost.com.

The Economist. 2008. "Iraq War: Eying the Wages of War." March 13. www.economist.com.

Edwards, John. "Edwards Lays Out Comprehensive Proposal to Enact His Plan for Iraq." John Edwards for President, February 14. http://johnedwards.com/news/headlines/20070214-iraq-plan.

Fallows, James. 2006. *Blind into Baghdad*. New York: Vintage Books.

Filkins, Dexter. 2008. "Exiting Iraq, Petraeus Says Gains Are Fragile." *New York Times*, August 21. www.nytimes.com.

Finan, William W. Jr. 2008. "Rethinking Iraq and the Region." *Current History* 107, no. 713: 443–445.

FOXNews.com. 2008. "McCain: Opposition to Iraq Withdrawal 'Seminal Event' in History." March 13. www.foxnews.com/politics/elections/2008/03/13/mccain-opposition-to-iraq-withdrawal-seminal-event-in-history.

Frosch, Dan. 2007. "Fighting the Terror of Battles that Rage in Soldier's Heads." *New York Times*, May 13. www.nytimes.com.

Fukuyama, Francis. 1995. "The Primacy of Culture." *Journal of Democracy* 6, no. 1: 7–14.

Galbraith, Peter W. 2008. *Unintended Consequences: How the War in Iraq Strengthened America's Enemies*. New York: Simon & Schuster.

Gallup. 2008a. "Iraq." www.gallup.com/poll/1633/Iraq.aspx#3 (accessed March 15, 2008).

———. 2008b. "Gallup's Pulse of Democracy: The War in Iraq." www.gallup.com/poll/1633/Iraq.aspx?version=print (accessed March 15, 2008).

Glanz, James, and Alissa J. Rubin. 2007. "Future Look of Iraq Complicated by Internal Migration." *New York Times*, September 19. www.nytimes.com.

Gordon, Michael R., and Adam Nagourney. 2007. "McCain Sees 'No Plan B' for Iraq War." *New York Times*, April 15. www.nytimes.com.

Hanley, Charles J. 2008. "Studies: Iraq Costs U.S. $12B Per Month." *Huffington Post*, March 10. www.huffingtonpost.com/2008/03/10/studies-iraq-costs-us -1_n_90694.html.

Herszenhorn, David M. 2008. "Bailout Plan Wins Approval; Democrats Vow Tighter Rules." *New York Times*, October 4. www.nytimes.com.

Hodge, Charles W., Carl A. Castro, Stephen C. Messer, Dennis McGuirk, Dave I. Cotting, and Robert L. Koffman. 2004. "Combat Duty in Iraq and Afghanistan, Mental Health Problems, and Barriers to Care." *New England Journal of Medicine* 351, no. 1 (July 1): 13–22.

Howard, Michael. 2007. "Children of War: The Generation Traumatized by Violence in Iraq." *Guardian*, February 6. www.guardian.co.uk/world/2007/feb/ 06/iraq.topstories3.

Icasualties.org. 2009. "Iraq Coalition Casualty Count." http://icasualties.org/Iraq/ index.aspx (accessed January 31, 2009).

Ibrahim, Saad Eddin. 2007. "Toward Muslim Democracies." *Journal of Democracy* 18 (April): 5–13.

IVAW (Iraq Veterans Against the War). 2008. http://ivaw.org.

Johnston, Tim. 2007. "Ally of Bush Is Defeated in Australia." *New York Times*, November 25. www.nytimes.com.

Jones, Jeffrey. 2008. "Majority Continues to Consider Iraq War a Mistake." Gallup, February 6. www.gallup.com/poll/104185/Majority-Continues-Consider-Iraq-War-Mistake.aspx (accessed March 15, 2008).

Joseph, Edward P., and Michael E. O'Hanlon. 2007. "The Case for Soft Partition." *Saban Center for Middle East Policy at the Brookings Institution*, Analysis Paper 12, June. Washington, DC: Brookings Institution. www.brookings .edu.

Kucinich, Dennis. 2007. "The Kucinich Plan for Iraq." January 10. www.informa tionclearinghouse.info/article16123.htm.

Landler, Mark. 2008. "US Investing $250 Billion in Banks." *New York Times*, October 14. www.nytimes.com.

Lalate. 2009. "Obama Iraq Speech Transcript!" February 27. http://news.lalate .com/2009/02/27/obama-iraq-speech-transcript.

Leonhardt, David. 2007. "What $1.2 Trillion Can Buy." *New York Times*, January 17. www.nytimes.com.

Levy, Clifford J. 2008. "Russia Backs Independence of Georgian Enclaves." *New York Times*, August 27. www.nytimes.com.

Libal, Kathryn, and Scott Harding. 2007. "The Politics of Refugee Advocacy and Humanitarian Assistance." *Middle East Report* 244 (Fall): 18–21.

Lindsey, Lawrence B. 2008. "What the Iraq War Will Cost the U.S." CNN, January 11. http://cnnmoney.com (accessed March 14, 2008).

Luo, Michael. 2007. "Antiwar Groups Use New Clout to Influence Democrats on Iraq." *New York Times*, May 6. www.nytimes.com/2007/05/06/washington/ 06left.html.

MacInnis, Laura. 2007. "Traumatized Iraqi Children Lack Needed Care: U.N." *Reuters*, May 23. www.reuters.com.

Mazzetti, Mark. 2006. "Spy Agencies Say Iraq War Worsens Terrorism Threat." *New York Times*, September 24. www.nytimes.com.

Mulrine, Anna. 2008. "Pentagon Plans to Send More than 12,000 Additional Troops to Afghanistan." *U.S. News and World Report*, August 19. www .USnews.com.

National Priorities Project. "The War in Iraq Costs." 2008. March 14. www.national priorities.org/costofwar_home (accessed March 14, 2008).

Newport, Frank. 2008. "Americans Concerned About Impact of Leaving Iraq." Gallup, March 14. www.gallup.com/poll/104977/Americans-Concerned -About-Impact-Leaving-Iraq.aspx.

New York Times. 2008. "Election Results 2008, House of Representatives Map." 2008. December 9. http://elections.nytimes.com/2008/results/house/map.html.

New York Times/CBS News Poll. 2007, September 4–8. www.nytimes.com/packages/ pdf/national/09102007_pollresults.pdf.

Obama, Barack. 2008. "Five Years Later: A Plan for a Safer America." www .barackobama.com/issues/iraq/index.php (accessed March 19, 2008).

Parsons, Tim. 2006. "Updated Iraq Study Affirms Earlier Mortality Rates." *John Hopkins University Gazette*, October 16. www.jhu.edu/~gazette/2006/ 16oct06/16iraq.html.

Pessin, Al. 2008. "US Army Suicide Rate Continues to Rise." Voice of America, May 29. www.voanews.com (accessed September 9, 2008).

Rashid, Ahmed. 2007. "Letter from Afghanistan: Are the Taliban Winning?" *Current History* 106, no. 696 (January): 17–20.

Reuters. 2006. "US Soldiers' Suicide Rate in Iraq Doubles in 2005." December 19. www.alertnet.org/thenews/newsdesk/N19303337.htm.

Richardson, Bill. 2007. "The Richardson Plan for Ending the War." December 17. www.richardsonforpresident.com/issues/iraq.

Risen, James. 2006. *State of War: the Secret History of the CIA and the Bush Administration*. New York: Free Press.

Rohde, David. 2007. "Taliban Raise Poppy Production to a Record Again." *New York Times*, August 26. www.nytimes.com.

Rohde, David, and David Sanger. 2007. "How a 'Good War' in Afghanistan Went Bad." *New York Times*, August 12. www.nytimes.com.

Rubin, Alissa, and Campbell Robertson. 2008. "Iraq Backs Deal that Sets End of U.S. Role." *New York Times*, November 28. www.nytimes.com.

Sanger, David E. 2006. "N. Korea Reports 1st Nuclear Arms Test." *New York Times*, October 9. www.nytimes.com.

———. 2007. "With Korea as Model, Bush Team Ponders Long Support Role in Iraq." *New York Times*, June 3. www.nytimes.com.

Sariolghalam, Mahmood. 2008. "Iran in Search of Itself." *Current History* 107, no. 713: 425–431.

Schamis, Hector E. 2008. "Argentina's Troubled Transition." *Current History* 107, no. 706 (February): 71–76.

Sciolino, Elaine, and Victoria Burnett. 2008. "Socialists Re-Elected in Spain, After a Bitter Campaign." *New York Times*, March 10. www.nytimes.com.

Shane, Leo III. 2008. "Veterans Groups Offer Different Views of Conflict." *Stars and Stripes*, March 16. www.stripes.com.

Sontag, Deborah, and Lizette Alvarez. 2007. "For War's Gravely Injured, Challenge to Find Care." *New York Times*, March 12. www.nytimes.com.

Stiglitz, Joseph E., and Linda J. Bilmes. 2008. *The Three Trillion Dollar War: The True Cost of the Iraq Conflict*. New York: W. W. Norton.

Stout, David, and Thom Shanker. 2008. "Next Year's War Costs Estimated at $170 Billion or More." *New York Times*, February 6. www.nytimes.com.

Suskind, Ron. 2008. *The Way of the World*. New York: HarperCollins.

Susman, Ina. 2007. "Iraqi Policewomen Are Told to Surrender Their Weapons." www.latimes.com/news/nationworld/world/la-fg-policewomen11dec 11,0,6920725.story?coll=la-home-center.

Tavernise, Sabrina. 2007. "Well-Off Fleeing Iraq Find Poverty and Pain in Jordan." *New York Times*, August 10. www.nytimes.com.

———. 2008. "Violence Leaves Young Iraqis Doubting Clerics." *New York Times*, March 4. www.nytimes.com.

Times of India. 2007. "Children Pay High Price of Iraq Violence: UNICEF." December 21. http://timesofindia.indiatimes.com.

Todd, Chuck, and Sheldon Gawiser. 2009. *How Barack Obama Won: A State-by-State Guide to the Historic 2008 Presidential Election*. New York: Vintage Books.

Unger, Craig. 2007. *The Fall of the House of Bush*. New York: Scribner.

United Nations. 2003a. Security Council Resolution 1472. March 28. www .un.org/Docs/sc/unsc_resolutions03.html.

———. 2003b. Security Council Resolution 1483. May 22. www.un.org/Docs/ sc/unsc_resolutions03.html.

Urbina, Ian, and Ron Nixon. 2007. "Veterans Face Vast Inequities Over Disability." *New York Times*, March 9. www.nytimes.com.

VAIW (Veterans Against the Iraq War). 2008. www.vaiw.org/vet/index.php.

White, Deborah. 2007. "Hillary Clinton's Thoughtful Plan to End the Iraq War." July 10. http://usliberals.about.com/od/extraordinaryspeech2/a/HillaryIraq.htm.

White House. 2008. "President Bush Visits National Defense University's Distinguished Lecture Program, Discusses Global War on Terror." September 9. http://merln.ndu.edu/archivepdf/iraq/WH/20080909.pdf.

Wittes, Tamara Cofman. 2008. *Freedom's Unsteady March: America's Role in Building Arab Democracy*. Washington, DC: Brookings Institution Press.

Yaphe, Judith S. 2008. "Iraq: Are We There Yet?" *Current History* 107, no. 713: 403–409.

Zoepf, Katherine. 2007. "Desperate Iraqi Refugees Turn to Sex Trade in Syria." *New York Times*, May 29. www.nytimes.com.

Glossary

Abu Ghraib prison: a prison in Iraq where US personnel were photographed abusing Iraqi prisoners

Agha: Kurdish tribal chief

Ahali Group: 1930s Iraqi leftist intellectuals who favored social reforms and the Iraq First policy over Arab nationalism

Al' Ahd (The Covenant): a secret organization of mainly Syrian and Mesopotamian officers within the Ottoman Empire that played an important role in the Arab Revolt against the Ottomans; some Mesopotamian officers became prominent figures in British-dominated Iraq

American exceptionalism: the belief that US culture, and political and economic systems, are inherently superior, giving the United States the unique right to promote certain features of its society around the world

Anfal: the Iraqi military repression of Kurds in the Kurdistan region of Iraq in 1987 and 1988 during the Iran–Iraq War

Anglo-Iranian (Anglo-Persian 1908 to 1934) Oil Company: British-dominated company that exploited Iran's oil under the Iranian shah's government

Ansar Al-Islam (Supporters of Islam): a Sunni, mainly Kurdish Islamist movement in Iraqi Kurdistan favoring a fundamentalist version of Islam and an Islamic fundamentalist Iraq

Arab League: international consultative organization of twenty-two Arab countries

Arab nationalism: the political ideology that all people who speak the Arab language and share Arab culture should unite, ideally in a single Arab state

Al Qaeda: initially an organization of Islamic volunteers who fought against the Russians in Afghanistan during the 1980s led by a Saudi, Osama bin Laden; later it engaged in terrorist attacks against the United States

Al Qaeda in Mesopotamia (AQM), also called Al Qaeda in Iraq: Islamic fundamentalist-oriented groups in Iraq composed mainly of Iraqis with some foreign volunteers who self-identified with Al Qaeda and fought US and US-allied forces in Iraq after the 2003 invasion

Ashura-tenth (of Muharram): Shia commemoration of the martyrdom of Imman Hussein

Asymmetric warfare: warfare between opponents initially differing greatly in strength in which each side benefits most by using tactics suitable to its unique capabilities and limitations

Awakening movement: the US-supported organization of mainly Sunni Iraqis that opposed Al Qaeda in Mesopotamia

Axis of evil: President George W. Bush's characterization of Iraq, Iran, and North Korea in his January 29, 2002, State of the Union address

Ayatollah: sign of Allah; a high-level Shia cleric

Baath Party (Renaissance Party) or Arab Baath Socialist Party: anti-communist Arab nationalist party founded in Syria; Saddam Hussein eventually gained control of the Iraqi branch of the Baath Party

Badr Brigade: SCIRI's armed forces

Baghdad Pact: 1955 pro-British alliance involving Iraq's monarchy, Turkey, Iran's monarchy, and Britain that was strongly opposed by Iraqi leftists and Iraqi Arab nationalists

Balfour Declaration: the British government's November 2, 1917, declaration of support for establishing a homeland for the Jewish people

Barzani rebellion: the intermittent Kurdish rebellion against Iraq's central government led by Mustafa Barzani from 1961 to 1975

Bedouin: nomadic Arab of the Middle Eastern or North African deserts

Blackwater: the private company based in the Great Dismal Swamp area of North Carolina that trained military and law enforcement personnel and provided security services in postinvasion Iraq and Afghanistan; changed name to Xe in 2009

Blowback: unanticipated effects of foreign policy, including war, on either the country originating the action or the target country

British Mandate: League of Nations mandate for British rule of Iraq, 1920–1932

Bush Doctrine: the concept of preventive war; interpreted as the US right to use military force against governments that might constitute a threat to the United States or its interests in the future

Caliph: the concept of a leader of all Islam

Central Command (CENTCOM): US military command for the Middle East and parts of central Asia and East Africa

Clan (subtribe): extended family typically including second, third, or fourth cousins

Coalition of the Willing: Bush administration expression for the coalition of nations participating in or supporting the US-led invasion of Iraq; also called the Coalition for Operation Iraqi Freedom

Coalition Provisional Authority (CPA): the occupation authority led by L. Paul Bremer that governed Iraq from soon after the 2003 invasion until approximately the end of June 2004

Council of Representatives: Iraqi parliament after 2005

Counterinsurgency: measures taken to defeat an insurgency

CPA Order Number 1: the Coalition Provisional Authority's de-Baathification order issued on May 16, 2003, removing thousands of people from government positions because of their Baath Party membership

CPA Order Number 2: the Coalition Provisional Authority's May 23, 2003, Dissolution of Iraqi Entities order, eliminating preinvasion Iraqi armed forces and security agencies

CPA Order Number 17: the CPA order that made members of the coalition occupation forces and international consultants and others immune from Iraqi legal process

Dawa Party (Islamic Call Party): a Shia political religious organization founded around 1958 and led by Muhammad Baqir al-Sadr

Dujail Massacre: the execution of dozens of Iraqi Shia men accused of attempting to assassinate Saddam Hussein at Dujail in 1982; this mass killing was the specific charge for which Saddam was sentenced to death and executed

Fatwa: an authoritative opinion provided by a recognized Islamic scholar on an issue relating to Islamic law

Fedayeen Saddam: Saddam's Martyrs (Saddam's Men of Sacrifice); Saddam Hussein's paramilitary force

Four Colonels (Golden Square): four Iraqi colonels who defied the British during World War II; after a brief war, Britain reoccupied the country and reinstalled the pro-British regime that executed the colonels

Free Officers: the secret group of officers in the Iraqi armed forces, including General Qasim and the Arif brothers, which conspired to successfully overthrow the Iraqi monarchy in 1958

Fundamentalism: the tendency to hold firmly to a perceived set of original beliefs; fundamentalism in religion often includes belief in the literal truth of sacred texts and that religion should play a powerful role in society, including government

Fursan: the pro-Baghdad Iraqi Kurdish militia

Governorates: provinces of Iraq

Green Zone: fortified area of Baghdad where US civilian occupation authorities resided

Gulf of Tonkin Resolution: the 1964 congressional resolution influenced by distorted information that in effect authorized the Vietnam War; the 2002 congressional vote for the Iraq War authorization bill affected by false claims of Iraqi WMD appeared similarly based on underlying deception

Gulf War of 1991: US-led military effort that was successful in making Iraqi forces withdraw from Kuwait

Hamas: Sunni Islamist movement among Palestinian Arabs

Hezbollah of Lebanon: Shia Lebanese political party reportedly aided by Iran

Hawza: a Shia center of religious study

Hijab: traditional head covering for women in Islamic societies

Hussein-McMahon Correspondence, 1915–1916: the exchange of letters between Sharif Hussein ibn Ali of Mecca and the British high commissioner in Egypt, Sir Henry McMahon, dealing with organizing the Arab Revolt against the Ottomans and the future of Arab lands in the Middle East

al-Ilah, Abd: pro-British regent for the Iraqi monarchy between the death of King Ghazi in 1937 and the installation of Faisal II in 1953; killed in the 1958 antimonarchy revolution

Imam: the leader of prayers in a mosque; an Islamic religious leader; for Twelver Shia, one the twelve infallible leaders of Islam after the Prophet Muhammad who were descendants of Ali and Fatima

Imam Hussein: grandson of the Prophet Muhammad who was the third Shia imam; commemoration of Imam Hussein and his martyrdom are central features of Shia Islam

Improvised Explosive Device (IED): explosive devices built by antioccupation Iraqi insurgents to attack coalition forces

Interim Iraqi Government (IIG): the group of Iraqis approved by the occupation Coalition Provisional Authority on June 2, 2004, to replace the IGC and serve as Iraq's government when occupation authorities declared Iraq sovereign at the end of the month and serve until the election of an Iraqi national legislature in 2005

Intifadas: Shia and Kurdish uprisings in the south and north of Iraq, respectively, following Iraq's defeat in the 1991 Gulf War

Iran-Contra scandal: episode during the Iran–Iraq War involving the United States' secretly violating its own ban against selling weapons to Iran and using profits from weapons sales to aid counterrevolutionaries ("contras") trying to overthrow a leftist revolutionary government in Nicaragua

Iraqi Communist Party (ICP): Iraq's first mass membership party; helped overthrow the monarchy but was later persecuted by Baathists

Iraqi Constitution of 1924: the constitution of British-dominated Iraq structured to guarantee that Iraq fulfill British interests

Iraq Development Fund: UN-authorized postinvasion fund derived from the sale of Iraqi energy resources to which the CPA had access

Iraq First policy: the political perspective that favored uniting all Iraqi ethnic and religious groups in a common Iraqi patriotism; conflicted with the Arab nationalist orientation

Iraq Governing Council (IGC): The group of Iraqis appointed (July 13, 2003, to June 2, 2004) by the CPA to provide advice and serve as a limited Iraqi provisional government until Iraq was declared sovereign

Iraq National Oil Company (INOC): the Iraqi government oil company established under General Qasim

Iraq Petroleum Company (IPC): British-dominated company that developed and exploited Iraq's energy resources

Iraqi Rebellion of 1920: the widespread multiethnic, multisectarian Iraqi rebellion against British occupation

Islamic Fadhila (Virtue) Party: the Sadrist movement led by Ayatollah Muhammad al-Yacoubi, who refused to follow the youthful and less religiously certified Moqtada al-Sadr

Islamic Movement of Iraqi Kurdistan (IMIK): Kurdish Islamic fundamentalist movement supplanted by Ansar al-Islam

Islamic Revolutionary Guard (IRG): Iranian Shia Islamic fundamentalist volunteer force

Islamic Supreme Council of Iraq (ISCI): new name for SCIRI after May 2007, also known as the Supreme Iraqi Islamic Council (SIIC)

Istikhbarat: Iraqi military intelligence under the Baathist regime

Istiqlal Party (Independence Party): An Arab nationalist–oriented party that opposed the Iraqi monarchy's government

Jash (young donkeys): Kurdish nationalist term for members of the Fursan pro-Baghdad Kurdish militia

Jewish Institute for National Security Affairs (JINSA): organization established to bolster US support for Israel

Jihad: a struggle on behalf of Islam; a holy war

Joint Resolution to Authorize the Use of United States Armed Forces Against Iraq: the October 2002 resolution to give President George W. Bush the authority to invade Iraq; supported by majorities in both the US House of Representatives and the Senate

Karbala: an Iraqi Shia religious city where the shrine of Imam Hussein is located

Kurdish Civil War: the violent conflict between the Kurdish Democratic Party and the Patriotic Union of Kurdistan from 1994 to 1996

Kurdish Democratic Party (KDP): Kurdish nationalist party historically led by the Barzani family and characterized by a right-of-center political orientation

Kurdish Regional Government (KRG): the Kurdish government of Iraq's Kurdish autonomous region

Law Governing the Rights and Duties of the Cultivators: 1933 law of the monarchal period that effectively enslaved many peasants to large landowners

League of Nations: predecessor to the UN; gave Britain control (the British Mandate) of the territories that became Iraq

Levies: Assyrian Christian soldiers hired by the British during the British Mandate over Iraq who were viewed as mercenaries by many Arab and Kurdish Iraqis

Low-Intensity Warfare: usually a combination of intense economic pressure and military attacks carried out over a long period of time to undermine a people's morale and support for their government

Mesopotamia: a Greek term meaning "the land between the two rivers," but more broadly virtually all the land, including modern Iraq, bordered by the Persian Gulf in the south, the Zargos and Anti-Taurus mountains to the west and north, respectively, and the Arabian peninsula on the southwest

Mahdi: for Twelver Shia, the "hidden" twelfth Shia imam who will one day return to the faithful

Mahdi Army (Jaish Mahdi): multifaceted paramilitary organization led by Moqtada al-Sadr

Mossad: Israeli intelligence agency

Mukhabarat: Baath Party intelligence agency

Mullah: Islamic preacher, cleric

Muslim: one who submits to Allah; one who embraces Islam

Najaf: a main Shia religious city in Iraq where the shrine of Imam Ali is located

National Council of Revolutionary Command (NCRC): the council that dominated Abd al-Salam Arif's Arab nationalist regime in Iraq after the overthrow of Qasim in February 1963

Nikah Mut'ah: the Shia concept of fixed-time marriage

North Atlantic Treaty Organization (NATO): US-led alliance that includes many European nations

Office for Reconstruction and Humanitarian Affairs (ORHA): US organization led by General Jay Garner that initially dominated postinvasion Iraq until replaced by L. Paul Bremer and the CPA

Operation Desert Shield: the large-scale deployment of US forces to Saudi Arabia and other locations in the Middle East to deter further Iraqi attacks after Iraq invaded Kuwait

Operation Desert Storm: the US-led military effort to expel Iraqi forces from Kuwait

Operation Iraqi Freedom: the 2003 US-led invasion of Iraq

Operation Provide Comfort: international effort to aid Kurds following the crushed Kurdish rebellion in the wake of Iraq's defeat in the 1991 Gulf War

Pan-Arabism: the movement, inspired by the ideology of Arab nationalism, for the unification of Arab peoples and countries

Partition of Palestine: 1947 United Nations plan to divide Palestine into separate homelands for the Jewish and Arab Palestinian peoples

Patriotic Union of Kurdistan (PUK): Kurdish nationalist party historically characterized by a left-of-center political orientation

Pentacle House: expression for five allied Shia political parties in Basra

Personal Status Law of General Qasim's government: 1959 reform that significantly improved women's rights in Iraq; opposed by many political and religious conservatives

Peshmergas ("those who face death"): Kurdish nationalist fighters

Policy Counterterrorism Evaluation Group (PCEG): an intelligence committee within the US Department of Defense that attempted to analyze intelligence data in the period leading up to the Iraq War

Preemptive war: a war launched in anticipation of an imminent attack in the belief that it is advantageous to strike the hostile nation planning the attack first

Predator: remotely piloted aircraft used by US forces in Iraq and Afghanistan to detect, observe, and destroy enemy leaders and forces

Preventive war: a war launched against a hostile nation that is not currently preparing an imminent attack in order to defeat it while it is relatively weak and incapable of effectively defending itself with the goal of removing a potential future threat

Psychological Operations (psyops): US military units using psychological techniques to win the support of Iraqi civilians and military personnel

Public Law 80: General Qasim's seizure of 99.5 percent of the concession territories of foreign-owned oil companies in Iraq

Quran (Koran): the word of Allah as revealed to his Prophet Muhammad; Islam's holy book

Republican Guard: a force created by General Abd al-Salam Arif initially to safeguard his government from a possible military coup; later greatly expanded to become whole elite divisions within the Iraqi armed forces

Revolutionary Command Council (RCC): Baathist governing council

Revolution: a social movement that accomplishes structural change (institutional change) in society such as in the form of a society's political system or economic system

Rightly Guided Caliphs: the first four leaders of Islam following Muhammad who had actually known him

Salafis: fundamentalist Sunni Muslims who believe that Muslims should follow the form of Islam that existed in the early years of the religion

Salvador Option: expression referring to the use of death squads to eliminate insurgents or their supporters

Samarra: Iraqi city where the Shia al-Askari golden-dome mosque was blown up in 2006, temporarily intensifying sectarian violence

Shah: Iranian king

Sharia: Islamic religious law

Shatt al-Arab (Arab River): previously contested border between Iraq and Iran

Shia: followers of Ali; members of the Shia branch of Islam

Sheik: leader of an Arab tribe

Sole Leader: a title given to General Qasim by many of his supporters

Special Operations Forces (SOF): US soldiers trained to operate in special circumstances such as behind enemy lines

Status of Forces Agreement (SOFA): the agreement between the United States and the postinvasion Iraqi government approved by the Iraqi parliament on November 27, 2008, which permitted US troops to remain in Iraq past the UN-authorized deadline of December 31, 2008, until December 31, 2011

Suez crisis: the international crisis caused by conflict over the Suez Canal involving the British, French, and Israeli invasion of Egypt in 1956

Sunnis: members of the Sunni branch of Islam

Supreme Council for the Islamic Revolution in Iraq (SCIRI): anti-Baathist Shia political-religious alliance formed in Iran by Iraqi Ayatollah Muhammad Baqir al-Hakim and his associates

Supreme Iraqi Islamic Council (SIIC): new name for SCIRI after May 2007, also known as the Islamic Supreme Council of Iraq (ISCI)

Sykes-Picot Agreement: British-French agreement to divide Arab lands after World War I that had been parts of the Ottoman Empire

Taliban: Sunni Islamist movement that achieved control of most of Afghanistan in 1996; allowed Osama bin Laden and Al Qaeda to operate in Afghanistan until defeated by US forces in late 2001; then fought US and NATO forces occupying Afghanistan

Thalweg: the center line of the deepest channel of the Shaat al-Arab, the location where Iran historically demanded that the border between Iran and Iraq be located

Thunder Runs: two high-speed US armored forays deep into Baghdad that proved the remaining Iraqi resistance forces there were incapable of effectively defending the city

Transitional Administrative Law (TAL): Iraq's postinvasion temporary constitution formulated during the presovereignty period when Iraq was controlled by the CPA and the IGC it appointed

Transitional National Assembly (TNA): the assembly elected by Iraqis on January 30, 2005, to create a permanent constitution for Iraq to replace the TAL

Treaty of 1922: treaty intended to create the impression that British presence and actions in Iraq were the result of a mutual agreement between Britain and Iraq

Treaty of 1930: treaty between Britain and Iraq to replace the 1922 treaty on the eve of Iraqi independence; allowed Britain to hold on to its military bases in Iraq

Tribe: a set of clans, often four to six, whose members are typically believed descended from a common ancestor

Twelver Shiism: the form of Shiism that is dominant in Iraq and Iran that holds that there were twelve infallible leaders of Islam after the Prophet Muhammad

Ulama: Islamic clergy, religious scholars

UN Monitoring, Verification and Inspection Commission (UNMOVIC): UN agency that resumed weapons inspections in Iraq in 2002; successor to UNSCOM

UN Security Council Resolution 687: UN resolution ending the 1991 Gulf War that required Iraq to recognize Kuwait's independence, eliminate all weapons of mass destruction, and accept and cooperate with UN weapons inspections

UN Security Council Resolution 1441: November 8, 2002, UN resolution that identified the situation in Iraq as a threat to world security but provided Iraq with the opportunity to avoid war if its government cooperated with UN weapons inspectors

UN Security Council Resolution 1472: March 28, 2003, UN resolution stating that those causing the Iraq War "should meet the humanitarian needs of the civilian population"

UN Security Council Resolution 1483: May 22, 2003, UN resolution that gave the United States and the United Kingdom collectively the authority to govern Iraq, sell Iraqi oil, and use the resulting revenue with UN oversight

UN Security Council Resolution 1546: June 8, 2004, UN resolution giving support to the transfer of sovereignty from the CPA to the new Iraqi government by June 30, 2004, and support for the January 2005 election of the TNA

UN Security Council Resolution 1790: December 18, 2007, UN resolution that permitted US and allied multinational forces to stay in Iraq until December 31, 2008

UN Special Commission on Disarmament (UNSCOM): UN post–1991 Gulf War agency to search for weapons of mass destruction and long-range missiles in Iraq

United Arab Republic (UAR): temporary union of Egypt and Syria, 1958–1961

United Iraqi Alliance: Shia political coalition, including SCIRI, the Badr Organization, Dawa, Moqtada al-Sadr's movement, Islamic Fadhila, and other parties that won the largest number of seats in the December 15, 2005, election for the Iraqi parliament

United National Front: an Iraqi antimonarchy alliance that included the Iraqi Communist Party (represented by the Peace Partisans), the leftist National Democratic Party, and the Arab nationalist Istiqlal and Baath parties

Vietnam Veterans Against the War: anti–Vietnam War organization of Vietnam War veterans, one of whose members was Senator John Kerry of Massachusetts

Vilayat-e faqih (guardianship of the [supreme Islamic] jurist): the principle of the Iranian Islamic Republic's political system that gives supreme political power to a religious leader selected by other clergy

Wahhabis: members of the Saudi Arabian fundamentalist branch of Islam founded by Muhammad ibn Abd al-Wahhab; Shia in Iraq often use the term to refer to any Sunni fundamentalist extremists

al-Wathbah: term for the anti–Portsmouth Treaty demonstrations of 1948

Woodrow Wilson's Fourteen Points: President Wilson's principles for the post–World War I world; many believed point twelve included support for democratic self-determination for the Arab people

Zionism: the movement to establish a homeland for the Jewish people, which led to the creation of the nation of Israel

Major Personalities

Aflaq, Michael: a Christian Orthodox Arab Syrian who played a leading role in the founding of the Baath Party

Allawi, Ayad: Iraqi secular Shia exile opponent of the Baathist regime who headed the Iraqi National Accord (INA) and later was appointed by the CPA to the postinvasion Iraq Governing Council; then served as prime minister of the interim government, June 28, 2004, to May 3, 2005

Ali, Sharif Hussein ibn: leader of the Hashemite family of Mecca, which cooperated with the British in organizing the Arab Revolt against the Ottoman Empire; his son Faisal became the British-sponsored king of Iraq

Annan, Kofi: secretary-general of the United Nations at the time of the US-led invasion of Iraq that the UN refused to authorize

Arif, Abd al-Rahman: brother of Abd al-Salam Arif who became leader of Iraq in 1966; overthrown by a Baathist-led coup in 1968

Arif, Abd al-Salam: a major leader of the antimonarchy revolution in 1958; led Iraq after the overthrow of General Qasim's government in 1963

Aziz, Tariq: a Chaldean Catholic Baathist leader and member of the Revolutionary Command Council whom Shia extremists were accused of attempting to assassinate in a 1980 bombing attack

al-Bakr, Ahmad Hasan: older cousin of Saddam Hussein who preceded Saddam as president of Baathist-controlled Iraq from 1968 to 1979 and appointed Saddam as a top party leader and organizer

Barzani, Masoud: son of Mullah Mustafa Barzani and leader of the KDP; president of the Kurdish Regional Government

Bin Laden, Osama: son of a Saudi billionaire, bin Laden fought the Russians in Afghanistan, where he and associates founded Al Qaeda, which later attacked the United States

al-Bitar, Salah: a Sunni Arab Syrian who played a leading role in the founding of the Baath Party

Blair, Tony: British prime minister, allied with US President George W. Bush who led his country into the Iraq War

Blix, Hans: head of the UN Monitoring, Verification and Inspection Commission (UNMOVIC)

Bowen, Stuart: Bush administration official who reported wrongdoing in postinvasion Iraq

Bremer, Louis Paul III: head of the Coalition Provisional Authority

Bush, George H. W.: US president from 1989 to January 1993 whose administration organized Operations Desert Shield and Desert Storm against Iraq

Bush, George W.: forty-third president who led the United States into the Iraq War

Butler, Richard: head of the UN Special Commission on Disarmament (UNSCOM) 1997–1999

Chalabi, Ahmed: secular Shia leader of the Iraqi National Congress (INC), later a member of the Iraq Governing Council (IGC)

Cheney, Dick: George W. Bush's vice president and a major proponent of removing Saddam Hussein's regime

Clinton, Hillary: senator from New York who narrowly missed becoming the 2008 Democratic presidential candidate; she voted in favor of Bush's October 2002 war resolution and was appointed secretary of state by President Barack Obama

Curveball (Rafid Ahmed Alwan): an Iraqi exile who provided false information that Iraq had mobile biological weapons

de Mello, Sergio Vieiro: UN human rights commissioner sent to Iraq after the US-led invasion; killed by a bombing attack on UN headquarters there on August 19, 2003

al-Douri, Izzat: Baathist former vice president of Iraq, member of the RCC, thought to have been a leader of the antioccupation insurgency

Ekeus, Rolf: executive chairman of UNSCOM between 1991 and 1997

Faisal I: the first monarch of the ruling dynasty installed in Iraq in 1921 under the British Mandate; died in 1933

Faisal II: third and last king of Iraq; killed in the antimonarchy revolution of 1958

Feith, Douglas: a major neoconservative official in the Pentagon under President George W. Bush

Franks, General Tommy: commander of US forces during the 2003 invasion of Iraq

Galula, Colonel David: French officer who authored a classic work on counterinsurgency

Garner, Jay: former US Army general put in charge of the US occupation of Iraq before being replaced by L. Paul Bremer

King Ghazi: son of Faisal I and second king of Iraq; became a vehement opponent of British polices and died under mysterious circumstances in 1939

Glaspie, April: US ambassador to Iraq who met with Saddam Hussein in 1990 shortly before Iraq invaded Kuwait

al-Hakim, Abdul Aziz: leader of SCIRI after the assassination of his brother Ayatollah Muhammad Baqir al-Hakim; later a leader of the Shia United Iraqi Alliance coalition of political parties

al-Hakim, Ayatollah Muhammad Baqir: Iraqi Shia clerical opponent of the Baathist regime who went into exile in Iran before the Iran–Iraq War where he helped found SCIRI; he returned to Iraq after the US-led invasion but was assassinated by a car bomb in August 2003

Hussein, Saddam: president of Iraq from July 16, 1979, to April 9, 2003; accused of repression, starting wars, and crimes against humanity; executed on December 30, 2006

Hussein, Qusay: Saddam Hussein's younger son who was given major responsibilities, especially after his older brother, Uday, manifested repeated criminal tendencies and was badly injured in a bomb assassination attempt

Hussein, Uday: Saddam Hussein's oldest son

al-Ilah, Abd: pro-British brother-in-law of King Ghazi who became regent when the anti-British Ghazi was killed in 1939

al-Jaafari, Ibrahim: An Iraqi Shia leader of the Dawa who lived for years as an exile in Iran; served as prime minister of Iraq from May 3, 2005, to May 20, 2006

Kamal al-Majid, General Hussein: Saddam Hussein's son-in-law who defected to Jordan in 1995 and claimed that Iraq was concealing information about its weapons programs although he also claimed that Iraq had destroyed all its weapons of mass destruction and long-range missiles

Kazzar, Nazim: Shia Baathist head of Iraq's security police, accused of torture and murder, who attempted a mass assassination of Iraqi leaders including President Ahmad Hasan al-Bakr and Saddam Hussein in 1973

Kerry, John: senator from Massachusetts who voted in favor of President George W. Bush's October 2002 Iraq War resolution and then ran unsuccessfully as the 2004 Democratic candidate for president against Bush

al-Khoei, Grand Ayatollah Abd al-Qasim: a top Iraqi Shia religious leader who opposed the level of clerical involvement in politics advocated by Iran's Ayatollah Khomeini and instead supported the Shia quiescence tradition

Khomeini, Ayatollah Ruhollah: religious leader of the 1978–1979 Iranian Revolution

Lawrence, Thomas Edward ("Lawrence of Arabia"): British representative in the Middle East who helped organize the Arab Revolt against the Ottomans

Makiya, Kanan: an Iraqi secular Shia exile and author who opposed the Saddam Hussein regime

al-Maliki, Nouri: a leader of Dawa who lived in exile in Syria for many years and returned to Iraq after the US-led invasion to become prime minister on May 20, 2006

Mandela, Nelson: the major leader of the South African prodemocracy movement who, after over twenty-seven years of imprisonment, was elected president of South Africa in 1994; he opposed the 2003 US-led invasion of Iraq

Mossadeq, Mohammad: Iranian prime minister who was overthrown in a British- and US-supported coup in 1953

McCain, John: senator from Arizona who supported the Iraq War and was the unsuccessful Republican candidate for president in 2008

Nasser, President Gamal Abdel: leader of the 1952 Egyptian antimonarchy revolt and later president of Egypt who defied the British; a hero to many Arab nationalists

Obama, Barack: senator from Illinois who opposed the Iraq War; the Democratic Party's successful candidate for president in 2008

Perle, Richard: a neoconservative official in the George W. Bush administration who served as chairperson of the Defense Policy Board; he advocated overthrowing Saddam Hussein's regime

Petraeus, General David H.: appointed commanding general in Iraq in January 2007 and served in that position from February 10, 2007, to September 16, 2008; expert on counterinsurgency warfare

Pope John Paul II: head of the Catholic Church who helped bring democracy to his native Poland and Eastern Europe but opposed both continued UN sanctions against Iraq and the 2003 invasion

Powell, Colin: former US Army general and chairman of the Joint Chiefs of Staff; George W. Bush's secretary of state January 20, 2001–January 26, 2005, who unknowingly presented false claims of Iraqi WMD to the UN before the invasion of Iraq

Qasim, General Abd al-Karim: leader of Iraq from the 1958 antimonarchy revolution to his death in the 1963 Arab-Nationalist military coup

Rice, Condoleezza: national security adviser and then secretary of state during the George W. Bush administration

Rumsfeld, Donald: US secretary of defense January 20, 2001–December 18, 2006, who played a major and controversial role in the Iraq War

al-Sadr, Ayatollah Muhammad Baqir: a major Iraqi Shia religious leader who inspired the development of the Shia political-religious movement; viewed as the possible leader of an Iraqi Shia fundamentalist revolution shortly after the Iranian Revolution, he was killed by the Baathist regime on April 8, 1980

al-Sadr, Moqtada: the leader of the Sadrist Mahdi Army who was the son of Ayatollah Muhammad Sadiq al-Sadr and the second cousin of Ayatollah Muhammad Baqir al-Sadr

al-Sadr, Ayatollah Muhammad Sadiq: Shia religious leader who set up a network of charities and social service programs to aid lower income people. Murdered in 1999. His son Moqtada al-Sadr inherited much of his organization and popularity

al-Said, Nuri: Arab Revolt participant who became Britain's most highly valued Iraqi politician during the Iraqi monarchy, serving repeatedly as prime minister and foreign minister; killed in the 1958 revolution

Shinseki, General Eric: US military leader who before the invasion recommended deploying a much larger force than what the Bush administration sent to Iraq

Sidqi, General Bakir: powerful Kurdish Iraqi general who staged Iraq's first military coup in 1936; he favored the Iraq First policy but opposed leftist reformers; assassinated by Arab nationalists in 1937

al-Sistani, Grand Ayatollah Sayyid Ali: major religious leader of Iraqi Shia since the murder of Ayatollah Muhammad Sadiq al-Sadr; Sistani called on occupation authorities to allow creation of an elected Iraqi government

Taguba, General Antonio: US general who investigated charges of American abuse of prisoners at Abu Ghraib prison

al-Talabani, Jalal: leader of the Kurdish PUK, member of the IGC, and president of Iraq after the 2005 parliamentary election

Vincent, Steven: freelance reporter for the *New York Times* murdered in August 2005 in Basra, apparently by men dressed in police uniforms, after reporting on charges of human rights abuses by British-trained Basra police

Westhusing, Colonel Theodore: US officer sent to postinvasion Iraq who became severely discouraged at perceived abuse and corruption

Wilson, Joseph: US official who investigated whether Iraq was attempting to purchase uranium oxide from Niger but found no evidence for the claim

Wilson, Valerie Plame: wife of Joseph Wilson who was the CIA's head of operations of the Counterproliferation Division's Joint Task Force on Iraq; some believe her CIA position was revealed to punish her husband for raising doubts about the claim that Iraq was seeking uranium oxide for a nuclear weapons program

Wolfowitz, Paul: neoconservative advocate of removing the Baathist regime who served as deputy secretary of defense in the George W. Bush administration

al-Yacoubi, Ayatollah Muhammad: a follower of Ayatollah Muhammad Sadiq al-Sadr who refused to accept the leadership of the young Moqtada al-Sadr and instead organized his own Sadrist movement, Islamic Fadhila (Virtue) Party

Yusuf, Yusuf Salman (Comrade Fahd): legendary leader of Iraq's Communist Party; executed by the monarchy's government in 1948

al-Zarqawi, Abu Musab: Jordanian-born leader of the Al Qaeda network in Iraq who was killed by a US air attack on June 7, 2006

al-Zawahiri, Ayman: Egyptian reported to be second in command to Osama bin Laden in Al Qaeda who supported attacking the United States

Zinni, Major General Anthony: US Marine general who was commander of CENTCOM from 1997–2000

Chronology of
the Iraq War

1533   The Ottomans conquer the territory that later becomes Iraq and maintain control, except for a short period in the seventeenth century, until World War I

1914–   Britain seizes Ottoman territories, including the Ottoman provinces later
1917   joined to make the nation of Iraq

1920   April 25: The League of Nations places Iraq under British Mandate. This is followed by a widespread multiethnic, multisectarian rebellion against the occupying British forces, convincing Britain to modify its approach to controlling Iraq

1921   August 23: Faisal, son of Hussein ibn Ali, the sharif of Mecca, crowned as Iraq's first king

1921–   After the British install the ruling family, they convince or pressure
1924   some Iraqis to accept a treaty and constitution that serves Britain's interests

1927   Oil is discovered in the Kirkuk area of northern Iraq and soon in southern and central Iraq

1932   October 3: Britain declares Iraq, dominated by the British-installed monarchy and pro-British Iraqi landowning and business elites, a sovereign nation; Iraq is admitted to the League of Nations

1936   Iraqi Kurdish General Bakir Sidqi stages a military coup and favors a comprehensive form of Iraqi nationalism. The next year he is assassinated by Arab nationalists in the armed forces

1939   April: King Ghazi, who repeatedly criticized British policies, is killed. The official explanation is an accidental car crash; most Iraqis, however, suspect he was actually murdered as the result of a British plot. He is succeeded by his four-year-old son, Faisal. But in reality his pro-British brother-in-law dominates Iraq as regent, along with pro-British Iraqi politicians like Nuri al-Said

1941   April: A military coup installs an anti-British government. The British invade, defeat the Iraqi armed forces, and establish a new occupation. Abd al-Ilah and other pro-British Iraqis, who had fled, return

1948   January: After representatives of the British and Iraqi governments negotiate a new treaty permitting Britain continued long-term access to military bases in Iraq, massive demonstrations against the treaty, the wathbah, take place, forcing the treaty to be abandoned

1948   After the state of Israel is established in May, war breaks out; Arab forces, including those from Iraq, are defeated; these events contribute to undermining the Iraqi monarchy

1955   February: Iraq joins the so-called Baghdad Pact, a treaty with Iran, Pakistan, Turkey, and Britain giving Britain, under the guise of the multinational alliance, continued military access to Iraq. This enrages many Iraqis, further weakening the monarchy

1956   Egypt's President Nasser nationalizes the Suez Canal; Britain, France, and Israel then attack Egypt. This prompts new Iraqi protests against the monarchy's collaboration with Britain

1958   July 14: The secret revolutionary Free Officers movement, led by General Abd al-Karim Qasim, stages a military rebellion that eliminates the monarchy. Iraq is declared a republic with General Qasim as its leader

1959   Baath Party militants, including Saddam Hussein, believing that the Iraqi communist movement is gaining too much power and that General Qasim is betraying Arab nationalism, attempt to assassinate him. Qasim is wounded but survives. Would-be assassin Saddam is also wounded and temporarily flees the country

1961   December 11: Qasim's government enacts Public Law 80, which expropriates almost all the concession areas of foreign oil companies, leaving them only the 0.5 percent actually producing oil

1963   February 8: Arab nationalists in the Iraqi armed forces stage a new military revolt and kill Qasim. Abd al-Salam Arif, an officer who played a leading role in removing the monarchy, becomes president

1963   November 18: Abd al-Salam Arif and his supporters remove most Baath Party members from the government

1966   April 13: President Abd al-Salam Arif dies in a helicopter crash. On April 17 his brother, Abd al-Rahman Arif, becomes the new president

1968   July 17: The Baath Party and its Arab nationalist allies stage a successful takeover

1968   July 30: The Baath Party carries out a new coup, removes non-Baathists, and takes complete control of the government. Baathist General Ahmad Hasan al-Bakr becomes president. His younger cousin, Saddam Hussein, reorganizes and expands the Baath Party

1972   Iraq nationalizes the Iraq Petroleum Company

1973   July: Nazim Kazzar, the head of the Baath government's security department, attempts unsuccessfully to seize control by massacring top Baathist leaders, including President al-Bakr, Saddam Hussein, and others

1975   March: Saddam Hussein successfully negotiates an agreement with the Iranian shah. In return for Iran's ending support for rebelling Iraqi Kurds, Iraq agrees to Iran's demand that the boundary between Iran and Iraq at the Shatt al-Arab be the middle of the deepest channel. Without Iranian aid, the Kurdish rebellion quickly ends

1979   January–April: The Iranian Revolution succeeds in ousting the shah. Iranian Shia fundamentalists led by Ayatollah Khomeini triumph over other groups in the anti-shah revolutionary alliance and begin the process of transforming Iran into an Islamic republic

1979   July: In the wake of the Iranian Revolution and the growing threat of Iraqi Shia fundamentalist rebellion against the Baathist regime, Saddam Hussein, previously vice president, becomes president

1980   April 8: Ayatollah Muhammad Baqir al-Sadr, advocate of establishing an Islamic regime in Iraq, is executed

1980   September 22: The Iran–Iraq War begins. Saddam and his advisers mistakenly believe that initial overwhelming Iraqi attacks and advances into Iranian territory will destabilize Iran's Islamic regime and force Iran to quickly make peace on terms favorable to Iraq. In reality the war will continue for eight disastrous years, taking hundreds of thousands of lives and devastating both countries' economies

1988   August 20: Iran, realizing it could not defeat Iraq as long as Iraq is aided by the United States and other countries, agrees to a cease-fire. Iraq declares victory but is more than $80 billion in debt to Saudi Arabia, Kuwait, France, the Soviet Union, and other nations

1990   August 2: Iraq invades Kuwait, an action opposed by the United States and most nations. The UN imposes economic sanctions against Iraq

1991   January 16–17: A US-led military alliance, including Britain and France, attacks Iraq (Operation Desert Storm), eventually forcing Iraqi forces to withdraw from Kuwait

1991   March 3: Iraq accepts UN requirements for a cease-fire

1991   Early March: In the wake of Iraq's defeat, Shia dissidents in the south and Kurdish nationalists in the north rebel but are defeated by early April. Due to international intervention, Baghdad loses control of its Kurdish provinces

1991   May: The UN Special Commission on Disarmament (UNSCOM) and the International Atomic Energy Agency (IAEA) begin weapons inspections and removal or destruction of WMD

1992   May–July: Elections in Iraqi Kurdistan result in the establishment of the autonomous Kurdish Regional Government

1994–   Civil war breaks out between the major Kurdish parties, the KDP and
1996   the PUK

1995   August: Saddam Hussein's son-in-law General Hussein Kamal al-Majid defects to Jordan, where he provides information suggesting that Iraq has not fully cooperated with weapons inspectors, but he also claims that Iraq did destroy all its WMD and long-range missiles

1996   June: Iraqi security agents destroy a coup conspiracy planned by the Iraqi National Accord, a US-aided anti-Saddam exile group, involving dozens of officers within elite Iraqi military units

1996   August–September: Iraqi government forces assisting the KDP in the Kurdish civil war capture Arbil and devastate forces of the Iraqi National Congress, another US-aided anti-Saddam exile organization

1998   November: After Iraq stops cooperating with UNSCOM inspectors on October 31, claiming that some are spies for Israel or the United States, UNSCOM pulls out of the country

1998   December 16–19: The United States and Britain conduct air strikes against Iraq called Operation Desert Fox

1999   February 18: Iraqi Grand Ayatollah Muhammad Sadiq al-Sadr and two of his sons are assassinated in a machine-gun ambush

2001   September 11: Al Qaeda attacks New York City and Washington, D.C., prompting a widespread desire to retaliate, which the Bush administration harnesses to gather popular support for an invasion of Iraq

2002   January 29: In his State of the Union address President Bush refers to Iraq, Iran, North Korea, and "their terrorist allies" as components of an "axis of evil"

2002   October 7: President Bush gives a speech in Cincinnati claiming that Saddam Hussein has WMD

2002   October: Majorities in both the US House of Representatives and the US Senate vote in favor of President Bush's Iraq War authorization resolution

2002   November 8: UN Security Council Resolution 1441, drafted primarily by the United States and Britain in consultation with China, Russia, and France, states that Iraq is in violation of the Gulf War cease-fire terms stipulated in UN Resolution 687. But Resolution 1441 gives Iraq the opportunity to avoid war through cooperating with the UN Monitoring, Verification and Inspection Commission (UNMOVIC) and the IAEA. UN inspectors return to Iraq, and Iraqis, hoping to prevent the coming invasion, provide a high level of cooperation

2003   January 28: President Bush again asserts that Iraq has WMD, in violation of UN Resolution 687

2003   February 5: Secretary of State Colin Powell delivers a presentation to the UN containing false information concerning WMD in Iraq

2003   March 17: Just before the invasion, President Bush addresses the American people and the world and again claims that Iraq has not disarmed; he says that the UN Security Council has failed to live up to its responsibilities. Bush gives Saddam Hussein and his sons forty-eight hours to leave Iraq or "military conflict" would begin

2003   March 20: The US-led invasion of Iraq begins

2003   April 9: US forces capture Baghdad

2003   April 14: US forces seize Tikrit, Saddam's hometown

2003   April 16: President Bush announces that "Iraq has been liberated"

2003   April 21: Former General Jay Garner arrives in Iraq to supervise the US-led occupation

2003   May 1: On the deck of the US aircraft carrier *Abraham Lincoln* President Bush declares the war in Iraq has been won

2003   May 12: Louis Paul Bremer III arrives to replace General Garner and heads the Coalition Provisional Authority (CPA)

2003   May 16: Bremer issues CPA Order Number 1, the de-Baathification order

2003   May 22: UN Security Council Resolution 1483 gives the United States and UK the temporary authority to govern Iraq and sell its oil

2003   May 23: Bremer issues CPA Order Number 2, disbanding the Iraqi armed forces

2003   July 13: Bremer appoints the twenty-five-member Iraq Governing Council (IGC)

2003   July 22: Saddam's sons, Qusay and Uday, are killed by US forces in Mosul

2003   August: Vehicle bomb kills Ayatollah Muhammad Baqir al-Hakim

2003   December 13: Saddam Hussein is captured in Tikrit

2004   May: Photographs are published of US troops abusing Iraqi prisoners at Abu Ghraib

2004   June: The United States and UN announce that Iraq is again officially sovereign; the CPA is declared replaced by the Interim Iraqi Government (IIG)

2004   November: US forces crush resistance in the insurgent-dominated city of Fallujah

2005   January 30: Transitional National Assembly is elected to develop a new constitution for Iraq

2005   Summer: Awakening movement begins when US forces start working with Sunni tribes in Anbar province against Al Qaeda in Mesopotamia (AQM)

2005   October 15: National referendum approves the new constitution

2005   December 15: Iraq's new parliament, the Council of Representatives, is elected

2006   February 22: Sacred Shia al-Askari mosque in Samarra is badly damaged by a bomb. Sectarian violence increases

2006   March: Public opinion surveys indicate that most Americans no longer support the Iraq War or consider it justified

2006   May 7: A broad coalition, including the KDP and PUK, assumes control of a unified Kurdish Regional Government (KRG)

2006   Summer: US forces shift significantly to the clear-hold-build counterinsurgency approach

2006   June 7: US air strike kills AQM leader Abu Musab al-Zarqawi

2006   October 9: North Korea, which Bush had included in the "axis of evil" with Iraq, detonates a nuclear weapon, widely interpreted as, in part, an effort to deter a US invasion

2006   November 7: Anti–Iraq War sentiment contributes to the Democrats' taking control of the US House of Representatives and the Senate

2006   December 30: Saddam Hussein is executed

2007   January: General David Petraeus becomes commander of US forces in Iraq; the surge in US troop strength soon begins allowing for more effective clear-hold-build counterinsurgency operations

2007   August 29: Moqtada al-Sadr orders his Shia Mahdi Army to cease-fire

2008   January: The Iraqi parliament approves allowing some former members of the Baath Party to apply for government positions. The World Health Organization, after interviewing over 9,000 Iraqi households, estimates that between the start of the invasion on March 20, 2003, and the end of June 2006 about 151,000 Iraqi civilians died from violence

2008   September: US forces officially hand over Anbar province to Iraqi government control. The Iraqi parliament enacts a provincial elections law but omits disputed Kirkuk and the three KRG provinces so that elections could be carried out elsewhere

2008   October: Thousands of members of the Sunni Awakening movement begin being paid by the Iraqi government instead of the United States

2008   November: Barack Obama, who had opposed the Iraq War, wins the US presidential election

2008   November–December: As the UN authorization for US forces approaches its expiration date of December 31, 2008, the Iraqi government approves the Status of Forces Agreement with the United States that allows US troops to remain in Iraq, but also states they should leave the country at the end of 2011

2009   January 31: Election for provincial councils in fourteen of Iraq's eighteen provinces results in losses for the ISCI and victories for candidates with more moderate and secular outlooks favoring a relatively strong central government

2009   February 27: President Barack Obama announces in a major speech at Camp Lejeune that "by August 31, 2010, our combat mission in Iraq will end" and that he intends "to remove all U.S. troops from Iraq by the end of 2011"

Selected Documentaries

On Iraq, Afghanistan, Iran,
the Middle East, and Terrorism

Purchase or Rental Sources

AETV	Arts and Entertainment Television, www.store.aetv.com
AFSC	American Friends Service Committee, www.afsc.org
AFV	American Family Voices, www.americanfamilyvoices.org
AGAT	Agat Films & Cie, www.agatfilms.com
AMZ	Amazon.com, www.amazon.com
BIO	Bio True Story, www.biography.com
CD	CD Universe, www.cduniverse.com
D&C	DOC & CO, www.doc-co.com
DISC	Discovery Store, http://shopping.discovery.com
FMK	Filmakers Library, www.filmakers.com
FRIF	First Run Icarus Films, www.icarusfilms.com
GNN	Guerrilla News Network, www.gnn.tv
HBO	Home Box Office, www.hbo.com
IAS	I Am an American Soldier homepage, www.iamanamericansoldier.com
IND	Independent Film and Documentaries, www.indiedocs.com
INF	In Focus, www.infocusproductions.co.uk
JP	Director John Pilger's Web site, www.johnpilger.com
MC	Military Channel, www.military.discovery.com
MEF	Media Education Foundation, www.mediaed.org
OTW	Outside the Wire, www.outsidethewire.com
PSU	Pennsylvania State University, www.medianet.libraries.psu.edu
PBS (PVS)	Public Television Video and DVDs, www.pvs.org
RAI	Italy's Public Broadcasting Service, www.rai.it
WCH	When I Came Home homepage, www.whenicamehome.com
WMM	Women Make Movies, www.wmm.com

Iraq

About Baghdad. 2003. 90 min. Exiled Iraqi poet and writer Sinan Antoon returns to Iraq to make this film recording Iraqis' opinions after Saddam's fall. CD.

Arlington West: The Film. 2006. 74 min. Soldiers' experiences in Iraq; interviews with soldiers and with members of Gold Star Families for Peace. AFSC.

Back to Babylon. 2002. 52 min. Previously exiled Abbas Fadhel returned to Babylon to direct this film about the effects of war, sanctions, and Hussein. AGAT.

Baghdad Blogger. 2004. 78 min. An Iraqi architect uses the Internet to post an informative and insightful diary about Iraq and Iraqis during the occupation. FMK.

Baghdad ER. 2006. 64 min. The Iraq War from the perspective of an emergency room in Baghdad. AMZ.

Baghdad Surge. 2007. An alternative to the mass media's portrayal of the surge. OTW.

Battleground: 21 Days on the Empire's Edge. 2006. 82 min. Filmmakers gather information in Iraq that highlights the humanity of all sides. IND; AMZ; GNN.

Bearing Witness. 2005. 60 min. Five female journalists risk their safety covering the second Gulf War. AETV.

Blood and Oil. 2008. 52 min. Michael T. Klare, *Nation* magazine defense correspondent, demonstrates that oil has been central to US political and warfare strategy. MEF.

Body of War. 2008. 87 min. Iraq War veteran Tomas Young, paralyzed from his service, speaks out against the war. AMZ.

The Boys from Baghdad High. 2007. 90 min. Four high school students were given cameras to make this film over the course of a year. HBO.

Bush's War. 2008. 270 min. Describes the war from the initial decision to go to war to later challenges, both in Iraq and within the US government. PBS.

Buying the War. 2007. 90 min. Media veterans discuss the mainstream media's failure to question the Iraq War and present information clearly to the American people. PBS.

Call Sign Vengeance. 2005. J.D. Johannes, former marine, returns to Iraq with a camera instead of a gun. OTW.

Confronting Iraq: Conflict and Hope. 2005. 86 min. Presents important questions to clarify major issues concerning the war. IND.

Fahrenheit 9/11. 2004. 122 min. Michael Moore examines the facts behind the George W. Bush administration's dealing with terrorist attacks and the war in Iraq. AMZ.

Fallujah: The Hidden Massacre. 2005. 27 min. Addresses the use of white phosphorus and the issue of war crimes. RAI.

The Ground Truth. 2006. 78 min. Documentary by Patricia Foulkrod that includes interviews with about two dozen Iraq War veterans describing their experiences after returning home. AFSC.

The Gulf War. 1996. 4 hours. History of how it began; includes interviews with military and governmental officials. PBS.

Gunner Palace. 2004. 85 min. Soldiers of the 2/3 Field Artillery share their experiences from their camp in one of the palaces that Saddam built. AMZ.

Hijacking Catastrophe: 9.11, Fear and the Selling of the American Empire. 2004. 64 min. How the Bush administration exploited a fearful public after 9/11. MEF.

Honor Betrayed. 2004. 34 min. This film questions the Bush administration's support of US troops. AFV.

Hunt for Osama and Saddam: Tracking Down the Killers. 2006. 50 min. Describes methods used to catch Saddam; analyzes their effectiveness in efforts to catch Osama bin Laden. AETV.

I Am an American Soldier. 2007. 101 min. Follows the 101st Airborne Division from their leaving Kentucky through a year of service in Iraq and back home again. IAS.

In Shifting Sands: The Truth About UNSCOM and the Disarming of Iraq. 2001. 92 min. A film by former UN weapons inspector Scott Ritter. AFSC.

Independent Media in a Time of War. 2003. 35 min. Amy Goodman of Democracy Now powerfully criticizes the mainstream media's coverage of the Iraq War. MEF.

Inside Iraq: The Untold Stories. 2005. 80 min. Includes interviews with soldiers and Iraqi citizens. IND.

Iraq Diary (Alpha Company). 2006. 180 min; 3 parts. Three months with the Marines 3rd Reconnaissance Battalion in Iraq. MC.

Iraq for Sale: The War Profiteers. 2006. 75 min. Describes companies that made huge profits off the war and had connections to decision-makers in Washington, D.C. AFSC.

Iraq in Fragments. 2006. 94 min. The country from the perspectives of Iraqis who must repair the damage. AMZ.

Iraq Occupation. 2006. 103 min. A town-hall meeting involving Scott Ritter and Ray McGovern. AFSC.

Last Letters Home. 2004. 60 min. Ten families share their stories and the last letters written home by their loved ones who died in the Iraq War. AMZ.

Leading to War. 2008. 72 min. News and television interviews documenting political leaders' weak case for going to war in Iraq. AFSC.

Marine's Iraq Experiences. 2005. 29 min. A marine talks about his experiences in Iraq and reversing his support for the war. AFSC.

Meeting Resistance. 2007. 87 min. Interviews with eleven insurgency fighters in Iraq; provides a close-up perspective of why they fight. AMZ.

My Country, My Country. 2006. 90 min. Laura Poitras spent eight months filming daily life in Iraq. AMZ.

No End in Sight. 2007. 30 min. Interviews with top officials revealing mistakes and mishandling of the war in Iraq. PBS.

Noam Chomsky: Impacts of the Iraq War, Political, Social, and Economic Consequences. 2008. 80 min. AFSC.

Occupation: Dreamland. 2005. 78 min. Filmed in Fallujah in 2004; includes footage of Iraq civilians and the 82nd Airborne Division. AMZ.

Oil in Iraq: Curse or Blessing? 2003. 53 min. An overview of Iraq's history with respect to oil production. FMK.

Operation Homecoming: Writing the Wartime Experience. 2007. 81 min. Actors read veterans' letters, essays, and poetry. AMZ.

Outside the Wire: Anbar Awakens. 2007. The movement against Al Qaeda in Iraq's Anbar province. OTW.

Private Warriors. 2005. 60 min. The role of private companies in the Iraq War. PSU.

Saddam Hussein. 50 min. Biography. BIO.

Saddam's Revenge. 2004. 53 min. A look at the Sunni tribes after Saddam, their battle with Shia, and their orientation toward the occupation. FMK.

Shadow Company. 2006. 86 min. Nongovernmental and private military involvement in Iraq; includes interviews with security contractors. AMZ.

The Soldier's Heart. 2005. 60 min. Describes the war's effects on soldiers and post-traumatic stress disorder. PBS.

Standard Operating Procedure. 2008. 116 min. The Abu Ghraib incidents using photographs and interviews with soldiers. AMZ.

Taxi to the Dark Side. 2007. 106 min. Describes mistreatment of people in the Iraq and Afghanistan conflicts. AMZ.

Uncovered: The War on Iraq. 2004. 87 min. Analyzes reasons for invading Iraq. AMZ.

Voices of Iraq. 2004. 80 min. One hundred and fifty cameras were distributed to Iraqis to document their lives. AMZ.

War Feels Like War. 2004. 60 min. Journalists enter Iraq behind the coalition of invading forces. INF.

War Made Easy. 2007. 72 min. How administrations have promoted wars from Vietnam to Iraq. MEF.

The War Tapes. 2006. 97 min. The story of several soldiers from predeployment to Iraq to their return home. AMZ.

We Iraqis. 2004. 52 min. An Iraqi French director visits family in Iraq, filming them before the invasion, then returns several months after the start of the war. D&C.

Weapons of Mass Deception. 2005. 98 min. With Danny Schecter, analyzes media coverage that sometimes contradicted itself and the truth. IND.

When I Came Home. 2006. 70 min. Using one soldier's story, this film addresses a lack of support and benefits for Iraq War veterans. WCH.

Why We Fight. 2006. 99 min. An interesting look at the role of the military in US politics. Directed by Eugene Jarecki. AMZ, PSU.

Afghanistan

Afghan Massacre: The Convoy of Death. 2003. 45 min. Investigation of the deaths of 3,000 Taliban prisoners. AFSC.

Afghanistan: The Lost Truth. 2003. 64 min. A look at the Afghani people across the country. WMM.

Afghanistan: Captives of the War Lords. 2001. 52 min. Arthur Kent films with hidden cameras to reveal life in Afghanistan under the Taliban regime. FMK.

Afghanistan Unveiled. 2003. 52 min. A female film crew documents women's circumstances in Afghanistan after the Taliban. WMM.

Return of the Taliban. 2006. Taliban resurgence in Afghanistan. PBS.

The Taliban Legacy. 2001. 35 min. Aspects of the Taliban and the situation of Afghan refugees in Pakistan. FMK.

The War Briefing. 2008. 60 min. Review of the situation in Afghanistan that President Barack Obama inherited. PBS.

Iran

Anatomy of a Coup: The CIA in Iran. 2000. 50 min. CIA actions in Iran in 1953 in support of the shah. AETV (History Undercover).

Iran: The Most Dangerous Nation. 2006. 90 min. Ted Koppel explores Iranian society including Iranian views on the Iraq War, Afghanistan, and Israel. DISC.

Iran: The Next Iraq? 2005. 50 min. Explores Iran's possible futures as a great power or a possible terrorist state. AETV.

Iran: Veiled Appearances. 2002. 58 min. Describes Iran twenty-three years after the Islamic Revolution from opposing viewpoints within the country. FRIF.

Middle East

Not In My Name. 2000. 43 min. Aspects of US involvement in the Middle East before 9/11. AFSC.

Party of God. 2003. 50 min. Hezbollah in Lebanon. PBS (*Frontline*).

Saudi Arabia: A Complicated Ally. 2003. 100 min. Analyzes the conflicted relationship between the United States and Saudi Arabia. AETV.

Saudi Time Bomb. 2001. 60 min. Saudi Arabia and Wahhabi international educational activities. PBS (*Frontline*).

The Women of Hezbollah. 2004. 49 min. Describes the commitment of two female Hezbollah activists to the Islamic Party of God. FRIF.

Terrorism

The 9/11 Hijackers: Inside the Hamburg Cell. 2007. 50 min. About the students turned terrorists who planned and carried out "the planes operation." AETV.

100 Years of Terror. 2000. Four parts, each 50 min. An overview of terrorism as a strategy in modern times. AETV.

Al Qaeda. 2006. 50 min. Investigation into the organization and its history. AETV.

America at a Crossroads: Jihad: The Men and Ideas behind Al Qaeda. 2007. 120 min. Hosted by Robert MacNeil. PBS.

Breaking the Silence: Truth and Lies in the War on Terror. 2003. 50 min. This Australian documentary examines various issues about the war on terrorism and asks whether the US government has been responsible for some acts of terror. JP.

Brotherhood of Terror. 2007. 50 min. Examines the Muslim Brotherhood, which some say might be a strong ally in the war on terrorism, but others say shouldn't be trusted. AETV.

Distorted Morality. 2003. 115 min. Two lectures by Noam Chomsky in which he discusses the issue of a war on terror. IND.

In Search of Al Qaeda. 2002. 60 min. An effort to find leaders of Al Qaeda after they dispersed following the 9/11 attacks. PBS (*Frontline*).

Inside the Mind of a Suicide Bomber. 2006. 50 min. Interviews with psychologists and failed suicide bombers. AETV (*History Undercover*).

Inside the Terror Network. 2002. 60 min. Investigation of three of the terrorists involved in the September 11 attacks. PBS (*Frontline*).

The Man Who Predicted 9/11. 2005. 50 min. Describes the evacuation plan he designed that saved an estimated 3,000 lives, although he lost his own. AETV.

Osama bin Laden. 50 min. Biography. BIO.

Osama's Hideouts. 2006. 50 min. Osama's hideouts and the suspected route he took out of Afghanistan. AETV.

Shootout: Hunt for Bin Laden. 2005. 50 min. Tells about weaponry, strategy, and events during the hunt for bin Laden. AETV.

Son of Al Qaeda. 2004. 60 min. From terrorist training camps to Guantanamo to the CIA, this man's story provides insight into the minds of Al Qaeda supporters. PBS (*Frontline*).

Targeted: Osama bin Laden. 2004. 100 min. Osama, from young man to leader of an international terrorist organization. AETV.

Terrorism: A World in Shadows. 2006. 5 hrs. and 35 min. Seven-part series. An overview of terrorism throughout history, including causes, ideologies, and terrorist rationales. IND.

Trail of a Terrorist. 2001. 60 min. Information obtained from the Algerian terrorist caught with explosives and a plan to blow up Los Angeles airport. PBS (*Frontline*).

Understanding America's Terrorist Crisis. 2003. 70 min. Asks why the United States is the target for terrorists' hatred. With Gore Vidal. MEF.

The Uses of History and the War on Terrorism. 2006. 60 min. A talk by Howard Zinn in Madison, Wisconsin, produced by Democracy Now. AFSC.

The War Against Al Qaeda. 2006. 50 min. A look inside efforts against the worldwide terrorist network. AETV.